W9-COZ-249

Civic Culture
and Urban Change

Civic Culture and Urban Change

Governing Dallas

Royce Hanson

Wayne State University Press
Detroit

Manufactured in the United States of America.
06 05 04 03 02   4 3 2 1

Library of Congress Cataloging-in-Publication Data

Hanson, Royce.
Civic culture and urban change : governing Dallas / Royce Hanson.
p. cm.
Includes bibliographical references and index.
ISBN 0-8143-3080-0 (alk. paper)
1. Dallas (Tex.)—Politics and government—20th century. 2. Political culture—Texas—Dallas—History—20th century. 3. City planning—Texas—Dallas—History—20th century. 4. Urban policy—Texas—Dallas—History—20th century. 5. Dallas (Tex.)—Economic conditions—20th century. I. Title.
JS803.2 .H35 2003
320.9764'2812—dc21   2002010175

ISBN 0–8143-3080–0

∞The paper used in this publication meets the minimum requirements of the American National Standard for Information Sciences—Permanence of Paper for Printed Library Materials, ANSI Z39.48–1984.

For Mary, Brooks, Mark, Juliette, Lisa,
Caroline, Diana, Sarah, and Grace Anne

CONTENTS

Part IV Civic Capital: The Political Life of Dallas

Part V Conclusions and Reflections

PREFACE

THE ISSUES ADDRESSED IN this book began to occupy me two decades ago, when I served as study director for the National Committee on Urban Policy of the National Research Council. The committee focused attention on the transformation of America's urban areas brought about by the triple revolution of economic restructuring, demographic change, and information technology. The report limited its recommendations to policies designed to address the implications of this transformation for national and regional urban policies, but its findings raised questions in my mind about the capacity of large cities to adapt their governance institutions to the new circumstances in which they found themselves.

The opportunity to explore this question in a concrete way arose when I moved to Dallas in 1987 to serve as dean of the School of Social Sciences of the University of Texas at Dallas. The city was then in the midst of its most serious post-World War II recession. The entire region was undergoing a wrenching transformation in the wake of the savings and loan debacle and the collapse of the real estate market. It faced a crisis in race relations, exacerbated by the use of deadly force by its police and the killing of three police officers in confrontations with minorities. The city was being sued in federal court to force redistricting of Council seats and for discrimination in its public housing. The school system was in constant turmoil as it entered a fourth decade of federal court supervision under desegregation orders. The failures of the education system were the more troubling as the high technology sector was leading the regional economy into a new era, much as cotton and oil had done in earlier times. It was an era, however, that would demand knowledge workers. The convergence of these conditions produced multiple crises of leadership, legitimacy, and competence.

There appeared to be a general recognition that something had to be done. The mayor had recently created Dallas Together, a broad-based citizens committee, to examine the most urgent of these issues, dealing with employment opportunities, economic development, and representation of minorities on the City Council. In March of 1989 I organized a conference at the university on the challenges that would face Dallas by the end of the century. What was remarkable at the conference was the general equanimity with which most of the participants addressed these and other problems. While there was substantial concern about race relations, education, policing, and the way in which political power in the city had been closely held, the general tenor of remarks was that Dallas was a city that worked, the evidence to the contrary notwithstanding. One of the clear impressions to emerge from the conference was a sense of belief by city leaders, including many of the minorities, in the exceptionalism of Dallas.

In the months immediately following the conference, the capacity of the city's leaders to resolve problems was put to test as a charter review committee, then the Council, voters, and ultimately the federal district court grappled with bringing Council representation in conformity with the federal Voting Rights Act. While I was working as a *pro bono* adviser to the committee, the idea for this book began to take shape. Having spent a decade in local government, served on a charter committee and as a delegate to a state constitutional convention, and put in many years as a teacher of local politics, I was fascinated by the way in which the problem was approached by both those resisting and those urging change. They clearly worked within limits imposed on themselves by their perception of what was appropriate and how Dallas was supposed to work. Later, serving on a Greater Dallas Chamber of Commerce Committee on education I discovered that some of the city's most innovative business executives resisted proposals for making fundamental changes in a clearly failing school system as contrary to the Dallas way.

In serving on other civic bodies—Dallas Alliance, the Board of the Greater Dallas Citizens Planning Council, and the Council of Leaders of the Community of Churches—or working on strategic planning with the Community Council of Greater Dallas, one could sense the need for an analysis of how the Dallas system of governance worked that went beyond the stories its civic leaders told each other. In particular there was a need for an analysis that connected the governance system to the capacity of the city to deal with the problems brought about by both the transformation of its environment and its own institutional design and operations.

Unlike many of the nation's largest cities, there was little scholarly research on Dallas. That which existed was not widely accessible to active and latent civic leaders. And most of it was descriptive rather than analytical. As one of the nation's newer metropolitan areas, largely built after the advent of the automobile and air conditioning, Dallas provided an excellent opportunity for a natural experiment in how a post-industrial city copes with change. This would require systematic monitoring of the changes that were taking place.

With the help of faculty colleagues with long experience in urban research, including Brian J. L. Berry, Donald A. Hicks, Irving Hoch, and Ronald Briggs, and the support of Alexander L. Clark, then the academic vice president of UTD, we approached the David Bruton Charitable Trust and secured funds to establish the Bruton Center for Development Studies. Its initial mission was to provide an independent source of information on and analysis of the population, economy, and development of the Dallas-Fort Worth region. Under the direction of Paul Waddell, the Center became the catalyst for a wide range of studies of the Dallas regional political economy. Work performed at the Center informs much of this book.

A few years later, George Farkas created the Center for Education and Social Policy, which directed its attention to the problems of teaching reading skills to disadvantaged students. Other members of the faculty and a number of doctoral students undertook research on a wide variety of policy issues, ranging from the response of the real estate and banking industries to economic change, to implementation of compensatory education programs in the public schools, housing needs, and the organization of the Dallas nonprofit sector. I am indebted to them for insight into these arenas of policy and organization.

In devising the research, I have benefitted greatly from the new generation of scholarship on urban governance and political economy represented by the regime theorists and their synthesis of the work of elite, pluralist and public choice theorists. Several histories of Dallas published since I started work on the book have been indispensable in helping me understand the economic and political development of the city. Of these, Patricia Hill's *Dallas: The Making of a Modern City,* deserves special mention for its analysis of the evolution of the business oligarchy that governed the city for much of this century. Darwin Payne's *Big D: Triumphs and Troubles of an American Supercity in the 20th Century* provided a rich chronological narrative tracing the growth of Dallas.

The core of my research, however, involved an effort to immerse myself in the civic folkways of the city. I was engaged as a participant observer in a number of organizations and civic activities during the decade I lived in the Dallas area. These activities gave me an invaluable opportunity to observe how city decision makers went about their work. I conducted more than 250 hours of videotaped interviews over a six-year period with key actors and other observers of Dallas affairs. The interviews were open-ended and designed to gain perspective and an in-depth sense of how the respondents understood the city's governance system to function, and how they had gone about dealing with problems on their watch. Reviewing these interviews and reflecting on the striking similarities in the meanings attributed to events and institutions by a diverse set of respondents led me to make the tension between civic culture and urban change the theme of the book. The interviews are listed in the bibliography. I have quoted sparingly from them, using direct quotations only where the words of the interviewee make the point better than a paraphrase or summary.

To the extent that the experience of Dallas is similar to that of other great cities, I hope this book can help in addressing a series of questions:

- Why is it so difficult to adapt local political institutions to the transformations that have occurred in population, economics, institutions, and technology?
- How have these transformations affected who participates in governance in the central city and the capacity of cities to adapt to these and other changes?
- Are there any measures that a city like Dallas can take to enhance its capacity for effective local self-government in the face of these pervasive shifts in its environment?

This book, then, is both analytical and argumentative. In the analysis, I have used an eclectic approach that attempts to capture the complexity of the city as it performs its critical governance functions. I have interpreted the evolution of the Dallas political economy in a way that attempts to account for the interplay of chance, choice, accidents, and opportunity in shaping the civic culture of the city, which occupies the central role in my exposition of why Dallas operates as it does. I also apply a "policy tools" approach to the analysis of each of the principal functions of city governance—provision of the major public services of education and policing; urban development; and the fostering of civic capital. Having engaged in a critique of the city's policy tools and the outcomes of their use, it seemed only fair to answer the question: "If that is so, what would you have us do about it?" I have, therefore, sketched out some thoughts in the final chapter about how things might be done to improve the city's prospects for adapting to its changed circumstances. These may seem unduly structural to those who belong to the school that disdains structure as irrelevant to governance. I do not, although I concede that it is hardly the sum and substance of it. If not sufficient, it is necessary.

Any project that has been as long in preparation as this one has hundreds of debts to acknowledge. While I cannot list all of them here, special thanks are due those busy officials and civic leaders who endured long interviews and other more casual conversations with me over the years and to colleagues at the University of Texas at Dallas who listened to me think out loud and were then rewarded with requests to read parts of the manuscript as it went through repeated revisions. A number of graduate assistants and Clark Fellows (high school students who won the dubious distinction of working with me on the research during summers) assisted in the historical research in newspaper files, participating in interviews, and preparing data. Theresa Daniel, who assisted me in most of the interviews and whose own research on minority leadership in Dallas was invaluable, and Shane Hall, who helped me develop the ideas at the core of Chapter 12, deserve special thanks. Brian Berry, Irving Hoch, George Farkas, Don Hicks, Anthony Champagne, Ted Harpham, and Paul Waddell read early drafts, caught errors of fact and judgment. Harvey Graff and Henry Bain read a complete draft and offered valuable suggestions for its improvement, as did three anonymous referees. I am grateful to the president and provost of the University, who granted me a year free of teaching to work on the research for this book following my retirement as dean, and to the several reporters and editors of the *Dallas Morning News* who have been as much sources for me as I for them in our common effort to understand Dallas. All remain blameless for errors too cleverly concealed and good advice ignored.

ROYCE HANSON
DECEMBER 2001

I

Civic Culture, Institutions, and the Dallas Political Economy

1

Urban Regimes and Change

> Governance involves *developing an adaptive political system,* one that copes with changing demands and changing environments.
>
> JAMES G. MARCH AND JOHAN P. OLSEN

The Institutional Mismatch

Change was universal in American cities during the last third of the twentieth century. Most experienced dramatic changes in their populations as a consequence of geographic and economic mobility, suburbanization, and shifts in age structure and fertility rates. Increased concentration of racial minorities and the poor in central cities produced fiscal stress and intergroup conflict. Many central cities lost population. Even if the population grew, as it did in Dallas, the metropolitan share of both people and jobs steadily declined.[1] The restructuring of the national economy and the spatial dispersion of local business weakened long-standing relationships among the private, public, and independent sectors of cities. Urban public education systems designed for an industrial age struggled to meet the demands of a new information-based economy while still trying to overcome a legacy of unconstitutional racial discrimination. Within a generation, federal assistance to cities expanded and then contracted but left cities subject to an almost exponential increase in unfunded mandates regulating how they conduct their affairs and vulnerable to litigation aimed at protecting individual rights and procedural fairness.

In the face of these transforming forces city governments modeled on machine-age corporations seemed anachronisms, even in performing their traditional roles as administrative subdivisions of the state. Yet city governments are expected to provide services equitably, enhance their resources, improve amenities, and avoid crises at the local level.[2]

This book is about how the governance regime of the City of Dallas adapted to these challenges, regardless of whether they were set in motion by forces beyond its control, or were consequences of its own actions. "The governance regime of the City of Dallas" encompasses more than the official organs of city government and the school system. In the words of Clarence Stone, an "urban regime" is "*the informal arrangements by which public bodies and private interest function together in order to be able to make and carry out governing decisions.*"[3]

The concept of regime governance comprising both public officials and private interests is based on the fact that the urban political and economic systems are inseparable. In a large, complex city the political influence of economic interests is exercised with few intermediaries, such as lobbyists or trade associations. Business leaders frequently play direct and prominent roles in both the economic and political sectors. The close relationship of property and business to political power is cemented by the heavy reliance of the city on property and sales taxes, and by the dependence of business and property owners on public services, infrastructure, and an amenable regulatory environment. Consequently, the productivity of private capital is a central preoccupation of a city's officials even if business interests are poorly mobilized to exercise political influence.[4] The sunk capital investments in existing firms and homesteads ensure a deep interest by owners in policies that protect values and expand markets and the tax base.

Although the urban economic and political systems are entwined, they cannot be fully synchronized because they are institutionalized in different ways. The urban economy, while affected by public policies, operates through thousands of firms and billions of transactions. Large numbers of firms and jobs can be created and destroyed in relatively short periods in response to shifts in demand, technology, industrial organization, and entrepreneurial imagination. Following both broad trends and beneath the surface shifts,[5] the urban economy expands spatially and changes structurally. It may be transformed over long cycles of growth and technological change.[6] The urban economy is a result, not an entity.

In contrast, urban governments are organized and bounded by positive law. Their physical limits are established by official survey, which are as indifferent to economic geography as to the natural landscape. A city's jurisdiction can be altered only by law, regardless of changes in its demography, settlement patterns, and economic conditions. The urban polity is an entity, not a result.

Consequently, as the urban economy spreads beyond city limits into regional and global markets, the "political" side of the urban political economy rarely follows. New jurisdictions and agencies may be formed but the outgrown and obsolete units are unlikely to go out of business. Even when the formal structure of government is changed, many of the actors remain and retain their old habits and routines. The institutional mismatch between the unremitting forces of economic change and the turgid inertia of going political concerns produces a pattern of sticky polities and fluid markets. Although changing times seem to demand that urban regimes adapt, they often cannot do so.

Regimes, Institutions, and Civic Culture

The pressures of change influence the formation, maintenance, and evolution or extinction of urban regimes as their principal components devise strategies for coping with the consequences. Economic interests are concerned with maintaining the value of their sunk investments, increasing their market shares, and shifting the burdens of paying for services to others. They can achieve these goals only through the use of public powers. Officials want to attract private investment and improve their competitive position among suburbs and other cities, and provide revenue to meet the demands of constituents for services and jobs. The confluence of these interests provides the motivation to form a regime, but does not guarantee its successful establishment. A regime is more than a convenient and transitory alliance formed in response to environmental conditions that confound routine approaches to problem solving. It connotes an arrangement that is widely acknowledged as the city's governance system.

A regime may be "pure"—structured so that it reflects the interest of a single group or faction—or complex, reflecting a variety of interests. It may be strong and stable over time, or fragile and unstable. It may evolve from a pure and stable arrangement into a more complex and volatile form.[7] Reciprocal benefits for its members allow some regimes to remain resilient and adapt to a changing environment.[8] Others founder in the face of mobilized opposition or shifts in underlying economic or political conditions.[9] Urban regimes differ in their policy objectives and in the extent to which they are aggressive or defensive in style.[10]

Understanding a city's regime is the key to explaining "how . . . cooperation [across sectors of community life] is maintained with an ongoing process of social change, a continuing influx of new actors, and potential break-downs through conflict or indifference."[11] Thus, a city's regime is best understood as a *political institution,* which embodies systematic patterns of behavior that reflect the collective experience of those parts of the private and public sectors that compose it. It manages access and information. It has well established, if unwritten, roles and rules that govern the relationships among its members and set the boundaries within which governing actions may occur. It purposefully melds economic and electoral power, interprets the public interest of the city, makes and keeps its rules, structures public life, performs civic rituals, and infuses them with meaning. The regime provides "the framework within which politics takes place."[12] It shapes interests, values, and roles, and in turn, is shaped by them.

Stories about the accomplishments of the regime contain the lessons or morals of an implicit "theory of action," which inform and guide its governing decisions. A stable and enduring regime may weave these stories into a civic myth that celebrates the city's creation and the achievements of its leaders. As the regime's interpretation of civic history diffuses throughout the city, its lessons produce a civic culture or creed—a set of pervasive values and rules—that become the guides people follow to do what they are supposed to do in light of the positions they hold and the situations they confront. Thus, the civic culture establishes the rules and tools of civic engagement. To the extent the attentive publics of a city, including the principal figures of the regime, imbibe the culture, they are socialized to behave in ways that are deemed appropriate.[13]

This "logic of appropriateness"[14] helps explain the policy choices and public actions of regimes with regard to services and development, especially those that do not seem to be "rational" when measured against external standards of economy or efficiency. It may also help explain the character of the regime itself and why it is often so difficult for it to adapt to changes in its economy or demography.

The rules of engagement and the standards of appropriate action imbedded in the civic culture of a regime also raise basic questions about how well the city's governance corresponds to the ideals and functions expected of cities in a democratic republic. As a practical arrangement to get things done, the first test of a regime's effectiveness is not its ability to exercise *power over* others in order to exact compliance, but its *power to* engage members of the regime in social production—"the capacity to assemble and use needed resources for a policy initiative."[15] In other words, can it solve important urban problems?

But Mussolini's regime made the trains run on time. Democratic values demand more. The concept of social production embraces the notion that in solving problems, those who participate in making governing decisions learn from experience and increase their capacity to deal with future problems. Surely, if a regime cannot deal with the practical problems of services and development it is unlikely to retain the support of a broader public upon which its sustainability ultimately depends. Still, such a regime may offer little more than commercial transactions, supplying good value per tax dollar but failing to expand civic learning beyond its elite members.

Democratic theory suggests that the most important function of urban governance is neither supplying local services nor managing development but the formation of civic capital by fostering citizenship that is competent and empowered for self-government. This involves providing direct experience in governance that nurtures trust and those other "habits of the heart"[16] that equip citizens for effective participation in republican government: informed and reasoned argument, deliberation, toleration, respect for the equal dignity of others, and compromise. Stephen Elkin echoes John Stuart Mill and Alexis de Tocqueville, arguing that municipal institutions are the principal means through which people learn and practice the arts of citizenship,[17] and should be viewed "as formative of the sort of citizenry that is necessary if a commercial republic is to flourish."[18] The thrust of his argument is that the "commercial public interest" is too important to be left to a regime focused narrowly on the interests of business: "a commercial republic is not the same as a republic dominated by businessmen."[19]

The concept of social production addresses the civic capital problem for those who participate in the coalition that composes the regime. Stone concedes that even in Atlanta where the coalition of white business executives and black politicians has a long history, the regime " . . . is centered around a combination of explicit and tacit deals."[20] Thus, it protects the privileges and interests of the coalition partner with the greatest and most fungible resources. This restricts meaningful participation in the coalition, limits the public agenda and curtails the social learning that is so critical to the development of civic capital. Making the regime more inclusive and its weaker members less dependent upon the concentrated wealth and slack resources of the economic elite becomes the great conundrum for the institutions of urban governance if they are to fulfill their civic function. A regime may solve problems in the technical sense that it is capable of making hard choices and carrying them out but still fail to develop civic capital, thus producing institutional entropy in the city and a cynical citizenry with few civic skills.

Cultivation of an informed citizenry engaged in sharing responsibility for resolving public problems can be justified on its own merits as valuable to the maintenance of a democratic system. Moreover, as Robert Putnam's work on Italian regional governments shows, regimes with civic cultures that foster an engaged citizenry are also more successful in economic development than those regimes with cultures built on patronage and dependence. He concludes that "economics does not predict civics, but civics does predict economics, better indeed than economics itself."[21]

The Plan of This Book

This book has three nested objectives. The first and most basic of these is to describe the Dallas way of governing and solving the problems it confronted during the last decades of the twentieth century. This entails an understanding of a unique civic culture and the way in which it is both the product of an urban regime formed before the World War II, and the wellspring of motivation, logic of appropriateness, and structure for policy choices as that regime and the city have evolved. Accordingly, the book deals with the great crises that have gripped the city since its recovery from the trauma of the assassination of President John F. Kennedy in 1963: achieving equity and quality in public education, police-minority relations, sustaining economic growth, and the distribution of political power. All involve elements of racial conflict. They also provide an opportunity to examine differences in regime behavior in the three functions of urban governance: service provision, management of development, and formation of civic capital.

The second objective is to analyze the extent to which the Dallas regime engaged in social production and civic capital formation as it addressed these service, development, and power distribution issues. This aspect of the inquiry is concerned in the first instance with whether the problems addressed were resolved. Regardless of the primary outcome, the secondary effects of the experience concern whether it resulted in institutional learning that increased the capacity of the regime or its adversaries to address similar or subsequent problems. The last stage of this inquiry examines whether problems were approached in ways that made the regime more inclusive or reflective, and thus formative of broad-based civic capital.

The third objective is to explore the implications of the findings for the future of effective democratic governance in Dallas and other large cities. As a practical discipline, political economy should offer more than a description of things as they are. Drawing on democratic theory, it should offer modest suggestions for how things might be made to work better. Elkin argues that: "When great political questions arise, especially when citizens run around in the streets raising them, it would be pleasing if political science offered something more than what a newspaper columnist well versed in recent polling data and electoral statistics can muster."[22] I pursue his aspiration to think of ways that could foster an urban regime that not only can get things done, but could be "formative of the sort of citizenry that is necessary if a commercial republic is to flourish."[23]

These objectives are pursued through the parallel use of several approaches. Historical and case analyses are employed to explicate the extent to which the governance institutions of Dallas engaged in social control or social production, manifested in fostering the capacity of regime participants to solve policy problems. Institutional analysis is used to illuminate the role of civic culture in influencing policy choices and in shaping judgment about the appropriate roles of actors, approaches to issues, and use of particular solution sets for dealing with critical problems. The bureaucratic typology developed by James Q. Wilson is useful in explaining the behavior of some of the organizations engaged in the policy problems.[24] Finally, I have adapted "tools analysis" to analyze various policy choices and approaches to problem solving. This method posits that decision makers choose policy "tools" that they deem appropriate for the tasks at hand. These "concrete mechanism[s] for achieving a policy goal"[25] include organizations, regulations, incentives, public-private partnerships, third party contracts, litigation, and other means. Examining why a particular approach was selected in the context of civic culture and regime politics, how it worked, and its consequences for social production and the formation of civic capital provide a richer analysis than can be squeezed from a traditional case study. Moreover, when particular approaches are used repeatedly in culturally patterned responses, they form "solution sets"[26] that reflect the lessons a city has learned from its experience and can tell a great deal about the capacity of the city to adapt to the exigencies of changing conditions.

Most regime studies lay out a history of the city in chronological order, followed by an analysis of the regime. This has advantages when the focus is primarily on one function of the city—usually development, because of its significance as a basis for formation and maintenance of a governing coalition. This book is organized in a different way. Because it examines each of the city's governance functions, I have kept the relevant historical material close to the institutional analysis it supports. While this sacrifices the coherence of a unified chronology of events, it avoids excessive repetition or the need to stretch memory to recover historical context for analytical commentary. The remaining chapters of Part I, however, introduce the reader to the civic culture of Dallas and provide a general history of its political economy and governance institutions. They describe how economic and political power were fused to form the "pure entrepreneurial regime"[27] that governed Dallas for most of the twentieth century and how recent shifts in economic structure and demography have modified these arrangements. Together, these chapters put urban flesh on the conceptual skeleton outlined above and introduce the ideas and institutions that matter most in understanding why Dallas responded as it did to the challenges it faced.

Parts II, III, and IV focus, respectively, on each of the principal functional policy arenas of urban governance: the provision of vital local public services, urban development, and the formation of civic capital. I have deliberately begun the examination, in Part II, of how the city adapted to change in two traditional urban services—schools and policing. These activities of local government, more than any others, define a city's governance system. As quintessentially *public* institutions with unique and strong organizational cultures of their own, their performance profoundly influences the perceptions of a city held by residents and investors. They consume by far the greater part of all local revenue and make up the largest components of the public work force. Teachers and police have the most frequent and direct contact with residents. In Dallas, as in many other big cities, they have been at the center of policy crises generated by internal demographic transformations and external shifts in economic structure, law and social mores. Thus, they offer an opportunity to examine in depth the ways in which civic culture shaped the city's responses to mounting pressures from local minorities, federal courts, and other agencies for justice in the provision of these vital services. Because schools and police are so important to the city but "off center" of the development and growth basis for the urban regime, their administration provides insight into the limits of power exercised by official and informal governance institutions and the influence of civic and organizational cultures on policy choices and the capacity to resolve problems of performance and equity in a rapidly changing environment.

Part III traverses terrain more familiar to observers of urban growth machines. Its three chapters are concerned with evolution of the relationship between the economic and governmental sectors and the influence of Dallas civic culture in urban planning and development decisions in the face of spatial dispersion, cyclic disruptions, and structural upheaval in the Dallas economy. The shift in the city's demography, and with it intensifying demands for redistribution of the benefits of growth and amelioration of its impacts on communities became a new force in development politics and directly challenged the legitimacy of the regime. The power of civic culture in shaping the city's responses to these forces of change suggests possibilities for the emergence of new governing coalitions, different and more influential roles for public officials as catalysts of development projects, as well as raise critical issues about the way development policies are made.

The earlier portions of the book having assayed the ways in which Dallas dealt with its service and development problems, Part IV addresses the effects of this experience on the formation of civic capital. Chapter 10 reviews the relationship of the civic culture of the city to the vitality of peak associations, civic networks, minority institutions and leaders, and participation in elections and bond referenda. This is followed by a detailed case study of the resolution of the 1990 City Council redistricting crisis that substantially increased the diversity of the Council and altered the rules of political engagement.

The story of how the city responded to minority demands for equal representation in city government and court enforcement of the Voting Fights Act illuminates how civic culture conditions choices and limits both the advocates and opponents of change. As with the experience in education, it also reveals the necessity and limitations of judicial intervention in city governance.

Part V reflects on the practical and theoretical issues raised by the book, and explores the implications of the findings for the future of democratic governance in Dallas, a convenient and instructive venue for contemplation of those prospects. It is the center of a prosperous and growing region that contains some of the most advanced industries of the new economy. Its business leadership has shown remarkable, even exemplary, capacity to adapt to the changing tides of the economy and technology over the course of its history. But these same leaders built and maintained a regime that for most of the twentieth century resisted comparable transformations in governance. This makes Dallas a good place to look for answers about why it is so difficult to adapt to transformations of its population and economy and to speculate about what it would take to institutionalize the capacity for change and foster a citizenry equipped to govern a great city.

2

The City That Invented Itself

> Every culture has its characteristic drama. It chooses from the sum total of human possibilities certain acts and interests, certain processes and values, and endows them with special significance, provides them with a setting, organizes rites and ceremonies, excludes from the circle of dramatic response a thousand other daily acts which, though they remain part of the "real world," are not active agents in the drama itself. The stage on which this drama is enacted, with the most skilled actors and a full supporting company and specially designed scenery, is the city. . . .
>
> LEWIS MUMFORD

A GREAT CITY IS MORE than stone and steel. It is also an act of civic imagination. Fact and allegory fuse in a civic myth that interprets experience, justifying the city's history and uniqueness. The civic myth is a story of the city's founding, its heroes, and core values. It is important not because it is true, but because believing it gives meaning to civic endeavors. It helps its keepers explain the city to strangers. It reflects the culture of the city—the rules and folkways by which the city operates—of which it is both author and product. It is the city's soul.

"A City with No Reason to Exist"

The core sentiment of the Dallas civic myth is that the city grew from a desolate river crossing into one of the nation's ten largest cities by an act of will imposed by visionary leaders on a hostile environment. Figure 2.1 contains one of the purest statements of that myth. Two aspects of the statement are remarkable. The first is that it is ahistorical—a product of modern public relations. Dallas historian Patricia Evridge Hill found the first expression of the myth of "a city with no reason to exist" in a 1949 article in *Fortune* Magazine, extolling the role of the "Dydamic Men of Dallas"—the Dallas Citizens Council.[1] This view of a city created by the benevolent, if not quite invisible hands of its leading businessmen served their interests and self-image well. Second, like all successful propaganda, the myth came to be believed by its authors. It is offered as historical evidence that the city can conquer its problems because its people (at least those who matter) aspire to greatness and are imbued with a practical spirit that can transform dreams into realities.

The civic myth has had its practical uses. It was invoked to rally support in 1961 for the peaceful, if symbolic, desegregation of Dallas's schools. Mayor Erik Jonsson drew heavily on its appeal to civic exceptionalism to restore the city's self-confidence and image following the 1963 assassination of President John F. Kennedy. With its good people and a "world class" destiny, the virulently reactionary sentiments of some of the city's wealthiest and most outspoken citizens could be marginalized along with the president's itinerant killer, Lee Harvey Oswald. Jonsson used the myth to build consensus for his "Goals for Dallas" strategic planning initiative, which laid out a set of projects designed to position Dallas as a beacon of civic progress and an engine of economic growth. Jonsson was no naïf when it came to understanding what it took to engineer change, but he described it in terms that made it sound like a miracle of civic goodness:

> How could this one-time trading post at a river crossing have grown so large with no navigable waterway, no rich deposits of minerals nearby, no mountains, no natural lakes,

Profile of Dallas. It is a city that was founded in the middle of nowhere. It had no natural resources. Unless, of course, you count the determination of its people. Through sheer determination, the city grew until it is the eighth largest in the United States with influence that stretches to every corner of the globe.

The city is a financial center, a center for commerce and culture. The technology and transportation leader of the Southwest; an insurance and convention capital.

Such a city does not just happen. It takes people. People with energy, with vision, and with guts. People who dream. And people who can take time from building a magnificent city to provide a place of thanksgiving in the very center of their city.

It took people just like you to make Dallas what it is today. And people just like you will make Dallas what it will be tomorrow. A city with no limits.

RepublicBank
Dallas

Source: Reprinted in Donald F. Mitchell, ed., *Profile of Dallas: Love Affair with a City* (Dallas, Texas: Turtle Creek Gallery, 1981), p. 38

Figure 2.1. The Dallas creation myth

no breath-taking vistas to lure people? Its climate is generally mild although often its summers are so hot and dry that its detractors say it's the ideal place to train for the Nether Regions Mark Twain called "the Ever-Lasting Tropics."

The answer is simple and straightforward. It can be found in the spirit of the pioneers who established a crossroads settlement here 140 years ago and the nature of the generations which followed. . . . Heedless of hardships,

> lack of capital or other resources, they had only their own physical strength and indomitable courage to meet the tremendous odds and challenges of their time. . . . Their responses to these barriers were heroic, though they certainly gave no thought to themselves and their deeds in such terms.[2]

Having imagined the selflessness and dedication of the city's pioneers, Jonsson turned to its modern achievements in buildings, highways, sports, cultural attractions, scientific and educational institutions, and air transportation, and to his own tenure as mayor:

> During those years [1964–1971], we made progress, building on earlier cornerstones. During that "most of a decade," cities all across the country were beset by rioting and burning, but we had none of that here. Herculean efforts of the past to right old wrongs, to communicate among the races, to achieve as one people became linked to a new program, Goals for Dallas. Through it thousands and thousands of citizens from all walks of life, all parts of the city, pooled their ideas of what Dallas should make of itself in the years to come. Each had a voice, a vital component in a program which also brings analysis, synthesis, order, discipline into the stream. With it we do more than bemoan serious, complex, difficult problems as terrifying or unsolvable. Solvable they are, but it requires communication and exploration with *all* the citizenry, not pat, overnight solutions. . . .
>
> Ah, those Dallas people! Friendly, hardworking, industrious, concerned for their fellowmen. . . .
>
> . . . Dallas is indeed a city with a heart. What more could one ask?[3]

If Jonsson's encomium improved on history, it furthered an image of Dallas its notable citizens liked to see: pulsing with energy and ambition, friendly to commerce, well ordered, led by enlightened and generous businessmen. It fit the need for the city to see itself as good—where the assassination was an aberration, the act of a deranged transient; an alien to the positive, building spirit of Dallas. It also captured well the credo of its public spirited but not public-regarding business leaders: unlike ordinary cities that rose to greatness as a consequence of the lucky confluence of historic forces,[4] Dallas was a conscious act of will.

This view contrasted sharply with the national image of Dallas as a "city of hate," fostered by the national media following the Kennedy assassination. Later, national popular culture embraced an image of *Dallas* as the domain of the crass and hedonistic Ewing clan of the television series.[5] The more uplifting RepublicBank version survived both the television series and the bank itself, which vanished into the maw of bankruptcies, receiverships, and mergers that reorganized Dallas financial institutions in the 1980s and 1990s. The city "created from nothing but the determination of its people;" the city that dared to dream great dreams; the city that works; the "can-do" city became a matter of faith for a generation of city officials, business and civic leaders. Dallas was a city that invented itself.

In 1997, two years after Jonsson's death at the age of ninety-four, Ron Kirk, the city's first African-American mayor, echoed the words of its once great bank and greatest mayor: "Dallas is one of the most entrepreneurial cities in the country. The evidence is the fact that we're here. We're not a port. We don't have mountains. We don't have oceans. There is no reason for us to be here except the fact that we decided that since we're here we're going to make this the biggest city in Texas. . . ."[6] Then, he added a codicil: "Our challenge is to embrace globalism in an everyday living, cultural and religious sense of what it means to be one of the most pluralistic cities in the world. . . . I start with the presumption that cities that are more diverse are going to be more competitive and more successful in this new world economy than cities that are less so."[7]

Heroes

Dallas' heroes have always been businessmen. Except for Texans who became presidents, it is the names of business leaders that adorn the city's freeways, plazas and public buildings. Publisher George Dealey, who stood against the Ku Klux Klan and engineered the home rule charter in 1930, is memorialized by the plaza where Kennedy was shot. Interstate 30, traversing the city from east to west, is named for R. L. "Uncle Bob" Thornton, Chairman of Mercantile Bank, impresario of the Texas Centennial, founder of the Dallas Citizens Council, and four-term mayor. The central library is Erik Jonsson's monument.

In times of crisis, business leaders rose to the occasion. Jonsson, CEO of Texas Instruments, agreed to become mayor following the Kennedy assassination. Jack Evans, another former mayor, and CEO of the Cullum companies, a local grocery chain, continued the tradition into the 1990s, when he was called from retirement to serve as interim director of the troubled Dallas Area Rapid Transit (DART) agency. For more than two generations, such men guided the slack resources of corporations to civic causes, shaped public opinion through the skillful use of public relations, and imposed their will on the city through the exercise of raw economic and political power. Unquestionably devoted to Dallas, they blended enlightened self-interest with a deep ethic of community service, rooted in their shared belief in the reciprocity of a great city and business prosperity. More than a few would explain their extended involvement in city affairs as a repayment to a city that had done so much for them. Erik Jonsson wistfully remarked: "Dallas had been good to me. That's why I can't refuse to do any job for Dallas that is asked of me." Rancher and developer John W. Carpenter expressed similar sentiments: "I feel a very personal obligation to repay my community for the advantages it has afforded me. It is my duty to plow back as much good as I can."[8]

It was to this tradition that Sandy Kress, on retiring as President of the Board of Trustees of Dallas Public Schools in 1995, appealed. A lawyer and former Dallas County Democratic Party Chairman, Kress had been elected with the backing of business leaders to "reform" the schools, which were perceived as contributing to a bad business climate for Dallas. In his two terms on the school board, Kress found that few of his business constituents had much stomach for the racial politics and bureaucratic infighting that suffocated substantial reform and lasting change. Kress called for business leaders to step forward and tackle the difficult and complex task of improving a public school system that had demonstrably failed to meet the challenges of diversity suggested by Mayor Kirk. The *Dallas Morning News* editorially joined his plea for business saviors: "His decision raises a major challenge for the Dallas business community. The city's civic leadership must view Mr. Kress' departure as a clear sign to step up their involvement in educational issues, not let up. . . . There is a crying need for board members with management experience and links to business groups."[9] None stepped up.

The comments of both Kirk and Kress sharply evoke the myth of a city where business giants could make things happen through sheer will power, business acumen, and the ability to raise capital with a few phone calls to colleagues. The editorial comment on Kress' retirement was a nostalgic appeal for return to that mythic age when such leaders existed and could deliver.

Core Values

The civic myth reflects the values of the civic culture. Those values shape much of the language of the city's political discourse, how the issues that can come onto the public and institutional agendas are framed and discussed, the ways in which the system works, and the tools its leaders choose to carry out policies.

A Privately Held Public Interest

The civic culture of Dallas is anchored in a strong preference for the private corporate over the public political sector. Over several decades, the national business press has celebrated its hospitality to commerce.[10] Since the good things in city life flowed from business, maintaining a friendly business climate was the epitome of public interest. It was central to the ongoing campaign to attract relocating firms.[11] In the words of Mayor Ron Kirk: "Our business is making money."[12]

In such a city, it followed that business leaders would have a better grasp of the public interest than mere politicians would. And throughout its modern history Dallas has looked to business for leadership of civic initiatives, funding for important projects,[13] and legitimatization of policies. This privately held public interest was wary of the use of local government for any but routine tasks: keeping the peace, protecting property values, providing services that kept the city clean, safe, and up-to-date, and holding tax rates down. With rare exceptions, mayors were business executives and Dallas developed no separate political class.

Minimalist Government

Accordingly, the city government was limited in scope and modest in ambition. For many years, the Dallas City Council refused to apply for federal grants-in-aid that would have required matching funds for expanded or new public services. Municipal services were basic, nonpartisan, and competently delivered. City planning was confined to facilitation of private development.

Aversion to active government did not extend to the use of public resources in support of private development. Infrastructure was built with surplus capacity to support unlimited growth. Business leaders backed bond issues to construct a series of water reservoirs to provide an ample supply to support growth well into the twenty-first century. They eagerly lobbied for federal funds to build levees so they could reclaim the Trinity River floodplain for development, build highways, and even construct public housing.[14]

Government in Dallas is not only minimal; it is diffused among a bewildering array of institutions and officials. Ten independent school districts serve students who live in Dallas. The city sprawls into three counties, which have concurrent jurisdiction with it over many activities, and primary responsibility for hospital services, mental health, welfare, courts, correction facilities, and some roads. In addition there are a number of special purpose districts, such as the Dallas Area Rapid Transit (DART) and the Dallas Housing Authority (DHA).

Amateur Officials

The Dallas civic culture placed a high value on the obligation for public service by its leading citizens. This included a duty, if called upon by one's peers, to accept a tour in elected office. But to ensure that busy business executives could spare the time for official duties, city council and school board positions were structured to require as little time as possible away from one's private profession or business. At worst, holding public office was expected to be comparable to service on a corporate or nonprofit organization's board of directors. Elected office should not, of course, be sought or considered a career. Rather, it was both a duty and an honor bestowed in recognition of prior service. Accordingly, council members were parsimoniously paid and rotated back into private life after two or three terms. Consistent with reform dogma, elections were nonpartisan, and city government was expected to be untainted by politics.

During the first forty years of council-manager government, "people of the best sort"—almost invariably successful business executives or financially independent citizens sympathetic to business interests—were recruited to serve on the city council. There they devoted a day or so a week to setting general policies for the city's affairs and superintending an administration of neutral competence.

The amateur culture has persisted. Repeated efforts to increase the pay of the mayor and council members above the $50 per meeting set in the charter have regularly been rebuffed at referenda. The most recent charter amendments, in 1989, limited both the mayor and members of the council to eight consecutive years of service. Few members of the city council have regarded it as a launching pad for a political career,[15] although two were subsequently elected to the U. S. Congress[16] and several have served in the Texas Legislature. The charter's requirement that a member who seeks another office must resign from the council upon filing for partisan nomination is a further impediment to political careerists, but proved no deterrent for Mayor Ron Kirk, who resigned in 2002 to seek the Democratic nomination for the U.S. Senate.

The city charter makes the mayor the ceremonial head of the city government and the presiding officer of the city council. Thus, the mayor can influence the council agenda, and appoint council standing committees and chairs of city commissions. Since 1991, as the only member of the city council elected citywide and for a four-year term, mayors have used the prestige of the office to influence public opinion, and when sufficiently skilled in the arts of persuasion, a shifting majority of the council colleagues.[17] Dallas mayors have no personal staff,[18] and no direct administrative authority. Most have, with the acquiescence of the council, established a close working relationship with the city manager, which former mayors generally list as a key to their effectiveness.[19] Equally important, however, are their reputations with peers in the business and social communities of the city, and in recent years, their ability to work amicably with minority groups.

Managerialism

A culture that relies on amateur officials, but expects efficient and economical government, necessarily depends heavily on professional managers. Extending the corporate metaphor to city government and the school system, the city manager and general superintendent of Dallas Public Schools are the chief executive and operating officers of their respective governments. They have full control, without formal approval by their elected bodies, over the appointment, assignment and dismissal of all department heads and other personnel. They provide all staff support for the elected officials to whom they report. They prepare and submit the budgets for approval.

In his study of Dallas, Stephen Elkin observed a natural symbiosis between the commercial interests of business executives in growth and orderly government and the interests of city managers in their professional reputations.[20] The affinity of managers with the Dallas business elite is evident. Many of Dallas's managers and assistant managers have entered the executive suites of local corporations or consulting firms upon leaving city hall, rather than moving to other cities.[21]

The cultural preference for the manager system extends well beyond business leaders. Minority and neighborhood representatives elected to the council are among its strongest supporters. They fear the concentration of political power by an elected mayor, even one that is a member of their group. Thus, they opposed a suggestion by Mayor Kirk in 1997 to create a charter commission to study strengthening the mayor's office.[22] Few council members envision themselves as mayor, and the manager system makes the mayor their equal in any matter that must be decided by vote, notwithstanding the higher visibility and public prestige of the office. They see in the manager system an opportunity to form logrolling alliances to convince managers to improve services to their constituencies, and feel they have the ability individually to influence decisions affecting their districts, in spite of the city charter's prohibition of instructions to city staff by individual council members.

Managerialism produces a subculture of its own. The pervasiveness and complexity of the city's problems, frequent lack of clear political direction, and sporadic outbreaks of racial division in the governing bodies encourages defensiveness, bureaucratic sluggishness, obsessive concern for control over programs and processes, and reflexive resistance to sharing power with community groups and elected officials.[23] Particularly in recent years, elected officials have not had the political cohesion born of long seasoning in the lesser "chairs" of the old business-civic system. Those who have won election without substantial prior business or political responsibilities have sometimes lacked the decisiveness or affinity of business executives for delegation of details to professionals. Consequently, the two managers of the big public enterprises of Dallas find themselves operating in an environment that ironically grants them less deference but more independence in making decisions on behalf of the city or school system.

Single Option Policies

One of the features of the entrepreneurial regime that governed Dallas for most of the twentieth century was its cohesion. The coterie of homegrown executives saw their business successes as inseparable from "their" city. They knew it intimately. They made it what it was. They needed no expert advisers or analysts. Their passions, interests, and experience guided them in the design of projects to enhance the city. Their *in camera* decisions were presented as sole options—the consensus of wise, beneficent, and experienced city fathers. As the ends of government were agreed upon by the best of the city's corporate citizens, the only issue of importance was selection of the most efficient and cost effective means of achieving them. If there were controversies, the business leaders would settle them quietly and in a way that reflected credit on the city's reputation as "a city that worked." Problems were not necessarily denied, but their causes and possible responses to them were not publicly discussed until business leaders had agreed upon a single option and said grace over it.[24] Analysis was unnecessary; none was welcome.[25] Studies were commissioned to support solutions, not to evaluate proposals.

Consumerism

Dallas civic culture views local government in business metaphors. In this sense, city government and the school system are regarded as service vendors. Residents are seen as individual customers seeking value for their taxes, rather than as citizens who share responsibility for balancing the city's tax-service package. The result of this attitude is to approach public policy as a marketing problem instead of an open deliberative process. It also encourages disdain for government, especially among those who can buy comparable services in the private market, reducing enthusiasm for taxes even below levels common among American localities. This, in turn, constrains the public sector, fulfilling prophecies of its inadequacies.

Projects that enhance the world class image of Dallas, but cannot be readily justified as necessary or cost-effective, such as a sports arena, symphony hall, or a rail transit system, can still be "sold" to the limited group of consumers that participate in bond referenda. They are marketed as prestige goods that will enhance individual enjoyment, satisfaction, or status, and thus, attract business and raise property values. A proposal may also be represented as a "bargain," involving no increase in taxes while enhancing service, amenity, or economic opportunity. Some projects may be structured to offer city taxpayers a free ride by shifting their costs to nonresidents.

Consumerism encourages passivity toward city affairs. This is reflected in voting participation in city elections, which is remarkably low, rarely exceeding 25 percent, and often falling below seven percent of those registered. When options are limited to a single choice and debate is discouraged, there is little to attract the ordinary citizen to become engaged in city affairs.

Obsession with Image

Consistent with the civic culture, officials and business leaders have boasted that Dallas "can do" whatever it sets its collective mind to. Its achievements and projects are measured against a "world class" standard that automatically adjusts to the metric of the proposal at issue. Anything that diminishes this carefully cultivated image is quickly disparaged or removed. Thus, in 1994 homeless "street people" were banished from the central business district in advance of the World Cup Soccer tournament games played in Dallas. When the parade celebrating the 1993 Superbowl victory of Dallas Cowboys degenerated into a mini-riot, emergency meetings and editorials called for tight control of future events to avoid injury to the city's image. Subsequent parades were well-policed and orderly. Part of the folklore of economic promotion efforts in Dallas is the apocryphal video of a raucous Dallas Council meeting being played for a relocating industry's executives by competing boosters from Atlanta.

Concern for image produces a superficial, symbolic approach to urban issues. When problems are framed as threats to the city's image, the logical response is a public relations campaign to restore its luster. The impulse is to label as anti-Dallas those who dissent from the single option, and to urge all right-thinking citizens to unite to keep Dallas world class.

There is a tendency to marginalize rather than reconcile differences and to defer efforts to resolve problems by addressing their causes. The other effect of this hyper-boosterism is the constant need for reinforcement and confirmation of the city's goodness and that of its civic icons. Dallas maintains a continuous awards procession that moves among the city's hotel banquet halls, where the interlocking civic organizations congratulate themselves and their leaders for their devotion to the commonweal.

Hidden Transcripts

In any society, there are some that do not adhere to or are left out of the dominant culture. They may outwardly conform most of the time because there is little choice, but they also engage in strategies that are subversive of it. These dissenters and doubters read from a "hidden transcript"[26] of resentment that is largely invisible to the keepers of the civic myth but widely understood by the civic underclass.

In Dallas, the dominant civic culture was the creation of the Anglo economic elite. The existence and role of the city's minority communities—principally blacks and Hispanics—were only slowly and reluctantly acknowledged. For most of the city's history, its minorities were ignored, suppressed, or patronized. The legitimacy of minority leaders depended upon their recognition or designation by business executives as "responsible" representatives of their communities. Minorities ostensibly accepted this practice, but took strategic advantage of it by using "rabble rousers" and "outside agitators" to make credible threats to the city's image, followed by visits from the designated peacemakers seeking incremental concessions from the establishment to restore the appearance of order. In the words of a prominent African-American leader: "The establishment was always willing to do what was good for business. . . . They would try to stop it [social unrest] from happening. . . . We were aware of that, so the strategy was, keep the outside pressure on, and have someone negotiating on the inside."[27]

In this light, Mayor Kirk's diversity amendment was a significant effort to bring minorities at last into the rhetoric of the civic culture. In one sense it is consistent with the culture's obsession with image: a world class city must deal in a diverse world and, thus, must appear to value diversity. At a deeper level, however, it suggests that the price of sustaining the dominant culture will be to include minorities and their authentic leaders, as they gain political power in the city, as full partners in setting the city's agenda.

Summary

Dallas civic culture rests on a creation myth that celebrates the acumen of its business leaders. The interests of business are equated to the public interest. Maintenance of a privately held public interest requires a consensus gained by suppressing, or failing to recognize as legitimate, alternative visions of the city and different points of view about policy. By subordinating, even scorning politics, the civic culture supports a minimalist government, presided over by amateur officials and administered by professional managers whose most urgent work is maintenance of the city's image as a haven for business. Citizenship is reduced to consumerism; self-governance to bargain hunting. Even minorities have assimilated the culture, learning to eke out accommodation by playing on the city's vulnerability to threats to its own myth.

Addendum

Effective October 2001, compensation for the Mayor and Council changed from the $50 per meeting rate described in this book to $37,500 for members of the Council and $60,000 for the Mayor.

3

The Transformation of the Dallas Economy

> [T]here can be no study of city politics without the study of city economy.
>
> STEPHEN ELKIN

DALLAS CIVIC CULTURE AND the persistence of its myth can be understood best in the context of the evolution of the city's political economy. Each of three major eras in Dallas economic history has occasioned a transformation of its functions and the extent of its physical dispersion. This history suggests that the civic myth may have improved on history in its celebration of private self-reliance and sheer will power as the moving forces in the city's development. Entrepreneurs were undoubtedly a critical element, but public decisions and investments, along with good luck and immutable national economic and social forces, also played a large role in shaping modern Dallas.

From Frontier Settlement to Regional Center

Land speculation was the constant companion of the westward course of the American Empire. The dream of quick and sustained riches energized wave after wave of ambitious men to found towns and lure others to participate in their dreams and schemes of building great new centers of commerce. Hardly a settlement in Texas did not imagine itself a metropolis of tomorrow, however inhospitable its location to realization of that ambition. A few succeeded, usually because they were located on natural harbors, well-worn trails, or navigable rivers. Others prospered because through luck or schemes they became rail centers or military outposts. The plains are dotted with ghost towns where the trains did not stop or the army did not stay.

Dallas's early settlers saw it as an opportunity to get rich. John Neely Bryan, Dallas's founder and first land speculator did not pick his homestead on the banks of the Trinity River by dumb luck. There was a good low water crossing where he could operate a ferry. He knew that the Texas Congress had plans for a military road connecting Austin with the Red River country, which would cross the Trinity at its northernmost navigable point, not far from his cabin. Bryan, who ended his days destitute and insane, imagined Dallas as the terminus of steamboat trade on the river, connecting North Texas to Galveston.[1] Subsequent investors in Dallas shared his dream. Three steamboats eventually made it all the way up the Trinity to Dallas in those early years. Two ran aground and sank and with them the illusion that the Trinity could be made navigable all the way to Dallas for any but small shallow draft vessels.[2]

By the end of the Civil War several major post and stage routes passed through town but railroads initially had little interest in serving Dallas. The Houston and Central Texas Railroad located its station a mile east of town (along the route of today's North Central Expressway) in 1872 only after residents paid it $5,000 in cash, and the city granted it 115 acres of land, together with a free right-of-way into town.[3] This is the first recorded instance of private fundraising in Dallas to secure relocation of a substantial firm. It also provided an early lesson in how the public interest and enlightened self-interest could be fruitfully joined. Some of the civic-minded subscribers who brought the railroad to the city incidentally benefited from enhancement in the value of nearby property. Eventually the Central Texas built track north to Denton, where it connected to the Missouri, Kansas and Texas Railroad, providing service to St. Louis and the northeastern United States.

Dallas's second rail line, the Texas and Pacific (T&P), was an even less willing participant in the development dreams of the town's property owners and merchants. Its planned route was within a five-mile variance of a straight line along the 32nd parallel from Tyler west to the Brazos River. This alignment would have missed Dallas by at least eight and perhaps as much as eighteen miles, a distance too far from town to enhance property values.

Legislative chicanery supplemented the guts, brains, and imagination of the city fathers in adjusting the route to serve Dallas. State Representative John Lane, a former mayor, slipped an amendment into the state's right-of-way grant, which required the new railroad to pass within a mile of Browder Springs. While this seemed a thoughtful adjustment in an era when steam locomotives needed to stop frequently to take on water, Browder Springs supplied water for Dallas, and was located just a mile south of the county court house. Even then, the city had to sweeten the pot with $100,000 in cash and twenty-five acres of land to persuade the T&P to build the rail line into the heart of the city, along what is now Pacific Avenue, rather than a mile south of the spring.[4]

In 1909, the Legislature was again instrumental in bending the rails to suit city interests. A law was enacted requiring the railroads to construct a union station in Dallas, rather than maintain five separate stations—one for each line. By the beginning of World War II, Dallas was served by eight rail systems, and was one of the most important rail centers in the southwest,[5] positioning it as a key distribution center for the nation.

The interruption of railroad construction in Texas after the financial panic of 1873 made Dallas the southwestern end of the lines. As a consequence, it was the regional terminus for the ginning and shipment of Texas short staple cotton, wheat, and milled flour. By 1875 Dallas was the busiest market in the world for buffalo hides, as the slaughter of the herds progressed across the Great Plains. With the railroads providing access to eastern and northern suppliers, hides and cotton money generating a lot of disposable income in Dallas, and a growing market of settlers to be served in towns and on farms spreading across Texas, Dallas became the region's chief merchandising center. Enterprising merchants like the Sanger Brothers, who arrived with the railroads, set up networks of "drummers"—traveling salesmen who took orders from farmers and small town storekeepers—and began establishing the first department stores in Dallas.[6]

The Dallas economy's evolution from a simple export terminal for raw materials to a major manufacturing and distribution center was facilitated by two unique immigrations. The Peters Colony was a land speculation and settlement scheme, which lured farmers from Tennessee and Kentucky to north central Texas with tales of a benign climate and rich soil without mentioning the hardships of life on the blackland prairie. Many of these small farmers, who settled in and around what is now Farmer's Branch, created a local market for farm implements, harness and saddles. Alexander Cockrell, a Peters Colonist, bought out Bryan's holdings in 1852 and organized a company to build a bridge across the Trinity, securing Dallas's dominance of the local market for farm produce and creating, in the bridge company, a ready buyer for lumber produced by Cockrell's sawmill. After his death, Cockrell's widow established the area's first flourmill.[7] By the beginning of the Civil War, Dallas was a major milling center for Texas and served as breadbasket for the Confederacy, shipping raw grain and milled flour throughout the South.

In the early 1850s, French, Swiss, and Belgian followers of the utopian communitarian, Charles Fourier, founded Reunion, across the Trinity from Dallas. The commune was a failure, but the colonists included artisans, mechanics, merchants and professionals who provided the nucleus of skilled labor and entrepreneurs necessary to begin making things that Dallas had previously imported, selling them locally and to customers in other cities.[8]

Cotton Capital and Financial Center

Awash with money from the trade in cotton, wheat, and hides, merchants and brokers gravitated to Dallas, creating a thriving wholesale center, a cotton exchange, and retail stores to serve the growing city and its hinterland with consumer goods and farm equipment. As the nineteenth century closed, the buffalo hide trade ended, but the cotton industry expanded with the local manufacture of an improved cotton gin, development of the cottonseed oil industry, and textile and clothing manufacturing. Farming and the cattle industry supported the manufacture of harnesses and saddles, farm implements and machinery.[9]

All of this capitalism demanded banks to secure cash surpluses and finance new enterprises and shipments. Insurance companies were needed to underwrite the risks of transporting valuable cargoes, losses from fire in a town of wooden buildings, and the hazards of life at the edge of the southwestern frontier. Texas law forbade the sale of insurance by companies that did not have offices and invest a high percentage of their revenues in the state. The initial effect of this law was to drive out-of-state insurers from the state, leaving a clear field for the formation of Dallas-based companies. The rapid growth of commerce soon made Dallas home to the largest concentration of insurance firms in the southwest. As Texas and its insurance markets grew, the major national underwriters returned to the state and set up offices in Dallas. By the beginning of World War II, Dallas was the fourth most important insurance center in the United States.[10]

The diversity and adaptability of the Dallas economy made it less susceptible to bank failures during the several financial panics that seized the country in the last quarter of the nineteenth century and the early years of the twentieth century.[11] Texas law also discouraged out-of-state banks and flows of capital from the region. Consequently, Dallas banks accumulated large pools of capital and were on the lookout for profitable local investments. By the time the railroads arrived, Dallas banks, through mergers and acquisitions, had metamorphosed in to a stable financial sector, eventually dominated by three commercial banking giants—First National, Republic, and Mercantile.

Dallas was already an important financial center by the turn of the century. Its position as the regional financial capital of the southwest was assured when it was designated as the site for one of the twelve regional Federal Reserve Banks created in 1914. Political connections were essential in securing the Fed for Dallas over rival cities Fort Worth, Houston, San Antonio, El Paso and Oklahoma City. Colonel Edward M. House, a Texan who was President Woodrow Wilson's closest adviser, and Postmaster General Albert S. Burleson intervened on Dallas's behalf with the Secretaries of Treasury and Agriculture, who selected the cities for Federal Reserve Banks.[12]

From Oil Patch to Silicon Prairie and Air Transport Hub

Bank autonomy and the availability of a large uncommitted capital pool were critical to the ability of Dallas to make a transition from an economy swathed in cotton to one greased with oil. Eastern banks already had close ties to the major oil companies. As the east Texas discoveries occurred, Dallas bankers realized that if they were to be players in a new, energy-based economy, they would have to finance the independent producers. Their innovation was to lend money to independent producers, such as H. L. Hunt and Clint Murchison, allowing them to use their petroleum reserves as collateral.[13] The independents, in return, located their headquarters in Dallas, attracting oil field equipment manufacturers and suppliers, lease brokers, lawyers, and contractors. Their demand for office space and housing helped foster the construction industry, producing, in time, some of the largest property development and management firms in the world, such as the Trammell Crow Companies, Lincoln Properties, and Venture Corporation.

The oil industry attracted to Dallas a small firm then known as Geophysical Services, Inc., co-founded by Erik Jonsson, Cecil Green, and Eugene McDermott. Initially a manufacturer of seismic and other exploration instruments, the firm changed its name to Texas Instruments (TI) after moving to Dallas. During World War II, it segued from production of sensitive seismic instruments to precision military electronics. Its laboratories developed the integrated circuit, and TI became the foundation for the transition of the Dallas economy from the machine to the information age, anchoring the concentration of telecommunications firms in northern Dallas and southern Collin Counties.

The presence of so much insurance talent in the city had fostered innovation in the industry. One such innovation was the creation of the Blue Cross-Blue Shield system of health and hospital insurance for school employees.[14] The rapid growth of Blue Cross and its need to keep track of claims led it to contract with another innovator, Ross Perot and his fledgling EDS Corporation, for computing services, propelling the city further into an information-based economy.

Civic myth and economic reality had a closer convergence in the development of the Dallas area as an aerospace and air transport center. The city had its share of early airplane eccentrics and visionaries, and like many medium sized cities throughout the country, the airplane was an object of financial speculation and mass entertainment. Seizing an opportunity, the Dallas Chamber of Commerce bought the land that is now Love Field in 1917 and leased it to the Army to train pilots. When World War I ended and the Army declined to purchase the field, the Chamber decided to develop it as an aviation-oriented industrial park, and succeeded in attracting a number of civil aviation firms. In 1926, when airmail service was being established, the Chamber offered carriers incentives of free rent and a guarantee of mail traffic to Chicago. With its central location, Love Field became a regional air cargo center.

Its role as a passenger terminal began in 1927, when the Chamber sold Love Field to the city of Dallas for $432,500, as its municipal airport.[15] Braniff Airlines moved its headquarters there, and Dallas received regular service from American and Delta Airlines as the demand for air passenger service grew.

The good flying weather, land availability, and a skilled labor pool that had evolved from the carriage and wagon business through automobile manufacturing, made the Dallas-Fort Worth area a good location for military aircraft manufacturing during World War II and the ensuing Cold War years. Defense-related industries in aeronautics, electronics, and communications grew into a major sector of the regional economy.

Dallas and Fort Worth had been bitter rivals for air service for many years. But rising costs, FAA pressure, and constraints on expansion of Love Field eventually led Dallas business leaders, spurred by Erik Jonsson's Goals for Dallas, to agree with their counterparts in Fort Worth to build Dallas-Fort Worth International Airport half-way between the two cities.[16] With the construction of D/FW, American Airlines moved its headquarters to Fort Worth. The creation of a major international airport made Dallas into a "port" of far greater importance than any imagined by early promoters of river navigation. While Love Field was restricted to serving non-stop destinations in Texas and adjoining states, it became the home base for Southwest Airlines, the nation's most successful discount short haul carrier.

The Automobile and Greater Dallas

The automobile shaped the physical form of modern Dallas. In 1920, Dallas was a compact city of only twenty-six square miles and 159,000 people. Some expansion had occurred by annexations of Oak Cliff, an independent town south of the Trinity, and East Dallas. A few subdivisions had developed along electric streetcar lines radiating from the central business district. Dallas resembled other up-and-coming midwestern cities, growing by a combination of population increases and annexation of neighboring settlements. As Table 3.1 shows, growth slowed during the Great Depression but spurted during the Second World War and the post-war era. Between 1945 and 1960, further annexations increased the city's land area six-fold,[17] as shown in Figure 3.1.

By 1930, the transcontinental U.S. highway system had more routes passing through Dallas than any other Texas city. Dallas loved roads. George Kessler, the city planner retained in 1911 to draw up a plan to guide the expansion of the city, had recommended the replacement of the Houston and Central Texas Railroad tracks with a great north-south thoroughfare, to connect Mexico and Canada via Dallas.[18] When it was finally

Table 3.1 Dallas Population Growth 1900–1990

Year	*Population*
1900	42,638
1910	92,104
1920	158,976
1930	260,475
1940	294,734
1950	434,462
1960	679,984
1970	852,255
1980	904,078
1990	1,003,298

Source: U.S. Census

completed in the early 1950s, the Central Expressway was the major catalyst for the first significant shift in retail and office locations in Dallas. In the name of "slum clearance" the expressway also displaced black residents living along the Texas Central tracks,[19] forcing their move to the only areas open to them, white working class and Jewish neighborhoods in South Dallas.[20] A long period of disinvestment in South Dallas began, accelerating the economic disparities between Anglo and minority neighborhoods.[21]

By the mid-1970s, four major federal interstate highways (20, 30, 35-E, and 45) traversed Dallas. The division of the city by the tracks on Pacific Avenue had been replaced by a new barrier, the Woodall Rogers Freeway, which connected the already overburdened Central Expressway to the downtown "mix master" of elevated ramps entwining three of the Interstates. The LBJ Freeway (I-635) ringed the city, connecting the international airport with the northern and eastern interstate routes. "Greater Dallas" now sprawled far beyond the city limits, and into adjacent counties in every direction. Residential development moved outward in concentric bands from the old city center, accommodated by the new transportation arteries. Commercial and industrial development followed.

When Erik Jonsson took office as mayor in 1964, a remarkable change had already taken place in the structure and spatial organization of the Dallas economy. Major businesses, including Jonsson's own Texas Instruments, were building headquarters campuses outside the compact perimeter of the central business district. The completion of the Trinity River levees and I-35 alongside them opened the formerly flood-prone "Stemmons Corridor"[22] to extensive industrial, office, and hotel development. Republic Bank and the Southland Corporation built their new office towers at opposite ends of an expanding "downtown." Ray Nasher built the region's first enclosed mall at the intersection of the North Central Expressway and Northwest Highway, just north of the Park Cities, taking the first step in the suburbanization of the comparison

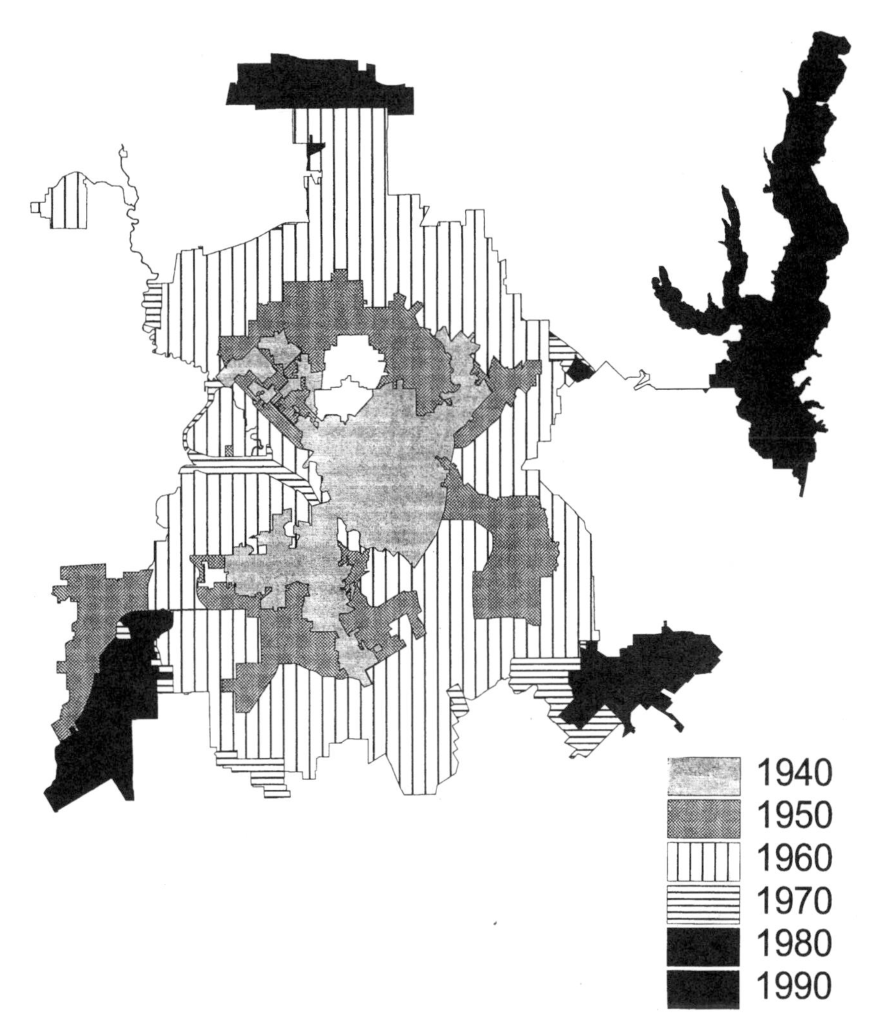

Figure 3.1. Dallas boundary expansions, 1940–1990

retail industry. In its annual economic roundup in January 1964, the *Dallas Morning News* reported that:"There has been a widespread dispersion of business throughout Dallas County in the last few years. Where only a few years ago, the business heart of the community was downtown, it has now spread and branched all over the county. . . ."[23]

The dispersion of economic activity and population continued through the next three decades, unabated by business cycles.[24] By 1990, the share of total regional employment in the Central Business District had dropped to about seven percent, and was continuing to fall.[25] Dallas had become a polycentric city, with several new centers of economic activity located beyond the city limits. It was an exemplar of the Sunbelt conurbation—sprawling, low density, with widely dispersed economic activity.[26]

During the 1970s and the first half of the 1980s, home and commercial development boomed, fueled by unprecedented population growth and a deregulated financial industry. Large scale planned communities and office parks blossomed on former ranches east of the airport and north of Dallas. A continuous strip of commercial, office, and residential uses bordered the Central Expressway, the North Dallas Tollway, and the LBJ. By 1979 the Dallas area accounted for two percent of all U.S. commercial development.[27]

Convenience retailers were the first to follow their customers to the suburbs. The department stores followed as new suburban malls were built, and gradually national specialty chains operating in malls and "big box" superstores began to supplant local merchants. In 1990 fewer than three of every ten employees in retail or wholesale trade in the Dallas Primary Metropolitan Statistical Area (PMSA) worked in firms located in the City of Dallas, in contrast with seven of every ten in 1962.[28]

The shift in the location of business was accompanied by institutional changes in the retail industry. By 1985, national retail chains had acquired all of the locally owned department stores. Only Nieman-Marcus retained a store in the central business district after 1990. Although the J.C. Penney Company moved from New York City to the Dallas area in 1988, it built its new corporate headquarters in Plano's Legacy Park, over 20 miles north of the central business district.

Although there was a great increase in office construction in the central business district between 1960 and 1985, total employment in the central business district shrank even as it burgeoned in the new uptown and suburban office parks. Manufacturing firms were also moving from the city to the suburbs or urban fringe. Those that remained downtown employed fewer people as new technologies increased productivity and changed the amount and kind of labor required. In 1962, 86 of every 100 people employed in Dallas County worked in the city. By 1990, only 46 of every 100 did.[29]

The dispersion of business activity during the last third of the century was accompanied by a fundamental shift in economic structure.[30] Manufacturing employment had accounted for 20 percent of all employment in Dallas in 1970 but dropped to 14 percent by 1990. And in absolute numbers, fewer workers were employed in manufacturing inside the city limits in 1990 than in 1970. In contrast, employment in services rose over the same period from 22 percent to 34 percent of the city's labor force. In the 1980s, the fastest growing industries were business, legal, and health services and telecommunications.[31] The Metroplex ranked third in the nation in Fortune 500 corporate headquarters.[32] It contained two-thirds of all high technology manufacturing employees in Texas and had the fourth highest volume of information flows of U.S. urban centers.[33] Many of the new corporate headquarters were located in the suburban office parks, however, rather than in Dallas. EDS and Frito-Lay moved their headquarters from Dallas to Legacy Office Park in Plano, which was being developed by Ross Perot, Jr. Frito-Lay had become a division of Pepsico. General Motors had acquired EDS.[34] GTE and EXXON moved their corporate headquarters from other states to Las Colinas, near D/FW Airport.

In the real estate and banking "bust," which struck Dallas in the mid-1980s, every major Dallas bank was declared insolvent by federal regulators and was merged into national banking systems headquartered in other states. Even the Trammel Crow organization was forced to restructure much of its debt in order to hold on to its most valuable Dallas properties, including its hotels and trade centers in the Stemmons Corridor.

The Southland Corporation, owner of the Seven-Eleven chain of convenience stores, built only half of its projected City Place development on the edge of the downtown district, and was taken over in a friendly acquisition by its Japanese partner.

Another significant but less apparent change was also occurring. Beneath the surface of net increases or declines in employment and firms, an "economic churn," was at work, destroying and creating firms. In his study of the Dallas economy from 1986 to 1989, Donald A. Hicks found that more than a third of the jobs in Dallas at the beginning of the period had disappeared from the economy by the end of it. In their place, new jobs that had not existed in 1986 accounted for 28 percent of the city's 1989 employment.[35] This creative destruction, which coincided with an economic recession, reorganization of industry, and the coming of age of new information technologies, contributed to both the diversification of the Dallas economy and to its spatial dispersion. All net job growth in Dallas during this three-year period occurred in service sectors and high tech manufacturing. The only service sectors to lose employment were finance, insurance, and real estate,[36] the primary victims of the banking-real estate collapse.

Summary and Conclusion

Dallas's first great expansion and diversification, in the late nineteenth century, was made possible by the development of the national railway system. It became, through the fortunes of location, the guile and side payments of its promoters, and the good luck of temporarily being the end of the line, the southwestern hub of north-south and east-west railroad traffic. As the buckle of the Texas Cotton Belt and the dominant point for the trans-shipment of buffalo hides, Dallas evolved into a wholesale and distribution center. A thriving market in perishable goods and captive capital made it an insurance and financial center. With surplus money to invest in new enterprises, a diversified economy developed, branching into retailing, manufacturing, and business services.

While the city experienced rapid growth during the period from 1870 through the first two decades of the twentieth century, it was still a moderately sized provincial commercial capital at the end of World War I. Because Dallas had developed a diversified economy, it was less vulnerable to the Great Depression than many other cities. Its financial institutions, industries and the labor force were well positioned to adapt to transitions in the economic base, first to energy and aviation, and then to information, catapulting Dallas into the front rank of American cities. While the energy, vision, and guts of Dallas private entrepreneurs celebrated in civic myth deserve credit for seizing the opportunities presented them, public funds and political skills were also critical at turning points in the city's history.

As one traces Dallas's progress through three great cycles of economic and technological change, the most impressive discovery is not how unique its development was, but how closely it followed the classic path of urban economic development. Its economy adapted to changes in the economic and technological environment by substituting locally made products for those formerly imported, processing raw materials from the hinterland for export, moving on to business innovations and invention of new products, and exporting its goods and services to other regions throughout the world.[37]

4

Economic Structure, Demography, and Political Power

Business operates Dallas.

A. C. Greene

Dallas . . . has been an exhibit of fragmentation for the entire decade of the 1990s. Once it was a prime example of the opposite: a place where decisive mayors and city managers worked quietly and efficiently with a single-minded business establishment to set clear community priorities. . . .

But that Dallas power structure succumbed to its own weaknesses. . . . When the establishment expired, it set in motion a long period of chaos, during which the newly-enfranchised elements jostled for power. . . .

Rob Gurwitt

The Dallas economy was transformed in the last third of the twentieth century but the city's civic culture remained remarkably constant and its institutions of governance changed little. The civic culture and institutions owe their inertia to three factors: the reputation of a once-dominant business oligarchy; the lingering effects of racial segregation; and devolution of power to professional managers of governmental and civic organizations.

The Rise of the Pure Entrepreneurial Regime

The business oligarchy is the most celebrated of these factors. Through its interlocking organizations it controlled major financial decisions and credit, city council and school board elections, selection of city managers and school superintendents, the management of the news, the work of charitable contributions, and even the designation of "leaders" in minority communities. This "pure entrepreneurial regime"[1] managed the civic agenda, allocated civic resources, and legitimated its own influence through the civic culture it manufactured. Its pervasive influence was exercised through the Dallas Citizens Council, the council-manager system of city government, and the city's major newspaper.

It had not always been thus. For its first sixty years, Dallas experienced the vigorous commercial competition and political conflict one would expect in a boomtown full of adventurers and entrepreneurs in hot pursuit of the main chance. A crossroads and entry point into Texas for migrants from both the Confederacy and the north, Dallas was tolerant of different opinions and persuasions. Its Jewish residents, for example, were relatively free from discrimination and a significant number of them played leading roles in civic and commercial life, including service in elective office. A robust labor movement flourished, as the Knights of Labor and the American Federation of Labor competed to organize Dallas workers. A variety of newspapers offered readers a full spectrum of editorial opinion.

In the late nineteenth and early twentieth centuries, prominent business leaders engaged in bitter battles for control of the city government.[2] They united in 1906 to replace the aldermanic ward system of local government with the then fashionable commission system. This coalition was maintained for most of the next fifteen years in the form of the Citizens Association, which nominated candidates for positions on the city commission. Independent, Socialist, Populist, and Democratic candidates often vigorously contested these elections. For a short time during this period, the business coalition broke down over personalities and style more than ideology or program. Loyalties were divided between two local parties, the Citizens Association (Cits) and the People's Independent Party (Pips).

The black citizens of Dallas played almost no role in city affairs. They were restricted to segregated neighborhoods of unpaved streets and substandard housing; the poll tax and Jim Crow laws limited black political and economic power. They were largely dependent upon their employers and the few white men of conscience, such as the Socialist lawyer-journalist-publisher, George Clifton Edwards, to advocate their interests.[3]

After World War I, the Ku Klux Klan emerged as a powerful force in Dallas. The city harbored the largest klavern in the country. Klan membership included many Dallas notables, including the sheriff, the police commissioner, the Democratic Party chairman, and for a time, banker R. L. Thornton.[4] By 1923, the Klan controlled most of the offices of city and county government. "Ku Klux Klan Day" at the State Fair drew an estimated 75,000 Klansmen and a record-setting throng at the Cotton Bowl watched more than 5,000 new members in a mounted ceremony, complete with burning crosses at each end of the field, swear fealty to the invisible empire.[5]

The foundations for the entrepreneurial regime and the style of local politics it produced were laid in opposition to the Klan. Many of the business leaders who had organized the Citizens Association, led by George Dealey, the publisher of the *Dallas Morning News,* were alarmed by the Klan's bigotry and lawless brutality. It had indulged in mob lynching, beatings, and intimidation of blacks, Jews, Catholics, and businesses it suspected of being owned by or employing anyone who was an object of the Knights' hatred. Others who had been involved in the earlier business coalitions realized that national publicity about the Klan posed a serious threat to Dallas's image as a progressive, cosmopolitan city. Few questioned racial segregation; none publicly. The Klan simply was bad for business.[6]

Declaring that neither white supremacy nor the existing moral order was in danger, the *Dallas Morning News* and its companion evening paper, the *Journal* denounced the Klan as backward and subversive of the growth of the city. The Klan retaliated by urging its members to boycott the paper, harassing its editors, employees, and agents, successfully damaging its subscription and advertising revenues. Joined by Dallas's smaller and more vulnerable labor-oriented press, Dealey persisted and used the statewide connections of his paper to help defeat Klan candidates in gubernatorial races in 1924 and 1926.[7] Governor Marian "Ma" Ferguson's vigorous use of the Texas Rangers to arrest Klansmen and suppress their activities ended Klan attempts to seize control of state government. Increasingly rejected by a public appalled by its vulgar excesses, the Klan receded to the paranoid margins of Texas political life.

The experience with the Klan taught Dallas's business elite an important lesson: their division could lead to "the wrong people" controlling the city at a time when its economy, riding the Texas oil boom, seemed to be taking off. In the past, their divisions had merely resulted in a choice between two somewhat different sets of businessmen. But the Klan was beyond the control of any business faction. The remaining progressive and pro-union forces in the city also learned that without sufficient votes to elect city officials on their own, their support of slates separate from those favored by the business leadership could result in the election of candidates even less well disposed to their interests.[8] A third lesson was imbedded in the minority community as a result of the Klan experience. Although they had no interest in improving the lot of minorities' condition for its own sake, the city's economic elite would take actions that benefited minorities if convinced the image of

Dallas as an orderly, progressive city, hospitable to business, was at risk.

As the Klan crisis passed, Dealey and his paper crusaded for a change in the form of city government. The commission system was redolent of the Klan. It was inefficient and riddled with political patronage. Commissioners engaged in internecine intrigues as they competed for power and resources. Once the ideal of reformers, commission government was rapidly being replaced in the progressive pantheon by the council-manager plan.

The *News* ran a series of articles and editorials, beginning in 1927, promoting the virtues of the council-manager plan as a cure for Dallas's governmental problems. It argued that Dallas had outgrown the commission form, which could no longer cope with the complexities of a large municipal corporation by depending upon partisan elected officials with questionable talents and inadequate experience to manage large public agencies. Dealey and his allies found the doctrines of the council-manager plan reflective of their experience as heads of large corporations. The business of the city should be conducted as a business. Its board, the city council, should be composed of men of widely recognized business judgment and broad experience. With a professional city manager to run the municipal corporation, such notable citizens would be freed from direct responsibility for day-to-day management of operating departments of the city government, but could still control it. The manager would be responsible for all administrative operations, including the employment and dismissal of all employees on the basis of merit alone.[9] Thus the ideology of the plan separated policy from administration and government from politics.[10] It promised a clean and orderly city within which business could thrive.

Business leaders united behind the movement for a new council-manager city charter. Remnants of the city's progressive Left joined them in 1927 to form a Non-Partisan ticket to oppose the City Democratic nominees. Both slates pledged to submit the charter reform to the voters. The Non-Partisans won all offices, and the mayor appointed a committee, which duly proposed a council-manager form of government. Council members were to be elected at large on a nonpartisan ballot. One of the Council members would be selected to serve as mayor, to preside over the Council and serve as ceremonial head of government. The Council would appoint a professional city manager as chief executive officer. Council members would receive only nominal compensation for their part-time service.

Submission of the new charter to the voters was frustrated when rival business-backed slates and a proliferation of independent candidates in 1929 resulted in the election of J. Worthington "Waddy" Tate as mayor. A drug store owner and an eccentric and perennial mayoral candidate, Tate signed the pledge to call a referendum for the council-manager charter, but he had not promised "when." He vetoed the proposal when it was submitted to him. Confronted by agitated civic and business leaders, he pulled out his trademark yo-yo and entertained himself. His visitors were not amused.[11]

Reacting to their oscillation on Tate's yo-yo, the reformers formed the Citizens Charter Association (CCA), which organized a petition drive and took the new charter directly to the voters. All the city's newspapers joined the *Dallas Morning News* in editorial support. A campaign manager was hired. Speakers bureaus were organized and deployed. The Chamber of Commerce and other business and civic associations fell in line to back the new form of government. Women's clubs endorsed the plan and helped organize the precincts. In an October 1930 special election, the voters overwhelmingly approved the new charter.[12]

The business leaders now determined to maintain the CCA to ensure election of a council that would fulfill the new charter's promise of efficient services, low taxes, and a good climate for business. The executive committee of CCA selected a full slate of council nominees in closed-door deliberations.

The basic rule was that "the office should seek the man, not the man the office." Care was taken to choose business and civic leaders of experience and integrity, who would accept council service as a civic duty. No one was expected to serve more than three two-year terms. Active partisans were to be avoided. The first CCA slate had no platform, its candidates made no speeches and offered no promises. Their few opponents were invisible, scarcely mentioned by the press. The *Dallas Morning News* helpfully told voters how to vote for the full CCA slate.[13]

For the next forty-five years, until it dissolved itself in 1975, the CCA dominated council politics in Dallas. It failed to elect a majority of Council members only twice: in 1935 and 1937, during the early years of the new system. Its candidates for mayor lost to independents only three times.[14]

After its losses to candidates of the rival Catfish Club in 1935 and 1937, the CCA metamorphosed into the political arm of the Dallas Citizens Council. R. L. Thornton, the self-made, shrewd, and folksy chairman of the Mercantile Bank, created the Citizens Council following his successful leadership of Dallas's effort to capture the 1936 Texas Centennial Celebration. In that triumph of salesmanship over history, Thornton mobilized support from his fellow bank chairmen, Nathan Adams of First National and Fred F. Florence of Republic Bank, 500 other business and civic leaders, the Board of Directors of the Chamber of Commerce, and the mayor and council. With Dallas's relative prosperity during the Depression, Thornton was able to secure commitments of cash from the banks and business leaders to underwrite the costs of the Centennial and produce a winning bid for the exposition.[15] When it turned out that he had underestimated the costs and needed more money, he assembled the heads of the leading corporations in Dallas and, with the help of his banking colleagues, extracted the necessary additional commitments.[16]

The success of the Centennial convinced Thornton and his fellow bankers that a permanent organization of the most powerful business executives in Dallas could achieve other important objectives. His idea was simple: bring together in one room only those men who headed the largest corporations and could say "yes or no" to a proposal and commit the financial resources or employees of their firms necessary to accomplish the tasks required.

Thus, the Dallas Citizens Council was organized in 1937 as a nonprofit organization for a "wholly educational and civic purpose." Once described as a "collection of dollars represented by men,"[17] membership was by invitation only and restricted to CEOs or presidents of the top firms doing business in Dallas. Initially it had only one hundred members, but as the city's economy expanded, it grew to over two hundred. No lawyers, accountants, physicians, ministers, public officials, or labor leaders were allowed. Members had to be able to make firm commitments without checking with anyone else. None could send a substitute to a meeting. An executive committee of some twenty-five members, including the executives of the largest banks, utility companies, retailers, manufacturers, and newspapers, set policies.[18] Political ideology was unimportant. Asked how a liberal Jew managed to be a part of this inner circle, composed largely of very conservative WASPs not famous for their social sentiments, Stanley Marcus responded: "Well, it helped to be rich."[19]

During its first thirty years of existence there was little turnover among members of the executive committee. The founders were relatively young in 1937. Almost all of them had built their own businesses. Few had been to college or had experience in other cities.[20] None followed careers in which Dallas was only a temporary stop on the corporate fast track. Most of their businesses depended on the growth and prosperity of Dallas. Their devotion to *their* city was absolute.

Citizens Council members seamlessly dominated the CCA and the Chamber of Commerce through overlapping memberships. Members were expected to "move through the chairs" of civic and charitable organizations to demonstrate their commitment to the city before being invited to serve on the executive committee or recruited for a tour of duty on the city council or as mayor.

The power of the Citizens Council rested on its ability to control the civic agenda.[21] To do so, as with charter reform, it offered only a single option.[22] As Darwin Payne notes in *Big D,* his history of Dallas, "If the Citizens Council could have had its way, no controversy would have reared its head to mar the city's reputation for collegiality."[23] The dependence of others on the bankers and other large corporations stifled dissent and ensured conformity. With the city's media executives imbedded in its inner circle, its views were assured favorable publicity. And with the ability to raise large sums of money quickly, the Citizens Council could underwrite advertising campaigns to shape public opinion on things that mattered to it.

The practice of limiting City Council members and mayors to no more than three terms (an exception was made for Thornton to serve four terms as mayor) prevented any from building an independent political base. The Citizens Council's reputation reinforced its power. Its endorsement was the stamp of legitimacy, and it fostered an environment in which almost all segments of Dallas society looked to it for guidance and approval.

The role of the Citizens Council in the governance of Dallas was most visible in the aftermath of the assassination of President John F. Kennedy on November 23, 1963. Prior to the assassination, Dallas had become a center of right wing radicalism. H. L. Hunt based his anti-Communist broadcasts and publications in Dallas. The John Birch Society had a strong presence. General Edwin Walker, a militant anti-Communist, made Dallas his base of operations after retiring from the army. The city was the home of the National Indignation Conference, which demanded U.S. withdrawal from the United Nations and the impeachment of President Dwight Eisenhower and Chief Justice Earl Warren. The city's most prominent divine, the Rev. W. A. Criswell, pastor of the country's largest Southern Baptist congregation, denounced racial integration as contrary to the teachings of the Bible and declared that the election of a Catholic as president would mean "the end of religious liberty in America."[24]

Republican Congressman Bruce Alger was an implacable foe of federal programs, the United Nations, and the Kennedy administration. Shortly before the fatal Kennedy visit, Alger led a group of screaming women who accosted Ambassador Adlai Stevenson, in town to address a U.N. Day meeting. Participants in another anti-administration demonstration spat at Vice President Lyndon Johnson and his wife during a Dallas visit. The *Dallas Morning News* lent its editorial voice to the extremist frenzy, but on the day of Kennedy's visit it published a generally gracious editorial welcoming the presidential party to Dallas. The paper also contained a full-page inflammatory advertisement paid for by The American Fact Finding Committee, a hastily concocted *nom de plume* for the usual assortment of Dallas right-wingers.[25]

The most prominent extremists—with the notable exception of the publisher of the *Dallas Morning News*—were not members of the Citizens Council. Whatever the political views of its members, the reactionary activities and pronouncements of the right wing zealots were of little concern to the *de facto* city fathers so long as they did not sully the reputation of the city as a good place to do business.

The assassination of the president, however, abruptly plunged the powerful men of Dallas, along with much of its population into what the *Dallas Times-Herald* characterized as "the dark night of the soul."[26] The Citizens Council swiftly reacted to salvage the city's reputation. With the promise of business support, Mayor Earl Cabell announced that he would run against Congressman Alger to purge the radical blot on the city's image. To do so, Cabell had to resign as mayor and from the City Council, which had to elect another member to complete the term as mayor and then fill the vacancy on the Council.

Key members of the Dallas Citizens Council concluded that none of the sitting City Council members possessed the vision and leadership skills needed to bring Dallas out of its "dark night." So they drafted their recent president, Erik Jonsson. But Jonsson was not a member of the City Council. Quietly consulting with the CCA-endorsed City Council members, and without informing the two independents, Jonsson's election was arranged. On February 23, after the regular Council meeting, Cabell announced his resignation. Council members immediately elected Jonsson to fill the resulting Council vacancy. Then they elected him mayor. Recounting the event, historian Darwin Payne observed: "The suddenness of Jonsson's accession and the behind-the-scenes, secretive maneuver, which preceded it, indeed were surprising. It was an example of the power structure working at its most efficient—and most exclusive—level."[27]

Jonsson brought to public office the formidable powers of persuasion and organization that had built Texas Instruments (TI) into an international business powerhouse. He organized Goals for Dallas, the strategic planning exercise designed to establish public priorities for moving Dallas into the front ranks of international cities. Encouraging wide public participation and using staff borrowed from TI and other corporations, he crafted an agenda of public works and institution building to restore the city's morale and forever change its landscape and economic function. He drove business leaders to overcome their resistance to working with Fort Worth to build the new international airport. He initiated plans for the great central library that would eventually bear his name, and a new city hall, designed by I. M. Pei. He convinced the Texas Legislature to convert the Southwest Center for Advanced Research, which TI had created on a thousand acres of land in North Dallas and Richardson, into the University of Texas at Dallas.

Twilight of the 'Garchs

Erik Jonsson's mayoralty was the "last hurrah" of the CCA. His administration marked a transition in both the monopoly power of the Citizens Council in city affairs and the power of the downtown, home grown business elite of Dallas. Jonsson operated in a business and professional world far different from his predecessors. CEO of a firm with a suburban headquarters complex and worldwide business interests, Jonsson's policies were regional and international in their scope and effect. Goals for Dallas, of which the new international airport was the centerpiece, involved the use of both public and corporate resources to produce the infrastructure needed to lead the economic restructuring already underway, and accommodate a new burst of population growth. The projects that facilitated the unprecedented growth in the 1960s and leveraged Dallas into the front rank of U.S. urban regions contributed to the dispersion of economic activity and the inevitable disintegration of business solidarity.

When Jonsson left office in 1971, Wes Wise, a local radio personality, defeated the CCA-endorsed candidate. By 1975 the CCA had disbanded, unable to control nominations for the City Council in the face of court-imposed single-member districts for eight of its eleven members. Business interests would continue to be the strongest single influence in civic affairs and in elections of mayors, but they would never again be able to exercise the sort of unchallenged monopoly power or enjoy the legitimacy they had before 1971.

The changed geography, massive restructuring, and institutional transformation of commerce began to be reflected in increased pluralism in the Dallas business community. As the first generation of Citizens Council leaders faded from the scene, the organization reinvented itself as more inclusive and metropolitan in scope. The Chamber of Commerce metamorphosed into the Greater Dallas Chamber. Rival sub-regional chambers of commerce and specialized business associations proliferated, reflecting localized business interests. It became increasingly difficult for any single institution to claim to represent *the* Dallas business community.

The construction boom of the 1970s and 1980s brought developers, builders, and savings and loan executives to prominence. Their names began to appear on the executive committee of the Dallas Citizens Council. As locally owned department stores were absorbed by mergers and acquisitions, another key set of business executives of the old oligarchy were replaced by branch managers of national chains based in other cities. The CEOs of all the national and multi-national corporations of Greater Dallas were inducted into the Citizens Council and each dutifully endorsed good works. But they lacked the intense personal and economic attachment to the City of Dallas of executives of the Thornton-Jonsson generations. They presided over firms that depended less on the Dallas region than the worldwide markets in which they competed. Their "Dallas" was not the central city but the Metroplex. They had to balance demands for charitable contributions and civic time between the city and suburbs where they located their new headquarters and where they and their employees lived. They used the city in a different way than their predecessors, thinking of it primarily as a base of operations and an environment for recruiting and retaining key employees rather than as a necessary and reciprocal component of success for their businesses and their personal careers. The multi-national CEOs with a deep commitment to Dallas and the resolution of its most urgent problems tended to be those with deep personal or corporate roots in the city.[28] Even in these corporations, changes in the executive suites could produce an abrupt decline in involvement. Many of the new high technology company executives headquartered in the Richardson-Plano Telecom Corridor tended to avoid Dallas civic involvement altogether.

The real estate and banking "bust" that struck Dallas in the mid-1980s further weakened business leadership. While the new bank managers assumed prominent roles in Dallas civic affairs, including positions on the executive committee of the Citizens Council, they, like so many of the new generation of Dallas executives, no longer had autonomy to say yes or no in committing corporate resources to civic endeavors. The devastation of the banking and real estate sectors removed a number of once-powerful executives from civic play entirely as they became consumed with financial woes and lawsuits. Survivors had less time to devote to the concerns of the city.

The combined effects of these spatial, structural and institutional transformations of business leadership in Dallas were profound. For decades, the leadership of the business community had been stable. Table 4.1 shows that the median tenure of members of the Board of the Dallas Citizens Council declined from eight years during the 1950s to three years during the 1980s. Another measure of leadership stability is the percentage of Citizens Council Executive Committee members who are newly seated in each year. Table 4.2 shows that following a major turnover in members at the end of each decade, few new members were added in the sixties or seventies. In some years none were added. From 1982 to 1990, however, a fourth of the total executive committee members in an average year were newly elected. Some of this churning of membership can be considered salutary, bringing in new generations of executives with new ideas, and diversifying what had been an exclusively Anglo male organization. But

Table 4.1 Median Tenure of Dallas Citizens Council Executive Committee Members

Decade	*Median Tenure*
1952–61	8 years
1962–71	5 years
1972–81	3.5 years
1982–91	3 years

Source: Dallas Citizens Council

Table 4.2 Percentage of New Members and Members with More than 10 Years of Service on the Dallas Citizens Council Executive Committee

Year	*Pct. New*	*Pct. > 10 Yrs.*	*Year*	*Pct. New*	*Pct. > 10 Yrs.*	*Year*	*Pct. New*	*Pct. > 10 Yrs.*
1950	21	38	1964	14	21	1978	69	0
1951	13	46	1965	7	22	1979	3	0
1952	0	46	1966	15	27	1980	6	6
1953	4	44	1967	4	16	1981	6	21
1954	13	39	1968	4	16	1982	26	20
1955	0	36	1969	4	16	1983	27	12
1956	0	36	1970	0	19	1984	31	3
1957	12	31	1971	20	19	1985	22	6
1958	0	52	1972	38	28	1986	17	7
1959	4	52	1973	10	24	1987	36	3
1960	0	60	1974	0	24	1988	13	3
1961	5	71	1975	0	31	1989	24	3
1962	64	28	1976	0	34	1990	34	3
1963	21	21	1977	0	34	1991	13	5

Source: Dallas Citizens Council

it also reflects the increased pluralism and reduced solidarity among business executives. The Citizens Council made an enduring imprint on the development of Dallas and an even longer lasting impression on its political system and civic culture. But its near absolute power—in matters of interest to its members—spanning two generations, gradually dissipated as the city and the business community itself changed around it.

The Legacy of Segregation and the Politics of Dependency

Suburbanization and economic restructuring were accompanied by a massive shift in demography. The Civil Rights revolution, propelled by the Supreme Court decisions on school desegregation, public accommodations, and equal representation, raised issues of equity the aging and parochial oligarchy could not fully understand or "fix" with symbolic actions supplemented with incremental concessions and side payments to maintain calm or conformity.[29] A new generation of more assertive minority leadership forced the Citizens Council and its designees to accommodate these new and unfamiliar demands or face destruction of the facade of efficient cooperation they had spent so long erecting. Dallas was no longer the city they knew.

Exclusion of Blacks from Power

Racial segregation was a fundamental force in shaping the social, economic and political geography of Dallas. For much of its history, black Dallas was virtually invisible. The WPA Writers Project's *Dallas Guide and History,* completed in 1942, devoted only six of its 408 pages to the black population. A fifth of the population was dismissed with the comment: "From his advent in the community the chief contribution of the Negro to the economic life of Dallas has been labor."[30]

From the end of the Civil War, black residents were confined to segregated neighborhoods, except for domestic servants that lived on the property of their white employers. Most settled near the Central Texas railroad tracks in Freedman's Town (today's State-Thomas District), Stringtown, alongside the tracks, and Deep Ellum, east of the Central Business District. Others lived in Frogtown, on the Trinity floodplain in west Dallas, and Elm Thicket, the area that was to become the Love Field neighborhood. In all aspects of social and economic life, racial segregation in Dallas was absolute. It was enforced systematically by law and custom, economic sanctions, official repression, and on occasion, organized private terror.[31]

Figure 4.1 maps the distribution and concentration of the black population of Dallas from 1950 to 1990, showing the endurance of patterns of segregation. Although considerable dispersal of the middle class households occurred in the 1980s, most continued to live in census tracts that were over three-fourths black. As a result of the migration of more affluent black families from the ghetto in southern Dallas, the number of census tracts with high rates of poverty doubled in the 1980s.[32]

The black middle class in Dallas was small compared to those of Washington, Baltimore, or Atlanta, where vibrant black middle classes were led by well-educated graduates of local black colleges.[33] It consisted primarily of small merchants and the few black professionals serving black clients. Teachers for the segregated schools were carefully screened by the all-white school board and closely monitored to weed out "trouble makers." In his memoir of black Dallas, Dr. Robert Prince, a physician who grew up in Freedman's Town, wrote:

> The complete isolation of Dallas' African-Americans generated a culture within a culture. The black man was governed by and worked in, a white society with folkways and mores dating back a millennium. The Negro was forced to develop a sub-culture that addressed his human needs. . . . The white man's world was his standard. . . .
>
> The Negro began a period of commercial intercourse that kindled racial pride. The black man who did not depend upon the white man for his income, was respected. Businessmen, physicians, gamblers, dentist [sic] and educators were in the upper strata. The common laborer was in a different stratum, with sub-stratification depending upon personality, education and personal wealth. The domestics were in a pecking order that was directly proportional to the social and financial status of the whites they worked for and emulated.[34]

The poll tax and white primary excluded black citizens from participation in elections. Even if they had fully participated, with a population that never exceeded 30 percent

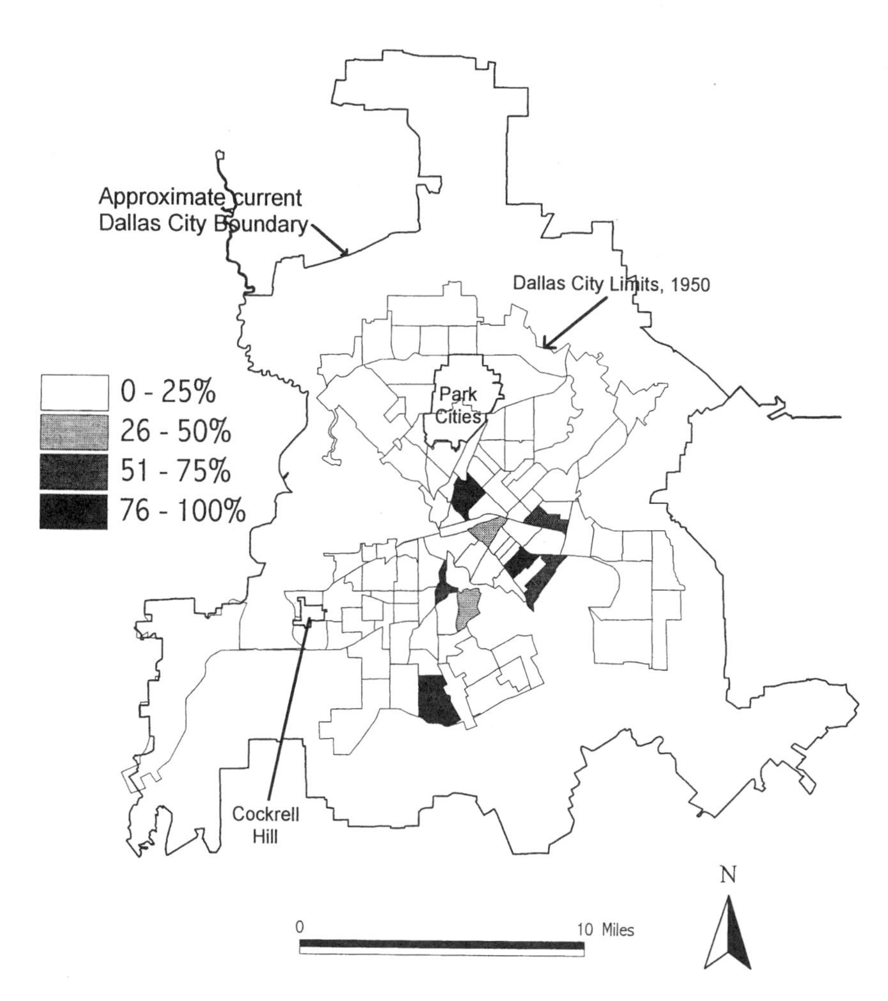

Percentage of black residents by census tract, 1950

Figure 4.1. Black residential patterns in Dallas, 1950–1990: percentage of Black residents by census tract

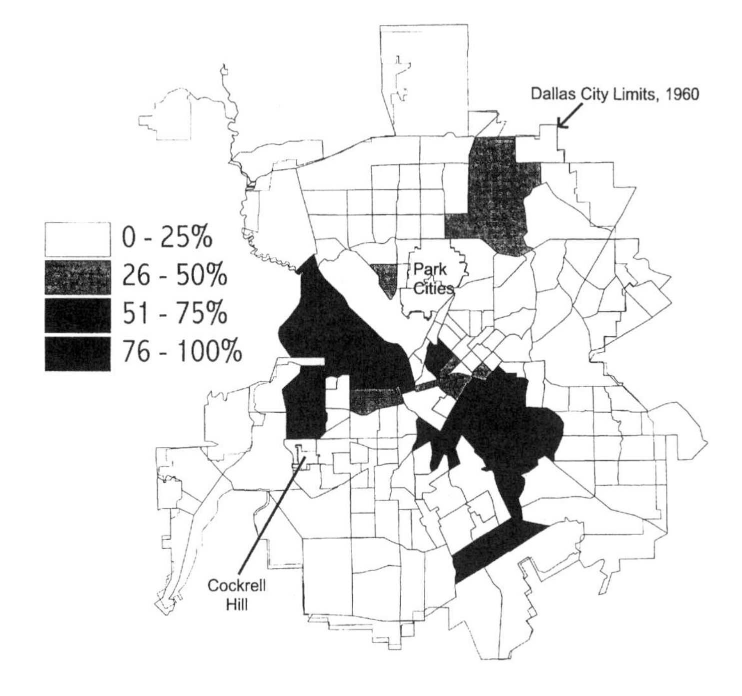

Percentage of black residents by census tract, 1960

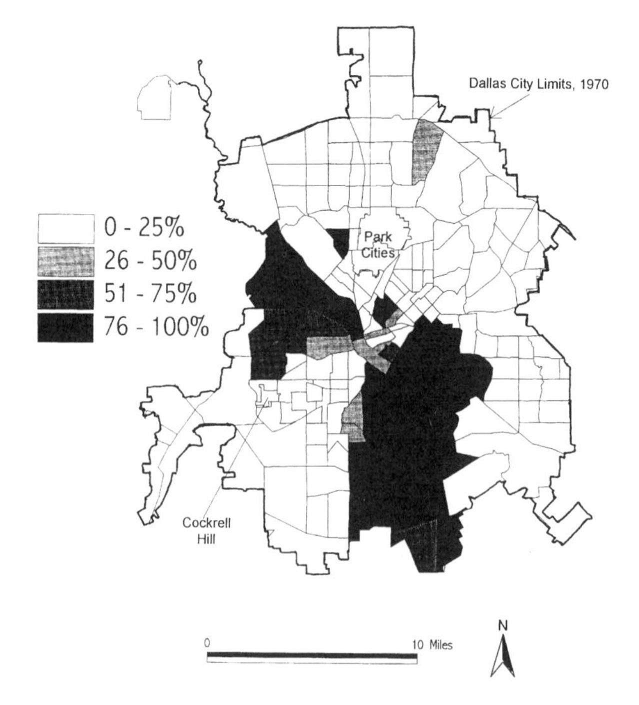

Percentage of black residents by census tract, 1970

Figure 4.1. Continued

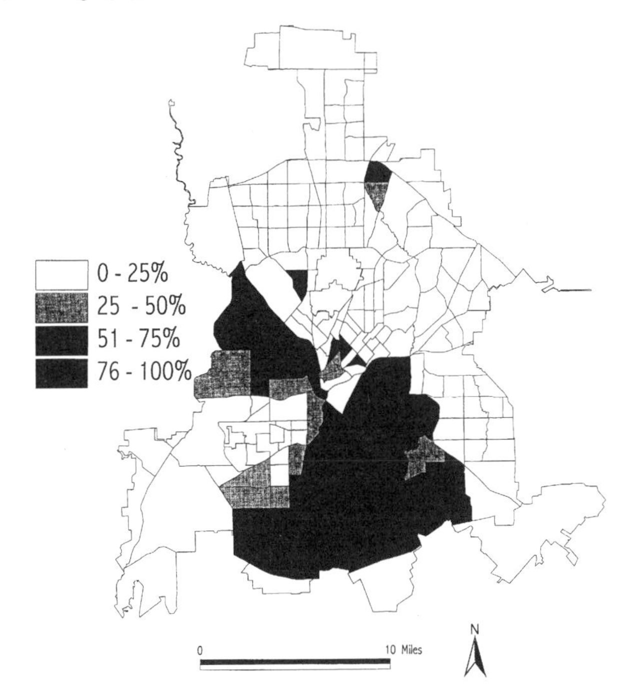

Percentage of black residents by census tract, 1980

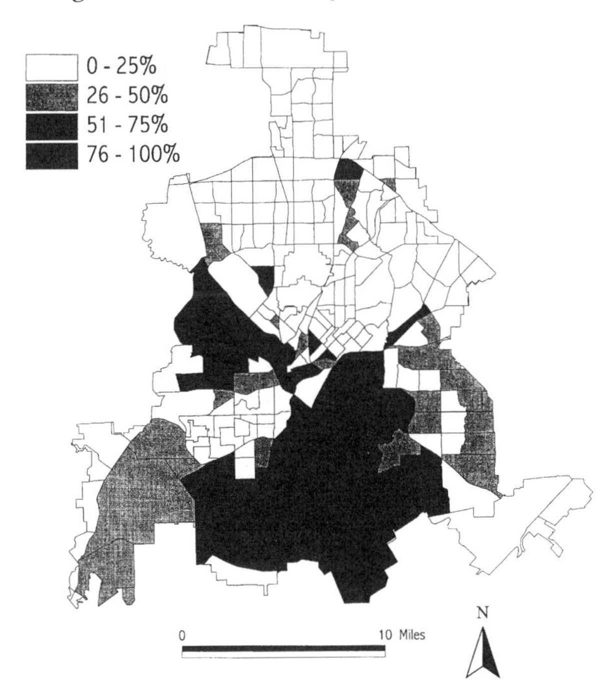

Percentage of black residents by census tract, 1990

Figure 4.1. Continued

of the total, at-large elections for numbered seats on the City Council would have diluted their the electoral strength. Black voters were a decisive factor in only one mayoral contest—in 1937—because of the temporary split of white voters between the CCA and the Catfish Club slates. Otherwise, until its demise in 1975, the CCA slate was virtually unchallenged, so it was unnecessary for its candidates to bargain for black support.

On the few occasions when credible black candidates for city council or school board appeared likely, economic pressure was applied to discourage them. The possibility of Rev. Maynard Jackson, Sr. running for the school board in 1944 was met with black domestic workers being told that if he won there would be bloodshed and massive firings of black people who worked for whites. A decade later, following the Supreme Court's decision in *Brown v. Board of Education,* the Dallas Council of Negro Organizations sponsored a prominent black attorney, C. B. Bunkley, as a candidate for the school board. Bunkley withdrew after he was summoned to a meeting with several white business leaders and was told that some members of the group had bought his mortgage.[35]

The powerlessness of blacks was reinforced by the absence, until the most recent decade, of a critical mass of independent professionals, managers, intellectuals and business owners who could provide community leadership and function as peers of the white elite. A survey of the Dallas-Fort Worth workforce conducted in 1989 found that only 17 percent of blacks were employed in administrative, professional and technical jobs, while 32 percent of Anglo workers held such positions.[36] The brutal crushing of attempts to organize industrial labor unions in Dallas in the 1930s[37] left blacks with almost no mainstream or main street avenues of political influence open to them.

For years, if any attempt to assert black influence could not be suppressed, it was punished. In retaliation for the Negro Chamber of Commerce's support of a black candidate to fill a legislative vacancy, white business leaders rejected its request to build a Hall of Negro Achievement at the Texas Centennial. Maceo Smith, the Negro Chamber's president, secured the exhibit only by appealing to Vice President James Garner, who saw that the congressional appropriation supporting the Centennial included $100,000 for the project, along with a rider that made the overall federal funding contingent on its construction.[38] After the centennial, the Negro Hall of Achievement was the only building demolished before the 1937 Exposition.[39]

Until 1953, blacks were allowed to attend the Fair only on two days—Negro Achievement Day, commonly called "Nigger Day"[40] by resentful whites, and Juneteenth (June 19), the anniversary of publication of the Emancipation Proclamation in Texas. Even after the Fair was opened to blacks for its entire run, no restrooms were available to them, they were not permitted on the midway, and many restaurants and food vendors refused to serve them. Even in 1955, when the midway was finally opened to them under threat of a black boycott of the fair, two rides remained closed. Fair officials were apparently concerned that white and black revelers might touch each other while enjoying "Laff in the Dark" or "Dodge 'em Scooter," and endanger public health or safety.[41]

Dallas had no black police officers until after World War II, although Council candidates supported by black voters in 1937 promised them. Even after "apprentice" officers were appointed in 1948, they were restricted to patrols in black neighborhoods and ordered to avoid contact with whites except in emergencies. Blacks were excluded from grand juries until 1951, when three black professionals were appointed to a grand jury, otherwise composed of Citizen Council notables, to investigate bombings of black homes in previously all-white neighborhoods of South Dallas. The grand jury returned indictments of several lower level participants in the attacks, alluded to a conspiracy that "reached into unbelievable places," but declined to indict the unnamed leaders for lack of sufficient evidence, and was discharged. None of those indicted was convicted.[42]

The Rise of the Hispanic Minority

Unlike Houston, San Antonio, or Fort Worth, Dallas did not contain a large Hispanic population until the 1970s. The *WPA Dallas Guide and History* devoted even less attention to Mexican-Americans than to blacks. A few pages were devoted to "Little Mexico"—a ten-block-square barrio north of downtown, formerly the red light district. Developed about 1914, the barrio contained about 10,000 residents in 1920, but had declined to 6,000 or fewer by 1940.[43] The *Guide* noted the "patient resignation of their race" with which its residents endured the poverty, squalor, and diseases of their community.[44]

Hispanics were classified as white for purposes of schooling, but were highly concentrated in the schools serving their neighborhoods. Like blacks, they were not a part of Dallas Anglo society. Most were blue-collar workers, and some, such as the Pedro Medrano family, were active unionists,[45] a calling that did not endear them to Anglo business leaders. A few had started small businesses.

The rapid growth of the Hispanic population began after World War II. No accurate estimate of its size was available until the 1970 census, when Hispanic respondents were first asked to identify themselves. By that time, the Hispanic population of Dallas had ballooned to 68,000. In 1990 it reached 200,000 and has continued to grow. Figure 4.2 shows, however, that Hispanics have not been as highly concentrated as blacks, accounting for 75 percent of the population of only a few census tracts in any period. Dispersion has increased with each decade, although several census tracts in Oak Cliff, West Dallas, East Dallas, the Love Field area, and a few others are more than 50 percent Hispanic. Much of the Hispanic population is younger than eighteen years old, and by 1998 Hispanic children comprised a majority of students in the Dallas Public Schools.

Even fewer Hispanics than blacks—just one in ten—hold administrative, professional or technical jobs, although Hispanics are moving into a wide range of higher status occupations in the private sector as well as into prominent governmental positions. In 2000, both the city manager and school superintendent were, for the first time, Hispanic.

While discrimination against Hispanics was never as intense in Dallas as that against blacks, they were largely excluded from the organized bar until the 1960s, when the first three Mexican-American lawyers were admitted to practice in Dallas.[46] Few Hispanic lawyers, even in the 1990s, were members of major law firms. Like blacks, Hispanics were also excluded from grand juries until the 1960s, and denied dignity and respect by the Dallas Police.

The geographic dispersion of the Hispanic population and its relative youth has made it difficult to translate growing numbers into political power. Single-member districts underrepresented Hispanics on the city council and school board. Hispanic officials found themselves in accord with blacks on a variety of substantive issues, but dependent upon alliances with Anglos for political power. As the total Hispanic and school-aged population grew, tensions developed with black political leaders as the two minority groups jockeyed for control of school policies, top positions on the school board, and appointment of the superintendent.[47]

The Politics of Dependency

Discrimination against blacks and Hispanics produced separate institutions in the minority communities. Many mirrored those of Anglo society, from the Black and Hispanic Chambers of Commerce, professional and fraternal societies, to churches. Many of these institutions are vibrant, but they are not equal.

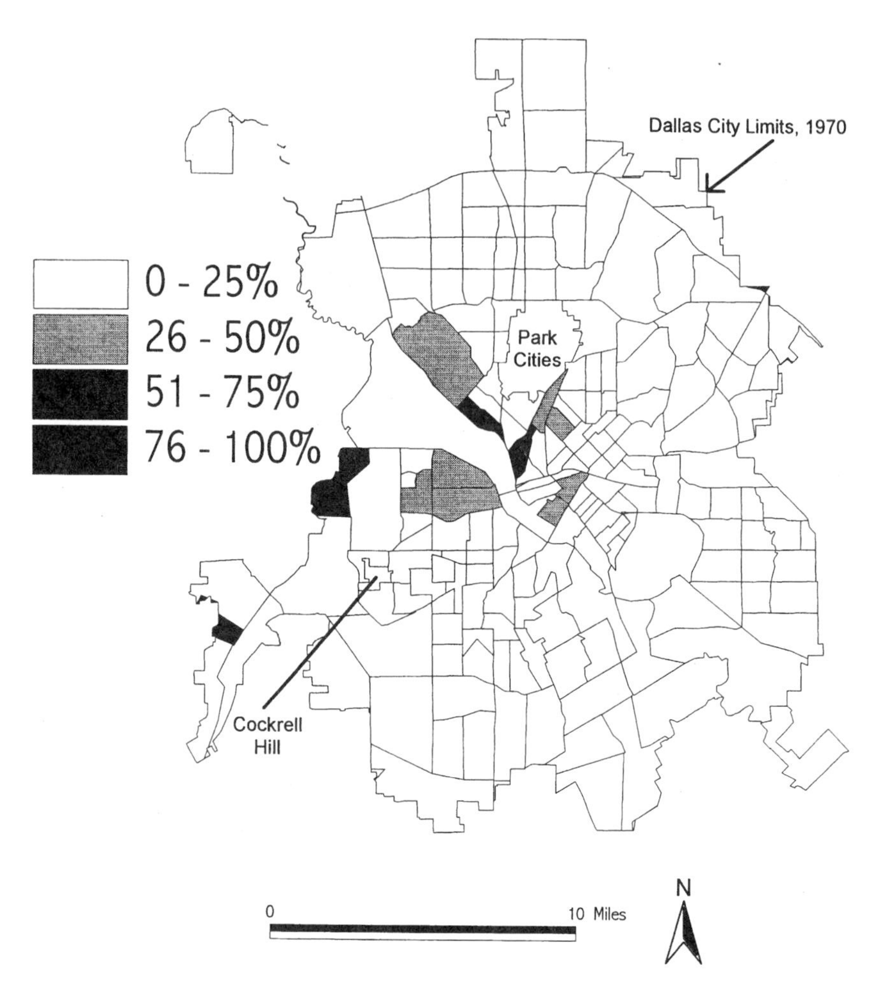

Percentage of Hispanic Residents by census tract, 1970

Figure 4.2 Hispanic residential patterns in Dallas, 1970–1990: percentage of Hispanic residents by census tract

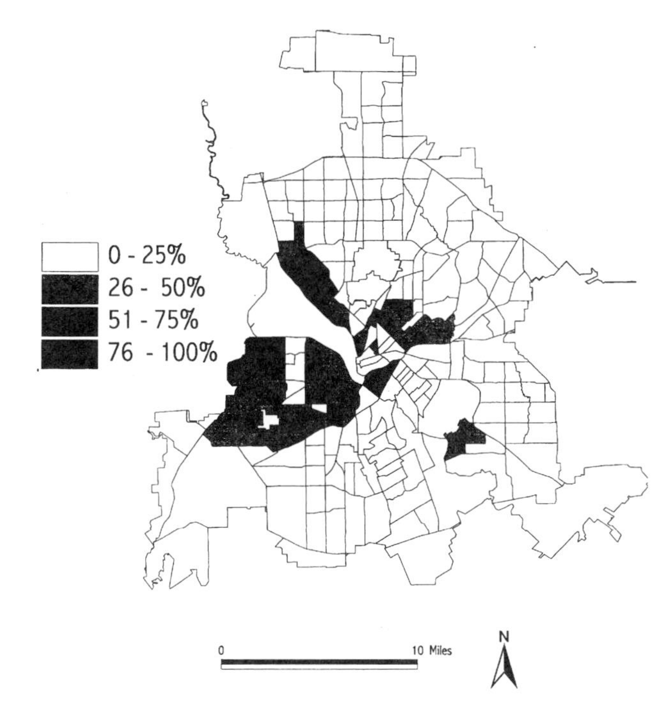

Percentage of Hispanic Residents by census tract, 1980

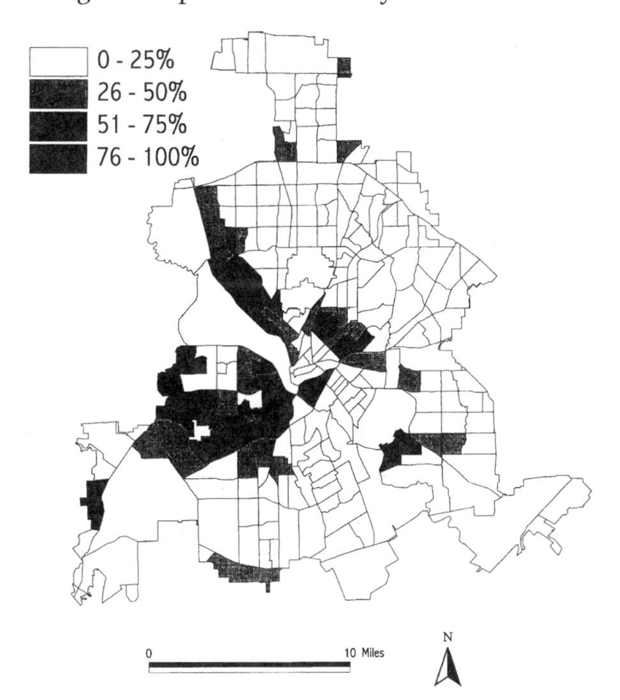

Percentage of Hispanic Residents by census tract, 1990

Figure 4.2 Continued

Many remain dependent, directly or indirectly, on white patrons, constricting their independence. Co-option was widely practiced through appointments and on occasion, direct financial subsidies and "gifts."[48] When selective benefits and side payments did not work, threats and sanctions were applied to induce conformity.[49]

Blacks and Hispanics were excluded from elective office until the 1960s, and when some were finally elected, it initially was with the endorsement of the Anglo business leaders. Only "safe" minority candidates received endorsement and financial support from the entrepreneurial regime, a necessity for success in the at-large election system. After federal courts ordered the creation of single member districts for election of most, and finally all members of the city council except the mayor, some minority candidates were elected who had bases of community support independent of elite business interests. They remained insufficient in number to form a stable governing coalition in a nonpartisan government in which some of their minority colleagues had received significant financial support from Anglo business executives who did not live in their districts, or in some cases, in the city.[50]

Frustrated by their own powerlessness, the resistance of the regime to sharing power, and its sluggish or hostile responses to their grievances, some minority activists turned to protests and litigation as means of gaining recognition for their interests. Protests were hard to sustain because of the frailty of the economic resources of the minority communities and the regime's tactical countermeasures. Demands were often met with symbolic concessions that offered slight advances, dampened mobilizations, and returned the city to the quiet business of business. In this environment, minority activists increasingly turned to litigation as a political stratagem for inducing substantive action on equity issues. Ultimately beyond the influence of the local economic elite, federal courts conferred a legitimacy on minority plaintiffs and the "class" they represented that was beyond the patronage or control of the regime.

The Managerial Regency

The Atlanta political regime described by Clarence Stone was based on a stable coalition of white downtown business leaders and black middle-class politicians. To achieve their goals, each needed the resources or power available only to its partner.[51] During its forty years of hegemony the Dallas regime needed no partner. It was based on cohesive economic interest, racial segregation, and the professional management of city affairs, reinforced by a widely accepted civic culture.

The first two bases dissipated as the economy restructured and *de jure* segregation ended. In the first stages of the transition, the weakened regime moved toward accommodation. It did what it had to do to maintain order and prevent damage to the business-friendly reputation of the city. As the transition progressed from the old "yes and no" oligarchs to a new generation of career executives with less stomach for the exercise of raw power, the style of business leadership in Dallas shifted from being engineers of accommodation to serving as policy brokers. Key executives could still be mobilized to use their good offices to bring the necessary actors to the table and reach consensus on how to address urgent problems. Committees of business notables could still be formed to recommend policies, even if those policies were no longer certain of execution. If neither policies nor leaders could now be anointed if they were unacceptable to significant minorities, the editorial blessing of the *News* and the support of other business icons remained important indices of legitimacy, even for politically ambitious minorities. The halo of the entrepreneurial regime hovered in the civic atmosphere.

In contrast with the social production process Stone described in Atlanta, in which coalition participants built social capital,[52] the legacy of the Dallas regime was weakness in other civic institutions. The local one-party system of the CCA was never supplanted by any new system for endorsing slates of candidates and mobilizing publics across the city. No institutions developed to transcend the identity basis of the new City Council's politics or set a public agenda.

City charter amendments supported by business organizations in 1989 marginally strengthened the role of the mayor as presiding officer of the Council, but left the office fundamentally a figurehead.[53] The Council, now elected from single-member districts became more reflective of the racial diversity in the city's population, more responsive and service-oriented than in the past. But it remained dependent upon the city manager for guidance on policy.

The rear guard of the oligarchy still raised money to support mayoral candidates and selected council members, but there were no public endorsements, for fear the association would harm the beneficiaries' electoral prospects. To the dismay of those who cherished the image of Dallas as the "city that worked," it frequently did not. In addition to racial conflicts, the continuing economic recession and dissention among business interests left Mayor Steve Bartlett, who was elected with support from downtown property owners,[54] without an agenda that had broad support. He declined to run for re-election.

Ron Kirk was elected mayor in 1995, again with the support of many business leaders, pledging to "end the blame game." As a symbol of black ascendancy in Dallas politics, and as a skilled mediator, he generally succeeded in lowering the decibel level of council meetings. He championed projects favored by business groups, tying them to values of the civic culture—economic growth and the city's world class destiny—but, critically for their success, he also linked them to new values of racial equity, promising jobs and business for southern Dallas. If Kirk did not wander far beyond the boundaries of the traditional civic culture, he was more visible and willing to take limited political risks than most recent mayors were. But he was not running the city—a fact of which he was acutely aware.[55]

By the early 1990s, most business leaders realized they no longer possessed the power to impose their unmediated will on the city. The complicated problems of the city often confounded even the most dedicated of them. Most issues could not be resolved by simple agreement on a course of action by a small group of corporate executives. They often required careful analysis and gathering of information and opinions from a broader cross section of experts and publics. Governing by amateurs and dilettantes was becoming increasingly hazardous, for both the city and the amateurs. The governance of Dallas fell to the professional managers of public and civic institutions—the sole survivors of the entrepreneurial regime. They alone still possessed the legitimacy bestowed by the civic culture.

Only the managers had the time, professional training, access to information, staff resources, and career interest in fashioning solutions to complex problems, negotiating the resolution of highly charged controversies such as urban development projects, police-community and other racial conflicts, service disputes, and settling interagency and intergovernmental brawls. Recent city managers have adopted a more deferential public demeanor and a more open style of management than followed by some of their fabled predecessors, but they also have become more autonomous and influential figures in their own right.

If the city government once emulated the business elite in the way it conducted its business, the major business and civic institutions now mimicked government in turning over much of the heavy lifting in local public policy to paid executives. Until 1971 the Citizens Council did not even employ a secretary.[56] It hired its first executive vice president in 1976.

Alex Bickley, a former city attorney, was so finely tuned to the interests of his employers that he operated within a wide band of discretion, carrying marching orders from the Citizens Council to the City Council. After Bickley's retirement and one false start, the Citizens Council in 1988 employed Jan LeCroy, the former Chancellor of the Dallas County Community College System, as its full-time president. LeCroy managed the day-to-day affairs of the Council, studiously avoiding personal controversy and guiding the board in the development of consensus projects, diversification of its membership and softening of its image by placing new emphasis on social and educational issues as well as economic development. His successor, Donna Halstead, had represented a northeast Dallas district on the City Council saw her role as a spokesperson and lobbyist for business interests and a bridge between the worlds of business and city politics.[57]

Other organizations, such as the Central Dallas Association, the Greater Dallas Chamber of Commerce, Dallas Urban League, The Community Council of Greater Dallas and the United Way of Greater Dallas, have become staff-led organizations. While business executives and other civic leaders involved with these organizations play their assigned roles in public affairs, few seek influence across a broad front of policies. Most have been content to negotiate their particular interests with the organizational bureaucrats and elected officials and to participate in task forces that tended toward the lowest common denominator in policy recommendations. Some freelance as policy entrepreneurs, building alliances where they can with key managers. Dallas evolved from the pure entrepreneurial regime of the Thornton-Jonsson era into a managerial regency.

Summary

The pure entrepreneurial regime of the Dallas Citizens Council could not maintain its hegemony in the face of the restructuring and spatial dispersion of the regional economy. Making decisions without public consultation or scrutiny and depending on consensus among a narrow set of corporate executives with common experiences, it was poorly designed to adapt to the racially charged, conflict rich, newly litigious politics of Dallas. The civic culture and values fostered by the Citizens Council during its long ascendancy have endured, however. The myth of a city with no reason to exist being willed to greatness by enlightened business leadership (amended to acknowledge diversity) remained a touchstone of public rhetoric and civic faith. The public interest was still identified with the maintenance of a favorable climate for business. Institutional barriers to effective political leadership, some of them imbedded in the city charter, and the cultural bias against active government remained. Officials still looked to business leaders to lend legitimacy to candidates for mayor and policy initiatives.

As *de jure* segregation collapsed from an onslaught of litigation and the oligarchy faded into the twilight of power, governance of the city gravitated to the remaining solid base of the old regime, the professional managers of public and civic institutions. The managerial regency's legitimacy rested on the perception of it as the rightful keeper of the civic culture's values of minimal, orderly, efficient services that protect the business climate and growth-friendly image of Dallas. The managers, however, have no independent bases of power, unlike the economic supremacy of the oligarchy or the electoral and interest group constituencies of the new class of politicians. Instead, their power rests on the deference the civic culture grants them and the extent to which distracted business executives, relatively powerless officials, and ordinary citizens accept their judgment, near monopoly of technical knowledge, and their aura of neutral competence as heads of hierarchical bureaucracies.

II

The Limits of the Public City: Vital Services

5

Power Failure: Public Education in Dallas

As currently arranged, education is prone to failure.

JOHN BRANDL

Introduction: Achieving Equality and Performance in City Schools

The Dallas civic culture's devotion to minimal government limits the public sphere to providing only those services the market and charities cannot produce more efficiently. "Politics" is regarded as an unseemly intrusion into the real work of delivering services. The job of elected officials is to "set policy," but leave to the professional administrators the determination of how best to carry it out. The cultural bias favoring limited government and its antiseptic management, however, has not protected basic public services from political conflict. Chief among these is education, with its matrix of racial and class issues that overlay neighborhood interests, property values, and educational policy.

The education budget for the Dallas Independent School District exceeds that of the entire city government. The quality of schools is regularly cited in citizen and business surveys as a leading consideration about whether to live in the city or reinvest in homes or firms.[1] And the public schools of Dallas, not unlike those of most major American cities, have been at the center of racial conflict. Some of Dallas's most prominent corporate executives, professional managers, community activists, and federal judges have all been involved in trying to resolve issues of equity, efficiency, and effectiveness in this most vital and costly of urban services.

The Dallas Independent School District (DISD) serves most of the school-age children and an overwhelming proportion of the minority children that live in Dallas. Nine other districts include some segments of the city, but the most significant are the Richardson, Plano, and Wilmer-Hutchins Independent School Districts. The Richardson and Plano districts serve mostly affluent neighborhoods in northern and far north areas of Dallas that were annexed after 1960. The Wilmer-Hutchins district serves poor black neighborhoods in southern Dallas and racially mixed working class towns along I-45 south of the city. Highland Park ISD, which is entirely surrounded by DISD, serves the tiny, high-income municipalities of Highland Park and University Park.

An elected Board of School Trustees governs each district. It adopts educational policies, sets its own property tax rate, and appoints a superintendent, the chief executive officer of the district, who is responsible for management of the system and policy leadership. State law establishes certain standards regarding curriculum, teacher qualifications and pay, the roles of board and superintendent, tax rate limits, and some other matters, such as the famous "no pass, no play" rule governing the eligibility of student athletes.

The most significant constraint on the autonomy and discretion of the Dallas Public Schools, however, has been federal court enforcement of the racial desegregation decisions of the U.S. Supreme Court. The Dallas school system has been in litigation since 1954, and under federal district court supervision since 1961. The court declared the district to have achieved a "unitary" system in 1994, but the case had not yet been dismissed as the 2000–2001 school year began.

Because the education system has such important implications for the economic well-being of the city, it is often a concern of those promoting urban growth and development. It does not follow, however, that concern will translate into support for the central city's school system when suburban schools offer better schools and less controversy. When education's intrinsic value and economic importance is infused with racial politics and constitutional law, a city is presented with issues of high salience and certain acrimony. An arena supposedly insulated from the baleful influences of politics by organizational and fiscal autonomy, nonpartisan elections, and expert management, becomes instead the vortex of intense, widespread, and continuing conflict over appropriate policies to deal with an interlocking set of demographic, legal, institutional, intergovernmental, and pedagogic issues. At the same time, the independent status of the district allows the city's elected and appointed officials to shirk political responsibility for the consequences of the educational policies pursued by the school district. The mayor, city council, and city manager are more spectators than participants in the most significant policy problem of the city.

It is difficult to imagine a more complex problem than dismantling a racially segregated education system and equalizing educational opportunities for minorities in a city of rigidly segregated neighborhoods, while adapting to changing demographics and meeting market demands for higher cognitive skills and work habits of high school graduates. All of these forces are moving targets, often changing before a policy designed to address them can be put in place. Furthermore, each policy intervention alters the situation and can generate unforeseen consequences, which must then be addressed.

Under the best of circumstances, school systems can be slow to respond to changes, especially ones as radical and unwelcome as desegregation. Deeply imbedded emphasis on rules and rights in the public schools personnel system produces vexing problems even for a superintendent deeply committed to desegregation or other reforms. The achievement of "balance" among faculties, staff, and administrators was a necessary element of a good faith effort to eliminate a dual system that had assigned only black administrators and teachers to black schools and only white personnel to white schools. Experienced teachers and administrators enjoyed "tenure." While they could be reassigned to eliminate the appearance of any one school having been designed for one race, it was not easy to move those with long associations with particular schools.

Achieving equality of educational opportunity in the schools across a large urban district requires that each school be staffed by competent teachers. This, in turn, assumes that administrators have standards for determining if teachers are competent, and that there are administrative procedures for removing those who perform below minimum standards.

Other features of the system, apart from its racial duality, were certain to complicate integration. The dual system had been built to serve segregated neighborhoods. School buildings are immovable objects. Thus, reassignment of students among school buildings, cross-racial busing, redrawing of attendance districts, and creation of new schools to serve both races were among the unpopular remedies that had to be considered.

To further complicate the process, during the first two decades of Dallas school desegregation, the school system was in the hands of boards and superintendents who were hostile to compliance with the Supreme Court's decision. They openly opposed desegregation and resisted court orders, urging board attorneys to delay compliance as long as possible, or agreeing only to token changes when no options remained. Later boards were often divided on desegregation strategy and other education policies, but they ranged from grudgingly compliant to supportive of the efforts of the courts and superintendents. And while the basic constitutional command to desegregate remained constant throughout the period, the views of the four successive federal judges with immediate jurisdiction over the Dallas case varied from outright opposition to strong support.

Civic Culture and the Constitution: Deliberate Speed—Dallas Style

An irony of the governance of American public education is that while local control of schools is voiced as a high ideal, no public service is more constrained by politics and law in its ability independently to choose how it will perform its function than are public school systems. The ideal of local autonomy is so deeply ingrained, however, that there is an almost reflexive resistance to policies imposed by superior organs of government, whether legislatures or courts. As a result, local school officials sometimes find themselves losing, through default or defiance, discretion over their own systems.

Immediately following the Supreme Court's school desegregation decisions in 1954 and 1955, the Dallas School Board, like most others that had operated separate systems for white and black students, technically had the authority—indeed a constitutional duty—to desegregate its schools. The initial refusal, followed by persistent delay in exercising its discretion, resulted in tighter and tighter court supervision of educational policy. The loss of autonomy to the court seems, in retrospect, an almost inevitable consequence of the Dallas civic culture and the inability of the city's governance institutions to adapt readily to the confluence of constitutional requirements and dramatic shifts in the city's demography and economy.

In the early 1950s Dallas was in the grip of its most serious episode of racial violence since the Klan era, occasioned by the post-war displacement of black communities and white reaction to the movement of blacks into previously all-white neighborhoods in South Dallas.[2] This coincided with the emergence of Dallas as the headquarters for well-financed right wing extremists and their organizations, which freely blended anti-communism, racism, isolationism, anti-federalism, nativism, and Christian fundamentalism.

The school desegregation decisions of the U.S. Supreme Court were denounced in Dallas by leading civic and religious figures, the daily newspapers, and W. T. White, the superintendent of schools. The school board, composed of members endorsed by the Citizens for Good Schools, an electoral arm of the Dallas Citizens Council, shared many business leaders' aversion to integration.[3] No minority interests were represented on the board, which was elected at-large. Blacks were elated by the decision, which also had initial quiet, and later open support of many white clerics and civic leaders. It is fair to say, however, that the idea of school desegregation was repugnant to those in Dallas with power to do something about it, including the first two federal judges to handle the local case.

Judge William H. Atwell was eighty-five years old when twenty-four black plaintiffs, represented by Thurgood Marshall of the NAACP Legal Defense Fund and local civil rights attorneys, petitioned his court to order the desegregation of Dallas public schools. Judge Atwell was not amused. He dismissed the case as premature, taking judicial notice that educational opportunities were equal in Dallas for white and black pupils, and that the Supreme Court's "all deliberate speed" rule gave local school officials time to work out a desegregation plan.[4]

The U.S. Court of Appeals for the Fifth Circuit reversed Atwell and remanded the case for a full hearing on the merits of the complaint.[5] After the mandated hearing, Judge Atwell denounced the Supreme Court's finding that segregated schools, *per se,* were unequal. He declared that Dallas school authorities were "doing their very best"[6] to desegregate "with all deliberate speed." Arguing that educational opportunities, though separate, were equal, Atwell wrote: "the white schools are hardly sufficient to hold the present number of white students; that it would be unthinkably and unbearably wrong to require white students to get out so that colored students could come in."[7] He again dismissed the suit, "in order that the School Board may have ample time, as it appears to be doing, to work out this problem."[8]

The Court of Appeals reversed Atwell once more. Noting that two of the plaintiff school children were denied admission, on the basis of their race, to a school four blocks from their home, requiring them to travel eighteen blocks across heavy traffic to a black school, the court recited the various excuses offered by the school system,[9] concluding: "It is not a sufficient answer to say that the school board has made 'a prompt and reasonable start' and is proceeding to a 'good faith compliance at the earliest practicable date.' . . . Faith by itself, without works, is not enough."[10]

Unable to conceal his distaste for the whole idea of desegregation and smarting from the higher court's rebuke, Atwell issued a sweeping injunction against the School Board "requiring or permitting segregation of the races in any school" after January 27, 1958.[11] The Board appealed the order, and the Court of Appeals again reversed Atwell, holding that their previous order had not required him to set a date certain for desegregation until he had given the school officials a reasonable opportunity to discharge their responsibilities. Moreover, the court noted that their earlier order had only forbidden the district from "requiring" segregation. The district court was ordered to retain jurisdiction, and after new hearings, to make a final decision.[12]

Atwell, now eighty-seven and thoroughly out of sympathy with the higher court, decided to retire, producing a temporary pause in the litigation. The School Board, however, did not come forward with a plan, and schools opened in Dallas in fall 1958 without so much as a token of integration.[13]

Early in 1959 Thurgood Marshall returned with the plaintiffs to the federal courthouse, where Judge T. Whitfield Davidson had taken over the case. Marshall asked the court to order the immediate integration of Dallas schools. Davidson denied the request, and recessed the hearing until April 1960. On appeal, the Court of Appeals required the school board to present a plan "for effectuating a transition to a racially nondiscriminatory school system . . ." within thirty days. It also ordered Davidson to hold a hearing on the plan within thirty days after submission of the plan.[14]

To comply with the court's order, the school board proposed a "stair step" plan, which would start with the first grade and then proceed, one grade level a year, to stop using race as a criterion for admission to the public schools. But even this was too much for Judge Davidson. Though he ordered the school board to proceed with desegregation of the schools, he ensured that it would not be accomplished so fast as to create confusion or disorganization. Thus, he rejected the school board's stair-step plan, which he concluded would "manifestly lead to an amalgamation of the races . . . ."[15] He approved instead a "salt and pepper" alternative, submitted by the school board at his request. This plan maintained racially segregated schools, but required the operation of integrated schools if parents of both races desired them.

Judge Davidson expressed his distaste for his duty in an opinion remarkable, even for its time, in condescension toward blacks, visceral loathing of integration and dread of miscegenation, apologia for segregation, and a harangue against the supplanting of local authority with federal power.[16] This opinion and those that followed after serial reversals by the Court of Appeals capture the myths and mindset that permeated southern politics at mid-century. Davidson excused the violence of the Klan, and denounced efforts to desegregate housing, schools, public accommodations, employment opportunities, and the voting booth. His opinions reveal acceptable attitudes at the highest social and political level in Dallas in the late 1950s and the early 1960s. And they reflect the pervasive influence of the civic culture even on the court, an institution that had higher and more legitimate claims on its loyalty.

In his first opinion, Davidson framed the question before him as whether "the white and black school children of Dallas [can] be presently and hastily integrated by force without frustration and injury to their educational opportunities."[17] He then conducted a grand misguided tour of history to demonstrate the virtue of racial separation and integrity and the dangers of forced integration to civilization. He described slavery as benign, even beneficent, and summoned his ancestors as exemplars of humane concern for the welfare of slaves, noting that his great-grandfather "never let a slave be whipped except on his own orders."[18]

Davidson denounced the ill wisdom of forcing suppression of long-established customs and the importance of racial integrity. Drawing lessons from the failure of the 18th Amendment and a pastiche of biblical, Jewish, and Greek history, cattle breeding, and contrasts between northern and southern Europe he proclaimed "Racial integrity . . . is a God-given right" that had saved Christian civilization.[19]

Having admonished the higher courts and warned the public of the impending calamities of forced integration, Davidson seemed cheered by the thought that even with efforts made in good faith, integration of the races might still fail. The final section of his order to the school board captures his obsession with miscegenation:

> Without purposely and intentionally discriminating between the races you may for any good cause or reason assign pupils to schools other than that nearest to them. Thus, to illustrate, if some pampered white boy, growing up without ever having been controlled or denied, enters an integrated school and by reason of his selfish propensities, pride or vanity or racial dislike creates a disturbance he may be transferred to another school. Likewise, if an overgrown Negro boy in an integrated school should be by premature growth inclined to sex and should write verses on the blackboard of an obscene character designedly for the white girls to read or should make improper approaches to them so as to provoke trouble in the school, he should be assigned to a school where the situation is different.[20]

Innocent of irony, he concluded by admonishing all parties that: "Not only in our schools but in our entire public relations should the two races be tolerant of each other and when exasperated from something that ought not to have happened just to consider something that's good."[21]

On appeal, the U.S. Court of Appeals characterized the "salt and pepper" plan as one that: "evidences a total misconception of the nature of the constitutional rights asserted by the plaintiffs. . . . to stand equal before the laws of the state; that is, to be treated simply as individuals without regard to race or color."[22]

The appellate court directed Davidson to approve implementation of the stair-step plan at the start of the 1961 school year, and to retain jurisdiction to determine if such a drawn-out period would be necessary to achieve full integration of the schools.[23] On June 27, 1961, Judge Davidson obeyed the court of appeals, but not without a final outburst of his displeasure at having to enter a decree of "forcible integration in disregard of the schools' plans and the constitution and laws of Texas."[24] He denounced the Supreme Court desegregation decision that led to the decree he was ordered to enter as "one of that line of decisions leveling and annulling constitutional limitation on arbitrary powers of government," bypassing the 10th Amendment "as though it had never been written." He expressed his dissent and distaste for the duty the Court of Appeals had imposed upon him, closing his opinion with advice to the parties and to the city: "One final word to the people of Dallas: Stand calmly by constituted authority. To the colored man, . . . [s]ound ethics and good manners tell us not to unnecessarily provoke the ill will of those with whom we live. . . . To the white man . . . do not, though you disapprove, resort to violence in any form. It injures your cause."[25]

Dallas at the Crossroads: Commerce or Segregation?

That Judges Atwell and Davidson could be counted on to do all they could to delay and frustrate desegregation was an important strategic consideration in the tactics of the school board.[26] Moreover, their opinions placed the moral authority of the local federal judiciary clearly on the side resisting desegregation, lending legitimacy to opposition and contributing ambiguity rather than clarity to the constitutional duty incumbent on the school board.

The school board was content with the status quo. With no political base independent of the Citizens Council, it was unaccustomed to taking policy initiatives on its own, and depended on the superintendent for guidance. Its job was to support the superintendent in maintaining good schools at modest cost and to avoid embarrassing the city. Superintendent White was an ardent defender of the dual school system and encouraged the board in its inclination to resist desegregation. Having no minority members, the board had no built-in "feel" for the concerns of the minority parents and pupils of the district.

Basically, the school board tried to position itself as neither in outright defiance of the law, therefore running a risk of inflaming popular resistance, nor capitulating to the demands of "outside agitators" like Thurgood Marshall. Thus, with the blessing of the district court, its initial response was to take maximum advantage of the "deliberate speed" granted it by the Supreme Court. It could claim a good faith effort at finding a workable way to preserve as much of the dual educational system as possible.

Opposition to school desegregation reinforced the growing radical conservatism among many of the Dallas elite. The Supreme Court mandate for school desegregation represented to these insular and independent men one more intrusion by arrogant and subversive outsiders into the conduct of local affairs. For them, *Brown v. Board of Education* was a socially unsound and morally wrong decision. But for others, whatever their opinion of its virtues, they could foresee that segregation, the second pillar of the oligarchy's hegemony, was about to collapse from the "outside" force of "judge-made" law.

Overt defiance of desegregation might have struck a populist cord in much of Anglo Dallas, but the recent history of racial violence in southern Dallas forced business leaders to weigh whether they valued segregation over commerce. By the time the case had been transferred to Judge Davidson's court, key leaders, especially Mayor R. L. "Uncle Bob" Thornton, had determined that violent white opposition to integration in Dallas could destroy all that Dallas's business leaders had so long and meticulously built. Federal enforcement of school desegregation in Little Rock, Arkansas against state resistance convinced them and their chosen school trustees that open resistance to the law of the land would be crushed—if necessary with federal troops—and that violent demonstrations and disruption of the civil peace could seriously damage the city's economy and its carefully nurtured reputation.[27] The Supreme Court also made it clear, in the Little Rock case, that no state law or action could stand against the higher claims of federal constitutional rights.[28] In Dallas, 300 white Protestant ministers now signed an open letter declaring segregation to be morally wrong and urging the city to prepare peacefully for desegregation. Thornton, anxious that Dallas should not become the next Little Rock, began quietly urging Dallas business leaders to prepare public opinion for the inevitable.[29]

If desegregation of schools could not be postponed indefinitely by taking full advantage of the turgid pace of the legal system, then it must be "sold" and implemented in ways that would minimize the damage. Desegregation became a commodity, which, if appropriately diluted and skillfully packaged, could be sold and swallowed with little harm to the city's peace and economy. Dallas's leaders did not know how to desegregate the schools, but they did know how to sell. They had sold the Centennial, the City Charter, and bond issues. This time they had three "customers:" the white citizenry, the courts, and black community leaders.

The "stair step" plan had the imprimatur of the local federal court. It fit the twin goals of minimal change and only slight disruption of going concerns. The plan signified compliance, but at a pace and scale that was not alarming. It did not call for busing white students to schools outside their neighborhoods. Rather, black students could simply apply, one grade level a year, to be assigned to the neighborhood school nearest their home and the school board would admit them without reference to their race. Given Dallas's pattern of residential segregation, the number of black students seeking admission to previously all-white schools could be expected to be few.

The Citizens Council, as a cohesive private association, could operate out of public view. Given its influence in the selection of members of the School Board and the City Council, and the fact that its founder, Thornton, was mayor until 1961, assured official ratification of its decisions. The economic power of the Citizens Council was sufficient to assure the compliance of merchants and other business people of the city. Citizen Council grandees owned the city's major newspapers, radio stations and television channels. While hostile to court-ordered desegregation, they could now be counted on to give editorial support to peaceful compliance and to suppress publication of inflammatory comments or events.

To gain support in the black community for their plan, and to suppress any racial confrontation, a biracial committee was appointed, consisting of seven key white business leaders and seven black businessmen and professionals, including one of the attorneys in the desegregation case. Weekly meetings were held to discuss how to accomplish the desegregation of schools and other facilities in Dallas, and how to prepare the community for the change. Essentially, the white leaders guaranteed peaceful enrollment of the first black children in previously all-white schools; the black leaders guaranteed no demonstrations or protests.

Achieving peaceful compliance—at least on a symbolic level—was approached as a mass marketing problem. A local public relations firm was commissioned to produce a film, "Dallas at the Crossroads," narrated by Walter Cronkite of CBS News, the most respected man in America. Shown over 1,000 times to community groups in Dallas, it stressed the harm that would accrue to the city from not obeying the laws and the unfairness of imposing the burden of resisting court-compelled desegregation on white school children. No blacks were featured in the film. The basic message of the need to obey the law was reinforced by editorials, statements by community leaders and from Dallas pulpits.[30]

On September 6, 1961, the police were ready in force for any disturbance as schools opened for the fall term. None occurred. Eighteen black first grade children were enrolled without incident in previously all-white elementary schools.[31] An "accommodation" had been reached with black litigants and community leaders that permitted both sides to claim victory and progress. Dallas had avoided a potentially ugly and damaging confrontation. It was a public relations success, which, in retrospect, can be too easily discounted. In the context of the politics of defiance of the Supreme Court that then pervaded the South, it was a substantial achievement to bring a major city with a history of racial bitterness to accept even the symbolic desegregation of its public schools. It also entered the folklore of the city, burnishing the reputation of the business elite for leadership in a time of crisis.

The crisis passed, but the basic issues of equal educational opportunity for minority remained unresolved. Blacks were frustrated by the slow pace of change, the poor facilities and lower quality programs in black schools, and the intransigence of the school board and superintendent in integrating the teaching staff or taking other measures to accelerate desegregation. In 1964 attorneys representing black plaintiffs petitioned Judge Davidson to order the immediate desegregation of the entire school system, accelerating the one-grade-at-a-time schedule begun in 1961. Davidson balked, contending that the 1961 Court of Appeals order had limited him to the twelve-step schedule. He counseled patience. On appeal, an impatient Court of Appeals said that Judge Davidson "should require the desegregation of grade 12 in 1965."[32] He interpreted the higher court's "should" as merely a suggestion, and declined to enter such an order.

Exasperated, the Court of Appeals took the unusual step of bypassing Judge Davidson and sent its order directly to the president of the school board, requiring the board to amend its plan to desegregate the twelfth grade in all Dallas high schools beginning in September 1965.[33] Two months later, T. Whitfield Davidson, aged eighty-nine, retired after twenty-nine years as a federal district judge.

The Court, the Regency, and Racial Politics

The 1964 Civil Rights Act[34] signaled a profound change in the attitudes of the nation's political leadership toward desegregation. Title VI of the Act made federal assistance to local schools contingent on desegregation.[35] An Office of Civil Rights was established in the Office of Education, and the Civil Rights Division of the Justice Department began to take a far more active role in desegregation and other civil rights issues. The national executive began to support the courts, and new federal judges appointed by Presidents Kennedy and Johnson took a less pinched view of both the desegregation decisions of the Supreme Court and their own equity powers to remedy segregated school systems.

A new generation of judges was willing to push for integration, rather than engage in delay tactics, narrow interpretations, or outright defiance of the law.[36] The U.S. Department of Health, Education and Welfare issued desegregation guidelines, and the Fifth Circuit Court of Appeals told district courts and defendants that they could not substitute more lenient court orders for the HEW guidelines.[37] By 1971, the Supreme Court had abandoned the "all deliberate speed" guideline of *Brown II*[38] and authorized lower courts to use their equity powers to employ the necessary tools, ranging from busing to attendance zones and integration of staff to "eliminate from schools all vestiges of state-imposed segregation."[39]

Dallas also was changing. A new biracial citizens group, the League for Educational Advancement (LEAD), gained a majority on the school board, displacing a Citizens Council-backed majority for the first time in twenty years.[40] The new majority included the first black trustee, Dr. Emmett Conrad. It supported a broad platform of educational reforms, including bilingual education, increasing the number of minority teachers and administrators, and improvements in curriculum and facilities. When W. T. White retired, Nolan Estes, a former associate commissioner of the U.S. Office of Education, was chosen as superintendent. Estes made substantial progress in integrating faculties, but little change occurred in attendance zones, so that by the end of the decade only two percent of the district's nearly 50,000 black students attended predominantly white schools.[41] Neither the board nor superintendent saw any need to act affirmatively to broaden or accelerate desegregation.

In September 1970, Sam Tasby, a black parent whose sons were bused past a nearby all-white school to a black junior high school several miles from their home, sought the assistance of the local Legal Services Corporation, which, on his behalf, filed a new desegregation suit in federal court. William M. Taylor, a former Dallas County Assistant District Attorney, Assistant City Attorney, and state judge, became the third federal judge to handle a Dallas case. Taylor found that Dallas still had a dual system.[42] He noted that the U.S. Supreme Court and the Fifth Circuit had authorized a variety of remedies for segregated schools. He then ruled that: "The Dallas School Board has failed to implement any of these tools or to even suggest that it would consider such plans until long after the filing of this suit and in part after the commencement of this trial."[43] The district was ordered to: "remove all vestiges of a dual system and at the same time truly provide a quality integrated educational system."[44]

In many respects, the remedies not chosen were as important as those that were. The court rejected massive busing of students, arguing that except for limited pairings, the residentially segregated housing patterns of Dallas precluded a successful busing program. Judge Taylor was skeptical of the desirability of extensive busing, especially of elementary school children, favoring neighborhood schools where it was feasible to retain them and still achieve the goals of desegregation. In particular, he was sensitive to the interests of black parents who intervened in the case, asking that neighborhood schools be retained, even if they remained all black, and to concerns that white residents might remove their children from the Dallas public schools rather than have them bused. Although Taylor's opinion acknowledged that the Dallas Public Schools were being unconstitutionally operated, his order relied heavily on incentives and enrichment programs to induce voluntary integration of Anglo and minority students.

There was one bizarre element in Taylor's otherwise straightforward order. In an effort to avoid busing elementary school children, he approved a "TV Plan," which would have linked pairs of white and minority elementary schools by simultaneous two-way television for at least an hour a day, supplemented with visits between the paired classes each week for at least three hours of personal contact.[45]

The Court of Appeals for the Fifth Circuit held the TV plan unconstitutional because "it does not attempt to alter the racial characteristics of the DISD's elementary schools."[46] In remanding the case to the district court, the circuit court observed that during the twenty years of litigation, "both the courts and the DISD have proceeded with 'all deliberate speed.' Endurance records, perhaps, but not speed records have been set in this and the prior litigation." The appellate panel noted that the 'all deliberate speed' timetable had been superseded by recent Supreme Court decisions, which "made it clear that ' . . . the obligation of every school district is to eliminate dual school systems at once and to operate now and hereafter only unitary school systems.' "[47] Judge Taylor was ordered to take the necessary steps, including busing of students in paired schools, to completely dismantle the dual system in Dallas by the start of the second semester of the 1975–1976 school year.[48]

In the two decades since the first desegregation suit was filed in Dallas, an entire cohort born in 1954 had passed through the school system. The racial composition of DISD students had also dramatically shifted. In 1955, about three-fourths of the students were Anglos. By 1971 they still made up 69 percent of students, but by the time Judge Taylor held an evidentiary hearing in 1975 to fashion a desegregation order, the Anglo student population had dropped to 41 percent. As the Anglo enrollment declined, Mexican-Americans became a significant ethnic minority in the city, and the court granted them protected minority status.[49]

This major change in the demography of the district, combined with the pattern of residential segregation in Dallas, long distances, natural and man-made barriers to access, and levels of traffic congestion, made the selection of desegregation measures such as busing more problematic than it might have been in earlier years. These were also years of rapid suburbanization. Most in-migrating Anglos joined their fleeing counterparts to settle in overwhelmingly white suburban school districts. These districts were safe from desegregation plans after the Supreme Court ruled in 1976 that suburbs could not be included in such plans if they had not maintained racially separate schools.[50]

In its search for a workable desegregation plan, the court entertained proposals from the parties and a growing list of minority and Anglo intervenors. As the basis for his order, Judge Taylor accepted a plan developed by the interracial Dallas Alliance, organized by Dallas businessman Jack Lowe, Sr. Lowe had worked with minority groups on housing and other issues, and enjoyed the confidence of leaders in both the business and minority communities.[51] Admitted into the case as *amicus curiae*, the Alliance's education task force of Anglos,

African-Americans, Mexican-Americans, and an American Indian spent several months in study and intensive debates to reach a consensus strategy for desegregating Dallas schools. As adopted by the court in its 1976 order, the plan contained the following basic elements:[52]

1) Division of the DISD into six sub-districts, four of which mirrored the racial composition of the entire district, and within which students could be assigned to nearby schools to achieve desegregation without the necessity of extensive cross-town busing. The other two sub-districts—inner city East Oak Cliff and semi-rural Seagonville in far southeast Dallas, were deemed to be too isolated and racially homogeneous to make the racial integration of their students feasible, given the time and distance required for busing, without unreasonable educational damage.[53]
2) Within each sub-district, schools were to be organized into a uniform, four-tiered system—grades K–3, 4–6, 7–8, and 9–12. K–3 children would attend their nearest neighborhood school, in which individualized and compensatory education programs would be emphasized. Grades 4–8 were to be located near the center of each sub-district and attendance zones drawn so that only short bus rides would be required to achieve desegregation of those intermediate grades.
3) Magnet high schools focused on vocations and professions were to be established in central locations and offer programs that would be attractive to students of all races. Open to all students in the district, admission to the magnet schools was to be racially balanced and free transportation provided. Enrollment at district-wide Vanguard Schools for grades 4–6 and Academies for grades 7–8 was also to be voluntary.[54]
4) A Majority-to-Minority transfer program was ordered, whereby students in the district could transfer from an

assigned school where their race made up the majority of the student body to any other school where their race was in the minority. Again, free transportation would be provided.

5) Bilingual education and English as a Second Language programs were to be expanded as rapidly as possible. Hispanic students could transfer freely to any school offering bilingual education programs if their assigned school did not offer one.
6) Exceptions to student assignment and attendance boundary changes were made for "naturally integrated" schools serving racially mixed residential areas, such as East Dallas, and for East Oak Cliff, where feasible boundary changes could not overcome its racial isolation.
7) All new facilities and improvements must be approved by the court, after review by the tri-ethnic committee appointed by the judge.
8) Schools and central administrative staffs were to be integrated to reflect roughly the racial mix of the district, and no school was to have a faculty or staff whose racial composition would permit an inference that it was designed to serve one racial group.
9) The district was to be held accountable for progress toward a unitary system by semi-annual reports to the court, covering all pertinent areas of program, personnel, facilities, and other matters pertinent to the desegregation order.

The Anglo majority on the board was sullenly compliant, and the district began implementing the court's order. Dallas was not ready to accept all aspects of the plan without further controversy, however. The NAACP appealed the modest busing element. It had resulted in few voluntary transfers of Anglo students to the new magnet schools. In 1977 the Fifth Circuit ordered Judge Taylor to reduce the number of one-race schools and to hold further hearings on the justification for the limited amount of busing. The School Board then petitioned the U.S. Supreme Court to reinstate Judge Taylor's busing plan. This action drew intervenors both in support and opposition.

Two years passed before the Supreme Court issued an anticlimactic opinion in January 1980, holding that the Dallas case was not properly before it.[55] This left the Court of Appeals decision intact, requiring Judge Taylor to take further evidence on busing and try to devise a plan that would result in a higher degree of desegregation. His attempt to persuade the parties to negotiate a consent decree was frustrated by dissension between Anglo and minority members of the School Board, and growing disagreement among counsel for local black plaintiffs and intervenors with attorneys for the NAACP Legal Defense Fund over two issues. The Legal Defense Fund lawyers wanted to press for more busing, consistent with the organization's national litigation strategy, while local counsel preferred to retain as many neighborhood schools as possible. The lawyers also disagreed over the NAACP's motion requesting Judge Taylor to recuse himself because of his former membership in the law firm now representing the School Board.[56]

Ten years after he began his supervision of the case, Judge Taylor recused himself, concluding that the issue of his impartiality could only precipitate appeals and further delay resolution of the case.

In the meantime, Superintendent Nolan Estes resigned. In addition to desegregation, his administration was afflicted with scandals in construction and facilities management. The School Board selected Linus Wright, a broadly experienced Houston administrator, to replace him. Wright had to clean up the financial mess and create an effective management system for the district. He confronted a hemorrhaging white enrollment in a district that had reached its statutory tax limits at a time when there was a growing gap between the performance of Anglo and minority students.

Assessing the situation, Wright demanded and got a contract that gave him full control over personnel selection and assignment. With the support of the majority of the board during the first five years of his tenure, he established a management system that held principals and teachers accountable for the performance of students, measured by standardized tests.[57] The measurement system was reinforced by strong leadership by Wright and his assistant superintendents. Principals and faculty were encouraged to participate in the redesign of curriculum and in setting achievable goals for their schools. External support was built through a wide variety of meetings with parent and community advisory groups.[58]

Poorly performing principals and teachers were first counseled, but if they did not improve they were transferred, or where possible, dismissed. Dismissal for incompetence under the schools' cumbersome and antiquated personnel system was extremely difficult, however. Wright recalled that it cost the district an average of $25,000 in legal expenses to fire an incompetent teacher and as much as $100,000 to get rid of an administrator in the early years of his tenure because of inadequate documentation of their performances.[59] Rather than confront these difficulties the district simply hired 500 additional minority staff, and kept most of the Anglos in their positions.[60]

Wright urged the board to adopt a desegregation plan the court could approve and return full control of the system to the district. Black trustees, however, did not want to end court supervision. They did not trust their Anglo colleagues to pursue a policy of equalizing educational opportunity. They saw the court's requirements as providing opportunities for the advancement of minorities in the system. Anglo members also resisted, fearing they would be blamed for support of busing and other desegregation measures.

Desegregating Dallas public schools now became the task of Judge Barefoot Sanders, selected by lot from the available federal judges. Sanders had deep roots in Dallas, where he was born, attended public schools, and served in the State Legislature. He had been the U.S. District Attorney for the Northern District of Texas, Assistant Attorney General for Civil Rights in the U.S. Department of Justice, and a candidate for the U.S. House of Representatives and the U.S. Senate. Judge Sanders began a month of hearings in April 1981 and issued his first opinion in August. He found that increased busing was not feasible, and directed the parties to present desegregation plans that emphasized magnet schools, majority-to-minority transfers, attendance zone changes, middle school desegregation, building improvements, and educational programs to reduce discrimination.[61]

As Sanders took over the case, the composition of the school board changed. After an absence of almost a decade from school affairs, business leaders associated with the Dallas Citizens Council organized the Committee for Quality Education (CQE) to reassert business influence in school affairs. It raised nearly half a million dollars for its candidates and elected five of the six candidates it endorsed in 1981. The new majority supported Superintendent Wright's accountability system, but opposed any busing of students to achieve desegregation. It rejected an agreement reached by the other parties to the case that provided for a financial supplement of $50 for each minority student and establishment of an office, paid for by the Board, to monitor efforts to improve the achievement of minority students.[62]

Sanders refused to accept a pure "neighborhood" plan, holding that it was inconsistent with the requirements of law. Transfers of minority students to north Dallas high schools were ordered, some schools were closed, the magnet school program was to be enhanced with construction of a new magnet campus, and enrichment programs were ordered for minority students. He established a monitor's office and ordered it to make semi-annual reports to the court on student achievement progress.[63]

The CQE majority initially voted to appeal the order, but after a meeting with the judge, two of the CQE members changed their minds and a racially mixed majority of the School

Board rescinded the decision to appeal. The NAACP, however, over the objections of its local chapter and the Black Coalition, appealed the order because of its apparent inconsistency with the organization's national strategy, which placed a greater emphasis on busing of students to achieve racial balance in schools. The School Board, once again reversing direction, appealed other aspects of the order. In August 1983, almost two years after it was issued, the U.S. Court of Appeals for the Fifth Circuit upheld all elements of Judge Sanders' order except for the boundaries of one attendance zone.[64]

With the basic framework for desegregation finally established by the courts, the district court's attention in the years that followed increasingly focused on the gap in achievement between minority and Anglo students. The performance system installed by Superintendent Wright resulted in substantial gains for both minority and non-minority students in the Dallas Public Schools, but when the CQE dissolved in 1985, as business interest in the schools once again waned, the board backed away from it. Achievement levels of minority and other disadvantaged students again declined, wiping out many of the gains made in the five years of measurement-driven management.[65] Wright could not convince Judge Sanders of the value and validity of his approach to improving minority student achievement. With the support of the court-appointed monitor and the minority board members, Sanders instead approved creation of special learning centers, where new techniques could be tried to improve student performance.[66] The district's own data showed that the longer disadvantaged minority children stayed in Dallas schools, the farther they fell behind their grade levels in reading and mathematics.[67]

When Sanders took over the case in 1981 it was already apparent that the diminishing number and proportion of white pupils in the system made extensive busing infeasible as a primary integration stratagem. During the 1980s the proportion of Anglo students dropped below 20 percent as Hispanic enrollment rose toward parity with African-Americans. Any prospect of racial balance, by any practicable means, evaporated. Most of Dallas's Anglo public school students were now served by other districts, such as Highland Park, Richardson, and Plano. Those districts, however, could not be included in any court-ordered desegregation plan, since they never had dual systems.[68]

The refusal of Anglos to transfer voluntarily to schools with heavy black or Hispanic enrollments necessitated other strategies. The court, therefore, placed increasing emphasis on facilities and programs—magnet schools, learning centers for K-3 pupils, bilingual education and compensatory education programs—as means of equalizing educational opportunity for Anglo and minority students.

In 1988, following the resignation of Superintendent Wright to accept appointment as Deputy Secretary of Education by President Ronald Reagan, the school board selected Marvin Edwards as his replacement. Edwards, an African-American who was Superintendent of Schools in Topeka, Kansas, had a strong reputation as an educator and conciliator of interracial conflict. The board continued to divide along racial lines, however, and while Edwards enjoyed the public support of the minority trustees, he was often at odds with them over personnel assignments, education policy, and his support of unitary status for the district. The court, however, was not willing to declare that the district had achieved unitary status while significant disparities in student achievement persisted, and the board failed to implement other aspects of the order with respect to magnet schools, the condition of facilities, faculty and staff integration, and educational programs.[69]

The establishment of single-member districts for the school board members, to conform to requirements of the 1965 Voting Rights Act, ensured election of three black trustees. Two members—Kathlyn Gilliam and Yvonne Ewell—rarely had opposition, and became permanent fixtures on the Board until the late 1990s.[70] Gilliam was consistently the most racially polarizing member of the board. She developed an extensive network of system employees who had benefited from her patronage. Ewell had been a successful principal of a middle school, and had been moved up to assistant superintendent and court monitor, based on her performance. After Wright found her work inadequate she resigned and was elected to the board in 1987. The third black seat turned over frequently. The other districts included one safe Hispanic seat, four safe Anglo constituencies, and one seat that alternated between Anglo and Hispanic trustees.

The consequence of this arrangement was a hardening of racial animosities among trustees, as blacks viewed Anglo members as almost always opposed to compliance with court orders, even as black enrollment grew to majority status and then was eclipsed by Hispanics. The three black votes formed a consistent bloc. Hispanic members were uncertain allies, because they often gained more by alliance with the Anglo members. In this environment the court remained the only sure source of support for the aims of the black trustees. Thus, they resisted any move to end court supervision, which would return the district to control by a majority that had an almost untarnished history of, at best, reluctant compliance with desegregation measures blacks favored.

In spite of these tensions, when Judge Sanders in 1990 asked the board to set a date for a bond referendum to finance the Townview Super-Magnet[71] and other long-delayed projects, the board briefly coalesced. It also agreed with a proposal by Trustee Yvonne Ewell to establish two task forces. The first was a response to reports from the desegregation monitor that little progress had been made in educational achievement of minority students and the threat of the Texas Education Agency to downgrade the accreditation of the district if it did not improve its governance practices. The Commission on Educational Excellence, the brainchild of Dallas attorney Sandy Kress and Robert Weiss, a program director of the Meadows Foundation, was given the task of making recommendations to the board for improving the quality of education for all children in the district. Kress, who enjoyed good working relationships with the black trustees and business leaders in Dallas, was asked to chair the commission.

The second group, a Task Force on Facilities, was charged with recommending improvements in the district's physical facilities, with a specific eye to projects to be included in the bond issue. Richard Knight, a former city manager, and the first African-American appointed to that post, was selected as chair.

The Kress Commission gave the School Board more than some of its members wanted. After a nine-month study of experience in other cities and examination of research on effective education techniques, the commission endorsed a strong emphasis on school-centered education. This recommendation reinforced proposals of Superintendent Edwards, which had been whittled down by the Board to a one-school pilot program at the insistence of Trustee Gilliam. The cornerstone of the commission recommendations, however, was an accountability system, modeled on the one used by Superintendent Wright, that would hold teachers, principals, and administrators responsible for improving the performance of their students, as measured by standardized tests.[72] Teachers and principals who did not perform effectively would be helped or dismissed. A key provision was that high-performing schools would receive financial rewards at an annual event, for which local businesses would raise the award money. Other features of the commission recommendations included community involvement in schools and greater classroom support for teachers. Widely praised by the *Morning News* and business organizations, such as the Dallas Citizens Council and Chamber of Commerce, the Kress report was endorsed unanimously by the School Board.

After the demise of the Committee for Educational Quality, some business executives had continued quietly to make campaign contributions to white and some Hispanic school board candidates. No formal or public endorsement group existed, but candidates were vetted by the informal "Breakfast Club" composed of like-minded business executives. Once more, business interests mobilized in 1991 to support the election to the Board of Kress and Rebecca Bergstresser, also a member of the Excellence Commission, as well as others who supported its recommendations. All of the Anglo and Hispanic board members were committed to implementation of the Kress Commission reforms. Only Gilliam and Ewell resisted. The third black trustee, Hollis Brashear, eventually sided with the Anglos and Hispanics in the organization of the Board, which elected Rene Castilla president and Kress as vice president. Kress was generally regarded as the leader of the board, and with a solid majority ready to follow his lead on policy, the coalition took perverse pride in being called the "Slam-Dunk Gang" by both friends and foes.

The majority approved a referendum for December 1992 on a bond issue to provide funding for the improvements necessary to comply with Judge Sanders' decrees. In order to avoid a tax increase to retire the bonds, and thereby assure support from the business community for the referendum, the Board scaled back the Townview Super-Magnet by almost half. This action angered Gilliam and Ewell, for whom the Super-Magnet was a long-sought symbol of resource equity. Sanders approved the scaled back proposal, but insisted on a contingency fund and ordered fines if the board failed to meet certain construction deadlines. The two dissenters now supported the bond issue and the voters approved it.

Shortly after the bond referendum, Edwards resigned to accept the superintendency of the Elgin, Illinois, school district. He had never gained the full confidence of the board, nor comfortably dealt with either the Anglo or minority members. Chad Woolery, the Deputy Superintendent, was named interim superintendent and eventually was appointed to the permanent position. Woolery was a veteran of the DISD and had well-established relationships with the black trustees, especially Yvonne Ewell. He had worked as assistant principal in an Oak Cliff middle school, and gained her support and Gilliam's, after showing that an Anglo could effectively manage a virtually all-black school in a low-income community.

Knowing the system and its administrative problems well, Woolery was an enthusiast of the new accountability system recommended by the Excellence Commission. He used it to demote or fire seventy principals at low-performing schools during his first two years on the job. Sandy Kress, in reflecting on the effectiveness of the system, said that it managed to get rid of the "D and F" principals, whose performance was such that even their patrons on the Board could not justify their retention.[73] But when the accountability system "began to reach the C-minus people, it began to run out of gas."[74]

It was apparent that one of the hard facts confronting any reform was that the Dallas Public Schools had become a job system for friends and supporters of trustees as well as an education system for children.[75] In this sense the racial and ethnic goals set by the court to assure integration of staff were an important source of power and patronage for minority trustees. Administrative positions in the schools and central office required racial balance. In addition, some programs had become sources for jobs of questionable utility. The $30 million federally funded Title I[76] compensatory education program for disadvantaged children was a good example. Kress observed: "Tons of people were hired who were less qualified . . . because federal funds were easy not to care about."[77]

The Title I program, however, was at the core of the effort to achieve a unified district by closing the gap in scholastic achievement between Anglos and minorities once it was apparent to the court that a achieving racial balance was impracticable. In the district's administrative hierarchy, the Title I program was managed by an administrator at the central office. The Title I administrator controlled the allocations to individual schools, and selected teachers as full-time Title I coordinators in schools. Like Title I programs elsewhere in the country, the Dallas program could reasonably be described as a federally funded employment program for redundant teachers and teacher aides with little discernible aggregate effect on student achievement.[78]

Before leaving Dallas Superintendent Edwards had initiated a "School Centered Education" plan[79] that gave individual principals authority to select and dismiss teachers and allocate their campus budgets as they saw fit. For the first time, principals operating under a site-based management concept were given control of their school's allocation of Title I and other special desegregation funds.[80] In turn, principals were to be held responsible for the performance of their schools.

With this new pressure on the individual principals to show improvement in reading scores, the Title I office began training its teachers in *Reading Recovery,* a "whole language" program that had a strong national reputation. Because of the large number of students in need of remedial education and the cost of well-trained and certified teachers, students were generally taught in groups of eight to ten, rather than individually tutored, which is far more effective.[81] Consequently, only a fraction of disadvantaged students could be served and the program was ineffective in significantly improving the reading abilities of those who participated. Some more cost-effective method of instruction was needed to reach the large number of under-performing elementary school children. The problem Dallas confronted, however, was finding enough qualified tutors for the large number of students needing help.

The Citizens Council's education committee, energized by the interest of Jerry Junkins, CEO of Texas Instruments, recommended trial of an initiative developed by Professor George Farkas of the University of Texas at Dallas.[82] Farkas' innovation was to recruit and train college students and community residents in techniques of reading instruction, employ them under close supervision, and grade their performance as tutors on written records of each session and reports charting the performance of the children they tutored. The children's progress would be measured with standardized tests. Improvement in reading by students participating in a demonstration of the program at an inner city school were comparable to nationally acclaimed programs, but at less than a fourth of their cost, suggesting that it would be possible to serve all the at-risk children in DISD with available Title I funds.

Within four years Farkas' *UTD Reading One-One* program had spread to thirty-two DISD schools, primarily by word of mouth among enthusiastic teachers and principals.[83] During the 1994–1995 school year, the program tutored approximately 2,400 at-risk children. It provided one of the inspirations for a reading initiative advanced by then Texas Governor George W. Bush[84] and was cited as an exemplary program in President Bill Clinton's 1996 reading initiative. By 1998 it had been introduced into a number of other school districts in Texas and other states. In Dallas the program was being quashed.[85]

It was opposed by the district's Title I administrator from its inception. It shifted control of Title I funds from the central office to principals, giving them discretion to purchase the services of UTD's tutors rather than support in-school Title I teacher-coordinators. Superintendent Woolery was cool to the program and resisted its expansion. He promoted the use of a computer-assisted program that used unpaid volunteers as tutors. Although almost all of the thirty-two principals whose schools used Reading One-One in 1994 seemed to prefer it, only eight continued their participation in 1995.

Principals opined that the central administration had reduced both their discretion and their resources. They were told that if they chose Reading One-One with their limited resources they would have to dismiss their school's Title I teachers. Few chose to go against the current even if they felt that Reading One-One was more cost-effective and had enjoyed both success and popularity in their schools.[86] The reversion to central control under Woolery gave principals no buffer between themselves and the central offices, and reduced the authority of some areas to experiment with less conventional approaches than those favored by the central administrative offices.

More Title I teachers were designated in more schools to manage the computer/volunteer tutor system. Elementary schools with high concentrations of at-risk students lost Title I funds they had used for Reading One-One as a result of legislative changes that allowed the system to use these federal funds for a wider array of services and programs. With almost all schools now sharing Title I funds, the administration and board could claim it was serving more students. Volunteer programs could symbolically engage the business community, providing critical political support to the administration and maintaining its access to slack resources for other selective benefits, such as computers and the annual performance awards event.

Asserting a broad effort (notwithstanding modest results) at improving minority achievement, the Townview Super-Magnet High School under construction, and Woolery's accountability system receiving good reviews, the board, with the black trustees still in opposition, voted to seek a judicial declaration that the district had achieved unitary status. Judge Sanders convened a hearing on the board's petition in May 1994. Two months later he declared the district unitary and agreed to release it from court supervision after three years, provided it continued to make progress in implementing his instructions.[87] The *Tasby* plaintiffs did not appeal.

New racial conflict ensued even before the judge reached his decision, and continued for the next six years. The first new controversy arose when René Castilla announced that he would not continue as president of the board, and supported Hollis Brashear as his successor, providing four votes for a black president. The four Anglos supported Kress, giving the deciding vote to the other Hispanic member, Trini Garza, who voted for Kress. Brashear became vice president.

The long-awaited opening of Townview in 1995 precipitated a second racial crisis. Woolery chose Ora Lee Watson, a black administrator close to Gilliam, Ewell, and County Commissioner John Wiley Price, to serve as executive principal of the new facility, at which six of the district's magnet schools were to be relocated. Watson immediately became embroiled in a public dispute with the principal of the Talented and Gifted (TAG) Magnet over the degree of autonomy this highly respected school would have at Townview. Although a majority of students in the TAG were minorities, it was regarded by some as an elitist school. It also had the active support of parents; the most vocal of whom were Anglos.

The dispute quickly escalated into a symbolic struggle over standards, equality, resources, and the self-image of minorities and TAG students. Trying to defuse the crisis at its new flagship campus, the board decided to move the TAG out of Townview, but the court refused it permission to do so. Woolery then reassigned the principals, but this only heightened the conflict. A number of TAG parents threatened to remove their children and start a chartered TAG high school under recently adopted state legislation.[88] Price entered the controversy, picketing the school and denouncing the Anglo TAG parents as racists. Price, the local NAACP chapter, and the New Black Panthers disrupted board meetings, forcing the board to adjourn. The controversy finally subsided after the principals were reassigned and new operating guidelines were developed for the individual magnet schools at Townview. It remained, however, a shadow grievance for both blacks and Anglos.

Racial tension on the school board descended from disagreement over desegregation strategy and administrative issues to personal recrimination in the Dan Peavey affair. An Anglo member of the majority coalition, Peavey relished his reputation as an outspoken antagonist of many of the pet projects of his black colleagues. In 1995, a neighbor intercepted and recorded conversations between Peavey and other unidentified persons on a cell phone, in which he used racial vulgarities in referring to black board members. The uproar resulted in his resignation, and effectively destroyed the legitimacy of the Slam-Dunk Gang, even though Kress and others deplored his comments and distanced themselves from him. After his resignation, Peavey was indicted but acquitted on unrelated charges involving insurance contracts he had negotiated for the school district as chair of its finance committee.

In 1996, Kress announced that he would not seek a third term. The board again divided along racial lines in choosing Bill Keever, an Anglo computer company executive who had replaced Bergstresser, as its president.

Judge Sanders' hope that the board might quickly resolve the remaining issues that would end court supervision was dashed when Superintendent Woolery surprisingly resigned to join Voyagers, a private firm that supplied educational materials and services to school districts across the nation. Keever's shortcomings as an interracial coalition builder, and even as a presiding officer, now became apparent. Cutting short a formal national search, the Anglo and Hispanic members decided to appoint Deputy Superintendent Yvonne Gonzalez to succeed Woolery. The three black trustees denounced the appointment as insensitive to the needs of black students in the system and an abuse of the selection process. They boycotted the session at which the formal appointment was made. Protesters led by Price, the NAACP, and the New Black Panthers began systematically to disrupt board meetings, chanting: "No justice, no peace!" Keever resorted to changing the meeting times to afternoons, and once had police expel protesters from the chamber. On several occasions, the board was unable to proceed due to demonstrations in the boardroom. Keever, ill and dispirited, retired at the end of his term, and was replaced in the chair by Kathleen Leos, a strong Gonzalez supporter.

Gonzalez, who had previously served briefly as superintendent in Santa Fe, New Mexico, moved quickly to consolidate her grip on the central administration. She removed several black administrators with ties to Gilliam and Ewell and began systematically to build political support in the business community and with teachers. She was an instant hero in the Hispanic community, as the highest-ranking Hispanic official in Dallas.

By the start of the school year in September 1997, Gonzalez appeared to have firm control of the system. She started the year with a rally of teachers in the Dallas Convention Center, at which she entered driving a bulldozer, symbolizing her determination to clear out the rubble of the system and build a great urban school system. Shortly after the rally, she dramatically announced that she was asking the FBI to investigate allegations of fraudulent practices in the system, and soon federal indictments were brought against fourteen employees. Then, claiming exhaustion from the racial stress and overwork, she took a short leave of absence, only to return in October to face a lawsuit by Matthew Hardin, the district's African-American chief financial officer, alleging that she had illegally bugged his car and sexually harassed him. In addition, he claimed that she had lied about the costs of renovations to her office and concealed the true costs from the board.[89]

At a dramatic evening press conference, a tearful Gonzalez denounced all the charges, but said that to clear her name and keep the focus on the education of the children, she would offer the board her resignation. Hispanics from across the city, led by Hispanic elected officials, rallied to her support at district headquarters, drowning out the black protesters supporting Hardin. The school board, over the strong objections of the black trustees, declined to accept her resignation pending resolution of the Hardin matter, and placed her on administrative leave with pay. A few days later, however, the U.S. District Attorney charged Gonzalez with misappropriation of district funds to purchase bedroom furniture for her apartment. The FBI recorded Gonzales instructing her administrative assistant (who was cooperating with the district attorney) to conceal evidence of the fraud. The board now accepted her resignation. Gonzalez pled guilty and was sentenced to federal prison.

The board now had to choose a new superintendent. Blacks and Hispanics each demanded that the new superintendent be from their ranks. Unable even to decide how to proceed, the board appointed a retired Anglo administrator, James Hughey, as interim superintendent, and eventually extended his contract through the 1998–1999 school year. Hughey seemed to bring calm to the system, although the board continued to struggle with the Hardin affair for several months, which had escalated into a defamation suit against President Leos. The board eventually agreed to a settlement with Hardin, which involved a cash payment in return for his resignation and withdrawal of the suit.

Meanwhile, the board remained embroiled in struggles over its presidency. The defeat of Kathlyn Gilliam in 1997 by Ron Price, a community activist backed by business interests and the *Morning News,* did not end the in fighting among members, or the racial polarization. Don Venable, an Anglo elected to fill a vacant position, tipped the power balance when he and one other Anglo member joined forces with the three blacks to replace Board President Kathleen Leos with Hollis Brashear. Yvonne Ewell's death a few months later left no one on the board that had been engaged in the early struggles for desegregation. Brashear, a former Corps of Engineers officer, was the only member of the board with substantial experience with large organizations. The board had become less volatile, but it had not become stable. It was without a permanent superintendent, and had no apparent plan for choosing one. Under the circumstances, it seemed improvident for the Board to request that Judge Sanders finally end his supervision of the district.

Although Hughey's interim administration was able to make some progress in standardized test results, the governance of the system remained in turmoil. The Texas Education Agency sent emissaries to lecture the board on its duties and admonish it against micro-management of the administration. At the behest of local business leaders, the Board hired a consultant to train it in good behavior.[90] As the superintendent search dragged into 1999, following the withdrawal of various candidates, State takeover of the system seemed a distinct possibility. Thus, as the century's end drew near, the education system of Dallas remained, as it had for over forty years, under the supervision of the federal court. And approximately three-fourths of its disadvantaged students—the overwhelming number of them blacks and Hispanics—could not read at grade level.

Lessons from School

The explanation for why the school system did not adapt well to its constitutional duty or the city's changing demography lies in Dallas civic culture and the institutions of school governance, including the federal courts. Policy choices were strongly influenced by the institutional roles key actors were assigned and the rules, customs, and practices governing their behavior rather than by rational calculations of the most efficient means to achieve a preferred outcome.[91]

The Dallas civic culture equated business welfare with the public interest and modeled its public agencies on private corporations. It was at its zenith when the desegregation crisis arrived. Even after the business leadership was no longer ascendant in school affairs, its legacy to the school system was a distinctive organizational culture that defined the roles of the board, administrators, teachers, constituents and clientele groups and the rules they followed. The School Board, once unhitched from business, proved incapable of finding a formula for interracial cooperation that could replace the old system of social control. Judges Taylor and Sanders, though dedicated to ending unconstitutional segregation, worked within the triple constraints of the judicial system, the managerial culture of Dallas, and a dysfunctional school system. Three lessons can be drawn from this experience.

Lesson One: Civic Culture Trumped the Constitution

The Supreme Court decision that ended the legitimacy of racial segregation in public education and, by the power of its logic, all forms of segregation, undercut one of the pillars of the Dallas entrepreneurial regime. It altered the distribution of power by transferring control of both the agenda and the venue in which key education issues would be decided from the quiet circle of economic leaders to plaintiffs and judges in open court. But the institutional culture of the courts, which made possible establishing the constitutional right to non-segregated public education, also made it enormously difficult to implement that right against the inertia of local civic and organizational cultures.

The federal court system is a highly specialized and unique bureaucracy, constitutionally independent of the other branches of government.[92] The federal district judge, although at the bottom of the judicial hierarchy, is in many ways the most independent actor in the system. Appointed to the bench because of close ties to the bar and political elite of the state, a district judge often draws legitimacy from a reservoir of deep community ties as well as from the constitutional authority of the office.

Appellate courts generally defer to findings of fact by the trial judge who hears the evidence and is assumed to be in a better position to assess its credibility and weight. They can overrule and scold, but they cannot remove an intemperate, lazy, recalcitrant, defiant, or incompetent district judge. Even after being admonished by a higher court a determined district judge may still find room to deflect its orders by parsing its ruling, as Judge Davidson did, reading "should" as a mere suggestion. When no room remains for distinctions of meaning, the norms of judicial behavior call for the judge to swallow personal preferences and follow the law as laid down by the appellate court, even if it is done with a final snort of disagreement.

For the first twenty years after *Brown,* the repugnance of the city's regime to desegregating its schools was openly shared by the first two federal judges assigned the Dallas case. Elderly and intransigent, they had spent their careers marinated in the racial prejudices of the south and "separate but equal" jurisprudence. Their rulings facilitated school board use of the judicial process to transform "deliberate speed" into deliberate obstruction. Even after the case was taken over by judges determined to carry out the Supreme Court's desegregation mandate, twenty more years elapsed before Judge Sanders decided that the district, having become nearly all black and brown, had achieved unitary status.

Courts are awkward forums for resolving complex problems such as school desegregation. They act by deciding the cases that come before them. Cases require adversaries. Plaintiffs, the initiating adversaries, choose themselves and define the issues to be tried. Defendants must respond even if they would have ignored the plaintiffs in a political forum. The defendant board and its allies retained certain tactical advantages, however. They had virtually unlimited financial and legal resources and, initially, a friendly court. They could both increase costs for their adversaries at little financial risk to themselves[93] and take evasive action, such as the 1961 symbolic desegregation, to buy time.

For plaintiffs, litigation against an entrenched government with popular support and deep pockets was lengthy and expensive. It was not unusual, therefore, for the NAACP Legal Defense Fund to provide support for the Dallas plaintiffs, including the services of Thurgood Marshall as lead counsel. The size of the city's school system and the significance of Dallas made a successful attack on its segregated schools important to the NAACP's overall strategy of demolishing separate school systems throughout the country. Pursuit of that strategy, however, led to disagreements between the Legal Defense Fund's attorneys and local counsel over acceptable remedies.

This led the court, appropriately, to admit intervenors into the suit to try to get a more complete understanding of the issues and obtain help in fashioning feasible and effective remedies for the constitutional violations. The number of interests represented, however, meant that a favorable ruling for one side would lead to an appeal by parties on the other side. A reversal or remand produced more hearings and revised orders followed by new appeals by a dissatisfied party, only to have the process repeated. The desegregation case became almost a career for some attorneys.[94]

Thus, what began as a straightforward legal controversy to end racially separate and unequal schools evolved into a multifaceted problem in educational equality among three major ethnic groups, compounded by a wide learning gap that involved class as well as race. The district court struggled to reconcile the Supreme Court's evolving doctrine on educational equality with practical problems in the use its equity powers to remedy a wrong with rapidly changing dimensions.[95]

Judges Taylor and Sanders were Dallas's shadow schoolmasters for a quarter of a century, spanning the tenure of seven superintendents; the only constant in the administration of public education for that entire period and the essential catalyst for change. When the school board had no viable plan for ending the vestiges of its segregated school system, the court adopted one proposed by the diverse and moderate business and civic leaders of the Dallas Alliance. In appointing a tri-ethnic committee to oversee implementation of elements of its order, the court broke the hegemony of the old guard in management of the school system and provided legitimacy independent of the business elite to a new generation of minority leaders.

As the case slowly evolved the court adjusted its involvement in the administration of the schools. It issued detailed administrative instructions and employed monitors and regular reviews to track progress in implementation of its decrees. A court-ordered audit first detailed the achievement gap between Anglo and minority students, providing impetus to subsequent accountability projects and a greater emphasis on performance-based management of schools.

The court-endorsed Majority-to-Minority transfer program and magnet schools fell short of the court's hopes for reducing the basic duality of the school system. Some magnets schools attracted a racially mixed enrollment and provided high quality academic programs but the rapid growth in African-American and Hispanic students accompanied by a decline in the number of Anglos was an "environmental" shift beyond the reach of court decrees and further limited the effect the magnets might have had.[96] The court was constrained by Supreme Court decisions and the territorial organization of Texas school districts from extending its desegregation jurisdiction to the suburban districts to broaden the market in magnet schools.

The centripetal instincts of the system's management and the court's need to find a way to fix responsibility for execution of its administrative orders seemed to lead inexorably toward the consolidation of the magnets at the Townview campus. Once relocated, the superintendent followed those instincts and created an administrative structure that precipitated conflict with the Talented and Gifted Magnet's efforts to maintain the uniqueness that made it competitive for the best students in the city. When the board attempted to ameliorate the crisis by returning the TAG magnet to its former campus, the court refused to allow it. It was not an appropriate response to the desegregation doctrine it had followed for many years.

In hindsight it is reasonable to conclude that the competition of the magnets for the most highly qualified and motivated students reinforced perceptions of many Anglos that their neighborhood high schools were going to decline in quality as a result of desegregation. Such perceptions were fed by a basic hostility to court intervention and reinforced by the twenty years of foot dragging by two federal judges, the school board and administration.

Through serial frustrations with the board and occasionally with superintendents, the federal court in Dallas stopped short of directly managing the system, as courts in other cities had done. From the perspective the school system, the intrusion was often regarded as oppressive. From the court's perspective, it was barely enough, and thus, just right.

The fits and starts of litigation, moving judicial standards of compliance, dissension among litigants, and racial conflict among members of the school board, added uncertainty and anxiety for parents with children in the public schools. Dallas resembled many other cities that were undergoing difficult desegregation experiences. As Alan Altschuler has pointed out:

> Regulated systems find it very difficult to move quickly enough to keep up with the inventiveness of the regulated parts. In school desegregation cases, . . . the school systems gradually respond to the judicial decrees, but meanwhile the people who prefer segregation are moving out of the central cities and are resegregating themselves in a societal sense. Here judicial intervention is virtually powerless to deal with the social facts of the case, where the only intention is the intention of individuals who have moved to segregated communities and taken advantage of preexisting jurisdictional arrangements as opposed to governmental entities having taken direct segregationist action.[97]

Court orders were directly responsible for the movement of black and Hispanic administrators into significant positions in the school bureaucracy and the largely successful integration of teaching staffs. The creation of ethnic enclaves in the school bureaucracy can arguably be traced to the court's endorsement of bilingual education and compensatory education programs. The homogenous staffing and relative ineffectiveness of these programs is more closely related to board politics, irresolute or inconsistent administration, and the availability of dedicated revenues, than to court directives.

The court was essential for vindicating the rights of minorities to a non-segregated education in the Dallas public schools. It was less well situated to deal with the second-order consequences of its decisions and orders, such as white flight or the creation of ethnic enclaves in bureaucracies created to provide special programs for minority students. The litigation process itself was, to a considerable degree, the prisoner of the parties. They framed the issues in forms the court could address, initiated proposed remedies, and decided whether to appeal. The court as supervisor of its decrees was the victim of its procedures and the institutional processes of the federal judiciary, which are not designed for efficient management but for full explication of legal issues. But part of the reason the court could not fully vindicate the rights of minority students in DISD lay with the organizational culture of the school system, and the administrative ineffectiveness of the managerial regency.

Lesson Two: Managerialism's Dirty Secret: "No One Is in Charge"

On paper, in the minds of judges, school board members, central office administrators, and most important, in the civic culture of Dallas, there was a school *system*. It was an orderly hierarchy of hierarchies. The elementary, middle, and high schools comprised a hierarchy of learning. Within each school there was a hierarchy of professionals—teacher aids, teachers, department heads, specialists and counselors, assistant principals, vice-principals and principals. A middle tier of area or "cluster" superintendents oversaw the schools in geographic sub-areas. At the top of the management pyramid the central administration contained an array of "line" assistant superintendents and staff agencies for functional areas such as budget, personnel, and research and evaluation. The Superintendent of Schools was at the apex; the most powerful and best paid managerial regent of the city. Lines of responsibility and accountability seemed clear. The system looked efficient. It appeared capable of turning out a product to meet centrally specified standards.

In reality, the school "system" consisted of two quite different types of organizations, joined in uncomfortable tension. Each inhabited a different world, responded to different constituencies, and lived by different rules and strategies. Neither was a *production* organization. Individual schools were *coping* organizations in which the activities of the classroom teachers are rarely observed directly by supervisors and performance is difficult to measure.[98] The effects of teachers on learning cannot readily be distinguished from other influences, such as poverty, the home environment, peer pressure, or racial isolation.[99]

Principals and teachers were expected to teach a curriculum they did not choose to students they did not select to make them proficient in skills and knowledge measured by tests they did not construct. As they carried out these tasks they were expected to maintain discipline and establish amicable relationships with parents and business "partners." They must also submit timely reports in proper form to mid-level and central office administrators, documenting their compliance with system rules and procedures. Principals' and teachers' careers were at the mercy of administrative superiors, the work of their colleagues and staff, contract negotiators, the good will of parents and random acts of charity, gratitude, caprice, misfeasance, stupidity, malice, and violence that make life interesting in a public school. Their working day revolved around the needs and behavior of children and adolescents confined in a structured environment.

Teachers generally, and a good many principals, regarded the central administration, headquartered on Ross Avenue, as out of touch with the grim reality of their daily lives; more of a brooding omnipresence than a constant companion and helpful guide to the 200 campuses. They saw it as addicted to imposing unachievable goals without concern for the practicalities of achieving them, meddling in matters best left to the campus staff, and consumed with avoiding blame for the dysfunction of the system. Many considered the rules they must follow and the reports they must prepare for the "higher ups" as mindless intrusions on their real work of teaching. They avoided or delayed as much of it as possible, and attended to the unavoidable with as little effort as was deemed acceptable.

Rather than seeing themselves as members of a great team spread across the city, led by the superintendent in pursuit of a common goal, teachers were more likely to search for strategies that allowed them to be left alone to do their jobs. This led to behaviors such as teaching to tests or excusing from testing those students who were likely to lower the average scores. This offended their sense of professionalism but it got the central office off their backs. They coped.

System administrators and bureaucrats lived in a different world. The administrative, political, and judicial superstructures were *procedural* organizations.[100] Their day was populated with advocates and appellants, state and federal operatives and auditors, regulations, boards and committees, meetings with principals and organizations of parents or teachers, budgets and reports, news reporters, and active or latent litigants. They crafted and issued directives, but could not control what happened in the schools. They approved curricula and texts, required lesson plans, and regulated class size, but they could not observe consistently how teachers taught or how students behaved and learned. So they resorted to rules, standards, tests, reports, and personnel sanctions to influence the behavior of the teachers. The rules existed because the board and superintendent did not trust the teachers to teach as they wished them to if left to their own devices and because the appropriate means of achieving accountability in bureaucracies was by insisting on procedural regularity—

following the rules.[101] The power of the central organs, and its limitations, lay in procedures.

In another important respect, the central administration was also a coping organization. It not only had to comply (or appear to comply) with the court's desegregation orders, but to cope with the changes in demography that were constantly eroding the capacity to comply. Central administrators also had to cope with a racially fractured board and the demands from minority trustees and their organized constituencies for more significant representation in the bureaucracy and more resources. At the same time, they confronted demands from local and citywide constituencies for better schools and schooling.

The uneasy co-existence of these two different types of organizations in the same system produced serial ambiguities in its management, as superintendents veered between attempting centralized control and site-based management. The central administrative offices were never comfortable with delegation of authority to the campuses and worked to retain control over critical decisions and resources, while joining the rhetoric of decentralization. Thus, in spite of declarations of decentralization, principals of individual schools did not know their budget allocations, even for formula-funded programs, library acquisitions, or supplies, until it often was too late to deviate from standard procedures. They rarely could depend on the same level of funding for the next fiscal year and remained dependent upon the central administration for resources and policy direction.

Notwithstanding observable tendencies toward dysfunction arising from its dual bureaucracy, the interests of most of the key actors in school governance were served by acceptance of the managerial myth that it was responsive to central direction. A centralized system was easier for the court to deal with than a decentralized one. Decrees could be directed to a single office that was assumed to have power to enforce compliance. During the early years of board resistance to desegregation, centralized administration ensured system-wide noncompliance. As the composition of the board changed, African-American trustees sought to maintain court oversight, and used the centralized administrative organs of the system to gain positions and resources as evidence of compliance with the court's orders. Decentralization might have advanced educational innovation and performance, but it could frustrate the ability to micromanage personnel decisions throughout the system.

Some of the programmatic remedies led to the establishment of new, specialized central bureaucracies dominated by African-American or Hispanic teachers and administrators. Title I programs mainly served black children and were staffed primarily with black personnel. Bilingual education and English as a Second Language programs tended to be staffed by Hispanics, although the program was chronically short of qualified bilingual teachers. Over time these organizations become mature ethnic enclaves and their members held tight to their satrapies even as their effectiveness seemed doubtful and the populations they were created to serve changed.

Central administrators subjected the Title I program simultaneously to the "Iron Law of Political Dispersion,"[102] and the "Law of Bureaucratic Survival." The federal money was spread thinly to more schools with scant regard for either cost-effectiveness or performance, but in a way that increased the reach and hierarchical control of the Title I Office.

For business leaders engaged in school affairs, seeing the school system as analogous to an industrial corporation with the superintendent as CEO meant solving the perpetual crisis in public education simply meant finding a CEO who could manage the system and calm the racial antagonisms of its board. Business leaders could then focus their efforts on supporting the superintendent without having to deal with the messy politics of urban public education.

But even within the central hierarchy, the superintendent's authority was illusory. Inertia, not the superintendent (or even the court), governed schools. As the school board drifted from its moorings in the business oligarchy, racial politics demanded close attention to the ethnic balance of key offices and positions. Personnel rules made discipline, transfer, or removal of the incompetent time consuming and costly; action against the merely inadequate was almost impossible. Because of their board and/or external support, some administrators and offices within the system were "untouchable," virtually autonomous of the superintendent. Constituencies and board patrons of neighborhood and magnet schools further constricted a superintendent's choices, as the Townview episode illustrated.

Superintendents set goals for schools, teachers, and students, but they could not make them happen. If anyone was "in charge" of what was taught children and how, it was not the court, board, or superintendent, but the teachers. This fact of organizational life was demonstrated by the contrasting approaches and success of the accountability projects launched by Superintendents Wright and Woolery.

Wright realized the limits of his power and chose a cooperative model that personally and directly engaged principals and teachers in sharing responsibility for setting standards and goals for their schools, designing curricula and methods of instruction. The system was designed to stimulate widespread achievement for all students. Incentives and rewards were largely psychic and symbolic rather than financial. Even with remarkable success in raising standardized test scores of both minorities and Anglos across the district, the project lost support from a board that wanted resources redirected to favorite projects and from a court that he could not convince that it was a better way to close the achievement gap between Anglos and minorities than the targeted facilities favored by the board.

In contrast, Superintendent Woolery's approach was built on the model of economic motivation borrowed from the corporate world. It assumed the superintendent was in charge of the system's overall performance and could apply incentives and sanctions to induce schools and teachers close the achievement gap. Ironically, the system created perverse incentives for teachers, the superintendent, and business supporters to report progress, whether real or not. Teacher coping behavior increased. Teaching to the tests became widespread, and some teachers were found to have provided answers to students in advance or to have prompted them during tests. Large numbers of students, most of them Hispanics, were not tested at all.[103] Schools showed "improvement" while a vast number of students fell farther behind and would eventually drop out of the system.[104] The cash awards for high-performing schools provided no incentives for schools unlikely to come into the money, and for whom punishment was the most likely prospect.[105] Whether the results were real or illusory, the civic culture's values of managerialism and image were appeased. Someone appeared to be in charge. But the children did not learn.

What made DISD a dysfunctional bureaucracy was not the incompatibility of the its coping and procedural components, but the institutionalized resistance to recognizing its dual character and devising strategies, as Wright had, to circumvent the problems inherent in such an arrangement. In spite of its achievements his approach ultimately lost support because it did not conform to the cultural norms of Dallas. Woolery's approach conformed to those norms and failed because it did. The Dallas school system was the very model of a modern major General Motors, circa 1950. And it was just as productive, circa 1980.[106]

Lesson Three: Social Production Is an Unnatural Act in Dallas School Politics

Clarence Stone argued that the governing coalition in Atlanta between the white business leadership and the black political leadership resulted in "social production"—a process that increased the capacity of the allies to resolve problems through the experience of assembling and using the needed resources.[107] The coalition members learned to engage in this process, rather than to struggle for social control. Stone included the peaceful desegregation of Atlanta's schools as one example of this process of social production. On the surface, it might appear that Dallas is an example of the social production model. Both cities achieved token integration of schools in 1961, using similar tactics.

The resemblance, however, is superficial. The black members of the biracial committee in Dallas were largely dependent upon the patronage of the business leadership for their legitimacy. Thus, a critical element of the social production coalition—the autonomy of the coalition partners—was missing. The Atlanta partners needed each other on a continuing basis. Blacks had become a political majority and had control of city government. There was no other game in town for the business establishment. Atlanta's blacks had political power, but relatively little in the way of slack economic resources. Cooperation with business was a necessity for the economic progress of blacks.

Control of the school board by a black majority was not possible in Dallas, given the configuration of electoral districts and the rapid growth of the Hispanic population. Anglos retained only a tiny remnant of the school enrollment but they continued to control the largest bloc of votes in the electorate and on the school board, consistently electing four members, and sometimes a clear majority. Even without a majority, they could usually ally with the one or two Hispanics, and occasionally a black, to form a temporary governing coalition. Anglos controlled almost all of the city's slack resources even if they were no longer willing to wield them as ruthlessly as in earlier times.

Emergence of the Hispanic enrollment plurality produced a new struggle between blacks and Hispanics over the allocation of resources and positions. The imminent end of federal court supervision, upon which African-Americans remained dependent for effective bargaining power, made protecting their gains more urgent. The relationship of African-Americans and Hispanics to the Anglos remained one of dependence rather than comity. There was never a consolidation of minority political power that was stable enough to induce those with economic resources to seek formation of a governing coalition. Instead, the Dallas school board's Anglos functioned as a social control group, exploiting the divisions between the two minority blocs and absorbing the costs of compliance. During the William Keever's presidency, this included disruption of school board meetings by black protesters and the boycott by the three black members of the meeting at which Superintendent Yvonne Gonzalez was selected. Rather than social production, the political economy of education in Dallas fostered a politics of racial identity and with it, an institutional incapacity for adapting to change.

To be sure, there were factors beyond the control of the court or the city that contributed to the decline of Dallas's schools. The metropolitan organization of public education facilitated abandonment of the central city district by Anglos and much of the business leadership of Dallas, leaving DISD a residual system for the lower middle class and impoverished residents of the city. This diminished the pool of stakeholders who might be most insistent on improvements in the schools. Although many remained residents or property tax payers in the DISD, they chose neglect over loyalty. Most corporate executives retained only an indirect stake in the effectiveness of Dallas Public Schools because they could recruit employees from a national labor pool and recent migrants to the Dallas area. Their participation in inner city educational affairs, therefore, continued the Dallas tradition of substituting symbolic for substantive action. Their practical interest shifted from how good the schools should be to reducing their cost, posing a long-term threat to the capacity of the system to conduct the enriched programs necessary to equalize educational opportunities for disadvantaged children and to compete with private and suburban schools.

Three features characterized business executives' behavior toward schools as the third generation of students since *Brown* entered its system. First was the lack of substantial and sustained involvement. Individuals and small groups of executives such as the Education Committee of the Citizens Council continued to try to influence school policies.[108] What characterized most of these efforts was their episodic, piecemeal or "project" orientation. The Dallas Citizens Council endorsed measures advocated by those few members who continued to care about the DISD but, with a few exceptions,[109] there appeared to be little staying power among the economic elite for school reform and almost no stomach for school politics. The Breakfast Club financially supported a few candidates from time to time, but there was no sustained, organized public effort by business leaders or any other group to recruit slates of candidates. When Sandy Kress, who had been elected with business support, called for business leaders to fill the leadership gap, he received no response.[110] After Kress left the board, there were marginal efforts to recruit strong candidates for election to the board. Failing that, some business leaders concentrated on defeating Kathlyn Gilliam by providing some financial and editorial support for her opponent.

Second, to the extent that business leaders became involved in school affairs, they tended to focus on supporting the managerial regency as the means of rescuing the system. Finding the right "strong" superintendent became a highest priority, consistent with the obsession of failing businesses to bring in a "turn around" chief executive. Given the Gonzales debacle, such concern was understandable. Business leaders brought in consultants to instruct the board on its proper role in school governance, i.e., making "policy" and letting the superintendent run the schools without micromanagement. There appeared to be little understanding by these executives—or for that matter by state education bureaucrats—that the function and organizational culture of a modern public school system make it impossible to run it like an industrial corporation. Here the civic culture of Dallas, with its reverence for managerialism, confused the preservation of a dysfunctional hierarchy with reform of the environment and methods of teaching and learning.

When reforms were endorsed, there was little follow-through, especially if they were resisted by the superintendent. A review of proposals by the Education Committee of the Citizens Council found that little had been done to implement its recommendations.[111] Even the most persistent of the business leaders in pressing for significant reforms, backed off when they met resistance from Superintendent Woolery to implementation of cost-effective reforms in reading education for at-risk children.[112]

Third, there was a continuing tendency among many business executives to approach issues of interracial educational equity and quality in Dallas as public relations problems. They wanted racial confrontations over personnel and policies to end, as they conveyed an image of an unstable environment for business. Their willingness to advocate serious measures was inhibited by fear that they or their firms would be accused of racism and become objects of protest demonstrations. Business executives do not like such public controversies.[113] They wished to be seen as good corporate citizens. Thus, they lent executives to sit on committees that support the school administration, and donated money and equipment for "Adopt a School" programs and raised cash for the annual performance awards. These shows of concern and benign support helped inoculate them against the "race card," and cost little. They were "appropriate" activities and conformed to the civic culture's deference to managers.

Conclusion

As the Dallas Public Schools began a new century and emerged from court supervision its formal governance and administration mimicked an industrial model long abandoned by most successful corporations and effective government agencies. A racially polarized governing board of amateurs with little experience in directing or devising strategy for a large-scale, complex organization charged with education of a diverse population with a high percentage of disadvantaged students was almost totally dependent on the professional staff for cues about the policy it supposedly made. It was of minimum help to the superintendent as either sounding board or guide. It did what it was equipped to do: kibitz, act as ombudsman for constituents, try to imbed preferences in programs and build patronage in schools and bureaus.

The organizational characteristics of the school system—its monopolistic behavior, its compromised hierarchy of procedural and coping organizations, its ambiguous centralization, and the racial representativeness of its bureaucracy—further limited the kinds of policies that were chosen and the extent to which the system could adapt to change. The superintendent, more than ever a managerial regent over an insular realm composed of unresponsive principalities, feared the racial balkanization of the district that could result from decentralization or the introduction of market-like competition by charter schools. That, and dread of not being in "control" perpetuated an administrative system that stifled innovation and relied on procedures and sanctions that produced perverse incentives in the coping organizations upon which the entire system ultimately depended to prepare the city's children for their adult responsibilities as citizens.

The captains of industry who continued to care about Dallas schools could be bestirred to endorse the latest reform or to put together a search committee composed of other managerial regents to look for a new superintendent to "take charge" of the system and turn it around. Some would contribute to campaigns for "the right sort" of School Trustees. Progress would be reported, celebrated, and rewarded.

Few big city school systems are models of constitutional

equity, administrative efficacy, or educational effectiveness. In this company of failures, Dallas hardly stands out. The account of how its powerful economic leaders and the civic and organizational cultures they fostered failed the Constitution and the children committed to its most vital public institution suggests the intricacy of the task of reforming systems of urban education upon which the future of great cities so heavily depends.

6

The Regency at Work: Redesigning Policing

The First Rule of Holes: When you're in one, stop digging.
MOLLY IVINS

THE MIXTURE OF BUREAUCRATIC and identity politics in the school system confounded the ability of either the fading oligarchy, the federal courts, or the managerial regency to adapt to the transformations of the Dallas economy and population and resolve the interrelated problems of minority rights, school governance, and educational quality. The other vital urban service, policing, generated parallel issues of race and governance. The Dallas Police Department had been slow to integrate minority officers into the force and had a reputation for unequal enforcement of the law in Anglo and minority communities. Actions of officers and the institutional behavior of the department and the Dallas Police Association produced some of the city's most dramatic racial confrontations of the last third of the twentieth century. The response to the crises in policing offers more insight into the capability of the Dallas governance system to adapt to the changing conditions of urban life.

The Police and Civic Culture: Making the City Safe for Commerce

From the earliest days of Charter government, the police were critical to the maintenance of the Dallas civic culture. Police corruption during Klan control of city government sullied the image of Dallas. The business oligarchy that engineered the council-manager charter reform placed a high priority on the creation of a professional and incorruptible police force. Dallas became one of the first U.S. cities to require some college education for its officers, and it established one of the southwest's first police academies. Texas law prohibited police from organizing to bargain collectively or to strike, constraining their ability to organize an effective employee union.

Under the charter, the city manager has the sole power to appoint and dismiss all department heads, including the police chief. The charter also restricts the ability of individual council members to communicate with any city employee other than the city manager on administrative or operational matters, and helps to insulate police officers and commanders from "parochial" pressures. Though generally committed to a public sector limited to municipal housekeeping, the value of minimal services never applied to the police force. By 1998 it included 2,845 sworn officers, with an operating budget of $227 million, far surpassing that of any other city department. In the Dallas scheme of limited government, order was the one necessary function; "public safety" was the only sacrosanct department. The police protected life and property, and people of property protected the police.

In a government of anonymous factotums, the City Manager and Chief of Police were about the only bureaucrats with widely recognizable names. And although the chief served at the manager's pleasure, a chief popular with powerful business leaders and the rank and file of the department achieved a degree of autonomy that made him almost an equal of his nominal boss. Some chiefs, such as Jesse Curry, the incumbent at the time of the Kennedy assassination, attained celebrity status. Until the late 1980s, all chiefs rose through the department's ranks, contributing to solidarity among police that reached from the street to headquarters. This combined with a unique mission and paramilitary organization to create an organizational culture that distinguished the police from other departments of city government.

Although no longer "political" in the old-fashioned patronage ways of the city commission, the police also gained autonomy based on bonds established between the officers and the clientele they served. Merchants were solicitous of police, encouraging them to visit or pass by their establishments while on patrol. Off-duty police officers were frequently employed as security guards for businesses and for community or private events, armed and in uniform. The department and police associations organized youth groups and sports leagues, and participated in school and neighborhood-based safety, anti-crime, and drug education programs. Police who were injured or killed in line of duty inspired spontaneous outpourings of official and public grief. Incidents of valor by police officers were celebrated at high civic occasions. Jurors and judges usually accorded a high degree of deference to police witnesses, accepting their testimony as highly credible.

The chief and organized officers capitalized on this public support and their image as "The Thin Blue Line" that divided civil society from chaos and evil to embellish their autonomy and build a political base independent of the manager and Council. One of the most serious charges that could be levied against a member of the Council or a mayor is that he or she was insufficiently supportive of the police in their life and death struggle against crime and disorder.

Police-Minority Relations: The Legacy of Segregation

The affection of the Dallas entrepreneurial regime for the police during the first forty years of charter government was not universal. By the end of World War II it was apparent that blacks regarded the all-white police force as at best uninterested in enforcing the law in their communities; at worst as enemies. Dr. Robert Prince, in his memoir of growing up in Dallas, reported that the police allowed gambling and prostitution to flourish unimpeded in black sections of the city, except for the open collection of shakedown money, or occasional sham raids when preachers or neighbors complained.[1] Crimes of blacks against blacks and whites against blacks went unsolved.[2] Returning black veterans who behaved "uppity"—with insufficient deference to white officers—were occasionally beaten.[3] The bombings of black homes in south Dallas in the 1950s were investigated but only a single low-level alleged participant was brought to trial and he was acquitted.[4]

The Mexican-American population of Dallas had a similar experience. Testimony before the U.S. Commission on Civil Rights and the Texas Advisory Committee on Civil Rights reported patterns of discriminatory police treatment of both minorities, including discourtesy, verbal and physical abuse, excessive use of force, unequal treatment compared to Anglos, and inadequate protection of residents and property.[5] Both of Dallas's largest minority groups tended to view the police as an occupying force, determined to control rather than serve them.

Black community and business leaders had pled with city officials for years to open the force to black officers. Although leaders of the Citizens Charter Association promised that black officers would be added to the police force in return for support of its candidates by the black Progressive Voters League in 1937, none were hired until after World War II, and they were restricted to patrols in black neighborhoods. Department officials claimed they could find no qualified recruits among either the black or the growing Mexican-American population. Serious recruitment of minority officers did not occur until well after the enactment of the 1965 Civil Rights Act. In 1970 there were only seventy blacks and thirty-six Mexican-Americans in a force of 1,912 police officers, although the two minority groups then comprised a third of the city's population.[6] Integration of the police force progressed far too slowly from the perspective of black and Hispanic residents, even though in 1973 the city, under federal prodding, announced a policy of hiring one minority for each new Anglo officer added to the force. With substantial expansion of the force and active minority recruiting, it was still disproportionately Anglo in 1990 when all minority groups combined exceeded 50 percent of the city's population.

By the end of the Jonsson mayoralty in 1971, Dallas was not just bigger, its population was fundamentally different. In each subsequent decade the differences from the past were accentuated. While some changes could surely be attributed to white flight, something else was also occurring. The Anglos remaining in Dallas were aging, the growth of the black population had slowed, and the burgeoning Hispanic population was predominantly young. A failing school system, high youth and male unemployment, and the decline of social and community institutions in the inner city combined with rising expectations and the ready availability of drugs to contribute to a dramatic increase in crime in Dallas, as in most large cities.

Dallas police were increasingly out of touch with minority residents. Naturally, few Anglo police officers lived in black or Hispanic neighborhoods. Many lived in the suburbs. The professionalism and specialization of the force furthered its isolation. The use of patrol cars to allow the police to cover larger areas and respond to calls more quickly meant that few officers knew residents and merchants personally, especially in minority neighborhoods. Specialized units, such as bomb squads and tactical response units, could deal with emergencies, high profile drug busts, and armed standoffs with consummate skill and intimidating firepower. But in much of black and Hispanic Dallas, the police were viewed as strangers who did not understand or care to understand the neighborhoods they patrolled. Merely being a minority too often made one an object of police suspicion, subject to being stopped, verbally hassled, or physically abused, even if not arrested.

Minority distrust of the police, combined with some racial bigotry and almost universal fear for their own safety among Anglo officers deployed in a sullen and unforgiving environment, was a volatile mixture. It existed during the most turbulent period of social dislocation and unrest in modern times, spanning the Civil Rights, anti-Vietnam war, and counterculture movements and the conservative and fundamentalist backlash against them.

In this unstable environment, a series of incidents forced a fundamental reassessment of whether a policing system with a history of institutional racism, and a relationship with minority communities characterized by reciprocal distrust, contempt, and fear, was competent to serve an increasingly diverse city.

In February 1971, three deputy sheriffs were killed by two Mexican-American burglars, triggering a week-long dragnet of legally questionable detentions and searches of people and homes in Mexican-American neighborhoods. The manhunt came to a climax early one morning when plainclothes police, acting on misinformation, kicked in the door at the East Dallas home of Tomas Rodriguez. In the ensuing confusion, police shotgunned and wounded both Rodriguez and his pregnant wife in front of their eight children. Rodriguez was later exonerated of any involvement, but the raid and his subsequent treatment—he had been chained to his bed at the hospital—inflamed the already tense relationship of law enforcement officers with Mexican-Americans in Dallas.[7]

Two years later, Dallas Police Officer Darrel Cain murdered twelve-year-old Santos Rodriguez (no relation to Tomas). Cain and his partner rousted the boy and his brother from their beds at 3:00 A.M. for questioning about a soft drink machine burglary. Cain spun the cylinder of his .357 Magnum and pressed the muzzle against Santos' head as he questioned him in the front seat of his patrol car. The second pull of the trigger following the boy's truthful denial of involvement, resulted in instant death from a massive head wound. Cain was suspended and charged with murder, but freed on $5000 bond.

Following Rodriguez's funeral, attended by an overflow crowd, Mexican-American community leaders organized a march through downtown Dallas, which was joined by more militant Hispanics and blacks. After exhortations to "Kill the Pigs!" the peaceful memorial parade spun out of control as demonstrators broke windows and burned two police motorcycles. Several police officers and a large number of demonstrators were injured. Thirty-eight demonstrators were arrested.

Under strict orders from the chief of police, the officers on crowd control duty refrained from using tear gas and other extreme measures. Following the melee, the City Council resolved to end dual standards of law enforcement in the white and minority communities, and gave its standing committee on public safety authority to investigate complaints of police bias. The Dallas Police Association, however, charged the chief with inadequate support of officers, leading to his resignation. Officer Cain was convicted of murder, but sentenced to only five years in prison.[8]

The two Rodriguez affairs marked the emergence of a more aggressive group of Hispanic political activists. A new generation of younger Mexican-Americans who were less dependent on Anglo patronage entered Dallas political life.[9] The Police Department increased the number of black and Hispanic officers, but these personnel changes were not commensurate with the pressure for improvement in police-community relations from the minority communities. The force remained overwhelmingly Anglo and discriminatory treatment of minorities continued, although the addition of black and Hispanic members to the City Council made it increasingly difficult for complaints of unequal treatment to be ignored.

During the 1980s the use of deadly force by Dallas police officers escalated, as Table 6.1 shows, from a low of three in 1982 to a high of twenty-nine in 1986. The overwhelm-

Table 6.1 Use of Deadly Force By Dallas Police 1982–1987

Year	*Incidents*
1982	3
1983	15
1984	10
1985	9
1986	29
1987	18

Source: Dallas Police Department

ing number of these cases involved blacks or Hispanics. Some could be justified as necessary and proper use of deadly force. Others were clearly suspect as racially motivated or serious breaches of discipline and discretion.

Michael Frost, an alleged drug dealer, was shot by a Dallas police officer in 1983 after he had been stopped for speeding. An autopsy suggested that he may have been handcuffed when shot, corroborating the testimony of witnesses. The officer involved, Cpl. M. D. Cozby, had shot five people in ten years. After an all-white Dallas County grand jury declined to indict him, Cozby sued Al Lipscomb, a black City Council member who had criticized him, for slander. Lipscomb issued a public apology to settle the suit.[10]

A black teenager, David Eugene Manning, was killed by a police officer investigating a prowler complaint. The officer's report of the incident stated that Manning took his gun, ran off, and fired a shot at him. There were conflicting claims that Manning was handcuffed and begging for his life when the officer shot him in the back. An internal police investigation found that the officer had made a "good shoot."

In 1984, police killed Guadalupe Martinez, who ran a roadblock while rushing his pregnant wife to the hospital. A shotgun blast was fired through the car's windshield. A mentally disturbed man, Darryl Armstrong, was shot in the chest when he allegedly tried to grab the arresting officer's flashlight after he had been stopped while walking naked on Kiest Avenue at 3:00 A.M.[11]

These incidents, and others, generated urgent demands for changes in police practices from civil rights leaders and black elected officials, including the two Council members, Lipscomb and Diane Ragsdale, and County Commissioner John Wiley Price. The department's leadership and the Dallas Police Association, however, continued to defend the officers and the department, and denounced their critics as hostile to the police and as rabble-rousers.

In 1986 the conflict between supporters of the police and minority elected officials came to a head. On March 20 of that year, Officer Gary Blair stopped Andrew Pigg and Charles Tillis in a parking lot for having an expired state vehicle inspection sticker. Pigg and Blair got into a fight, which ended with both men dead of wounds inflicted by the police officer's gun. Tillis was indicted for murder, on the police claim that he had assisted Pigg in gaining control of Blair's firearm by entering the fray, kicking and punching the officer, although there were no witnesses other than Tillis. A key witness for the defense was Blair's former partner, who testified that Blair had a reputation for confrontation with people he arrested.[12] Council Members Lipscomb and Ragsdale infuriated police by lending their names to a defense fund established for Tillis, who was acquitted. Five hundred officers and their spouses packed a Council meeting to denounce the two Council members for their support of Tillis.

Although the number of police shootings dropped to eighteen in 1987, minority anger was heightened by three incidents. A seventy-one-year-old crime watch volunteer was fatally wounded by police fire in May of 1987. Just a few months earlier, a seventy-year-old black woman, Etta Collins, had been shot to death on her front porch by police responding to her call to investigate a suspected burglary next door. Black elected officials used Collins' death as a rallying cry to demand a review of the police department's deadly force policy and the training of officers. At their insistence, a Committee of the U.S. House of Representatives held hearings on police brutality and misconduct in Dallas. While the officer who shot Collins was not indicted, Chief Billy Prince fired him, as he was in probationary status at the time of the incident.

Prince's action enraged the Dallas Police Association, to which 95 percent of the force belonged. It held an unprecedented poll of its members, with 58 percent of those responding indicating lack of confidence in the Chief and Assistant Chief Harold Warren. Richard Knight, the first African-American City Manager of Dallas, issued a public statement saying that he continued to have confidence in Prince's ability to lead the department. The chair of the City Council's Public Safety Committee made a similar statement. Then, in November of 1987, two more civilians were shot. An unarmed sixteen-year-old black girl was shot in the thigh by an officer and a sixty-two-year old Hispanic, Raymond Mendoza, was fatally shot. Chief Prince fired the officer who shot the teenager, along with another officer, accusing them of illegal searches and falsifying reports, and declared that he was "in control" of the department.

The Regency's Dilemma: Backing or Managing the Blue

In the meantime, the City Council, at the suggestion of Charles Terrell, the chair of the city's Citizens' Crime Commission, had engaged consultants to make recommendations on police-community relations and strengthening the Police Civilian Review Board. As a result of the consultant's work and their own growing anxiety over the deteriorating relationships between police and minorities, the Council adopted a package of reforms. They expanded the membership of the Review Board, and over the strenuous objections of both Chief Prince and the Dallas Police Association, gave it power to subpoena witnesses, unless the Council disapproved such a request within thirty days. In addition, the board was given the authority to employ its own investigators if it was dissatisfied with the report of the department's Internal Investigation Division.[13]

The Dallas Police Association denounced the new Review Board. It feared that the ordinance placed accused officers in an untenable position in which they would be denied their constitutional right against self incrimination if testimony they had given in the internal investigation processes of the department were subpoenaed by the board.[14] Of more immediate and understandable concern was the appointment of Peter Lesser to the new Review Board by Councilman Lipscomb. Lesser was the attorney who successfully defended Charles Tillis, and he had other actions pending against the police. Association leaders argued that Lesser had a conflict of interest and would be unable to judge fairly cases brought to the Board. Lipscomb refused to withdraw the nomination, and Lesser would not step aside.

While Chief Prince openly opposed the changes to the Review Board, the Police Association felt he had not been sufficiently supportive of their brother officers and the performance of the department. The DPA called for Chief Prince's resignation for failing to support them. Black council members demanded that he resign because they regarded him as too unwilling to make changes in the department's racial composition and its approach to race relations. Morale among rank and file officers was reported to be at its lowest point ever by both departmental officials and the Association. Divisions along racial lines within the department emerged as many black officers joined the Texas Peace Officers Association, a statewide all-black organization, because they felt unrepresented by the DPA. On the other hand, some 200 white officers who felt that the DPA was insufficiently aggressive in dealing with the city defected to form the Police Patrolmen's Union. The estrangement of the Association from the department's leadership was confirmed when Senior Corporal Monica Smith, the newly elected president of the Association, declined to be sworn in by Chief Prince, as was customary. Instead she asked Ross Perot to do the honors, a task the peripatetic Dallas billionaire accepted.

On January 14, 1988, two days after Smith was sworn in as president of DPA, James Joe, an off-duty black Dallas policeman, was shot to death while attempting to apprehend two burglary suspects. Nine days later, a white officer, John Glenn Chase, was killed after he stopped a vehicle for a routine traffic violation. A mentally ill "street person" intervened to wrestle Chase's gun from him. Begging for his life, Chase was shot three times in the face at point blank range. The impact of the brutal murder was heightened in the already tense atmosphere by published rumors that black onlookers had egged on Chase's assailant, shouting, "Shoot him! Shoot him again!" Although there was no eyewitness corroboration of this report, an agitated Chief Prince, in a television interview, asserted that criticisms of the police by Council members had created a dangerous environment for officers. "The atmosphere that's been created by negative criticism, I think, has contributed to a person who's been on the edge going through with it [shooting the police officer]," he declared. Characterizing Council and public criticism of the police as "constant bashing," he added: "All we can do is continue to follow our training and procedures, continue to solicit support from the community and politicians and it has to get better."[15] Once again, City Manager Knight and Mayor Annette Strauss expressed their support for the Chief. Council Member Ragsdale, who had been outspoken in her denunciation of police practices, received death threats.[16]

The Police Association, in shock and grieving the death of two officers, considered asking the two black Council members not to attend Chase's funeral. A new citizen's organization, Citizens Offering Police Support—COPS—was organized. Drivers were asked to show their support of the police by keeping their headlights on, and displaying "BACK THE BLUE" bumper stickers. A few weeks later, on February 26, a third officer was murdered when escorting a grocery store manager from the bank where he had made a deposit. They entered the store while a robbery was in progress. Officer Gary McCarthy intervened and was killed.

Declaring that its members were literally and figuratively "under fire," the Police Association's leadership decided to capitalize on the public arousal over the shootings and antagonism toward the black Council members. They began an effort to collect signatures for a referendum on the Civilian Review Board and to force the city to enlarge the force by 700 additional officers. Among its grievances with the city, the Association felt the city manager and Council had reneged on an earlier promise to increase the size of the uniformed force. They seemed determined to put the issue of policing the police to the voters. On March 8, 1988, Presidential Primary Day in Texas, the DPA deployed its members to polling places throughout the city and collected over 60,000 signatures, far more than the number necessary to force a referendum on both issues. All they had to do to put the matter before the voters was to file the petitions with the Secretary of the City Council.

A referendum on the Review Board was certain to produce a racially polarized vote and further inflame race relations in Dallas. The remnants of the entrepreneurial regime that were not busy salvaging their businesses from the worst recession in recent Dallas history retreated from the arena. They wanted to antagonize neither the police nor the minorities. They counseled restraint and urged all sides to avoid actions that would polarize the city. They left the problem with the city's first woman mayor, Annette Strauss, and its first black city manager, Richard Knight. Craig Holcombe, who chaired the Council's Public Safety Committee summed up the fears of city officials and other leaders: "I did not want the referendum. I was absolutely opposed to it. I felt like it would have ended up in a Dallas police officer versus Diane Ragsdale and Al Lipscomb vote. And I just thought that would be horrible for the city, absolutely devastating. It would be racial and it would be really ugly—bringing out the worst in all of us."[17]

Minority leaders on and off the Council warned that a repeal of the Citizens Review Board's powers would be viewed as a racist act and further alienate them from the police. The authority of the Council to establish policy for the city—including its police force—was being challenged by a group of insurgent city employees, who were going directly to the voters. The city manager's ability to "manage" the police department and to establish the city's budget and staffing priorities were also at stake in the proposal to require 700 new officers. Although the Police Association, through its petition drive, sought to restore the status quo, both Knight and Strauss understood the need to both defuse the immediate conflict and change the composition, culture, and management of the Dallas Police.

Chief Prince resigned on April 13, having lost the confidence of the officers ostensibly under his command, the city manager, and the Council. Knight announced he would undertake a nation-wide search for a new chief, a stance immediately denounced by the DPA, which opposed appointment of any "outsider" to head the department. No Dallas police chief had ever come from outside the department,[18] and the DPA saw Knight's position as both a slap in the face of its professionalism and as appeasement of minority agitators. Mayor Strauss, and especially Knight, were concurrently being assailed by the African-American community for failing to control police behavior toward minorities. Several black leaders, including the two council members, seemed eager for an electoral confrontation with the police association, if only to confirm the racism of the city. The city faced a rebellious police force and the real possibility of escalating racial conflict.

With the old establishment in disarray, the only major business leader to become involved in the controversy was Ross Perot, never a member of the inner sanctum of Dallas business power. Perot entered the affair from compassion for the police following the trauma of the Officer Glenn Chase's murder. Officiating at Monica Smith's inauguration as DPA president, he immediately recognized the incipient danger to the city. He gained the trust of the DPA's leadership through his sympathy and help in their time of grief and trouble. He made his private plane available to the DPA so officers could attend Chase's funeral in Ohio. He promised Smith and the DPA board that he would familiarize himself with the problems and complaints of the officers through a series of meetings, but that he would not be bound by any organizational positions of the DPA. Rather, he insisted on freedom of individual action in the joint interest of the officers and the city. Given his reputation for patriotism and support for the police, his pledge was sufficient for Smith and her board to entrust him with the tacit authority to negotiate on their behalf. They, of course, held the trump card: the ability to file their petitions and force a referendum on the Review Board and an increase in the force.

Knight took the position that he could not negotiate directly with the DPA under Texas law. He also did not want to do so on the grounds that it would compromise the chain of command that descended from the Council, through him to the Chief of Police. Perot agreed to serve as a trusted but independent spokesman for the interests of the officers in negotiations with Strauss, Knight, and African-American community leaders. As Knight later recalled:

> This was a politically expedient time for the issue to come to a boil. There were emotional highs and lows associated with the love, care, and nurturing of policemen. We owe a lot to the police. But they also know how to capitalize on the emotions of the people . . . There was a lull after the petitions. I don't remember if the Mayor called Perot or if Perot called the Mayor. But as a result of that conversation, Ross, the Mayor, [Tom] Luce [Perot's attorney], and myself

> brainstormed and discussed what Perot had found out with the police. At the same time I was being taken on by the black community for not standing up to the white man. The Chief had made remarks about a number of my bosses and the people on the street. My job, I felt, was to get something on the table.[19]

In addition to the hot potato of the Review Board and police-community relations in general, Knight faced a $38 million short fall in his budget estimates. A referendum that imposed an obligation on the city to hire 700 additional officers—a number far in excess of his estimate of the actual need—could have a devastating effect on other essential services. Success of the referendum proposals would compromise Knight's ability to set policy for the conduct of the police department at a time when he was persuaded that fundamental changes were needed. He believed they could not be accomplished by simply replacing Chief Prince with another product of the department's "up-through-the-ranks" system.

A compromise was hammered out in a series of meetings among Mayor Strauss, Knight, the city attorney, Perot, and Luce. The group was occasionally joined by Craig Holcomb, the chair of the Council Committee on Public Safety, Charles Terrell, the Dallas Crime Commission chair, and Pettis Norman, an African-American businessman, former Dallas Cowboys star, and member of the Mayor's Task Force on Crime, who had credibility with many black leaders. The DPA (which never was directly engaged in the meetings) agreed not to file its petitions to force the referendum. In return, Knight and Strauss secured agreement from a majority of the Council to amend the ordinance to weaken the Review Board's subpoena power and to change its membership requirements to exclude Peter Lesser or any other person who might have a conflict of interest in a proceeding before it. Knight agreed to recommend a smaller, but significant increase in the size of the police force. The agreement held. The crisis passed. But the hard work of changing the culture and practices of the police department remained.

Outside Chiefs and Departmental Reform

The Civilian Review Board, the proximate cause of the referendum crisis, ultimately proved to be of little significance, in spite of its symbolic importance to both police officers and African-Americans in 1987. Soon after the compromise was reached, Knight appointed Mack Vines as the first Chief of the Dallas Police Department who had not risen through its ranks. With a reputation for reform and strong community relations skills, Vines had served cities in Florida and North Carolina.

The new chief energetically set about trying to change the department. Its officers resisted just as energetically. Vines's civilian apparel and non-military manner were resented. His reforms were more threatening. He restructured the department to promote minority officers to precinct and departmental command positions over Anglos with longer service and, in some cases, higher test scores. He imposed new rules and training for the use of deadly force; and began an aggressive outreach effort to work with black, Hispanic, and Asian communities. These measures were consonant with Knight's wishes and had the support of a majority of the Council. With the new positions added as a result of the compromise agreement with DPA, Vines began to recruit new African-American and Hispanic officers, as well as other ethnic minorities. While many of his actions were popular with more reform-minded officers and with much of the public and press, he was despised by a substantial segment of the force.

After Knight left city government to pursue private business opportunities, Vines became entangled in a controversy over the truth of statements he made to the Civil Service Commission in a hearing on the firing of an officer. A Dallas County grand jury indicted Vines for misdemeanor perjury in 1990, leading Jan Hart, Knight's successor as city manager, to dismiss him.[20] Vines's uneasy two years in Dallas started important reforms in the Department, but he never gained the confidence of the rank and file necessary to implement the policies Knight and a majority of the Council had urged.

Hart followed Knight's lead, however, and sought the next chief from the national pool of accomplished police administrators. In January 1991, she selected William Rathburn, Deputy Chief of the Los Angeles Police Department, over internal candidates. Her decision reinforced the message that the old system was dead.[21]

Rathburn was a popular chief with both officers and community representatives, in spite of his non-local career. He continued the reforms started by Vines, but proved more adept at both internal and external advocacy of them. He worked well with minority council members, moving officers from low-crime north Dallas precincts to increase patrols in high-crime areas of south and west Dallas. The Council provided funds for a new police Academy during Vines' administration, and the new recruits received better training before being put on the streets. The number of incidents involving the use of deadly force sharply declined. The economy recovered as reforms in training, policing, and prisons were being implemented. The crime rate began to fall in Dallas as it did in most cities across the country.

John Wiley Price and his small band of civil rights "warriors" had picketed regional police stations for several years, demanding employment of more black officers and commanders. Price continued his confrontations, blocking traffic and creating disturbances that drew the attention of the city's television news. After a series of demonstrations at the southwest police district headquarters, Rathburn issued an order that no one but a sworn officer could enter a perimeter around the facility. Don Hicks, identifying himself as a council member, crossed the perimeter hoping to mediate the standoff between police and demonstrators. An officer ordered him to leave, citing Rathburn's directive. When Hicks refused and became verbally belligerent, he was arrested and handcuffed. While amends were made all around, the incident weakened Rathburn's support on the Council. His relationship with City Manager Hart also cooled. He resigned after less than two years as chief to head security for the 1996 Atlanta Olympics. His accomplishments in stabilizing the department and rebuilding community support drew favorable comments from a wide spectrum of officials and community leaders—including Price—as well as sour comments from police officers and some civic leaders about the inability of the city to retain a talented and effective chief.[22] There was some support for Acting Chief Robert Jackson, an African-American promoted from sergeant to assistant chief by Vines, and then made executive assistant chief by Rathburn, but Hart turned instead to Ben Click, Deputy Chief of the Phoenix Police Department to fill the top Dallas position.

Click became an exceptionally popular chief with both officers and the general public. Thoroughly professional and highly persuasive in dealing with police officers, community groups, the media, and other officials, Click's hands-on style of leadership and commitment to community-oriented policing gradually transformed the department and its relationships with minority communities.

Vines and Rathburn made changes designed to diversify the department. Both chiefs moved a number of minority officers into the command structure of the department, which, prior to the arrival Vines, had been almost entirely Anglo. In some cases they passed over Anglos with higher scores on promotion tests and longer service. A number of senior officers retired or took positions in other cities. The chiefs made aggressive use of the 500 additional positions authorized by the Council to recruit minorities and women. While these additional positions were important in changing the character of the department, the rapidity of the expansion resulted in appointment of some recruits who were not well suited to police work and gave the department a high percentage of relatively inexperienced officers.[23]

Rathburn, in particular, launched a number of high visibility special tactical programs, such as "zero tolerance" raids on drug dealers and creation of units to deal with growing youth gang activity. He initiated a coordinated neighborhood policing program in the Southeast Division. Neighborhood Liaison officers were appointed to work closely with local community groups. In the CBD, Rathburn worked closely with the Central Dallas Association, adding a task force of 85 officers to increase policing in the business district, including bicycle patrols and strict enforcement of new anti-loitering ordinances, aimed at removing the homeless and beggars from the sidewalks and alleys.[24] Each of these initiatives involved creation of special units within the department, creating more opportunities for advancement of effective minority officers.

Training of new officers and retraining of experienced officers stressed community and race relations, but when Ben Click arrived in Dallas to assume his new duties as Chief of Police, he found a department still deeply divided along racial lines. Minorities felt the old policies and practices had discriminated against them for years and that the reforms were not changing conditions fast enough. Anglo officers opposed new programs they viewed as giving unfair preferences to minorities and women, especially in promotions. Diversification of the force, though clearly necessary to the legitimacy of the police in the community, had not gained full legitimacy within the department.

Click refrained from an immediate shake up of the command system, giving people time to adjust to his presence, and he focused on certain basic elements. First, he wanted to send a strong signal to all officers that he would demand high standards of professional conduct and would play no favorites. Two days after his arrival in Dallas he had occasion to demonstrate his resolve. He fired a black officer who had filed a false report. At the same time Click affirmed his commitment to the importance of racial diversification in changing the department internally, facilitating the task of the police on the streets. He was convinced from his experience in Phoenix that if officers of different races worked together in a regime of high professional standards that the racial antipathy within the department could be overcome. From the beginning he made it clear that for the police to thrive, they had to develop a good relationship with the community. In public appearances before community groups he stressed the need for young people in the various communities of Dallas to "see themselves" as future police officers, rather than to be repulsed by the thought. He bluntly pointed out that in order for the department and its leadership to become more representative of the city's diverse population, there would be some short-term sacrifices by Anglo officers.

Click set up a committee of officers to produce a departmental mission and values statement, which was then posted in every police building and printed on wallet cards and issued to every officer. As he was shifting the department's orientation from responding to emergencies to community policing, Click made effective use of the uniformed traditions and discipline of the police. He made methodical use of the hierarchical, paramilitary structure of the department. "One thing [police departments] are good at," he later mused, "is following orders."[25] At headquarters he cracked down on deputy and assistant chiefs who reported for duty late and left early, or had slack attitudes toward attendance at office and community meetings. He demoted those he regarded as setting bad examples for the rest of department. He forcefully defended his personnel decisions before the Civil Service Commission, winning most appeals.

Click set about demolishing the bunker mentality that permeated the department. Realizing that the hierarchical structure and tribal loyalties of the department could both impede change and facilitate it, he pursued a "tight-loose" management strategy.[26] He tried to establish a balance between a brisk management style that assured consequences for unprofessional behavior with a "softer" approach that welcomed ideas and assistance from the ranks in structuring how officers did their jobs. He, therefore, established strict standards of conduct, balanced by an atmosphere of openness to ideas and accessibility to him and other police commanders by both officers and the public. Unlike Vines, Click was almost always in uniform, and he ordered the command staff to wear their uniforms almost all the time. He wanted to establish a common identity between commanders and officers, creating a more comfortable situation for informal communication in his visits to police stations and with individual officers.

Reflecting on the effect of the paramilitary hierarchy on his ability to change the department, Click concluded that it had been useful to a certain extent. "We can always make [commanders and officers] attend a meeting, but it is a different problem to make them like it," he said: "Often there is not enough structure in organizations, no uniformity, no discipline, no sense of direction. It is sort of like herding chickens. In our business that doesn't happen." But, he concluded, even a hierarchy cannot be managed entirely from the top down: "You have to let employees have input, they have to be heard, they need to help structure how the job is done."[27] Professing a dislike for micromanagement, Click tried to combine high, centrally enforced standards of conduct with substantial latitude for commanders, and ultimately for the officer on the street, to work within a framework of accountability for both means and results.

The more difficult task before Click was to overcome "almost an aversion" among commanders and officers to dealing with people who had been critical of the police, to treat them with respect, and to repair the strained relationships that had developed with black and Hispanic neighborhood groups. Police-community relations improved under Vines and Rathburn but they were still far from ideal. Commissioner Price and his "warriors" still picketed police divisional headquarters where they thought commanders were insufficiently sensitive to minority concerns or had too few minorities among in the command and officer contingents. Adding to the irritation at the Northwest Division, Price occasionally slow-marched his pickets across busy Northwest Highway during rush hour, blocking commuter traffic and eliciting stern lectures from the editors of the *Dallas Morning News*.

Click made it clear to the command staff that they must get out of their offices and become a part of the community. He expected them to be willing to work long hours, setting an example for the patrol officers by not only attending community meetings and listening to people, but by responding to their concerns. Early on, Click attended a community meeting in a South Dallas neighborhood that was so hostile to police that officers never entered it except in response to an emergency call, and then only with at least two patrol cars carrying four officers. The neighborhood contained a high level of drug and gang activity, and the dealers and gang leaders controlled its residents—most of them poor, all of them black—through intimidation and violence.

Click discovered that the residents who had to cope with daily robberies and shootings had no respect for the police. Officers came into the neighborhood only to respond to calls and never saw its residents except in a confrontational setting. Click began working with one of the neighborhood leaders who was intitally skeptical of his intentions and ability to deliver on his promises. She declared that she had no use for the police, but agreed to try once more. The chief and his commanders hand-picked a few officers who were willing to work with her and others to turn the neighborhood around. They stepped up police presence and helped residents organize to take back their streets. Four years later, the neighborhood leader still called Chief Click, but it was rarely to complain of a police problem; instead, she called to compliment officers, or to let him know of a new community activity.

By 1998, Click had converted much of the police department to community-based policing, using both city funds and federal grants. He estimated that his officers attended over 3,000 community meetings a year, and a large number of them were trained in meeting facilitation, stakeholder group organization, and problem-solving skills. Community police officers were assigned to neighborhoods where they got to know people on the streets they patrolled on foot or bicycle. Several mobile police "storefronts" were purchased, which could be moved into areas experiencing heightened criminal activity, to show a continuous police presence. Attention was paid to preventing low-level criminal activity, such as vandalism, graffiti, public drunkenness, rowdy behavior, and loitering. This "broken windows" approach to policing was supplemented by "weed and seed" raids on drug dealers and strong anti-gang programs.

Click's changes in the approach of the department to its policing task resulted in development of greater trust between the police officers and the community. By mid-1998, the city had about 500 active neighborhood crime watch groups. Sixty of these groups had organized citizen patrols of their neighborhoods with the encouragement of the community police officers. Officers assigned to the community policing unit and district commanders tended to agree that the approach had greatly improved police-community relations, and that having police involved in the community made their jobs easier.[28] People were more likely to report crimes and to regard police intervention, when necessary, as supportive. Use of the mobile stations appears to have had a positive effect on communities where they have been placed, reducing crime and helping build stronger ties between police and local merchants and citizens.[29] Police were better informed about activity in the areas they served and developed new working relationships with other city departments, such as Parks and Recreation, and job training programs at the Community College, which assisted them in dealing with youth and unemployment-related issues before they festered into criminal activity.[30] As Table 6.2 shows, Dallas serious crimes against persons and property fell from 1992 through 1999. Crimes increased slightly in 1997 in all police divisions except the southwestern and north central divisions, but resumed their downward trend all across the city by 1999.

Organizational Culture and Institutional Change in the Dallas Police Department

The Dallas police force had three core attributes, all of them common to police organizations: autonomy that verged on insularity, a paramilitary structure and discipline system, and solidarity that approached tribalism. Each reinforced the others. Diversifying the force and reforming the institutional behavior of the police required first understanding and then changing each of these attributes.

The DPD was a uniformed service of specially trained, armed, and sworn officers. Thus, "the city's finest" were immediately set apart from the rest of city employees and, by the nature of their role, from the rest of the city. All sworn officers entered at the bottom ranks and went through a common training experience. For most of its history the DPD excluded women and minorities. Once admitted, they had to start at

Table 6.2 Violent and Property (Part I) Crime in Dallas 1992–1999

Year	*Crimes*
1992	131,373
1993	112,211
1995	99,865
1997	101,665
1999	78,706

the bottom, so the number of female and minority senior officers and commanders was disproportionately smaller than the number in the force at large. Diversification was imposed on a generally unreceptive department. Many older Anglo officers had not reconciled themselves to it by the mid-1980s.

The promotion system relied strictly on test scores and tended to confine promotions to a small pool of Anglo officers. Deviation from the custom of promoting the officers with the highest scores was regarded throughout the ranks as detrimental to the quality and morale of the force. There was almost no means of lateral entry at higher ranks into the force from other cities or law enforcement services, and thus little cross-fertilization of experience except through in-service education and training programs. These included both local college and Southwestern Legal Foundation courses and participation of promising officers in the FBI Academy.

The result was a department that was well trained and abreast of the latest technology and techniques of policing, but also inward-looking, self-satisfied, and thus, unreceptive to change, particularly change that implied criticism of the ways in which the department had conducted its affairs. It was difficult to make personnel changes in the command structure because senior officers had civil service protection from dismissal or demotion except for cause. If previous assistant chiefs and deputy chiefs were routinely given high performance ratings, regardless of their actual performance, it was the official records that determined their vulnerability, not the impressions of a new chief. Unlike the military, where senior officers are regularly rotated among command posts, police command staff were likely to remain in place for many years, nursing aspirations to become chief or occasionally functioning as "virtual vacancies," gliding toward retirement.

Police departments, like schools, are *coping* organizations.[31] It is not possible for those at the top of the organization to observe directly what those on the street do or to determine the effect of their activity on the incidence of crime, as opposed to other factors. Police work frequently as individuals, in pairs, or small groups such as tactical squads. Individuals or pairs of officers on patrol have extraordinary discretion over which laws to enforce or how stringently to enforce them.

Whether working alone or in a group exercise, police procedures are highly regulated by a detailed disciplinary code, procedures, reviews, and *post hoc* investigations. Unlike other agencies of city government, the police department itself conducted investigations of misconduct or corruption of its officers through its Internal Investigations Division. A military-style chain of command enforced orders and imposed discipline from the top. Failure to follow departmental orders and regulations could result in stiff penalties, including suspension, dismissal, or the filing of criminal charges. Disciplinary actions could be appealed to the city's Civil Service Commission. Alleged criminal conduct was referred to a grand jury. Disciplinary actions were not uncommon. Indictments were rare; convictions rarer.

The distinctions of the police force from other services and its role in maintaining the values of the regime reinforced its autonomy within city government. Combined with the uniqueness of the disciplinary code and authority to police itself, autonomy metamorphosed into insularity. Within this bureaucratic cocoon, the mutual dependence of fellow officers for their safety or lives in stressful encounters with an increasingly alienated minority public generated solidarity. They could protect each other through the informal "code of silence," which discouraged officers from reporting breaches of the code of conduct, or even criminal wrongdoing.

Throughout its history, when assailed from "outside," the department turned inward, hunkering behind its institutional defenses and mobilizing its business and community allies. A single officer might have to be sacrificed as a "bad apple," but the department, having cleansed itself, could continue as before. Such was the state of the department in 1989 when the cumulative weight of the deadly force incidents and the shootings of police officers forced the issue of police-community relations to the top of the civic agenda.

The initial institutional response of the police department and the DPA was to call upon citizens to "Back the Blue," using the mystique of police heroism and barely coded racism to rally Anglo Dallas to resist efforts to change the way the department and its officers operated. Their insularity and inbred leadership generated an institutional insensitivity to the concerns of the city's minority communities. On the other side of the controversy, the hostility to police practices and inflamatory statements by Council Members Ragsdale, Lipscomb, and Commissioner Price only intensified the institutional paranoia of the police.

Monica Smith, the newly elected president of the Dallas Police Association, was confronted with her promise to make the Association an effective voice for the rank and file, without turning their sorrow over the loss of comrades and their bitterness toward their critics into an all-out racially polarized referendum. Unable to negotiate directly with the city manager because the DPA was not recognized as a bargaining agent, and alienated from the chief and other top commanders the Association felt had let them down in a time of need, she found bargaining power in the palpable threat of the referendum. Thus, an inherently weak organization, in its desperation, took an extreme position to defend the status quo with respect to the review board's powers and to augment its ranks with new recruits. It had to deliver something to its members, but its leaders did not want to be blamed for bringing the city to open racial conflict, undermining its image as a city that worked, and that of its police department as keeper of its peace. There was also some concern among the leadership of DPA that losing the referendum could end the Association's influence. It was in their interest to win concessions without having to test their influence in a referendum.

They placed their hopes in Ross Perot whose national prominence and well-known sympathies for the police gave the leadership of the DPA the ear of a potentially powerful protector. His meetings with officers to hear their grievances strengthened their confidence that he would fairly represent their interests in any negotiations to resolve the referendum crisis. In the Association's eyes Perot was a symbol of the business power that had ruled Dallas. His intervention gave them legitimacy. His counsel could not be ignored. At the same time, Perot served Knight and Strauss's interests in averting the disaster of a referendum on the review board and increasing the size of the force above Knight's estimate of need. Perot's systematic discussion with police officers allowed venting of their concerns about the review board and perceived lack of support from the chief and other city officials without creating a confrontation with Knight. It also allowed Perot and Tom Luce, his attorney, to obtain a sense of how far the DPA might go in its efforts to seek public justification for its position, and what concessions the city might make to avert a racially polarizing referendum. Perot's role was, therefore, enveloped in the civic culture's reverence for the business hero as problem solver, but it was also more complex and subtle. As was his custom, Perot made his own rules: he would support but not advocate, present his findings but not represent the Association, and remain free to offer his own advice to both the anxious city and its restive police.

Mayor Strauss quickly recognized the danger that a referendum on the review board posed. She engaged in a public exchange of statements with Monica Smith to discourage the Association from filing its petitions, and sought to rally editorial and other civic support for modifications in the review board's structure, membership, and powers. It appeared at one point that an agreement on changes to the Review Board's powers would lead to a withdrawal of DPA's threat to file the petitions. The Council adopted some conciliatory amendments, but these failed to satisfy the DPA board, which accused the Council of acting in bad faith. Smith again threatened to file the petitions. Black council members were unwilling to accept the further dilution of the Review Board's powers. More fundamentally, the mayor had no more authority than any other council member to negotiate with the DPA, and she could not be sure of holding a majority in support of any agreement she might reach. Nor could she be certain that the DPA could make a firm commitment. There was also the issue of council interference with the prerogatives of the city manager to deal with a city department in which a large portion of the employees appeared ready to defy official policy.

City Manager Knight had both a personal and institutional stake in the outcome. The attempt of the DPA to circumvent the budgetary process and use the threat of the referendum to increase the size of the police force was a direct challenge to his administrative authority. The mayor, other city politicians and the private sector leadership were deeply concerned about the danger of a bitter, racially charged election, which would probably be won by the police and their allies. This would further alienate minorities and reinforce the police. It would intimidate Anglo council members, and make more difficult the reforms of the department Knight believed could be achieved only with a new chief from outside the force who was resolved to diversify it and discipline the practices that had in large part precipitated the crisis.

Knight had earned his promotion from first assistant city manager to the top position in City Hall on the strength of his reputation as the city's "Mr. Fixit." With the retreat of the oligarchy to the anxious sidelines, Perot's ambiguous role as interlocutor between the police and the city government, and the mayor's inability to frame a resolution acceptable to the DPA and Council, the regency had been thrust upon Knight. Perot's role enabled him to feel out the DPA without having to deal directly with Smith and its board. The fact that he was black, combined with endorsement of his final recommendations by Pettis Norman would give them credibility with the black council members and the minority community. If Perot and Luce agreed, the DPA would have to go along or face losing the support of their most visible and important champion.

The compromise Knight fashioned guaranteed the rights of police officers to invoke their Fifth Amendment rights in Review Board proceedings and limited the board's subpoena power by making it subject to Council approval. Most importantly, from the DPA's perspective, it prohibited membership on the board by persons who represented officers, the department, or those, such as Lesser, who represented persons with actions against the police. Knight also proposed the creation of an advisory committee composed of experts in law enforcement to advise the board on police procedures and provide an independent base of professional judgment on which to base its decisions. He indicated his willingness to recommend an increase of 500 officers in the force.

These modifications had the immediate effect of allowing the DPA to claim that its main goals had been achieved and withdraw the referendum threat. The black City Council members were not pleased with the compromise, but were unwilling to oppose Knight publicly because he symbolized for them the long overdue recognition of blacks in Dallas governance.

Initially the compromise appeared to avoid any substantial adaptation of the department to the changing demography and character of the city. Knight's gambit relied, however, on four factors. The first was his own ability to select a chief from outside the department who could heal the breach with the minority communities and engineer a reorientation of the department's policing practices. Second, he counted on the command hierarchy of the department and the institutionalized tendency of police to obey orders even if they disliked them. Third, he expected the new chief to integrate the command structure of the department and use the additional positions to increase substantially the number of minority officers on the force, thereby gradually changing its racial perceptions and attitudes. Finally, he expected council members and others to distance themselves from the risk of blame for the volatile police-community relations problem, leaving him and the police chief as expendable regents if failure ensued. Near the end of his tenure as city manager, Knight said that he thought his appointment of Mack Vines as Chief of Police was the most important decision he made.

Vines clearly initiated a process of institutional change that continued under his successors. A first order of business for each of the new chiefs was to use his powers as commanding officer to revamp the command structure of the department, which had been a formidable barrier to change. Under Dallas's ossified civil service rules, none were able to bring key staff officers or assistants with them. Each had to make the best of what was there, reassigning a few commanders to different jobs, testing their abilities and resilience, promoting a few promising junior officers into newly created command positions, reorganizing the command staff and divisions to shake up the system.

The initial response to Vines among the old guard of the force was to wait him out, doing what was necessary to avoid being insubordinate, and hope for a return to the way things had been. City Manager Jan Hart's appointment of William Rathburn torpedoed that strategy. Rathburn's "cop's cop" demeanor made him more acceptable within the department, enabling him to build on the changes initiated by Vines. His departure after less than two years, however, produced uncertainty about policies and complicated the serious morale problems of a department that was still racially divided and contained many dispirited officers. Ben Click, however, stayed long enough to demonstrate the importance of sustained leadership in transforming a large, complex organization such as the Dallas Police Department.

Although the department seemed ideally structured to facilitate rapid changes of policy, it was, in fact, a far more cumbersome system. Paradoxically, the built-in mechanisms designed to insulate the police from political pressure and corrupt influences—civil service protections, preference for promotion from within, internal investigation of alleged misconduct, etc.—conspired with the shared dangers of the profession to isolate the police from the society they were sworn to protect and serve.

The factors that fostered solidarity and mutual obligation among officers up and down the chain of command immobilized rather than energized the department when the system came under attack. As a result, both Chief Billy Prince and the Dallas Police Association fundamentally misread the crisis of confidence and legitimacy arising from the shootings of police and use of deadly force against suspects. The DPA saw the problem as one of embattled officers, trying to do their duty but denied the support of their commander and the public. Prince, a product of the system, shared the view of many officers that what was needed was support for the efforts of one of the most professionally trained and technically well-equipped police forces in the country, not criticism. Both Prince and the DPA believed that it was the politicians and the city that needed to change, not the police.

By the time Ben Click arrived on the scene, most officers were resigned to having an outside chief. Click still had to overcome the basic inertia of the system. The support of Managers Jan Hart and John Ware, the City Council, and the business community could be counted on only so long as the city was at peace and crime rates did not rise. He recognized that his effectiveness in producing lasting change in the department's approach to policing, and in the attitudes of officers toward the diverse publics they served, hinged on his ability to persuade rather than command. This required an external strategy calculated to produce public support for the police as well as for the chief, and an internal strategy that reduced racial tensions among officers and changed police doctrine with regard to the role of patrol officers.

To succeed, Click believed he "had to move the soft end of social control from the department to the neighborhood."[32] The department did not have the resources or skills to keep the peace or conduct the surveillance required in every neighborhood and business district in Dallas. Police could, however, help organize neighborhood residents and merchants and work with them to reduce crime and to resolve problems before they escalated to criminal behavior. Previously, he observed, the police had created expectations for levels of safety they could not meet. This left people disappointed and skeptical if not hostile to the police, who withdrew into their police cars and 911 service. Isolated from the neighborhoods and uncomfortable, even fearful in entering them, "there was a lot of hatred." This often placed the individual officer under great stress and danger. Experienced officers were leaving police work due to stress from confrontations. Car patrols had made strangers of the police. The intimate knowledge of the beat cop about the neighborhood and those who lived in it had been lost, and with it the bonds of trust between police and public. Click thought that people should be able to know their community police officer. And that if he could show officers that his "broken windows" approach to policing would make the lot of the police a happier one, he could rebuild morale and at the same time make the city safer.

Click used the semi-military organization of the police, with its steep command structure and strict disciplinary code to change the department. But he did not mistake his official authority for effective control. Rather, he assumed *responsibility* for leading the department and for persuading officers up and down the chain of command to share that responsibility with him, and with the communities of the city. According to Click: "In this kind of organization, the key is spending a lot of time with your employees. The more time you spend with them, the more they will speak up, and the better your decisions will be. The same with the community. Structure helps carry out policies. When I look at other organizations, they could be well served by more structure. But you can't create it overnight."[33]

The Capacity to Resolve Problems and Adapt to Change

It was not clear in 1998 how much of the reduction in Part I offenses was due to changes in police approaches, and how much was the result of the drastic reduction in unemployment rates as the Dallas economy surged. Chiefs from outside the department introduced new approaches to policing and made cumulatively important strides in diversifying it. Restoring police morale was more problematic. Vines did not survive long enough to achieve material improvements in morale, and his management style exacerbated some problems of discipline and morale. Rathburn was more successful, but his premature departure truncated his impact on the department, although it helped prepare the ground for Click. Click won over most of the force, and in so doing, substantially enhanced the department's capacity for dealing with the race relations problem that had plagued it and the even more widespread problems of community support and trust.

Community policing was a major change in the way in which the department performed its function. It appears to have had a substantial and sustained effect on the levels of crime, the perception of safety in those communities where it was established, and in the way in which police officers and commanders practiced their craft. In instituting the change, Click did not simply order officers to operate in a different manner. In fact, many of the basic practices of the department continued much as before. He hand-picked the first community police officers, provided them with special training, and demonstrated their effectiveness. He created a community police support unit, attached it to police headquarters, and expanded the program as officers could be trained for it.

As an institution, the police department exhibited both a resistance to and facility for adaptation to its changing urban environment. In the skilled hands of Rathburn and Click, the command structure and paramilitary discipline of the department facilitated adaptation. But resources were also critical—

particularly the complement of new officers that facilitated diversification, and funding for the Police Academy and other training programs. The availability of federal funding for interactive community policing also helped turn the department in new directions.

Fear of crime and the police was not banished. Minorities still expressed much lower trust of the police than Anglos, but the palpable antagonism between minorities and the police had abated substantially by 1998. While the police force was not yet a reflection of the city's population, it was much closer than a decade before. The command structure had been substantially integrated. There were fewer complaints of racial harassment by police. And crime was down. Conversations with police officers and commanders suggested that more had occurred than mere compliance with orders.

Racial friction in the department had not ceased, but it was less pervasive. The Police Association and the Texas Police Officers Association had not merged. There were still complaints of preferential treatment for minorities in promotions. But there was general acceptance of minority and female commanders and far wider acceptance of the value of a diversified force. The organization seemed to have learned that it needed to work closely with neighborhoods and business associations. When it did, its job was made easier, more satisfying for both the residents of the city and the officers. A consensus had been reached that community policing worked, and that the old ways of reliance on force and fear did not. When Chief Click retired in 1999, his replacement was Deputy Chief Terrell Bolton, a black officer whose rapid rise through the ranks had been possible because of the outside chiefs.

Conclusion

Civic culture was an important ingredient in producing the crisis in policing in Dallas, but it was also a significant factor in its resolution and the reform of the department. A long history of segregation and concern for commercial safety while undervaluing the dignity of minority residents of the city produced the toxic environment that exacerbated the reaction of both minorities and police officers to the use of deadly force and the subsequent killings of police officers. The deference to managerialism allowed City Manager Knight to take on an overtly political role in fashioning a compromise that ended the incipient mutiny of the Police Association. Although the organized oligarchy was essentially absent from the field, Ross Perot's involvement provided the cover of business legitimacy to the outcome as well as a way for Knight to avoid recognition of the DPA as a bargaining agent for the officers. The hierarchical system and the organizational culture of the police made it possible, in turn, for the outside chiefs to institute a series of fundamental reforms in the way in which the department operated. It was clear from the way things first unraveled and then were reformed that neither the city managers nor the chiefs were, in Chief Prince's hopeful term, "in control." But they did find ways to be responsible and in so doing, managed to improve the responsibility and effectiveness of the Dallas Police.

III

Growing Dallas: Civic Culture and Development

7

Growth as a Public Good: The Dallas Growth Machine

> Local politicians, eager for relief from the cross-pressures of local politics, assiduously promote goals that have widespread benefits. And few policies are more popular than economic growth and prosperity.
>
> PAUL PETERSON

The Gospel of Growth

Land use and economic development occupy a large segment of the policy agenda of any economically active city. They engage the city's elite economic and professional institutions—its banks, utilities, merchants, mass media, lawyers, architects, engineers, and builders. Their impact is pervasive, affecting housing and traffic patterns, neighborhood and regional environmental quality, and fiscal capacity.

Development activity affects both private fortunes and the tax base. It cannot occur without a convergence of private capital and governmental power. The private sector is primarily responsible for development through its investments and disinvestments in capital stock and employees. But the extent and character of private investments are contingent on the exercise of the most formidable powers of government: the police power; the power to tax, spend and borrow; and the exercise of eminent domain.

Through its police power, the city regulates the location, density, character, and occasionally, the pace of private development. Improvement of property, or changing its use, because of its potential impact on neighboring uses and on the community at large, requires the permission of the government.[1] Proposed changes in land use frequently excite high levels of conflict among developers, adjacent property owners and community residents. The Plan Commission, Board of Adjustment, and the City Council become forums for the resolution of these conflicts and the development of policies designed to promote and shape patterns of growth and ameliorate its effects on established neighborhoods.

Tax and monetary policies are critical to building cycles and the kinds of development that occurs during them. During most of the boom years for development in Dallas, federal tax policies provided for accelerated depreciation on office and apartment buildings, encouraging a flow of capital into real estate ventures. Deregulation of savings and loan associations in the early 1980s, combined with policies that allowed investors to shelter income in real estate, encouraged the building bubble of speculative housing and commercial space.[2]

Through its power to borrow, tax, and spend, government provides the "vital systems,"[3] such as transportation and sanitary systems, schools and parks,[4] without which most private urban development could not occur. These public expenditures by federal, state, and local governments make the public co-investors in urban development. Over the course of time, the City of Dallas invested billions of dollars in infrastructure. At the end of the 1997 fiscal year, the city's balance sheet listed the depreciated value of city-owned property, plant and equipment, excluding the street system, at $2.5 billion.[5] The annual cost of debt service, operation and maintenance of public facilities and infrastructure networks represents, after public safety, the largest expenditures in the city budget.

Taxes on land and improvements are the most important source of revenue in Dallas. Slightly more than a third of the city's revenues come from its property tax.[6] Sales taxes, which contribute 28 percent of 1996 revenues,[7] are also related to development of commercial property, giving the city an interest in capturing high volume retail uses in the city, rather than have them locate in the suburbs. Such firms, in turn, depend upon growth in population and firms for their own expansion.

The acquisition of land for public facilities to accommodate new development or serve existing uses, and in some cases to assemble and sell land for redevelopment by private firms, frequently requires the use of the power of eminent domain. The power to condemn land and buildings may also be used to remove derelict structures from communities in an effort to prevent the spread of blight to adjacent properties. Again, whether used for a clear public purpose or a more ambiguous "public benefit," the power of government to take private property affects other land values and, hence, both private and public welfare.

There is, then, a natural reciprocity of interests among local public officials, taxpayers, and developers. Developers need infrastructure with excess capacity. Governments need revenue to meet service demands. Public facilities can be expanded through long-term obligations. Debt service on excess capacity induces a need for accelerated development to ameliorate tax burdens. This need encourages relaxation of restrictions on development that promises substantial revenue gains. If the gains do not materialize because the new residents and firms demand better services, the pressure increases to stimulate more development through tax and direct subsidies. If development does occur, but taxes do not decline, this is usually taken as evidence that even more development is needed; therefore, regulations should be further relaxed and more and better infrastructure should be provided. The language of urban development is that of economics and engineering—efficiency and best means. But its art is that of distributive politics—the narrow focus of benefits and the wide diffusion of costs.

The amount and character of development is also intimately connected to the image of the city its leaders and inhabitants hold. "City building, at its very core an activity involving capital investment and land use, is also very importantly an effort at image creation or preservation."[8] Thus, the capture or retention of a Fortune 500 headquarters, the threat to close a prestigious department store, and the construction of a new sports arena or concert hall take on far more political significance than their economic effects alone may justify. They symbolize the vitality and "greatness" of a city. They may occupy far more of the energies of city leaders and draw more heavily on the city's resources than less dramatic changes such as new business formations and expansions of existing firms, although these may actually produce more jobs and tax revenues than relocation of a corporate headquarters.

Because of the importance of development to the fiscal health and image of the city, it has a "special relationship" to city governance institutions.[9] Some argue that it is the central function of urban governance.[10] The slack resources that come from development and growth, whether in the form of tax proceeds or business support of community programs, make officials solicitous of development interests, and helpful in maintaining the growth machine—"An apparatus of interlocking pro-growth associations and governmental units. . . ."[11] The depth of this solicitude and the nature of the relationship between those with interests in development projects and public officials and civic leaders varies with the mobilization of pro- and anti-development opinion, which in turn is influenced by the civic creed or culture of a community.[12] So it is with Dallas, a city virtually synonymous with development as growth from its founding to the present day. Of 1907 Dallas, Darwin Payne wrote: "Growth and progress—that was what mattered. By most accounts, certainly in Dallas, the definitions of these two words were the same. Growth was progress and progress was growth."[13] Throughout its history, any interruption or flattening of the rate of growth was regarded as abnormal. From the early 1960s until the real estate bust of 1986, the construction crane was the unofficial "city bird" of Dallas. Even the trauma of the Kennedy assassination did not slow the pace of growth. Hundreds of thousands of square feet of office and commercial space were added to the city's inventory in years immediately following the darkest day in the city's history. Single-family homes and apartments rose from the blackland prairie of north Dallas, displacing cotton farms and ranches. Urban development spilled across the city line to create a seamless urban landscape between Dallas and Fort Worth, forty miles to the west, broken only by the meandering floodplain of the Trinity River and D/FW Airport. Rural villages found themselves transformed in the space of two decades into subdivisions and shopping centers. Second and third tier suburbs in the neighboring counties were reshaped as "edge cities" or exurbs.

Growth was confirmation by the marketplace of the Dallas myth and civic creed. Bigger signified better. It justified the investments made by the city's banks, newspapers, and other major businesses in securing federal, state, and local support for great public works projects that had facilitated and promoted growth—the Trinity Levees, D/FW Airport, the highway system, and the water supply system.

World Class Consciousness

The proprietors of Nieman-Marcus, the high-fashion Dallas emporium, realized there was a market for high quality merchandise among the newly rich cotton kings, oil barons, financiers, and speculators crowding the City of Dallas. They not only mined this local (and eventually an international) clientele with consummate marketing skill, but took on a mission of educating Dallas about the importance of the fine arts and cultural institutions in a great city. Gradually, a set of enthusiasts grew and fostered support for the visual and performing arts and for public amenities and design that offered variety and relief from the earnest commercial and cultural conformity of the city. This cosmopolitan vanguard gradually made headway against parochial and ideological fears that the contemporary arts might corrupt the city with immoral and communistic ideas and images by appealing to the vanity of city leaders eager not to be regarded as a bastion of rubes.[14] By 1997, Dallas drew the notice of an art world it once scorned when developer Ray Nasher donated to the Dallas Museum of Arts a garden to display his private collection of modern sculpture, considered the finest in the world, and sought by major U.S. and foreign museums.[15] The city's aesthetic appreciation had come far from the day Mayor R. L. Thornton characterized a modernistic metallic screen commissioned for the main library as "a bad welding job."[16]

Following the lead of its cosmopolitan mayor, Erik Jonsson, Dallas became more and more interested not only in being the biggest city in Texas, but in attracting and building "world class" commercial, scientific, and cultural facilities and institutions as integral components of a great city. Of these, the Dallas/Forth Worth International Airport was the most prominent, soon becoming the busiest passenger terminal in the U.S. The University of Texas Southwestern Medical Center rose from a marginally acceptable medical school, founded in the 1940s in renovated military barracks, to international distinction in research and medical education, with four Nobel Laureates on its faculty by 1995. Its achievements were clearly related to the generous financial support of local donors. The Dallas Cowboys (located in suburban Irving) designated themselves "America's Team."

The city remained reluctant to submit itself to the terrors of public planning and urban design, or to the visions of a more amenable city developed by the Dallas Institute of Humanities and Culture and local architect James Pratt. But it did embrace first rate architecture for several office and civic buildings.[17] Ross Perot, who chaired the funding drive for the Symphony Hall, insisted on two conditions for his participation: that it be named for his colleague, Morton Meyerson, and that it be a "world class" facility.

"World class" became the cliché of choice in describing the aspirations of Dallas leaders for its facilities and institutions, or justifying public support of major projects, whether provided by public or private funding, or some combination of the two. Thus, the creation of a rapid transit system for the city was premised on the assertion that all world class cities had one. Proponents of public participation in the cost of constructing a new arena for professional basketball and hockey teams argued that world class cities had professional sports franchises.[18] The region's political and business leaders enthusiastically embraced the Super Conducting Super Collider project, although it was eventually canceled by the federal government after land acquisition and the start of construction for the mammoth atom smasher in Ellis County, south of Dallas. Support for the project was propelled not only by the lure of massive federal spending to construct and operate the facility, but because of its uniqueness and the prospect that it would attract to Dallas "world class" scientists and enhance the opportunity for the further development of high technology enterprises. In the late 1990s, one of the arguments marshaled to support a multi-billion dollar program to develop the Trinity River, which bisects Dallas, as a recreational, transportation, and development corridor, was that world class cities had vital and development-attractive waterfronts.[19]

In many instances, the impulse for excellence that was manifest in the desire to propel Dallas into the front rank of international cities had a salutary effect on important amenities and facilities. On the other hand, passion for the grandiose resulted in the neglect of or withdrawal of support from institutions of substantial quality that did not achieve "world class" status as quickly as opinion leaders and major donors might have wished. Ross Perot temporarily withdrew a donation of $7 million from the Dallas Arboretum, reportedly because it was not conforming to his view of what was needed to make it "world class." Perot later reinstated the gift, when assured that the funds would be spent as he wished. One of Erik Jonsson's last acts was to liquidate the Educational Excellence Foundation, which he and others had established to endow the University of Texas at Dallas, and to direct most of its assets—some $35 million—to Southwestern Medical Center, where he had recently undergone cancer treatment. Jonsson was angered at the University's president and impatient with the slow pace at which its School of Engineering (named for him) had developed.

The definition of what was or ought to be world class was essentially arbitrary and nominees for the honor were rarely the result of rigorous analysis. With few exceptions—such as the airport, Super Conducting Super Collider, and the medical school—they often reflected whims of influential and wealthy figures rather than any strategic analysis of the city's needs. The rapid rail system, for example, could not be justified by any careful analysis of demand or population density in a highly dispersed region such as Dallas.[20] Similarly, there was no serious analysis of the costs and benefits or opportunity costs of the new downtown sports arena to justify city participation in its development.[21] And the quarter of a billion dollars in bonded debt for the city's contribution to the Trinity River Corridor project was approved by voters before feasibility studies had been completed on transportation, flood control, and recreational components that were keys to its success.[22]

Being world class had become an integral part of the civic culture, permeating civic discourse and going beyond mere commercial boosterism. The sentiment reflected pride in past accomplishments, but it also expressed the aspiration for recognition as one of the world's great cities.

Growth and Decline as Development Policy Problems

For four decades following the Second World War, Dallas grew. Even after the real estate bubble burst in the mid-1980s, property values dropped, and vacancy rates soared in the new monumental "world class" offices, growth slowed to a crawl but it did not stop. As the surplus space was absorbed, growth resumed, albeit at a less robust pace, and there were signs that the old self-confidence had returned. Mobil Oil decided to retain its headquarters in the central business district (CBD), and the Blockbuster Corporation returned its headquarters to downtown Dallas from its sojourn in Fort Lauderdale, Florida. Both received "incentives" from the city for locating in the CBD. In 1996 the first segment of the DART light rail system opened for service. Although a third of CBD office space remained vacant in mid-1998, 7.2 million square feet of new space was under construction in other parts of town.[23] The tax base stabilized and in 1995 began a slow but steady recovery,[24] reconfirming faith in the unmitigated goodness of growth.

As the city "built out," however, new issues arose involving the distribution of growth and its benefits. In 1990, the Oak Cliff Chamber of Commerce complained that the city had favored growth in northern Dallas to the neglect of public facilities and services in the southern sector of the city. The chamber released a flood of data to substantiate its charges and proposed consideration of a referendum to secede from Dallas.[25] Black and Hispanic activists repeatedly charged that the northward skewing of development activity was evidence of racism. Neighborhood groups opposed commercial and apartment projects, which they feared would affect them adversely. But the basic value of growth was uncontested.

At the end of the twentieth century, few large vacant tracts suitable for extensive employment centers or mixed-use development remained within the city limits.[26] The principal concern of the city's business and political leaders was competition with the suburbs and the under-utilization of office and commercial space in the central business district. The city's enthusiasm for virtually unrestricted growth had infected its suburbs, which offered other advantages in labor force quality, access to special markets, and cheaper land. The real problem for "Big D" now came from its own creation: Greater Dallas.

With a civic culture that was supportive of an expanding economy and population, the basic Dallas policy toward growth had been to accommodate and promote development. The traditional assumption of the city's economic elite was that all growth was good, and that the city would benefit if new development occurred anywhere on the Dallas side of the Dallas-Fort Worth Metroplex. The public facility networks of the city were designed with many years of excess capacity that could support growth beyond the city limits.[27] This excess capacity promoted dispersion of development and facilitated opening large tracts of land to development, first inside, and later outside the city with the enthusiastic approval of the city's economic establishment. This was because the same financial, retail, media, and utilities companies that profited from development in the city could now broaden the geographic scope of their activities. In some cases, there were fewer policy constraints on suburban development than in Dallas, and even fewer marketing problems.

All of this was of little concern to a city that had experienced few serious recessions in its development sector. As Charles Boortz pointed out, Dallas had experienced three extended real estate "booms" between 1945 and 1985. Although development was affected by national business cycles, Dallas had not suffered to the degree that other areas had at the end of the first two expansionary periods. This was a result of the region's general population growth and its oil-enriched economy, which benefited from the national stagflation crisis triggered by the OPEC energy crises of 1973 and 1978. With national tax policies that sheltered real estate investment, and banking laws that first restricted and then deregulated financial institutions, real estate offered the perfect hedge against the business cycle in a place where growth seemed inevitable and the local economy invulnerable to either inflation or recession.[28] Most development after the 1970s occurred outside the CBD and much of it outside the city,[29] but development inside the city still proceeded at a brisk clip. Six million square feet of new office space were added in the central business district from 1970 to 1980, and 18 million more square feet in the 1980s.[30] But even as new office space was being built, employment in central Dallas declined in both absolute numbers and as a percentage of regional employment.[31]

When the speculative bubble burst in 1986 with the collapse of the savings and loan institutions, the region had a glut of residential and commercial capacity that precipitated a sharp general decline in property values for the first time since the Great Depression. Every major financial institution in the city reorganized and changed owners and management.[32] Texas and regional unemployment figures rose above the national average. Male black and Hispanic workers, heavily concentrated in construction trades, experienced double-digit unemployment rates. The residential property tax base of the city contracted by almost a fourth between 1985 and 1995 before it recovered.

The suburbs were not as severely affected as Dallas. Many continued to grow, although almost every large-scale real estate project in the region experienced foreclosure and resale to new owners at distress prices.[33] The suburbs were increasingly competitive, actively recruiting new employers, and working closely with developers of large industrial and office tracts to attract headquarters of "world class" corporations to their new edge city campuses and technology corridors rather than to downtown towers.[34]

In response, the public and business institutions of Dallas shifted from a posture of accommodation of any growth anywhere to the creation of policies designed to capture more of the region's growth for the city. One of the strongest expressions of this change in attitude was a report commissioned by the law firm of Arter & Hadden as a vehicle for a mayoralty campaign by one of its senior partners, Forrest Smith—ironically, a former president of the Greater Dallas Chamber of Commerce. In the foreword to the report, *Dallas First,* Smith wrote:

> Dallas has the unique capacity to examine its challenges, and come up with its own solutions. At our lowest ebb in the 1960's, this community came up with "Goals for Dallas," a major turning point in our history. "Goals" paved the way for D/FW Airport, unquestionably the prime contributor to the continued growth of the D/FW Metroplex.
>
> Sadly, this growth has not treated all of the Metroplex evenly. There are a number of big winners. But the biggest loser is "Big D."[35]

The Greater Dallas Chamber of Commerce, under fire from city business leaders and the local chambers in Oak Cliff, North, and East Dallas for its indifference to where new industry located in the region, changed presidents and reorganized to place a stronger focus on the city.[36]

The growth of the city had always been taken for granted. So had the decline of some of the less affluent sectors of the city that were populated primarily by minorities. Decline in these areas was expected to be more than offset by the prosperity of other parts of the city—primarily, downtown and northern Dallas. The new ingredients, which now came to the front of the policy agenda, were decline of the CBD and the overall contraction in the economic health of the city. Decline was associated not only with the absolute and relative amounts of growth, but increasingly with the quality of the built environment and with a host of other factors, such as the quality of schools and public safety.

Civic Culture and City Building

Public Planning as a Private Enterprise

Texas's "independent-traditional" political culture[37] is predisposed toward limited governmental interference with the rights of private owners to use their property in ways that most benefit them.[38] In Dallas, the hold of the frontier's image of an owner's absolute right to any use he or she chooses evolved to accept basic land use regulations such as zoning and subdivision regulation, so long as they were applied to protect or enhance established property values. This tolerance of modest regulation of property rights did not presume that public plans should prevail over private preferences in response to market opportunities. Private owners and developers are assumed to have a better grasp of desirable and feasible development than public bureaucrats. When private preferences conflict with public plans, the latter should not bar the opportunity for a higher use and a greater gain.

The role of city government is to facilitate growth, not to constrain it or to nit-pick proposals. Rezoning of land can normally be accomplished in less than 120 days, assuming the applicant has obtained the assent of the neighborhood residents. The planning department of the city generally does not have the resources or experience to work with developers to solve development problems that are "outside the box" of established rules and practices. Dallas government has not been hospitable to aggressive planners[39] and a professional planner has not headed the department since the early 1980s. The position of Planning Director was left vacant for several months following the resignation of Michael Coker in 1994.[40] The planning staff has been given little latitude for creative policy initiatives, which tend to be left to consultants, private developers, and ad hoc efforts led by business executives. Its work focuses primarily on review of individual rezoning and subdivision applications and is confined to determining whether a proposal conforms to existing regulations and policies.[41] Staff members who are regarded by development interests as too rigid or hard to work with generally have a short tenure in the planning department, which is chronically understaffed. When developers are confronted with the need for innovation in ordinances or financing to make a desirable project work, their attorneys and consultants tend to work with the council member in whose district the project is proposed, often drafting the necessary text or map amendments for introduction by the member.[42] Since the mid-1980s, the department has not been involved in any master planning, comprehensive rezoning, or ordinance revision initiatives. It is almost entirely a procedural regulatory organization. Its job is to maintain a clean and working house.

A prominent real estate lawyer described the planning process in Dallas as "outside-in." Developers propose plans which the staff and Plan Commission adopt, as compared to a process in which staff and commission members set guidelines that developers are expected to meet.[43]

As Dallas developed, much of the available raw land was in large tracts, often resulting in large-scale residential and commercial development projects that might take many years to complete, requiring substantial organizational, planning, and financial capacity. This produced a remarkable group of developer-owners who could afford substantial investments in planning and design studies and who exercised considerable patience in developing their property.[44]

Because the larger land holdings were usually on the periphery of existing settlement, and in some cases quite far from it, the "accommodationist" and facilitating approach to growth produced a low density, polycentric pattern of development within the city limits and in the proliferation of municipalities ringing the central city.[45] Developments of large international development firms present a special problem in city policy. They employ design, engineering, and legal talent of the highest quality, and concentrate it on a single project.

They are prepared to make dazzling presentations to the public, city staff, the Plan Commission, and the City Council. Their lawyers are skilled negotiators and deal makers. And they hold out the tantalizing prospect of enriching the tax and employment base of the city. This array of talent and promises generally surpasses and often overwhelms the resources available in the short-staffed city planning department to review projects.

The importance of development in city affairs, however, does not depend directly on the interests of large land holders and others directly involved in the physical development of those tracts. Rather, it derives from the extent to which interest in and the costs and benefits of development are widely diffused throughout the urban economic system. That many have an interest in development does not mean that all have the same intensity or kind of interest. These distinctions are important in understanding what maintains the growth machine in Dallas, and in assessing its reach and influence.

Bankers, Builders, and Brokers

At the center of the pro-growth network are the bankers, builders, and brokers. They are interdependent but not always cohesive in their interests. Financial institutions compete with one another and out-of-state lenders to finance development. Builders and brokers often compete head to head. Because the financial and land markets are fragmented, the competitive impulse produces cycles of speculation and overbuilding.[46] The industry is especially vulnerable to shifts in national fiscal and monetary policy, which change the risks involved in real estate investment and the affordability of new space for buyers.[47]

Restructuring of the financial industry since the savings and loan crisis of the 1980s affected both capital flows into real estate investment and the interest of some of the largest Dallas financial institutions in local real estate development.

The merger of Dallas-based banks into national banking systems made new sources of capital available, but the experience of the banking-savings and loan crisis made financial institutions more wary of portfolios too heavily weighted with real estate investments. Reorganizations left Dallas bank managers with less discretion to finance local "deals" than in pre-bust years. Would-be borrowers in the years immediately following acquisition of Interfirst Republic by North Carolina National Bank (NCNB) commonly complained that the initials of the Charlotte, North Carolina, holding company stood for "No Cash for No Body."[48] As the economy rebounded after 1993, however, capital again flowed freely into Dallas area real estate development, although relatively little investment occurred in speculative commercial and office development for several years.

Another important change was noted by Max Wells, a former Council member and Chairman of The Oaks Bank, an uptown community institution that avoided the restructuring of the 1980s:

> One of the great changes besides just the economic recession, was the failure of all the major Dallas banks and the change in the banking rules. . . . We were a unit bank state and you couldn't have branches. The other side was that . . . the big banks were the institutions that brought people to town, and when they brought them to town they wouldn't let them go to [the suburbs]. Every major company that came to town until the 1980s immediately located in the central city. The big banks were the prime movers, and they didn't want them out there in Plano or Grand Prairie. Now, Nations Bank and Bank One don't care whether you locate in Plano or Grand Prairie; . . . they don't even care if you come to Texas. The second the big banks didn't care where you located, was when the core of the city began to suffer.[49]

While autonomous of local government, the various components of the development industry are interdependent.

There is little vertical integration in the industry, in part due to federal and state regulations against self-dealing by financial institutions. While these restrictions were frequently evaded through corporate shells, such practices were curtailed in the wake of the Savings and Loan scandals of the 1980s. Nonetheless, there were often long standing collaborations among lending institutions, development companies and builders, real estate brokerages, title companies, law firms, and construction contractors. It is fair to characterize the industry in most large cities, including Dallas, as *articulated,* if not integrated.

Growth-Dependent Industries

Closely allied to the core industries are others that are heavily dependent on them for income. These include public utilities, which extend their service areas and customer base as the city grows. General contractors, who build infrastructure as well as buildings, depend upon development for a steady flow of business. Skilled and unskilled construction workers are highly vulnerable to the development cycle. They provide a solid blue-collar constituency for growth. Real estate is one of the largest sources of advertising revenue for the local newspaper. The businesses of the other two principal buyers of newspaper ads, automobile dealers and retail merchants, grow with the city. A sizable segment of the legal, architecture and engineering, accounting, and public relations professions are regularly employed in making financial deals, preparing plans, securing governmental approvals, or marketing projects.

In Dallas, as in most regions, there are ties among the local financial institutions, developers, law firms, real estate brokerages, and related enterprises. Major developers and prominent attorneys have served on the boards of banks, savings institutions, and insurance companies. Where there were no formal corporate ties, there often were social and other business associations. Law firms, such as Jenkens & Gilchrist, grew from its work for the Murchison oil and real estate interests into one of the largest corporate law firms in Texas. The Ebby Halliday Real Estate brokerage grew from the same base.[50] Ray Nasher, who developed the North Park office and retail center, created his own bank.[51]

Helpers: Politics, Planning, and Public Works

Billions of dollars ride on development transactions in a great city like Dallas. Urban development is not simply a private matter, however. It requires at least the acquiescence of the local government, and often its active participation. No other industry is as directly or heavily dependent upon local policy and its administration. Its members, therefore, are naturally interested in the content and execution of policies and in the attitudes toward growth of the officials whose decisions can influence its pace, scale, location, and character.

Individuals and firms involved in development are an important source of campaign funds for local elective offices. Some of them invest a fraction of their slack resources in candidates who will advance their interests or, at worst, leave them alone. Surely some political contributions by development interests are motivated by personal relationships with candidates or because of political beliefs that transcend immediate financial concerns. Those in the development and associated industries are conditioned to contribute by habit as well as interest. More than most citizens, they are closely involved in the everyday operations of city government and aware of the capabilities and views of elected or appointed officials.

In Dallas, where the system of governance was designed to impede electoral mobilization and widespread participation, funding is crucial in closely contested races.[52] Unless a candidate possesses personal wealth or can draw upon a group of personal or ideological benefactors, developers and their associated interests are an important source of large campaign contributions. Those interested in development may have projects pending in several council districts. Even if they do not, multiple access can be important in land use cases deemed of city-wide importance where support must be obtained from members other than the one in whose district the project is located. On other occasions, it may be necessary to find a two-thirds majority to override the recommendations of the Plan Commission. Since the City Council has not contained reliable factions in recent years, active developers often contribute to candidates running in several districts. In the first two elections in which all candidates except the mayor ran in single member districts, three-fourths of the contributions to winning council candidates came from donors who lived or conducted business outside their districts. Even more significant, no council candidate won without support from donors who contributed to candidates in other districts.[53]

So pervasive is the culture of growth in Dallas, however, that there have been few scandals associated with the support of politicians for development projects. There has been little need for skullduggery in a civic culture predisposed to accept as wise the desires of real estate investors. Government was organized and staffed to "keep the dirt flying."[54] In 1997, however, Council Member Paul Fielding was convicted after pleading guilty to federal charges of extortion and abuse of office in connection with the rezoning of property in his district.[55] The Fielding case and the conviction of Council Member Al Lipscomb in January 2000 on sixty-five counts of extortion and bribery raised serious questions about the dependence of council members on outside income for subsistence in an era where fewer people of independent means sought election to the Council.[56]

Those concerned with development and economic growth have a strong interest in the composition of those public bodies and staff agencies that regulate development. The City Plan Commission reviews rezoning applications and subdivision plans. It may advise on master plans. Historically, it has been one of the places used to groom future Council and mayoral candidates. Composed of unpaid, part-time members nominated by the members of the Council, the City Plan Commission is the first line of public review for any important zoning or development proposal. Its recommendations can carry considerable weight with the Council because of its representative and "delegate" character. The Council can overrule its zoning recommendations only by a two-thirds vote. Consequently, one of the interests of the development industry is that Plan Commission members be, in general, favorably disposed toward growth. The best insurance for that interest is the election of development-friendly members of the Council, since each member appoints one member of the Plan Commission, and like the Council, commission members customarily defer to their colleagues on projects in their respective districts.

While the Plan Commission is passively procedural, responding to the matters brought to it by applicants, via the planning department, the public works agencies of Dallas are active production bureaucracies, which measure progress in miles and square feet of infrastructure built. They plan their own projects independently of the planning department, with which there has been little cooperation or communication, beyond that which is essential.[57] They have generally maintained a close and friendly relationship with developers. Their role is to facilitate development and to ensure that public facilities are provided to support and serve new growth.[58] In general, public works agency directors and the assistant city managers that oversee development activities have exhibited little interest in land use planning or urban design.

Pro-Growth NIMBYs

As a consequence of their insensitivity to community concerns, public works agencies and pro-development interests have occasionally incited fierce opposition to growth-serving projects from parties known as "NIMBYs" for the sentiment, "Not In My Back Yard." Reconstruction of North Central Expressway was delayed for at least a decade as alternative schemes, including one for double-decking the freeway, were rejected as aesthetic and economic disasters by adjacent property owners and residents. Voters turned down the ambitious rail plan proposed by DART in 1989, precipitating a crisis over the future of the agency. Proposals to widen streets in some areas were bitterly opposed by residents. In general, however, Dallas has harbored no significant or persistent anti-growth faction and development in the city has proceeded with broad public support and only sporadic resistance.

Working and middle class neighborhoods near Love Field organized in the early 1980s to protest noise from the airport and have remained vigilant in support of the Wright Amendment, which restricts flights from the in-town airport to service within Texas and adjoining states.[59] Neighborhood-based opposition to development projects occurred in the early 1980s in response to the speculative boom that fueled widespread efforts to increase residential densities and convert some residential land for commercial uses. Neighborhood-based organizations engaged in bitter battles with developers over projects they believed would change the basic character of this racially diverse, mixed-use uptown neighborhood. Lori Palmer, a neighborhood activist who later served on the City Council recalled: "For the first time, residential property-owners got involved. A lot of people were not interested in developing the land, just in up-zoning it and flipping it. This caused a lot of people to become outraged at what was happening. Heretofore there was nothing that would bring them downtown."[60]

Successful neighborhood opposition to major projects and the appearance of signs on telephone poles saying, "Save Oak Lawn, Shoot a Developer," led to negotiations among developers, land owners, and neighborhood advocates. They produced and the city adopted a consensus plan for a special zoning district that permitted development to continue that was in keeping with the character of the area.[61]

Across the city, neighborhood associations formed to oppose the excesses of the development frenzy financed by a deregulated savings and loan industry that was spinning out of control. The Dallas Homeowners League was formed, serving as a communications network among neighborhood activists. The neighborhood movement fought off a number of the most egregious projects, and in doing so made the city staff, elected officials, and the more stable developers sensitive to neighborhood interests, but it did not challenge the basic growth ethic of Dallas.

In Lake Highlands, in northeast Dallas, community leaders opposed high-density apartment projects, which were permissible in the "cumulative" zoning categories that had been placed on land in their area, which allowed such "less intensive" residential uses to be built in commercial zones.[62] The mobilized residents of this affluent area helped persuade the Council to adopt a new zoning ordinance in 1984 that made each category of land use exclusive to its zone.[63] Lake Highlands, however, eschewed alliances with other communities. According to Donna Halstead, who was a leader in the battle against the apartments, and later served on the DART Board, the City Council, and became, in 1998, the President of the Dallas Citizens Council: "There were alliances, but Lake Highlands was not actively involved. We never even joined the Dallas Homeowners League. We were not opposed to development; we were, in fact, in favor of it. But we were in favor of development that was sensitive to and integrated into the community so that it was an asset."[64]

Minority neighborhoods in South Dallas mobilized to oppose condemnation of homes for the expansion of Fair Park, and to demand restrictions on the number of liquor stores and billboards advertising liquor, but they were generally proponents of growth for their areas, viewing it as a source of economic opportunity. West Dallas residential neighborhoods waged a long and eventually successful campaign for the closing of a lead smelter and the cleanup of lead-contaminated soil from their community. And homeowners and other residents of the Bachman Lake area, North of Love Field devoted years to opposing adult-oriented clubs and bars in their community. In most of these cases, the overriding concern was fear of disinvestment, loss of property values, or community quality, rather than development.

In Dallas, NIMBYism is qualified. Some kinds of growth are welcomed. Some neighborhoods desperately seek growth in the form of redevelopment. Opposition is selective, and there is no effective citywide coalition of anti- or slow growth forces. All embrace the belief in the goodness of growth and the rhetoric of a world class city.

The Fourteen Little Zoning Czars

Individual neighborhoods have become critical players in the development process, however, following the charter changes that required all council members to be elected from single member districts. Neighborhood assent is crucial to any rezoning or development project that requires City Council approval. Local community opposition generally translates to opposition by the member of the Council who represents that neighborhood, and only in the rarest circumstances will a majority of the Council vote to override the wishes of the member from the directly affected district.[65]

In 1993, for example, the Council followed the lead of the member from a North Dallas district and overrode the advice of planning staff, the Plan Commission, and the City Attorney to refuse development permission to Cinemark Theaters to construct a 21-screen "Tinseltown." The property was zoned for commercial use and had contained a large discount retail chain store. The proposal met all the requirements of the zone. The developer had been encouraged by Mayor Steve Bartlett to build the theater, but as neighborhood opposition to the congestion, noise, and attraction to young people grew, the district council member opposed it, and the Mayor, who lived in the district, changed his position as well. After denial of its site plan, Cinemark sued the City for illegally denying its permit, ultimately settling the case for $5 million.

For all practical purposes, since the creation of single-member districts, Dallas has "14 little zoning czars."[66] There is almost no inquiry by the Council as a whole once it knows the wishes of the member in whose district the case arises. In a governance system that relies on private initiative, has a passive system of planning and project review, and a Plan Commission populated by council surrogates and without strong staff support, development projects can often be reduced to transactions between a developer and neighborhood groups. If the development occurs where there is no organized local group, it involves the developer and the district council member.

Summary

The Dallas civic culture's value of a privately held public interest is most clearly evident in the development function. The ambition to grow the city to "world class" scale and quality is widespread throughout the city. Private developers and their affiliates in finance, law, architecture, sales and other fields, are expected to be entrepreneurial and innovative and take the leadership in projects that would help the city achieve its ambitions. Government is expected to place no roadblocks in their path and to provide facilities and services as needed. It also serves as a cheerleader for major projects and offers subsidies for others. Neighborhood groups might oppose the location or scale of specific projects, but unlike those in some cities, they rarely question the basic value of growth. The result has been a policy system that is ad hoc and responsive to individual projects, but with little overall direction. Where the private sector leads, Dallas follows.

8

Making Development Policy the Dallas Way

> We are going to make Dallas a worldclass competitor in every way.
>
> DALLAS MAYOR ANNETTE STRAUSS

Introduction

The most striking difference between the development policy arena in Dallas and those for schools or policing is the continuing deep involvement of business interests. This is to be expected because of the direct stakes business leaders have in development, while public services only indirectly affect those interests. The way in which business interests engaged in development policy changed, however, in the twilight years of the business oligarchy.

The prime movers of the entrepreneurial regime had deep roots in the city, and it was the primary locus of their property and business activity. They controlled both its informal governance and its formal government. The most significant entrepreneurs, corporate executives, and investors of the new Dallas operate on a grander scale but with shallower interests in the city. They often control or have access to world-wide assets of greater value than the tax base of the city. They may be headquartered in the suburbs, other cities, and even other countries. Whether their residences and offices are based in the city or not, they are independent of it.

The last two decades of the twentieth century experienced increasing separation of tenancy and ownership of major properties in the commercial districts of Dallas. Shopping malls, which replaced the central business district for comparison shopping, are usually owned by an absentee real estate development company and operated by a management firm, which leases space to "anchor" tenants—national or regional department stores—and specialty stores. This system is a sharp contrast with the old Dallas downtown, where hometown department stores owned their buildings, and so did many of the smaller specialty merchants. In the restructuring of the banking industry banks became tenants in buildings they once owned. Even the venerable Trammell Crow development firm sold many of its properties and remade itself into a property management firm. All this changed the nature of the stakes of these major financial and business institutions in the city.[1] First, the initiative in development policy shifted from the tight circle of hands-on "yes and no" business executives of the Thornton era to the professional executives of the peak economic organizations—the private sector's managerial regents. These include the presidents of the Dallas Citizens Council, the Greater Dallas Chamber of Commerce, the Central Dallas Association, and the North Texas Commission. This closely allied network of association executives guides their boards of virtual leaders—well meaning but busy CEOs of national and global firms—carefully deferring to them in public utterances, and matching policy initiatives with CEO "champions," who can channel the limited time they have for civic work into those activities.[2] The association executives remain dependent upon the CEOs on their boards for their legitimacy, but within the tolerances of their boards and attention span of their chairs, they exercise wide discretion in fashioning and pursing development initiatives.[3] Thus, operating within the halo effect of the civic culture, they gradually displaced the old grandees of the entrepreneurial regime as the true development policy entrepreneurs of Dallas. The Dallas business executives committed to the city are few,[4] and of those that devote their time and resources to restoring the city's economic vitality through development projects, none has been willing to serve on the City Council or the School Board, in contrast with those of the earlier era.

Old customs are hard to change. With a tradition of aversion to public management of growth, Dallas naturally looked to the corporate sector for leadership in response to the problems of growth and decline. This bias was institutionalized in the privatization of city planning, third party management of complex development situations, ad hoc and reactive administration of development policies, and a decision-making process that relied more on consensus and symbolism than analysis. In recent years, however, the city government and city officials have played a more active, if ad hoc and idiosyncratic, role in development issues.

Privatization of Public Planning

Dallas's economic elite denigrated governmental planning but took pride in their strategic vision. The Texas Centennial was the lodestone of the pre-war generation. The modern prototype was Erik Jonsson's "Goals for Dallas." Institutionalized in an independent nonprofit organization, Goals for Dallas operated for almost two decades, through three planning cycles. Never absorbed into the city government, in 1991 it was collapsed into the Greater Dallas Chamber of Commerce and subsequently extinguished. Corporate funders, pinched by the recession, questioned the need to support several "planning" groups—the Dallas Citizens Council, the Greater Dallas Chamber of Commerce's economic development division, the North Texas Commission, and the city's Office of Economic Development.

During its life, Goals for Dallas provided a mechanism for the development of a long list of "goals," ranging in scale from neighborhood to region. Its business backing gave legitimacy to large-scale projects such as the international airport, expressway construction, and rapid transit. All were seen as boons to development, either through directly inducing it, or indirectly, by promoting the image of Dallas as a progressive, world class city.

Goals for Dallas was a consensus process. Its staff, after the first cycle of loaned executives from Texas Instruments returned to their corporate posts, consisted primarily of meeting facilitators and communications specialists. There was little analytical competence. It was a public relations triumph, winning Dallas an "All American City" designation from the National Civic League in 1970, advancing a favorable national image of Dallas, and confirming, in the eyes of the regime, the city's rehabilitation from the tragedy of the Kennedy assassination. In spite of its inclusive rhetoric and community outreach through group and neighborhood-level meetings throughout the city, Goals for Dallas was not a radical departure from the "single option" approach to policy initiated by the Citizens Council in the 1930s. And the consensus goals were never allowed to interfere with more immediate opportunities for development.[5]

Since the demise of Goals for Dallas, two other strategic exercises were conducted by business leaders. The Dallas Citizens Council established a strategic planning committee in 1989. Chaired by Jerry Junkins, the CEO of Texas Instruments (TI), and assisted by some retired TI executives who had assisted Jonsson in the original Goals for Dallas effort, the committee produced a strategic agenda for the Citizens Council to guide its activities.[6] The document was unique in that it contained analytical information about each of the issues it presented and placed the highest priority on education, job creation, and "governmental affairs,"[7] rather than public works. It was supposed to serve as a guide for the Citizens Council in using its influence and slack resources and as an educational reference for a new generation of corporate executives, rather than a decision tool for the city.

The business executives found, however, that achievement of the ambitious goals outlined in their strategic plan was more difficult to achieve than they had supposed. A 1994 review of the progress of the nine strategic priorities in the plan found that the Citizen Council's efforts had produced little change. One reason, the review suggested, was "the increasing complexity of issues. It is more and more difficult to make informed judgments regarding public policy."[8] Even in areas of traditional interest, such as the revitalization of the Central Business District, the Central Dallas Association had seized the initiative, leaving the Citizens Council in a supporting role.

Different aspects of the strategic plan took on lives of their own, led by executives who made them their personal causes. The Dallas Together Forum, co-chaired by William Solomon and Pettis Norman, set goals and monitored the hiring of minorities and women as employees, executives and board members for major Dallas-area corporations. Jerry Junkins' efforts in education reform, discussed in Chapter 5, were not carried on by others after his unexpected death in 1996. The major effect of the Citizens Council's influence was to stimulate new interest in improvement of the city's infrastructure as a means of attracting new growth.

Within a few months after the closing down Goals for Dallas, the chair of the Citizens Council's Committee on Public Planning Policy, Robert Decherd, CEO of the Belo Corporation, the parent company of the *Dallas Morning News,* persuaded Mayor Steve Bartlett to support production of a long range *Dallas Plan* for infrastructure. This plan, like Goals for Dallas, would be produced by an independent nonprofit organization headed by a prominent local businessman and funded by businesses and foundations. It would work for the city at no cost. The city would provide office space, but the Dallas Plan would not be part of city government. A professional staff director would be employed, as had been the case with Goals for Dallas, and business firms would loan staff specialists to undertake key responsibilities.

The City Council approved the process and agreed to act on recommendations made by the Dallas Plan. Robert Hoffman, CEO of the regional Coca-Cola Bottling Company was named to head the project. The Dallas Citizens Council recruited a nationally known planner, Richard Anderson, the former president of the Regional Plan Association of New York, as executive director. Decherd raised $400,000 from corporations and foundations to fund the first eighteen months of work on a comprehensive plan for improving the public facilities and communities of Dallas. Anderson and his staff, most of them loaned by DCC member corporations, explored the city's backlog of infrastructure projects, financing mechanisms, and key assets—facilities, areas, and undeveloped opportunities. Initially, they formulated three possible scenarios to guide the city's future: well-managed city (implicitly in decline); regional partners (sharing growth with the suburbs), and the city as investor in its future.

The Council, with relatively little discussion, selected the ambitious "city as investor" strategy, preferred by the Dallas Plan's sponsors and staff. This approach proposed using city capital investments to leverage funding from other sources—primarily the State and federal governments—to produce a backlog of neighborhood level improvements; protect core assets of the city; and undertake development initiatives in the CBD, southern Dallas, and the Trinity River Corridor. The task now became one of translating this broad concept into a plan with sufficient specificity to guide future Council decisions on bond issues and capital budgets.

In the fall of 1993, the staff prepared a "draft framework" Dallas Plan, which was published by the *Dallas Morning News* as a Sunday supplement.[9] This document was then discussed at an extensive set of neighborhood meetings set up by the staff. The broad strategic concepts of the draft were generally supported by participants in the meetings, which ranged in attendance from as many as seventy to fewer than half a dozen. Citizens participating in the meetings mainly wanted to know how the plan might deal with their complaints about unfulfilled promises made during prior bond elections. "They liked it, but wanted to know: 'what's in it for me?' " Anderson reported.[10] There seemed no way to reach a consensus with so many particular projects being proposed. "Everybody misunderstood the process. Everybody took the [draft] as the plan," Hoffman said.[11]

With no clear method of ranking requests, the planning process was turning into a laundry list. Reassessing their position, Hoffman and Anderson executed a "90 degree shift" in the thrust of the Dallas Plan. Instead of a thirty-year blueprint for infrastructure investments—their original charge—they converted the plan to a statement of "principles, goals, and objectives. . . . It seemed to be a breakthrough, and public opinion changed."[12] They now explained that the Dallas Plan was a new way of public sector thinking and behavior with regard to long-range planning, rather than another planning document destined to gather dust on city hall shelves. If the city could see itself in the context of the region and as using its capital expenditures to influence and guide the much larger investments of federal and state agencies, the recommendations for downtown or the Trinity River Corridor would be more readily understood and gain broad support. The Dallas Plan, in Hoffman's view, became a guide to a new active role for local government.

Its authors transformed the Dallas Plan into an agreement in principle, a "plan for planning," rather than a set of public policies of sufficient clarity that a reasonable person could tell if they were followed. Specific recommendations were avoided. For example, in discussing its recommendations for enhancing the city's core assets,[13] the Dallas Plan proposed six "policies":

1. Continue and enhance long-range planning to ensure that core assets will have the capacity to serve the community over time.

2. Use asset-specific task forces to define short and long-term programs for those core assets meeting the community's cultural and recreational needs.
3. Give the needs of existing core assets high priority when allocating city capital funds.
4. Invest city funding of core assets in projects that will most effectively leverage private and intergovernmental investments.
5. Create partnerships with other governmental jurisdictions, facility operators, and community organizations, where appropriate, to preserve and enhance these core assets.
6. Create physical and operational linkages between core assets and other key areas of the city.[14]

The recommendations for the library system, the first of the listed core assets, were not much more specific. The text of the plan laid out the costs of some proposed improvements, such as facility upgrades and a new automated information system, but left to the city government the task of deciding which projects to place in capital budgets and bond issues: "For planning through the year 2025, The Dallas Plan recommends that the Dallas Library consider strategies to provide convenient service locations. One possible method is to consider satellite facilities . . . . The Dallas Plan also recommends an on-going process of replacing and repairing branch facilities as they reach approximately 30 years of age."[15]

Some recommendations for action, either immediately or in a five-year period, were more specific. An important proposal was for the city to establish an economic development corporation. With powers to issue revenue bonds, assemble land, and work with public and private entities to bring projects to fruition, it would be the primary vehicle for carrying out a proposed comprehensive economic development plan for the city. When it was first suggested by Robert Hoffman in 1994, the proposal was greeted with expressions of strong support by the city manager and Council.[16] But it was never created.

The Dallas Plan had nothing to say about the importance or location of a new sports arena for the professional basketball and hockey teams, an issue that dominated public discussion of capital investments by the city from 1996 to 1998. Its comments on the other major public investment in the ensuing five years—the Trinity River Corridor—were sufficiently broad to cover almost any action the city might decide to take. The Dallas Plan subsequently endorsed both projects and the bond issues to support them as consistent with its strategies.

Changing the Dallas Plan from a thirty-year capital investment plan to a "plan for a plan" or a "way of thinking and acting" on capital investments made consensus possible. The plan was presented in December 1994 for Council adoption, which was accomplished with no debate and much praise for it as a transformative innovation. Anderson had left the project in the early fall, while the document was being redrafted. He returned to New York to become the executive officer of a professional association. Karen Walz, a planning consultant with experience in several cities, replaced him, and undertook a new round of neighborhood hearings to design a work program for implementation of the first year of the Plan. Its "25 for 95" proposal identified high priority projects to be funded by a 1995 municipal bond issue, designed primarily to address the city's construction backlog.

The corporate sponsors of the Dallas Plan pronounced it a success and committed funds to support it as a nonprofit corporation for an additional three years. Its self-perpetuating board was expanded from its three original members to seven, with two seats—the chair and vice-chair—reserved for the donors. The board selected other members from a variety of community organizations. Walz and her small staff managed a series of community meetings to gather new proposals and occasionally proposed strategic initiatives to the city government.[17] Beginning in 1995, they began to sponsor annual neighborhood fairs, at which neighborhood associations could display their successes and learn from each other through seminars and exhibits. They also assembled "partners" to work on various projects that were suggested by the Dallas Plan.

Taking its cue from the *Morning News* and Decherd, the business community peak organizations endorsed the Dallas Plan, the credibility of which was enhanced because it was not produced by the city government.[18] The neighborhoods that had been consulted to broaden the base of legitimacy for the plan also supported it. Sharing the civic culture's deep distrust of government, they accepted the idea that a plan advanced by business leaders was more likely to be carried out than one initiated by city officials. At the same time the civic myth of business power encouraged community residents who participated in the process to press for attention to their particular interests.

Placing priorities on proposals and projects was, however, beyond the reach of a plan for planning. The leadership of the Dallas Plan, with the concurrence of the city manager, chose not to undertake a thorough analysis of how changes in the demography and economic functions of the city might affect its infrastructure needs. In the absence of clear central themes, they were unable to sort conflicting demands into a coherent set of policies to guide choices of specific projects or to stage their construction over time. The superficial engagement of the City Council provided little guidance for a capital agenda and left the private planners with a dilemma. If they presented a plan containing choices that were certain to excite controversy, it quite likely would not be adopted. Thus, they reverted to a level of generality that ensured no dissent and could be used to justify virtually any project that did not violate the broad principles of the plan.

Goals for Dallas and The Dallas Plan are not remarkable in themselves. Many large cities have privately funded planning "associations," which prepare analyses and make recommendations on development and infrastructure policy. It is unusual, however, for a modern city to cede its *basic* long-range planning function to a private organization. The metamorphosis of the Dallas Plan from its original conception as an examination and prioritization of the city's infrastructure needs for a thirty-year period, to a general approach to thinking strategically about those needs was true to Dallas civic culture. It resisted entrusting the city government with the authority or responsibility of charting the city's future. It maintained the "outside-in" approach to development policy. It retained control of decisions in a small, trustworthy group, which kept development issues at levels of generality sufficient to ensure consensus, then incrementally shaped support for specific projects. It played at empowerment, but lived by endorsement, for it was the blessings of its corporate sponsors and the acquiescence of the neighborhoods that give it legitimacy. What was different was that, unlike in the days of the entrepreneurial regime, it needed both business and neighborhood endorsement to make it acceptable to a City Council with no capacity of its own for policy analysis to aid it in making a considered independent judgment.

Third Party Management of Complex Development Problems

Goals for Dallas and the Dallas Plan laid out broad, long-term goals for the city's development. Both addressed the two most complex development issues of Dallas: strengthening the central business district in the face of the centrifugal forces of regional growth, and reversing the racial isolation and economic decline of southern Dallas. Neither made specific policy proposals for resolving these problems. Both cases had already been entrusted to extra-governmental organizations.

The Central Business District

It is difficult to overstate the importance of the central business district (CBD) to the City. It contains a sixth of its property tax base. Beyond the fiscal effect of a serious decline in value of CBD real estate on tax and bond interest rates, physical deterioration of the CBD is almost certain to increase the cost of municipal services such as public safety and maintenance. Decline of the CBD tends to be more salient politically than decline in other areas because of its disproportionate share of the tax base, its public symbolism, and the economic power and political influence of its property owners and tenants.

Concern for the value of their downtown investments and businesses led the major property owners and employers in the CBD to create the Central Dallas Association (CDA) in the early 1980s to manage downtown revitalization.[19] The CDA is a private nonprofit organization of stakeholders who provide its core funding from annual dues based on the value of their properties or the size of their payrolls. In addition, it receives funds from management fees for activities it conducts and for the sale of products, such as maps, reports, parking/toll tags, and transit passes.[20]

In its capacity as an advocacy and public affairs organization, the CDA provides information about the CBD to prospective tenants and developers, promotes events in the city center, and works with public agencies and private owners to enhance services and facilities. In 1985, Larry Fonts moved to Dallas from Atlanta to serve as the CDA's full time president and executive officer. He worked with the board to develop a strategic plan, which focused on physical and functional measures designed to revitalize downtown and adjacent neighborhoods located outside the freeway ring enclosing the CBD. Key elements of the plan included in-town housing, passive and active amenities, public safety, transportation, and marketing of the central area.[21]

In 1993, the CDA persuaded the City Council to create the Downtown Improvement District (DID), in effect, "an awesome privately held government,"[22] financed by a special assessment on real property in the central business district. Revenue from the assessment supports enriched services, maintenance, and capital improvements,[23] including construction of vest pocket parks and plazas; street-scape improvements such as paving, banners, murals, and lighting; and special downtown events.

By far the largest expenditure from the special assessment—42 percent of the total budget—was devoted to measures designed to increase the reality and perception of safety in the business district. When city services were cut back in the recession of the late 1980s, crime rates in the CBD soared. Only two patrol cars were assigned to the area. Borrowing an idea from other cities, Fonts persuaded the police department to experiment with bicycle patrols, initially using three bikes and other equipment donated by CDA members.[24] The patrols were so successful[25] they were expanded within three months to nine officers, and by 1997, the bike patrol had expanded to thirty of the seventy-five officers assigned to the downtown area, including a small horse-mounted contingent. The CDA/DID purchases the bicycles and personal equipment, and pays for the extra hours of police presence. It also convenes private security directors, conducts public safety programs for businesses, and supports an "ambassadors" program, consisting of twenty-three employees who work the streets as additional eyes and ears for the police and provide assistance and information to pedestrians.[26]

Better policing was seen as essential for further development of downtown Dallas because the sense of insecurity discouraged businesses and their customers. A closely related problem was the concentration of homeless people and panhandlers on the streets. CDA worked with the city to develop, enforce, and defend in court an ordinance that prevented living on the streets and panhandling in the central business district.[27]

Over time, CDA developed a reputation for producing results, leading to increased reliance on it to solve problems in the Improvement District. Fonts described a call from Mayor Steve Bartlett, who said he had complained for several months to city staff about the unsightly amounts of loose trash he noticed near the downtown McDonald's restaurant. Bartlett wondered if CDA could do anything about it. By noon, Fonts was able to report to the mayor that his staff had acquired half the needed trash cans from Dallas Area Rapid Transit (DART), had them in place at the intersection, and had commitments to place the others by the following day. Focus on the area, the ability to work across departments and jurisdictions, and the involvement of the private sector and non-local agencies are keys to CDA's success.

The improvements in safety and amenities were important in changing the "feel" of the business district. They were clearly necessary in the short run to renew confidence that downtown was a good place to work and invest. By themselves, however, they were insufficient to fill vacant buildings and rekindle investor interest. This required public investments in infrastructure and the creation of financial incentives for the reuse of buildings that had become obsolete for their original uses as department stores and offices.

The most important long-term infrastructure decision influenced by the CDA was the agreement by property owners and DART on a surface alignment for the light rail line in the central business district, and the location of transportation transfer centers on the east and west sides of the CBD. In the words of a particpant:

> It was hard, tough negotiating . . . Talk about politics in City Hall, this was politics in the business community; who got the stations, who wanted them, who didn't. How do you play this? Is it going down Main, Commerce? . . It ended up on Pacific and Bryan in the line of best fit. We got an aberration behind the Plaza of the Americas, but there's a political reason for that: it's a future station for the Arts District back there; it's as close as you can get to the Trammell Crow ranch. It's a future station with a dogleg in the line.[28]

The transfer terminals on the east and west sides of downtown where commuters could change from buses to rail in safe and pleasant surroundings were initially opposed by DART. CDA had to "force feed" them. The key to gaining support was changing the position of J. B. Jackson, a black community leader who was on the DART board. Jackson had initially opposed the stations, fearing that they were an effort by businesses to prevent poor people from congregating at transit stops in front of their establishments. CDA persuaded him that they were instead designed to facilitate convenient transfers by patrons who had to use two modes of public transportation to go to and from work, and to give transit riders a pleasant place to wait out of the weather. By the time local support had materialized, the federal transportation appropriations bill with funds for such projects had already been enacted, so CDA asked U.S. Senator Lloyd Bentsen to insert the $13.7 million for the project in the budget reconciliation bill. Even then, DART reluctantly agreed to the transfer stations, as it had wanted all buses routed on Elm, Commerce, and Main, the three principal east-west traffic arteries in the CBD. Once the transfer terminals were built, however, transit patrons responded favorably to the safe, secure, out-of-the-weather stations.

CDA placed major emphasis on the reuse of older office and warehouse buildings in and near downtown for residential apartments. It spearheaded efforts to use various forms of creative financing to encourage developers to convert some of the beautiful but outdated buildings in downtown Dallas to new uses. With the help of key board members such as land use attorney Susan Mead, the CDA worked closely with the city's director of economic development to use federal loans, guarantees by the city, tax abatements, historic preservation tax credits, and purchase-lease-back arrangements to finance conversions. Approximately 10,000 new in-town housing units were constructed in the CBD and environs between 1990 and

1998. The average annual income of the new, mostly young households was $70,000.[29]

The housing brought a new constituency to the CBD, with a substantial stake in its improvement. The stakes increased in 1996 when the city designated the CBD as a Tax Increment Financing (TIF) District. This was expected to raise the tax base by $333 million and generate $140 million in revenue over 15 years for improvements in infrastructure in support of private development.[30] The CBD's new residents, however, may have had quite different priorities than the CDA Board for the use of resources available to the "real government of downtown," but no way of expressing their interests through the private government of their community. In anticipation of a divergence of interests between residents and businesses, CDA devoted additional resources to communications and amenities targeted to serve the new residents, but had no plans to represent them on its board or that of its clone, the Downtown Improvement District.[31]

The Central Dallas Association illustrates strengths and limitations of using a third party organization to stimulate and manage urban development. Founded as an advocacy organization, CDA evolved into a private government for the central business district. Although the tax levy imposed through the Downtown Improvement District must be approved by the City Council, CDA has wide latitude in deciding how to spend the revenues generated by it. In addition, it collects other revenues through dues and sales, solicits contributions from members and other donors, and applies them to its projects. Its ability to function as a contractor, selling some services to the city and buying others from it gives it great flexibility and the ability to seize opportunities and mobilize private resources.

As a membership organization, CDA engaged its members in understanding and devising practical approaches to solving or minimizing the problems of the central business district. Formulation of proposals and management of improvements through the CDA gave them greater legitimacy among its business constituents than if the same measures had been devised by the city government. Having prominent business or professional leaders serve as "champions" of a cause or program, such as downtown housing, better policing, or improvements to Main Street deepened the level of informed commitment and increased the credibility of actions in a city used to accepting business leadership.

At the same time, CDA was an interest group representing property holders and business tenants. This gave it substantial influence in shaping city decisions that affected the business district, including policies that gave a private association direct control over public revenues. Fonts recognized the potential problem his organization's dual role created, commenting: "I try real hard to keep us focused on the public interest." For a leader of a hybrid organization—pressure group, self-help organization, and self-perpetuating private government for development of the city's most valuable and vulnerable real estate—that was not always a simple matter. Free of most constraints placed on government agencies, CDA drew its strength and legitimacy from its membership and access to both private and public resources. The organization's narrow constituent base and focus, and its ability to move swiftly to strike deals in its private capacity, however, could also occasionally lead it, with the best of intentions, into problematic ventures. It then had to use these strengths to extricate itself and mitigate the damage.

A prime example was the Downtown Education Center. This project was entangled in the effort to find appropriate new uses for a multi-story building at the eastern end of downtown, which had housed one of the city's most important Main Street department stores. After it was acquired by a national chain, the old store was closed and the entire building left vacant, a silent rebuke to those who sought to arrest the decline of downtown Dallas.

After the building had been on the market for seven years without a buyer, Rick Douglas, the President of the Greater

Dallas Chamber of Commerce, approached Federated's management, suggesting that they give the building to a nonprofit subsidiary of the CDA for use as a downtown education center.[32] The upper floors were suitable for conversion into apartments with the use of various tax, guaranteed loan, and other incentives. But the residential uses needed the foundation of an institutional user to fill the seven lower floors that had housed the store, and to secure the bank loans necessary for the conversion to educational uses.

Without serious examination of demand or careful consultation with the local universities, Chamber and CDA leaders announced the opening of the Downtown Education Center (DEC). The public universities of the area, along with El Centro, the downtown branch of the Dallas County Community College, were expected to provide courses for students drawn from the CBD and nearby neighborhoods. The universities would each contribute to the cost of administration of the Center by the Alliance for Higher Education (AHE), an organization that had been established by the universities to manage a telecommunications system for distribution of televised courses.

The AHE managers had only tangential familiarity with the several universities' degree programs, administrative systems, and academic schedules. Their inept administration and marketing was compounded by the university presidents' reluctance to make commitments to a project in which they lacked confidence. The result was low enrollments during the first five years of the Center's existence. Administrators at the area's major public universities—the University of Texas Arlington and the University of Texas Dallas—regarded the DEC as a needless drain on scarce resources.[33] It tended to reduce on-campus enrollment at best, and at worst resulted in canceled classes and confusion. Alternative off-campus opportunities seemed more productive, but none of the local university presidents felt they could afford to alienate the prominent business champions of the project. Thus, they made token commitments of cash and courses, keeping the Center barely alive. After six years, it had attracted only a thousand enrollments a year. More classes were canceled than offered.

The low enrollment, inept management, and tepid interest of the universities raised the prospects of the Center's failure, marring the outstanding success of the apartment conversions on the upper floors, which were completely rented by 1997. The project had to be salvaged. Tom Dunning, a businessman with good connections in Austin and with the local universities was enlisted as the DEC's champion. Business leaders used their influence to obtain expressions of interest from the Texas A&M System's administration, which spurred the University of Texas System to pledge its devotion to the maintenance of the DEC. The University of North Texas and Texas Women's University, both in Denton, and Texas A&M at Commerce had interest in offering courses at DEC, which gave them a presence in the city. Unlike the UT system schools, these institutions did not see enrollment at the downtown center as a zero sum game, as they were located too far from Dallas for the DEC to compete with their home campuses. The business executives then used their contacts in Austin to secure special status for the Center from the Texas Higher Education Coordinating Board, permitting it to offer five off-campus degrees composed of combinations of courses offered by the participating universities.[34]

None of the local university presidents who regarded the venture as ill conceived and an unwise diversion of scarce resources was willing to incur the wrath of its supporters by speaking against it. Although its El Centro campus was only a few blocks away, the Dallas County Community College agreed to assume ownership of the first seven floors and to manage the Center. In return the Community College District received the property free of debt, together with a pledge of $500,000 in tax increment financing from the city, and $150,000 in cash. The note on the Center was retired with a Southwestern Bell grant of $250,000, which was matched by other donors, and agreement by the three banks that had financed the loan to write off $900,000.

The CDA had tried to provide an "educational supermarket," shifting the paradigm in higher education from individual campus control of offerings to one that allowed students to "shop" for courses at a central location. There was a superficial appeal to the contention that there was a need for an institution of higher learning in the heart of the city—world class cities supposedly had one—but there were substantial opportunity costs for the universities pressured into participating in such a force-fed consortium. Furthermore, there was a conceptual problem with a higher education venture that was essentially job training, where students were to take courses or even full degree programs from part-time faculty in a facility without a library or on-site laboratories. It proved more difficult than had been imagined to transform a real estate deal into an institution of higher learning.

Instead of a new approach to higher education, CDA found itself with a financial tar baby that proved hard and expensive to shake off. If it was naive about the problems of higher education, it was skilled in using political influence to secure Coordinating Board approval for a problematic academic enterprise, acceptance of the facility by the community college, and city acquiescence in using TIF funds to subsidize the transfer. It also was able to mobilize the slack financial resources of its members to extricate itself from its difficulties. Finally, the DEC illustrates the penchant of Dallas business leaders to act without prior analysis, to present and pursue a single option, and to paper over the mistake with cash—most of it other people's.

Southern Dallas

Roughly half of the area and 45 percent of the population of Dallas lies south of Interstate 30 and the Trinity River. The same area, however, contains only 17 percent of the city's business firms and 13 percent of the property tax base. Southern Dallas includes most of the city's African-American and Hispanic households, well maintained middle and working class communities, stable racially mixed neighborhoods, and the city's highest concentration of public housing (the West Dallas project) and all the high-poverty census tracts. It is dotted with small business districts and contains the Red Bird regional mall and general aviation airport. Two of the "core assets" of the city, Fair Park and the Dallas Zoo, are in southern Dallas, as well as two important hospitals—Veterans Administration and St. Paul Methodist.

Almost all of the undeveloped land in Dallas is south of the Trinity River. The area is inadequately served by grocery stores, pharmacies, branch banks, retailers, and consumer services. Unemployment has been chronically high in the southern sector, which contains the largest concentration of unskilled and low-skilled workers and the lowest levels of education in the region. Residents and business owners have regularly complained of neglect of their communities by the city, in contrast to the substantial investments in infrastructure to support development in northern Dallas.[35]

Long-festering resentments of people living in southern Dallas include failure of the city to extend the Trinity River levee system to protect low-lying black and poor neighborhoods, ineffective code enforcement against landlords of derelict properties, inadequate refuse collection, and general neglect of opportunities for economic growth. As southern Dallas gained representatives in the transition to single-member Council districts, the political demands for attention to the southern half of the city grew more insistent.

In response to these mounting concerns, City Manager Richard Knight in 1989 urged the City Council to create the Southern Dallas Development Corporation (SDDC), a nonprofit community development corporation, to foster business development in the area.[36] Jim Reid, an assistant city manager, moved from city government to become president of the new organization. It was "seeded" by a contract with the city government and charged with the task of using its initial capitalization of $5,000,000 in Community Development Block Grant funds to stimulate investment in small businesses and job creation in southern Dallas.[37] SDDC used these funds to leverage private and other government loan programs that were available to small businesses, and offered technical assistance to businesses to help them qualify for loans.

Reid and his small staff of experienced financial "deal makers" worked aggressively to expand and diversify SDDC's sources of funding. He used public resources and powers to secure private collaboration in specific development projects. He used the Community Reinvestment Act as leverage on lending institutions to increase their activity in southern Dallas, and to help him create a Southern Dallas Development Fund in 1992. Nineteen Dallas financial institutions committed $3.7 million for loans over a four-year period in an area of the city that had once been redlined. In the same year, Reid organized the Dallas Business Finance Corporation, which SDDC managed, to take advantage of the U.S. Small Business Administration's Section 504 loan program. SDDC was certified under a national Small Business Administration competition as a micro-lender, and received a $2 million grant from Texas Instruments, which qualified the donor for a tax credit under the federal Enterprise Communities program. By the end of 1995, SDDC had made 222 business loans.[38]

Focusing on making loans to established but undercapitalized minority firms, SDDC managed to pyramid its resources and influence, eventually generating more income from federal grant and loan programs and corporate and bank donations than from city hall.[39] By 1997, it had become substantially independent of the city government, and had become a developer itself, renovating a historic Oak Cliff office building that had been abandoned and vacant for many years. Reid estimated that SDDC would lend another $5 million during that year to leverage $7 million in loans from private investors.[40]

Total SDDC loan activity from 1989, when it was established, to May 1998 amounted to $21.8 million, which leveraged $36.3 million from other sources.[41]

Given the magnitude of the economic and physical development problems of southern Dallas, the SDDC represented a modest effort by the city. Its successes, the recovering economy, and the commitment of some key business leaders, southern Dallas Council members, and Mayor Ron Kirk, led to the establishment of a second nonprofit development corporation in 1997, the Dallas Initiative. The Initiative is governed by a board of nine members with equal representation from the political, business, and civic sectors. It was capitalized by loans from the city. Its mission was to act as a developer of city-owned land at Red Bird Airport in Southwest Dallas, and to plan and promote development on other vacant or underused privately owned sites.[42] Once market and potential users were identified for a dormant tract of land, the Dallas Initiative approached the owner and offered a joint venture proposition: using the city loan the Initiative would put in the infrastructure and market the parcel in return for half interest in the land. It then would use its interest in the land as collateral for a development loan, and as parcels are sold, the Initiative repays its loans, retaining any excess income to fund further activity.[43]

While the Dallas Initiative is another "private-public partnership" designed to stimulate development in southern Dallas, a variety of other private nonprofit and for-profit projects were launched in the late 1990s, marking an important though not yet dramatic change in investor attitudes toward this long-neglected part of town. McDonald Williams, chairman of the Trammell Crow Company and former chairman of the Dallas Citizens Council, created a foundation in 1997 to work with citizens in South Dallas-Fair Park to revitalize their community, one of the most distressed in the city. Williams commissioned a consultant study of business opportunities in the southern sector, which found extensive business opportunities and a suitable and well-motivated labor force. In April 1998, nine financial institutions signed a covenant with the city to provide $1.5 billion over a five-year period for home mortgages, business, and consumer loans in southern Dallas.[44]

By the end of the 1990s, two local grocery chains, Minyard's and Tom Thumb, opened or planned several new stores in southern Dallas. Several banks opened branches in areas where once only pawnshops, liquor stores, and check cashing storefronts had served neighborhood financial needs. The *Dallas Morning News,* Trammell Crow Company, and Frito-Lay announced plans for new facilities south of I-30. And Tom Hicks, owner of the Dallas Stars Hockey team, the Texas Rangers baseball franchise, and Chancellor Communications, announced that he was establishing a for-profit corporation to invest in business opportunities in the inner city. John Ware resigned as city manager to head this new venture capital firm.

After years of talk, there were signs of unsubsidized private investment. The question was whether it was too little to reverse the spiral of neglect, decline and disinvestment that had characterized the inner city neighborhoods of southern Dallas for over forty years. The level of commitment and activity, at long last, seemed more than token. Some private investors such as Williams, Hicks, and the banks (with the carrot of a secondary mortgage market at Fannie Mae and the stick of the Community Reinvestment Act) seemed convinced that there were unrealized opportunities for profitable investments south of the Trinity. The city, however, had not committed many of its own resources, either in direct subsidies to development, tax abatements, or tax increment financing to southern Dallas.[45] The use of nonprofit corporations such as the Southern Dallas Development Corporation and the Dallas Initiative offered low risk "partnerships" that provided an opportunity for small-scale experiments in economic development for distressed areas.

After the advent of single-member districts, the city increased some services in the area—particularly police protection—and used federal programs, such as Enterprise Communities, to supplement the community policing, small loan, and job training programs[46] of other agencies, including SDDC. The 1998 bond referendum allocated roughly half of all local infrastructure improvements to projects in the seven Council districts located predominantly in the southern sector.[47] In addition, much of the bond proceeds from the Trinity River Corridor project were to be spent in southern Dallas, including extending the levees to protect low-lying areas from periodic flooding. The project was expected to provide construction jobs for some residents of the area, and enhance outdoor recreation opportunities.

Institutional Aversion to Analysis

Lacking official public plans to guide development decisions, the government of Dallas responded to private initiatives as they arose, generally facilitating and accommodating growth. Only in a few instances, and at rare intervals, has the city attempted to rein in runaway development or manage growth. As a consequence of its relaxed attitude toward planning, the pattern of development has been one of low-density projects, by-passed parcels, dispersed activity centers and commercial clutter. Functionally related uses, such as convention, entertainment and dining districts, arts centers, and public markets are widely separated. Until quite recently, little attention was paid to public spaces and amenities.[48] The quality of uptown business or industrial centers has depended almost entirely on private covenants or associations. While some development is of very high quality, it suffers from poor articulation with neighboring uses. And, while weak planning alone certainly cannot account for it, new physical and economic development has been concentrated for the past thirty or more years north of the Trinity and I-30. In addition to a cultural predilection for letting the market take its course, several institutional features of Dallas governance contribute to this fragmented, ad hoc, and reactive approach to development.

Dallas's economic elite and elected officials have historically had an almost pathological aversion to any analysis that might challenge or delay private development proposals and thus diminish its reputation as one of the nation's most business-friendly cities. The best way to avoid such analyses is to avoid building the capacity for producing them in the city government and to discourage independent organizations from conducting studies or publishing such information. This attitude is congenial to the development industry, which retains the initiative in advancing projects and a near monopoly on technical information that may be used to evaluate the claims made for them with regard to their impact on the city's economy and fiscal condition. The business leadership's approach to decision-making was characterized by one close to it as: "Ready . . . Shoot . . . Aim." Analysis in Dallas more frequently follows than precedes decisions, and is designed to justify rather then inform them.

Few Dallas city managers have been schooled in planning. Most have risen from backgrounds as budget analysts, operations specialists, or administrative generalists. They tend to be action-oriented and driven by Council demands and the inbox of daily management and fiscal crises, citizen complaints, and official obligations. Many share the engineer's impatience with planning, regarding it as impractical at best, and trouble at worst. In Dallas, since there are no comprehensive and functional master plans and no mid-term capital improvements program, there are no institutionalized connections between planning and the annual capital budget for facilities. Plans are disparaged as generating unrealizable expectations, bitter site-specific controversies, or both. They are almost certain to conflict with some future developer-initiated proposals. Action-oriented managers often regard them as flaccid abstractions that impose constraints on their flexibility in solving problems. They require premature choices. Planning is often regarded as a necessary evil in the modern practice of city management, but it should be kept on a short leash, tolerated for its rare public relations value, but not taken seriously except as an occasional support for the regulation of development. The "real" planning is project planning for facilities.[49]

The Council and Mayor are part-time, term-limited, and devoid of independent professional staff. The City Charter sharply restricts their discretion over the administration of city affairs. Their obligation to hear development cases *de novo* after staff review and Plan Commission recommendations often absorbs a great deal of time on the meeting agenda. This leaves little time or inclination to deliberate complex concepts and information about economic, demographic, and physical changes or ideas for long-term approaches to dealing with them. Although almost all Council members considered planning, zoning, and other development issues an important or very important part of their official responsibilities,[50] the strong tendency in all except the most notorious rezoning cases was to follow the lead of the member in whose district the case arose. This custom greatly limited their ability to play an effective role in growth policy. The prevailing attitude appeared to be that growth was good if it was unopposed in one's political backyard.[51]

Dallas enjoyed a well-deserved reputation—at least until budget cutbacks during the 1986–1994 recession—for the quality and maintenance of its public facilities.[52] The requirement that bond issues be submitted to referenda produced a "lumpy" capital improvement process, however.[53] As a matter of practical politics, it encouraged city managers to distribute projects among council districts to ensure electoral support from enough sectors of the city to secure its approval.[54]

The Dallas "triple A" bond rating from Wall Street bond rating services has talismanic status in Dallas politics.[55] Any public action that could endanger the bond rating set off alarms in the city manager's office, the daily press, and business organizations. The only city of a million to receive such a high rating, it was seen as emblematic of the prudent fiscal management for which the city received repeated recognition.[56] While the rating affected the interest rate at which municipal bonds were sold, and thus, the debt service charged to the annual operating budget and the property tax rate levied by the city, it also operated as a brake on expenditures of all sorts.

Dallas, like most cities, relied heavily upon property taxes for revenue, so even though the income of resident households and corporations increased, property values did not grow apace in a city that was substantially built out.[57] The result of this revenue bind was an effort to avoid raising tax rates on a base that actually declined during the recession, and grew more slowly than the suburbs in good economic times.[58] With a static or declining tax base and unwillingness to raise taxes, capital improvements and, particularly, maintenance of the existing stock fell short of needs. This set in motion a spiral of declining urban quality. Following conventional wisdom, the city sought new development to arrest the decline in its property tax base. To compete with its neighboring cities, it often offered developers property tax abatements for an extended period (usually fifteen years) on the theory that the multiplier effect of the development would produce other property and sales tax collections to offset the abatement. It rarely did.

The first draft of the Dallas Plan gingerly suggested that the city should worry less about its bond rating and more about the adequacy of its facilities, enduring a short term increase in bond interest rates and taxes in order to achieve a long term improvement in services and values. The proposal faded in the glare of the bond rating's evil eye, disappearing entirely by the final draft.[59]

The cultural and institutional factors discussed above understandably produced a process of decision-making on development issues that is ad hoc and disjointed. It has patterns but no theme. With weak analytical ability and no institutionalization of effective urban planning or capital programming, the governance of development in Dallas relies on consensus among developers and officials and symbolism for the rest of the attentive publics. Procedurally, this is accomplished by a "two-meeting" process. As described by former Mayor Steve Bartlett, decisions were made at the first meeting about what to do by a small circle of powerful Anglo men. At the second meeting, tri-ethnic inclusion was simulated. Selected minorities and others were invited in, the issue was discussed, and in time, the decision was revealed for the expanded group to ratify.[60] Consensus, in this form, requires restricting access to the arena in which choices are made to those who were unlikely to polarize deliberations, i.e., public spirited, "constructive" citizens who can take "a citywide" view of things. These knowledgeable citizens tend to know essentially the same things. Consensus is facilitated by the absence of information or analysis that raises fundamental challenges to the agreed upon single option, thus restricting the range of likely disagreement.

As Dallas evolved, agreements reached in this manner were increasingly seen as less than legitimate. A more inclusive process was demanded. This was achieved in exercises like Goals for Dallas and the Dallas Plan by the extensive use of public forums, workshops and hearings at which citizens, including those with unconventional views, occasionally expressed in intemperate or polarizing language, could be heard. But hearings and forums were not designed for deliberation. Little detailed analytical information was provided. Votes were rarely taken. "Consensus" from individual meetings was reported, then reprocessed centrally to produce a final document that could claim to be the product of thousands of hours of meetings with citizens throughout the city.

These documents contain broad generalities with which almost no one could disagree, and laundry lists of wishes from constituencies throughout the city. But they are devoid of policy guidance sufficiently precise for a reasonable civil servant or citizen to know if it was being followed. Recommendations are specific only for projects or measures on which there is consensus, even though little or no supporting evidence is presented. Acquiescence is achieved through symbolic rewards and vague promises of future selective benefits. The legitimacy of the decisions rests, then, on the apparent openness of the process, the opportunity of all to be heard, and the public recitation of "needs" that were unlikely to be met. Moreover, since "plans" are produced privately, they have no official status, except as they are endorsed or "accepted" by the City Council, included in a bond issue, or used as a justification for further official action.

Public Officials and Development Policy

As Dallas grew, the role of government shifted. For most of the city's history, its role was passive. Gradually it moved from accepting and accommodating development through permissive regulation and production of infrastructure and services. As the city built out and the suburbs began to compete for high value projects as well as residential subdivisions, Dallas began to market the city's business climate and location advantages. Finally, the city actively tried to induce growth by offering financial incentives such as tax credits and abatements, grants and loans, improvement and tax increment districts, and directly participating in financing special projects.

The City Manager as Entrepreneur-in-Chief

The city's *laissez faire* approach to growth produced a sprawling, polycentric metropolis. As the city's share of new development in the region diminished, stimulation of growth became a central concern of city officials. The city manager, as chief executive of the city government, was given new responsibilities for economic development and wide latitude within the broad Council "policy" mandate to do what one could to generate growth.[61] Only the manager has official authority to negotiate on behalf of the city with financial institutions and other firms, and as power gradually shifted from mayors who were part of the economic oligarchy to the managerial regents, city managers have assumed increasing importance in major development issues.

John Ware, who was manager from 1993 to 1998, described one way in which he performed his role as policy entrepreneur for economic development:

> I took it as my role to get money into the economy. And that's why I only focused on big issue projects. I chose to use housing as an example. I went and sat down with Jim Johnson, the Chairman of Fannie Mae. This was in the winter of 1994 . . . I called him up, asked could I come and see him. He didn't know who I was. I told him I was the City Manager of Dallas. I flew up to Washington to see him. He had his top team there. He asked me what I wanted. I told him, "I want to give you an opportunity to hitch your wagon to Dallas' star. I need you to come into Dallas and buy 2 billion dollars in secondary mortgages." . . . He said, "Can you all absorb 2 billion dollars? I think you can only absorb a billion," and I said, "No, I think we can absorb a billion and a half," and he said, "Let's agree on a billion and a half."
>
> So, then I had to come back to Dallas and get the bankers together and say, "Look, fellas, I cut this deal, now y'all gotta help me make it happen." They were all tellin' me how hard it was going to be. So I said, "O.K., let's not talk about housing, let's talk about loan origination fees and service continuation fees." A light came on. As long as you can show people how they can make money, they'll do anything you need done. But they won't do it for altruistic reasons. If you can show them how to make money, then they can become more benevolent, with both their time and resources. . . . Twenty-seven lending institutions agreed to form a partnership with the city to provide mortgages for housing in Dallas.[62]

As Ware's story suggests, the city manager occupies the point position in economic development. The manager is the official who negotiates grants, loans or other assistance from federal agencies. In addition to the mortgage financing deal, Ware and his predecessor, Jan Hart, negotiated the federal financing for the in-town housing program and the Neighborhood Renaissance Program. The municipal bureaucracy under the manager's control applies for and dispenses federal program funds for housing and economic development projects. The administrative staff prepared the application for the city's participation in the federal Empowerment Zones/Enterprise Communities Program. The manager has the initiative in proposing bond issues and tax increment financing districts. The manager's recommendations on applications for tax abatements or other subsidies are rarely disapproved by the Council. The manager and the top assistant managers are the city's direct liaison with the business community and federal or state agencies. While many of the most visible decisions, such as improvement districts and bond issues, must come back to the Council for specific approval, the "policy" guidance under which the management of the city operates is so broad as to extinguish any meaningful distinction between policy making and its implementation. The operational fact of life is that the city manager is the chief development policy entrepreneur of the City of Dallas.

The Changing Role of the Mayor

The Mayor, as the ceremonial head of the city government and, since 1991, the only official elected city-wide, has also become engaged in negotiations with businesses and other economic development projects. Mayor Annette Strauss spent hours with the management of Nieman-Marcus, persuading them to keep their flagship store in downtown Dallas, in spite of its lower profitability than its suburban locations.[63] In the early 1980s Mayor Robert Folsom was a key negotiator with the town of Renner, resulting in the last major annexation to the city in far north Dallas.[64] Mayor Jack Evans negotiated directly with Trammell Crow for land in the Arts District.[65] Mayor Steve Bartlett was an active participant in discussions that brought quarter final competition for the 1992 World Cup in soccer to Dallas, along with part of the sport's international staff. He also played an important role in negotiations that convinced the owner of the Minnesota Stars to bring his NHL hockey team to Dallas and share Reunion Arena with the locally-owned Dallas Mavericks NBA basketball team.

Mayors have not always been able to deliver on their promises. A majority of the Council may not agree to a mayoral deal, especially if it has not given its consent in advance to him or her playing such a role, or if serious opposition surfaces. In the current Dallas Council-Manager system, the mayor controls neither a consistent majority of the Council, nor the manager. Managers have occasionally reminded the mayor that they work for the Council, on which the mayor has only one vote. It is easier for the Council to repudiate proposals by the mayor, who has few political sanctions available to discipline wayward colleagues, than it is to reject those of a manager it selected to be chief executive and has a mandate to act in its behalf.

Before the days of the managerial regency, mayors often had dual roles as economic and political leaders, and they had, until the 1980s, compliant councils that spent only a few hours a week on their council duties. The Council often received its marching orders from City Attorney Alex Bickley, who functioned as the conduit for the wishes of the Dallas Citizens Council. Bickley would often tell the City Council what "the boys" wanted them to do.[66] Recent mayors have remained sensitive to the interests of business, but it has been far more difficult for them to discern a clear and coherent business position on many key development issues. As a consequence the mayor has become a more independent force in setting development priorities and, especially, in mobilizing the necessary public support to bring off major projects. The involvement of Mayor Ron Kirk in two 1998 bond issues—subsidizing a new sports arena and the Trinity River Corridor Project—illustrates this changing role.

In 1994, the owner of the Dallas Mavericks, Don Carter, began to complain about the inadequacy of Reunion Arena, which had been built in 1980 in a deal that made the city its owner and carrier of debt, which had not yet been fully retired. Carter argued that he needed more space for luxury boxes, and that there were also problems in the modifications that he had to make to the basketball arena to accommodate the Dallas Stars hockey franchise, which was under a separate ownership. The Stars management was also unhappy with the joint use contract, which limited their sale of advertising space in the facility and they were threatening to decamp to some other city offering a better deal.

Few knowledgeable people expected Carter to leave Dallas, even for the suburbs, but the recently arrived Stars were another matter, and Carter was rumored to be looking for a buyer that might not share his allegiance to his hometown. Coming off a serious recession, the central business district lagged the general pace of recovery and there was growing concern among downtown economic interests that loss of the sports franchises would further damage the image of Dallas as the city that worked. The *Dallas Morning News,* through its sports columnists and editorial pages, urged the city to act so as not to lose the teams, as Houston had lost its NFL Oilers to Nashville.

The Council instructed City Manager John Ware to enter into negotiations with the teams to make "the best deal that he could to keep them in Dallas." The Council agreed to take that deal—whatever it was—to the voters for a final decision.[67] Ware commissioned a study of possible alternatives to Reunion Arena and the city's sports commission conducted its own inquiry into how best to keep the teams in Dallas.

When Kirk was elected mayor, he initially recused himself from arena matters, since his law firm represented Carter, and he remained dependent upon the firm for his income because Dallas mayors received only the $50 per meeting stipend allowed all council members. When Carter sold the Mavericks to Ross Perot, Jr. in 1995, however, Kirk began to play an active part in the discussions with both teams. In the meantime, investor Tom Hicks acquired the Stars, and he and Perot entered into a separate set of discussions over the joint use of any new arena. Both entrepreneurs skillfully played on the city's fears of abandonment, maintaining that while they wanted to keep the teams downtown, they were open to all possibilities. Perot heightened Dallas's anxieties by taking suburban mayors for rides in his helicopter to look at potential sites in their municipalities.

Council members feared that if they were to propose a general obligation bond issue to assist two billionaires in financing their sports palace voters would reject it, leading the teams to quit the city. To enable it to issue less politically risky bonds, the city sought authority from the Texas Legislature to levy a special tax on hotel rooms and rental cars to finance its share of any arena deal. Mayor Kirk actively lobbied the Legislature for the bill, but the final Act was the work of an Arlington representative and it gave the neighboring suburbs the same powers as the city of Dallas, thereby keeping them in competition for the arena.

It became clear fairly early in negotiations with the city that neither franchise owner was interested in modifications to Reunion. They wanted a new "world class" facility, which they expected the city to help finance, notwithstanding the debt it still owed on the old arena. Critical issues for the negotiators were whether to demolish Reunion and where to locate the new facility. The city owned Reunion and adjacent parking, which could be used. Perot was interested in controlling the environs of the arena, however, for additional development opportunities. He envisioned it as part of a new entertainment-oriented complex. The Dallas Plan gave no guidance, as the future of the sports franchises was not an issue it had addressed and its plans were too general to provide any hint as to the best location for such a facility. No advice was sought from the City Plan Commission.

A number of sites were considered, including the West End, a dining and entertainment district in converted warehouses at the edge of the CBD, the Farmer's Market area at the northeast edge of the CBD, with access from I-30, and the Reunion site. To the surprise of almost all observers, Perot, whose Hillwood Development Corp. would develop the arena, chose the site of an abandoned power plant separated from downtown by a freeway and rail lines. Although adjacent to I-35, there was no current access, but the city did have plans to extend a downtown street into the site. Perot said he expected to develop some fifty acres of the site into a new central gathering place, a "Times Square" for Dallas, which would, when fully developed, produce new revenues for the city treasury. While the choice of the power plant brownfield was, at best, problematic for proponents of a downtown location, they swallowed and praised the decision of the owners as a wise and valuable contribution to a vibrant downtown. The architecture critic of the *Morning News* dissented:

> After many intense days and nights of negotiations, . . . the choice was narrowed to one bad site. . . . "Bad" in this context means unlikely to do anything for downtown, when doing something for downtown was a major justification for a new arena in the first place. . . . [T]he TU site is too remote and too self-contained to be an integral part of anything. . . . [I]t is a freeway site that will make it easy for fans to drive to the game, then drive home again without setting foot in downtown.[68]

The choice, however, was true to the Dallas way of deferring to the preference of the developer. It was a practice that produced a central business district that constantly leaked from its container of freeways, diffusing most of its interesting attractions to its periphery and beyond, frustrating the possibility of creating a critical mass of interest near the center of town.

The agreement Ware negotiated with the owners was complex. In return for the teams agreeing to remain in Dallas for thirty years, the city agreed to contribute $125 million, approximately half the cost of constructing the new arena, and to build a 2000-car public parking garage. The teams would contribute $105 million to construction costs. The city would become the owner of the arena, which the teams would rent at $3.4 million a year, plus an additional million for improvements. At the end of thirty years the teams had the option of purchasing it from the city for $1 million or continuing to rent for $200,000 a year. The teams retain all revenue from ticket sales, luxury boxes, concessions, and advertising, including sale of the right to name the arena.[69] The city agreed to construct the planned roadway as a boulevard through the site and to condemn land, if necessary to complete assembly of the site. Hillwood would reimburse the city for its costs, including any litigation costs, with income drawn from a tax increment financing (TIF) district. This provision amounted to paying the city with its own money, since but for the TIF district, the additional property tax revenue generated on the site would flow into the city's general fund.

Perot's construction company would earn $8.4 million for managing construction of the arena, and Hicks' company would earn $1.6 million in financial management fees. Reunion Arena would not be razed, but would not be allowed to compete with the new facility for special events.[70] The teams were given the option of managing it for the city, which they later chose to do. Perot promised to develop the rest of the site, "as market conditions allowed."[71]

The mayor and manager placed the outline of the best deal they could get before the Council in November, just days before it had to decide whether to place the bond issue to finance the city's share of the project on the ballot for a January referendum date. With the mayor arguing: "This not only gives us the opportunity to keep the Mavericks and Stars in Dallas with a wonderful new arena, but also makes an otherwise unproductive piece of land an integral part of our downtown,"[72] the Council approved the referendum, with only three votes in opposition. A completed master agreement was not available for Council review until almost a month later.

In the Dallas tradition, a letterhead committee was formed to support the arena referendum, with tri-ethnic co-chairs and a list of business, civic, and political figures including all but one of the living former mayors, and the chairs of the peak business organizations. Endorsements were dutifully produced from the Dallas Citizens Council, Central Dallas Association, Greater Dallas Chamber of Commerce, and the Dallas Plan. Mayor Kirk assumed active and visible leadership of the drive for approval, financed by a $2.5 million campaign fund, all but $400,000 of it contributed by the franchise owners' companies.[73] Kirk's mayoral campaign consultant managed the advertising effort for the referendum, with heavy use of television commercials featuring the mayor and his predecessors, as well as other Dallas notables, such as former Dallas Cowboy quarterback Roger Stauback. The "Vote Yes!" campaign outspent a loosely organized group, "It's a Bad Deal!," by 28 to 1, but eked out victory by a mere 1,600 votes in a bitterly fought media and neighborhood campaign.[74]

The mayor's leadership and vigorous advocacy were decisive. The margin of victory came from precincts in southern Dallas, where the black churches mobilized the mayor's core supporters, who voted overwhelmingly in favor of the arena, demonstrating their solidarity with the city's first black mayor. Most Anglo voters in northern Dallas voted "no."

Within a month after the arena victory, City Manager Ware proposed that the Council schedule a general obligation bond issue of $543 million—the largest in the history of the city—for May. Almost half of the total, $246 million, was for the city's portion of the Trinity River Corridor Project, which the Mayor had declared his highest priority when he assumed office in 1995. Ware argued that by extending the development period over fifteen years, no new taxes would be required to support debt service on the bond package. The other ten propositions were largely non-controversial facilities, strategically distributed among the fourteen council districts, ensuring unanimous support for the entire package. A key "citywide" addition was made to the original package submitted by Ware: a new police headquarters to replace the antiquated old municipal building where the central offices of the police department had been housed. Although no site had been selected, costs were estimated and the support of the Police Association was assured.

Once again, the mayor assumed leadership, building in projects to avoid dissent from any members of the Council or the police department, and gaining assurances that there would be no tax increase, so as to solidify business and homeowner support. This time Kirk named himself chair of the "We Love Dallas" campaign for approval of the eleven propositions. His campaign consultant again took charge of campaign advertising and organization. While opposition was less well organized than in the arena referendum, the Trinity projects came under serious attack for their lack of specificity, questionable feasibility, and debatable claims of benefits. The campaign brochure, for example, asserted:

> With absolutely no tax increase to Dallas citizens, the Trinity River Project is the key to making 21st Century Dallas a world class city . . . an 8,500-acre greenbelt bursting with new business and entertainment. . . . It will build a system of toll roads and levees, lakes and forests, trails and recreation facilities that extend from South Dallas all the way north to Royal Lane. Also, the project means millions, if not billions, in positive economic impact from future development along the Trinity River Corridor.[75]

Kirk framed the Trinity issue to appeal to two critical constituencies—southern Dallas minority voters and pro-development interests. "This is our last, great hope to invest in an asset that will change our pattern . . . of outward growth, take the Trinity off the landscape as a negative asset . . . and make it our D/FW Airport in terms of economic impact,"[76] he argued to his business constituents, who strongly endorsed the project, envisioning solutions to long-standing traffic problems and new development opportunities.

He appealed directly to black voters, citing the extension of the levee system into southern Dallas, a long-standing symbol of neglect of minority and poor neighborhoods, and arguing that most of the money for the project would be spent in southern Dallas, protecting homes and creating jobs. The week before the election he told a gathering at a prominent black church: "We should give every family in Dallas, no matter their race and no matter their economic status, the comfort of going to bed at night and knowing they have the same flood protection as everyone else."[77] Kirk gained the support of John Wiley Price, a sometime adversary, and endorsement of five major ministerial groups.[78] Radio ads were targeted to the black and Hispanic communities.[79]

The mayor gave no quarter to critics of the project, characterizing those who disrupted a council meeting to protest the Trinity bond proposition as "rag-tag environmentalists," more concerned with media exposure than the interests of minorities in the flood plain of the Trinity. "I find it offensive, I find it racist, and I find it patronizing and I won't tolerate it," he declared, before having the president of the local chapter of the NAACP ejected from the council chamber for refusing to yield the microphone when his time had expired.[80]

With substantial defections of north Dallas voters, Kirk needed all the help he could get south of I-30, and once again, his core constituency came through. While the first ten propositions carried by large majorities—some by over 80 percent of the votes cast—the Trinity River proposal won only 52 percent of the votes—a 2,500 vote margin.

Earlier mayors were active supporters of bond issues but none risked as much personal and political prestige as Kirk did in the arena and Trinity bond elections. Few gained as much in reputation for effective leadership crossing racial and class divides. In winning, Kirk potentially changed the calculus of Dallas politics. In the past, north Dallas voters dutifully followed the lead of the city's prominent business executives and organizations, voting overwhelmingly for pro-growth measures. Black and Hispanic voters were essentially ignored. They were expected to vote against bond issues, but in numbers too insignificant to affect the outcome. In the two 1998 referenda, the core supporters remained the business interests, but Anglo voters could no longer be counted on to carry such controversial pro-growth issues. Ironically, affluent voters were more susceptible to populist alarms about corporate welfare than their disadvantaged minority neighbors. The campaigns, therefore, were designed to promise benefits for minority voters so they could be mobilized to produce substantial margins of support to overcome north Dallas defections. Because he enjoyed the trust of minority voters—particularly blacks—Kirk was able to rally their support, which, in other circumstances might have been indifferent or even hostile because of the sponsorship by the business elite.

The results of the arena and Trinity referenda suggest three different interpretations. The most optimistic is that the success of the electoral alliance laid a foundation for a sustainable social production alliance that could empower minorities and strengthen the city's capacity to address its most difficult problems. A second interpretation is that they merely offer evidence that minority voters are susceptible to skillful manipulation through promises of benefits and appeals to protect "their" mayor. A third is that they are the idiosyncratic work of an exceptionally talented politician cobbling together ad hoc support for projects he regarded as his principal legacy as mayor.

To gain minority support, much was promised. Sustaining that support could depend heavily upon whether the promised benefits are delivered. It would also appear to depend upon whether Kirk and others establish an alliance that can outlast his tenure as mayor. The larger lesson, however, was that endorsement of the business elite could no longer guarantee the passage of a major bond issue. An alliance of business resources and minority votes would be required for the Dallas growth machine to endure.

9

The Private Uses of Public Powers

> Those who think that the business of America is business need to entertain the idea that there is a commercial public interest from whose vantage point any identification of businessmen's satisfaction and the public good can be disputed.
>
> STEPHEN L. ELKIN

Introduction

Development and growth have occupied a large space in the political culture of Dallas. Some of the largest and most spectacular development projects are among the icons of the city. Fair Park occupies an emblematic role in the city's mythology and contains one of the nation's finest collections of Art Deco buildings. Ray Nasher's North Park Mall, one of the nation's first enclosed shopping centers, remains one of the most pleasant in the country, adorned with modern sculptures from Nasher's incomparable private collection. The Magnolia building with its famous neon-lighted flying red horse was long the universally recognized symbol of the city, visible at night far across the plains as one approached Dallas. By the 1980s, Pegasus was walled in by sleek new skyscrapers and displaced as the city's beacon by Reunion tower, which at night resembles a giant, teed-up, blinking golf ball. As Dallas matured, both the Magnolia building and its mythic symbol were given new life. The building was being remodeled and Pegasus' shadow was etched in stone at street-level in a new urban park on Main Street. The Crescent, Meyerson Symphony Hall, and Fountain Place joined the list of architecturally distinguished Dallas buildings.

Understatement is rarely regarded as a virtue in Dallas, where the longhorns and cowhands in the city's newest monument, Pioneer Plaza, are one-and-a-half times life-sized. This new park, the gift of Dallas master builder Trammell Crow, is adjacent to the sprawling Dallas Convention Center and the monumental City Hall, one of I. M Pei's most dysfunctional and, ironically, symbolic creations.

The building that attracts the most visitors and the most awe, however, is plain: the Texas Book Depository, where Lee Harvey Oswald fired the bullet that killed President John F. Kennedy in 1963. The city struggled for almost thirty years before coming to terms with the legacy of the building, finally refurbishing it as offices for the County government and constructing on its infamous sixth floor an outstanding memorial to Kennedy, explaining his assassination.

These structures, among others, reflect the complex and often contradictory character of the political economy of Dallas's development—striving for excellence and equating large or new with quality. Some of them are aesthetic as well as financial successes; others were disasters on both counts. All kept the dirt flying. The city that invented itself, above all else, kept remaking itself. Rhetoric about the magic of the market aside, the city government was far more than a passive observer and referee of development by private builders. It often was a direct financial participant and even more frequently played a vital role in facilitating specific projects and in fostering growth in general. The ways in which the city performed its development role had important consequences for its capacity to resolve economic and physical development issues. And the lessons its officials and private investors drew from that experience affected the capacity of the city to adapt to the changing needs of its people and economy, and the aging of its built environment.

Dallas, Inc.—Resolving Development Problems

The "pure entrepreneurial regime"[1] that governed Dallas from the adoption of the City Charter in 1930 into the early 1970s sustained a clear "supply side" development philosophy anchored in opportunistic private investment. The city's great public systems—air and highway transportation, water supply, and the Trinity levees—provided the access and opportunities for almost exponential growth throughout much of the twentieth century. The governance of Dallas resided with a small circle of business leaders, whose investments in land and buildings were supported by public infrastructure they devised and facilitated by benign regulations, which they supervised in their parallel incarnations as public officials. City government kept the growing household tidy and safe for those that mattered to the oligarchy. As the "establishment" that shaped modern Dallas dissipated, the physical stock it built and the institutions and practices it established continued to influence urban development.

Throughout Dallas history, growth meant progress. There was unity of purpose, not to mention personnel, in the public and private sectors. Dallas was viewed as a firm. Each shareholder-citizen was presumed to have the same interest in sharing the benefits of growth in proportion to each one's investment. There was consensus that growth would make everyone better off. The city was not concerned with redistribution of the immense wealth its growth machine was generating. But it was a machine with a sticky accelerator and no brakes. It roared into a speculative crash in the 1980s, and as the wreckage cleared, the city began to assess the consequences of unevenly distributed growth for critical sectors of the city where disinvestment and decline had been masked by the net citywide growth in incomes and property valuations. Now, as valuations fell, the disparities among sectors of the city began to have political resonance in a new political system that was no longer smoothly synchronized with the distribution of economic power.

A system designed to promote mainstream growth did not easily adapt to deal with the problems of areas being left behind, such as the central business district and southern Dallas. Being market-based, it contained neither the financial incentives nor regulatory constraints designed to guide growth to areas that conventional market wisdom eschewed. Good works could not always be mortgaged. They involved high risks, and the region's financial institutions had just been sold and reorganized as components of national banking systems as a result of failing to exercise due diligence in making speculative loans. Government action to reduce risk was necessary before new investment would occur.

Traditional measures, such as provision of infrastructure helped, especially in the central business district. Expansion of the convention center, construction of the Meyerson Symphony Hall, and renovation of the Farmer's Market generated additional downtown activity. The provision of the DART light rail line, creation of a downtown transit circulation system, and transfer stations improved accessibility and convenience. Additional safety and amenity measures were vital to stanching the flight of existing businesses and making downtown an option for new enterprises, but such measures violated city bureaucratic routines that called for the even distribution of such services across the city. For the city itself to enhance services in one part of town without a tax increase could be perceived as—and in fact result in—reducing services somewhere else. Clearly, some new means that did not violate the civic culture's abhorrence of active government was required to address effectively the problems of the hollowing core.

A private government for the central business district (CBD), the Central Dallas Association, was the appropriate response. Its members assessed themselves extra taxes through the Downtown Improvement District (DID) to pay for additional services and amenities. Tax increment financing (TIF) captured the growth in revenues within the CBD and applied it to further advance the CDA's downtown improvement objectives. As in the past, the initiative for growth-supporting services came from the private sector, but with a significant difference. Downtown property owners that directly benefitted from the enhanced services and amenities paid the marginal cost through their special tax assessment. With the addition of the TIF, the property owners received all the benefits of the revenue attributed to improvement in property valuations and new development in the CBD. Without the TIF, the growth in revenue from improved valuations would have gone into the city's general fund for distribution throughout the city. What emerged from the struggle to come to grips with the problems of the CBD was a private government with a dedicated source of public revenue and the power to tap it for purposes of its choosing.

Reuse of vacant offices and warehouses for in-town housing and development of new in-town housing at locations surrounding the CBD required governmental stimulation of the market through tax abatements, loan guarantees, and loans. Using federal programs, the city's Department of Economic Development, working with property owners, developers, and CDA, kindled a housing boomlet around the center of town. By 2000 this government-subsidized reinvestment program had created a thriving residential sector in the CBD and surrounding neighborhoods, materially altering the economic and social function of city's center.

These actions primed the pump for investment in conversion of other older buildings to new residential and business uses. The Greater Dallas Chamber of Commerce acquired a vacant office building to renovate it for its headquarters and to house the CDA, the Dallas Citizens Council and a number of other nonprofit business associations.[2] In each case, the city became a non-equity partner, but its position was subrogated to that of the private lender. In the past, public support of development was indirect, through infrastructure, services and benign regulation. Now, but for the city's financial participation through a combination of direct and tax subsidies, some of the deals could not have been made. Moreover, through its Department of Economic Development and the direct entrepreneurship of the city manager, the city proposed projects to developers and financiers, negotiated with owners, and brought federal and private funding to the table.

While the new role of government in financing development and the flexibility of the CDA, as a private government, were critical in addressing the complex issues of CBD resurrection, they raised other issues. Subsidies for investors have a narcotic effect on both their dispensers and the recipients. They are hard to stop. Developers begin to consider them an entitlement, and they become a pawn in the competition with other cities for relocations and investors.

For the city, making deals tends to displace comprehensive and strategic thinking about the use of public resources. Each deal is self contained, justified by a *pro forma* financial analysis that looks at return on investment and a superficial analysis of the number of temporary and permanent jobs it will "create." There is satisfaction, even pride, in bringing off a deal that produces a tangible result. Lacking a strong in-house analytical or planning capacity, however, city officials operated primarily on intuition. They gave little thought to the opportunity costs of their decisions or the cost-shifting effects of development subsidies on residents and firms in the remainder of the city.

Such long and mid-range planning as existed were products of superficial analysis, symbolic participation, and consensus bromides. The new generation of lightly engaged business executives was unable to fathom the complexities of the city or too timid to address development issues in anything but broad generalities. The result was improvisation without a sense of general direction. In such an environment, the grand project overwhelmed more practical, if prosaic ones. Research on the economic effects of sports facilities strongly suggests that $125 million in subsidies for the new sports arena—five times the size of the entire Section 108 in-town housing program—will do less for downtown than an equal investment in housing or the arts. Image remained a cultural preoccupation of city decision makers. Images were not subjected to critical analysis and informed deliberation.

In southern Dallas, years of disinvestment and landlord neglect ravaged many neighborhoods. The private market had long resisted investment in homes and minority-owned businesses. The city government turned to a nonprofit community development corporation to lead the effort to attract investment. The Southern Dallas Development Corporation produced an impressive return on the city's initial investment of federal Community Development Block Grant funds. Its assistance was critical to the expansion of minority businesses that banks initially refused loans. But the scale of SDDC's activity is minuscule in comparison to the development problems of southern Dallas.

The Dallas Initiative and the investments of private entrepreneurs such as Don Williams and Tom Hicks represented investors with a newly awakened interest in the economic potential of vacant land, small firms, and stable households south of the Trinity and I-30. Depending upon their perceived success, they could have a broad impact on other private investors. City officials heralded these private efforts, but did not rely on them to produce change. Government money was to be used explicitly to fill a gap left by a business establishment that had not provided loans or jobs in southern Dallas and to provide services long withheld by the old commercial regime. The arena and Trinity bond issues were positioned to appeal to voters in southern Dallas, promising that substantial portions of the proceeds of the bond sales would be used to improve public facilities, and provide employment to its residents and business for its firms. By such means, new for Dallas, the city government expected to create a wider distributive effect from its direct expenditures, further generating a stronger market for private investors in home mortgages and business enterprises.

The constriction of slack private and public resources during the recession years, accompanied by substantial shifts in the distribution of political power among the city's principal population groups, made the city more receptive to federal programs designed to stimulate development that provided specific benefits to minority and poor communities. This shifted the development focus of the city government and expanded participation in development politics beyond the boardrooms of banks and corporations to the professional managers and boards of private governments, community development corporations, city bureaucrats, and the City Council.

The old regime could pursue development objectives without much concern for how their actions affected minority communities, the environment, or neighboring jurisdictions. That day was gone, and with it a regime that rested on the enlightened self-interest and consensus of a tight circle of home grown business executives, who could reach quick, private agreement on plans of action and assemble the necessary resources to carry them out. It was replaced by a loose network of private and public organization managers, and a few individual corporate executives acting in their self-interest or selective community welfare impulses. Separate components operated in narrowly defined geographic areas of the city and there was no overall coordination or coherence to the system. One of the distinguishing features was the separation of most of its actors from those concerned primarily with the city's human capital. But new development policies and instruments that emerged from the economic crisis of the 1980s and early 1990s were more than a continuation of past practices. Serious concerns for urban decline elevated issues of equity to factors that city and business leaders had to address in order to build support for projects that mattered to them.

The civic culture continued to resist strong public leadership and planning, but pervasive rule by oligarchy was replaced by a system of mixed private-public governance of development. Business leaders and city officials reached consensus that the development problems of the CBD and southern Dallas could not be left to an unassisted private sector. Government created or enabled the new nonprofit development organizations to flourish, use public capital to stimulate private investment, and reduce risks.

With few exceptions, those engaged in development remained rooted to the notion that the answer to equity issues was to induce more growth. There was little discrimination about the type of growth, the kind of employment and related activity it would generate, or the offsetting impact it could have on demand for services and infrastructure. In spite of the "world class" rhetoric, there was little evidence that development decisions were designed to address strategically the massive shift in the Dallas economic base toward information and knowledge. In that context, making Big D bigger, even if it added marginally to employment and revenues, would not necessarily address its core economic development problems. Dallas's real competition was no longer with its suburbs for a new arena or industry headquarters, but with other major urban centers throughout the world to supply the human and physical capital the new economy's firms and consumers demand. "Over the long haul, an area's competitiveness will be determined by the characteristics of the area itself: the quality and quantity of its labor force and entrepreneurial talent, the quality of its infrastructure, the age and productivity of its capital stock, its access to regional and national transportation networks, etc."[3]

Dallas seems determined to maintain and improve its infrastructure. Clearly, it has an abundance of entrepreneurial talent, although its long neglect of its minority labor force and businesses means that it has a substantial gap to close to gain a competitive advantage with other diverse cities. It has yet to develop the capacity to address the education of its growing minority population. The isolation of the city's major development institutions from the far more complex and ambiguous issues of education and work force development separate some of the most energetic and creative talent of the city from the problem most in need of a sustained application of their intellectual energy and resources.

The Capacity to Learn and Adapt

Historically, Dallas decision makers relied heavily upon their experience, and drew lessons from it on "what works." This perspective, in private and public organizations concerned with development, stressed cumulative experience in the city's affairs. Key figures in these organizations, such as the Citizens Council or Chamber of Commerce, had long histories of involvement and close personal relationships with each other. They knew who could be trusted and where to exert pressure. They knew Dallas; they built Dallas; from their perspective, they *were* Dallas. During their hegemony they institutionalized their knowledge and values by bringing along younger men "through the chairs," mentoring them for higher responsibilities in their firms and civic organizations.[4] There was low turnover at the top of the Citizens Council, and the period for learning and maturation was long. It mattered little that there were term limits on service on the City Council or as mayor. Successors in office had imbibed the same lessons from the same stories. Everyone knew what to do without being told.

As the world of Dallas business became more complex and the old guard died, their firms merged into global enterprises and dispersed across the region and the world. They were replaced by a new generation of professional managers. The stories and folklore remained, but many of the lessons were lost. The high rollers that built the see-through buildings and ran the once-impregnable financial institutions of Dallas into the ground in the 1980s lacked any enduring attachment to the city. By the time the Resolution Trust Corporation had cleaned up their mess and left town, the stability of the past had been replaced by high turnover in key business and civic positions, and the learning curve became lower and slower. This was particularly the case in organizations that relied primarily on experience rather than analysis as the primary source of functional knowledge, due to the lack of a critical mass of members with broad and deep experience. In organizations with shallow staff pools and volunteer "champions" drawn from a rotating board, there were problems in collective institutional memory and organizational learning. Hence, the lament of the Citizen Council's leaders that things were too complex and they did not have enough information to know what to do.

City government mirrored the quandary of the private sector, with added complications. Tenure among the last four city managers averaged less than four years. This was ameliorated by the fact that all of them had prior experience in Dallas as well as other cities. But, beset by budget crises, police-community conflicts, and a City Council that increasingly demanded attention to the problems of individual districts, there was relatively little time to produce coherent long-term development policies.

A serious problem for development policy arose from the combination of term limits, lack of staff, and district elections for members of the City Council. Council members were less likely than the managers to learn from other cities' experience, to have access to technical information about development practices, costs and benefits, or to build a strong set of peer leaders on development issues. The shift in the membership of the Council to a political class from business people with direct experience in development meant that as members changed there was even less continuity than in the days when most shared a common view of the value of urban growth. Term limits imposed an institutional learning disability on council members, who often left office just as they gained enough experience to master the intricacies of development issues. The practice of deferring to the wishes of the member in whose district a project was proposed further limited critical evaluation of development proposals. In this environment of shared innocence, but incessant demands to "do something," mayors honed in on projects with high "announcement value" to show that the city was still a player in the region's development sweepstakes. Both city hall and the peak business organizations depended upon their managerial regents to define issues, suggest policies, and implement measures.

In creating the Dallas Plan, the Citizens Council and the city government recognized the need for a strategic intelligence capacity to inform and guide critical development decisions. They did not equip the Plan with enough staff or consulting resources, however, to provide sufficient information or an adequate public procedure to produce wise and legitimate choices. The resort to a conceptual plan for planning begged most of the substantive questions of development policy for the city, and provided but slight guidance for specific projects. What they learned was that the Goals for Dallas project had a reputation for success, and it had been privately funded and directed. They did not learn that the city had changed significantly, and that although there was still a high level of distrust of the government, there was no longer a consensus on development policy or infrastructure needs even within the business sector. The result was not a visionary "plan" for the first quarter of the twenty-first century, but a document of such generality it was almost impossible for any project to be inconsistent with it. While the small and energetic staff of Dallas Plan worked assiduously with neighborhood groups and its business sponsors to promote worthy projects, the Plan functioned principally as a public relations cover for subsequent bond issues. The lesson for its proponents was that in Dallas you can get away with exaggerated claims for very little, if everyone agrees not to notice.

They did not learn that effective planning in a changing city is intensely political, in both the rawest and best sense of that term. Separating the Dallas Plan from the city government drained it of political life. But it provided an excuse for not building a respectable planning capacity within the city. Such a capacity would include an institutional memory to advise the city's management and elected officials of potential pitfalls in schemes that replicate old mistakes. It would also include a "trustee for the future" role designed to examine opportunity costs of proposals and provide a means of informed public deliberation of alternatives. The Dallas Plan followed the path of least resistance toward the final resting place of Goals for Dallas—a pleasant civic memory, but no one can exactly recall its features. There is strong resistance in Dallas to getting smarter.

Implications

Development, unlike the provision of services, directly benefits a small class of investors, developers, builders, realtors and their supporting trades and professions. The effect of development activity on the whole city and on specific geographic sectors is immense. The indirect effect of growth and decline, registered through the property tax base and the job market, is pervasive. The distribution of benefits and costs from development on where, what kind, and how much growth or decline occurs has placed the development function at the center of urban political economy. Because politics matters so much to development, pro-growth and other related community interests mobilize around the selection of officials and administration of policies used to promote, produce, induce, or regulate it.

Great fortunes are at stake in development. So are smaller investments in homes, firms, and jobs, and, indeed, the welfare of the city, its neighborhoods and commercial districts. As Clarence Stone has pointed out:

> The political economy context means that development policy must attend to the fact that by and large, investment capital is privately held and mobile. There is nonetheless cause to believe that the particular arrangements of a community, informal as well as formal, fashion the form that attractiveness to investment capital takes. If so, there is reason to pursue how civic arrangements might best be designed to represent the full community they serve.[5]

It is clear from this analysis of development in Dallas that it would stretch the point to suggest that the "full community" was meaningfully engaged in the making of development policy, or in holding those that are involved accountable for its effects on the city, its residents, and firms. The engagement of neighborhood interests was at most episodic; often it was idiosyncratic. The Council delegated its zoning powers to its respective members. The privatization of planning and delegation of some of the most important development matters to private governments and other organizations enabled timely action without following all of the bureaucratic routines of city agencies. At the same time, these "shadow governments"[6] often regarded broad participation in decision making as a source of unnecessary dissension and an impediment to the flexibility required to bring off an important deal. As the arena fight suggests, the secrecy and "creativity" involved meant that one interest group's "flexibility" was another's "hanky-panky." Robert Stoker points out that:

> Organizations that create and implement development policy are engaged in significant political decision making. While the community has an interest in business success, there are limits to the congruence of the city's interest and that of its business community. The problem of governing is to develop a process that will facilitate the success of business without ignoring the city's other communities. This suggests the need for higher levels of citizen participation and for more open organizational processes than

> has been characteristic of the shadow government. What is needed is not simply an organization that can quickly and effectively pursue well-defined goals. What is needed is an organization that is capable of considering ends as well as means.[7]

Because development is a mixed good, with both private and public costs and benefits, the civic institutions that govern it deserve special attention. Private rights are at stake, and the integrity of the system by which they are balanced with values of fairness and openness lies at the heart of constitutional government and the legitimacy of both the processes and outcomes of decisions. The development of the city is imbued with public interests, and it is important, therefore, that development policy be developed and applied in ways that permit appropriate representation and due deliberation of those interests.

IV

Civic Capital: The Political Life of Dallas

10

The Phantom Publics of Dallas

> Many local governments have become depoliticized, with goals of service efficiency overriding any concerns for the democratic nature of the process by which decisions are made. Many municipal corporations today are run like corporations, and citizens play a role in municipal decision making equivalent to the role of stockholders in corporate decision making.
>
> TIMOTHY BLEDSOE

Anti-Politics and Civic Capital

Earlier chapters have described how Dallas dealt with educational and policing crises and the development of the city during its economic and demographic transformation in the last decades of the twentieth century. Several generalizations about the governance of Dallas can be derived from those accounts. First, each policy arena engaged distinct groups of actors and organizations and each operated with substantial independence from the others.[1] Second, the role of the business interests in these arenas shifted over the period from one of pervasive dominance to one that varied from general disengagement to substantial intervention by individuals or small groups. Third, the role of the professional managers evolved from one of neutral administration to policy entrepreneurship and advocacy. Fourth, race mattered in almost every situation that involved a major adjustment of resources or power.

Finally, the civic culture of Dallas limited participation and constrained effective action to resolve some problems, such as school desegregation and educational equity, and facilitated resolution of others, such as police reform.

Institutionally, Dallas governance is characterized by its diffusion of formal authority and responsibility for the performance of services and development. In recent years, the system became even more diffuse, with delegation of some of the most significant activities of the city to private governments. This reflects and reinforces a civic culture that denigrates the role of government, while using public resources to advance private interests. Dallas dreads robust political conflict as a threat to the business-friendly reputation of the city. The result is a public that is not even semi-sovereign.[2]

In each of the policy arenas discussed in the preceding chapters, Dallas slowly evolved from a pure entrepreneurial regime based on social control to a more complex system. But a stable and reliable governance coalition failed to emerge that could engender the rich networks of civic engagement that convert a place into a polity. The alliances that were developed failed to foster broad political and problem solving skills, encourage open deliberation, or to share power and responsibility for public decisions. Instead, a managerial regency evolved. Consistent with its civic culture, Dallas has produced few institutions whose object is to build civic capital—those "habits of the heart"[3] learned only by engaging citizens in their self-governance.

Civic capital formation involves more than ad hoc cooperation between those with votes and those with money to reach a particular goal, such as approval of the bond issues for the sports arena and Trinity River projects. Robert Putnam's research in Italy and the United States suggests that the development of a rich network of community-based associations ranging from political organizations to choral societies and sports clubs increases the vitality of democratic governance and prospects for economic growth.[4] These horizontal networks of civic engagement, based on mutual trust, Putnam argues, enable people to surmount the problems of collective action and achieve higher levels of social and economic production.[5] They provide an opportunity for people to take each other's measure; to gauge their trustworthiness, judgment and character. Participants learn to manage organizations and to recognize attributes and practice the arts of leadership. Some primary groups are quite narrow, homogenous, and exclusive, but intermediary institutions, such as parties, unions, faith-based organizations, and civic and business associations often encompass people of diverse backgrounds and points of view.

The practice common to most of these truly voluntary associations, and critical in the development of civic capital, is deliberation—public discourse that seeks to persuade by giving reasons that others are morally obliged to consider. This involves more than the mere aggregation of preferences or indoctrination. It assumes that preferences are not immutable, but subject to modification, even change, as a result of reasoned argument. The more diverse the group, the more important argument is, for in order to arrive at a decision that does not rend the organization, advocates must appeal to a collective, or public, interest. Frequently, this requires compromise, sub-optimizing the utility of individuals or factions. Participants learn from this experience how to frame and present issues, how to use the rules to advance their cause or frustrate that of their adversaries and how to assess risks involved in political bargains and alliances. They also learn the conventions of civic discourse, which make it possible for people to disagree on important matters without regarding adversaries as enemies. The civic skills learned in voluntary associations are those most useful in official forums. But in official forums additional ingredients are necessary. Decision-making bodies must be, and be perceived to be, designed to consider and represent salient interests and to operate in a manner that is regarded as fair by those who do not prevail.

Civic culture in Dallas has suppressed mediating institutions that could provide an open and public system of citizen participation and leadership development. Fear of "politics" animates even the most successful local politicians. Mayor Ron Kirk, when asked if he could see any advantages in elections of the city council on partisan on slate endorsements, responded: "The most refreshing thing about being mayor is that we can fix potholes. We don't need political parties."[6]

The mayor's comment reflects the triumph of traditional civic reform dogma. Discomforted by inefficiencies born of corruption and disdainful of the capacities of common citizens to understand their "true" interests, Dallas discarded civic republicanism and its messy politics to embrace a city government modeled on the industrial corporation. Severing municipal offices from partisan primaries and general elections insured lower voter participation and greater influence for the closely held Citizens Charter Association (CCA).[7]

Since the demise of the CCA there has been no local party or bloc within the Council, making it more difficult to pursue a coherent policy program for the city, but the tradition of offering a single policy option continued into the era of the managerial regency. Critical deliberation of even the single option, let alone consideration of alternatives, is impeded by the absence of independent policy analysis capacity for Council members.[8] Sharp criticism of a manager's proposals is regarded as bad form for a council member and an insult to the manager's professionalism or personal integrity. Thus, on the official level there is no tradition in Dallas of organized policy debate as a means of engaging a wider public in city affairs.

A battery of institutional barriers frustrates sustained leadership and public accountability for the performance of the city's government. Local government is segmented among the city, school districts, and the county. Single-member districts and the absence of political parties or stable endorsement groups make it impossible for Dallas voters to elect a government. Executive power is once removed from electoral review.

Neither the mayor nor any member of the Council can be fairly held accountable for the policies of the city. John Dewey argued that without officials there could be no public.[9] Dallas has officials aplenty, but at the dawn of a new century it has only a phantom public.

The Peak Associations and Civic Networks of Dallas

One function of civic institutions is the development of democratic leadership skills based upon reciprocity and trust rather than status, authority and compulsion.[10] For many years people associated with the entrepreneurial regime were prepared for leadership roles through serving in a "thick" network of associations and offices. Max Wells, one of the last of the business leaders to rise through the system and serve on the City Council, described his career:

> I was hired by the second largest Savings and Loan Association in Dallas, in 1951 by Frank Hoke. The week I came to work, he quit. Frank announced he was going to run for City Council. Frank won and I helped in the campaign. After the election Frank wanted me to be on the radio board [which oversaw the management of WRR-AM and FM]. . . . My second boss was a member of the Park Board. Don Wright and Jack Evans, who was chairman of the bank's executive committee, got me into the Dallas Assembly. Jack nominated me to many things. . . . The third bank I worked for was headed by Ralph Rogers, who was also helpful. He was the city troubleshooter. KERA was struggling and he took that over. Ralph was very dictatorial but people wanted him to take over things in trouble. He took over the Arboretum. This was the era you were expected to do civic things . . . .[11]

Jerry Bartos served on the school board and City Council after rising "through the chairs" to the vice chairmanship of the Greater Dallas Chamber of Commerce and chair of the North Dallas Chamber. His recollection squared with that of Wells: "For some reason there was a culture that when you started working in the business community that you gave. You didn't get—don't even expect to get." He then added: " That switched in the second or third generation of companies."[12]

The system Wells and Bartos described depended on those who rose through it to volunteer for civic endeavors because their personal wealth or corporate sponsors supported their public service. Term limits ensured frequent rotation in public office. But the turnover of officials was ameliorated by the continuity of an almost interchangeable civic leadership, each member of which had been steeped in the traditions and creed of the business elite.

Junior members of this establishment moved through a series of positions of increasing responsibility, much as Wells and Bartos did. This included apprenticeship on boards, such as the United Way, Red Cross, Greater Dallas and area Chambers of Commerce, the Dallas City Plan Commission and the Park Board—traditional stepping stones to a Council nomination by the CCA. Those who showed the greatest promise of carrying the values and interests of the business elite were inducted into the Dallas Assembly, created in 1962 by the Dallas Citizens Council to groom a new generation of business leaders to run the city and its major institutions. Membership in the Assembly allowed close association with the senior leaders of business and government, and participation in programs that familiarized members with the business perspective of the city and its issues.

This thick system existed only for the Anglo business and professional elite, and was almost exclusively male until the 1980s. As late as 1993, of 138 active members, twenty were African-Americans, fourteen were Hispanics, and one was Asian-American. The sixty-five Assembly alumni (those over fifty years of age) included only two African-Americans and one Hispanic.[13]

The peak organizations of the business establishment were neither inclusive nor transparent. They trained two generations of executives for public service in a way that built trust among their members but fostered distrust beyond their private councils. They used secrecy, economic power, and a governmental scheme and electoral system that reinforced their control of elections and public policy. Their members "gave," but essentially on their terms. In the quarter-century since the demise of the Citizens Charter Association, fewer of the economic elite have taken on the kind of public responsibilities that Wells and Bartos saw as their duty. A shadow group of executives continued to use its economic power to influence elections, however.

The Breakfast Club—described by one observer as "the street people; they have streets named for them"[14]—is composed primarily of members of the Citizens Council. It operates less openly and more informally than the CCA, interviewing candidates and encouraging its members to donate funds to campaigns. It makes no collective formal or public endorsements, however, and members do not always support the same candidates, although its more influential members generally signal their preferences among prospective candidates, as they did in the mayoral races in 1991 and 1995.

Contributions from members of the Breakfast Club were decisive in the 1991 defeat of Diane Ragsdale, the most controversial and outspoken black council member. The *Dallas Morning News,* whose CEO helped found the Breakfast Club, endorsed Ragsdale's opponent, Charlotte Mayes, a significant signal to voters entertaining doubts about or disenchanted with Ragsdale.[15] The Breakfast Club was also an important source of financial support for the school board campaigns of the "Slam-Dunk Gang."[16]

A 1990 letter to members of the Breakfast Club from its convenors suggests the value of the return on its investments. The letter reported that members raised or personally contributed "well over $350,000 to the individual campaigns of candidates of their choice during the spring 1989 election. . . . This was over 22 percent of the total contributions . . . and over 92 percent of the contributions went to the winners."[17]

The letter reported the fruits of the club's good citizenship: nominees suggested by the Breakfast Club had been appointed to four of the five positions on the Board of Adjustment; nine of fifteen positions on the Plan Commission; three of five positions on the Civil Service Board; and five of the seven positions on the Park Board. In addition, the group had recommended appointment of ten of the fourteen Dallas representatives on the DART Board and all three of the Dallas representatives to the D/FW International Airport Board. Finally, members were billed for their annual dues of $2,500 each.[18]

The Breakfast Club is not engaged in the development of civic capital. It does not recruit candidates, build a political organization, or hold public meetings or candidate forums. It is a device for a small, self-selected group of wealthy business leaders to use their financial resources quietly to influence elections and appointments without accepting any individual or collective responsibility for their actions. Candidates can accept contributions of individual Breakfast Club members without stigma that might attach to the same money if it came from a political action committee or with the open endorsement of the group.

Thinner, less influential, and more specialized networks evolved in Dallas for development of leaders that were not part of the business elite. Women's clubs, charitable societies, arts organizations, homeowners associations, Parent-Teacher Associations, regular party campaigns and clubs, church and civil rights organizations, professional societies, and ethnic chambers of commerce provided alternative bases for gaining civic experience and producing candidacies.[19] Each base, however, lacked the broad policy immersion and intensive mentoring of the old peak organizations. None commanded a comparable level of financial resources.

In recent decades, the Leadership Dallas program of the Greater Dallas Chamber of Commerce has become a rite of passage for younger business, government, and nonprofit organization executives and community leaders. An effort to broaden and diversify the leadership base of the city, the program has been valuable for new mid-level business and professional people moving into the Dallas area. It provides them a network of alumni and an opportunity to become familiar with important economic and political issues confronting the city and region. Leadership Dallas and its clones operated by subregional Chambers of Commerce add value to the civic capital of participants. Leadership Dallas remains, however, an elite program that does not reach deeply into the community at large.

Homeowners and community associations provided civic experience and core constituencies for several council members from both banks of the Trinity. Larry Duncan, who headed the Dallas Homeowners Association, built his successful campaigns in the city's Fourth Council District on member groups, and effectively used them as forums for the discussion of a wide range of public issues during his eight years on the City Council. They provided a way for Duncan, an Anglo, to persevere in a district that had a majority of non-Anglo voters, and draw solid majorities from black voters, even when opposed by black candidates. Council Member Lori Palmer's mid-city political base grew from the mobilization of owners and renters in opposition to development projects in their Oak Lawn neighborhoods. Homeowner groups were also important in the constituencies of Lee Simpson in East Dallas, and Donna Halstead in the Lake Highlands area of northeast Dallas. No lasting citywide federation of such groups was established, however. Their narrow focus and periodic lapses into inactivity after threats to their immediate neighborhoods receded made them an unstable base for aspiring leaders with interests beyond service on the City Council.

Minority Institutions and Leaders

The cool reception the Dallas Interdenominational Ministerial Alliance gave the Southern Christian Leadership Conference during the civil rights movement of the 1960s produced divisions among black churches. Combined with a tendency toward organizational independence and financial weakness, these divisions sapped the ability of black churches to act collectively or provide a solid base for political action. Congregations could be mobilized for some candidates and endeavors, but they have produced no clear collective program or voice, and no system for the development of political leaders. While many Anglo clergy and lay leaders joined minority congregations in supporting desegregation of schools and public accommodations, and in advancing other appeals to conscience, most communities of faith in Dallas have evaded sustained political engagement. The Christian Right has been more active in suburban school elections than in either City Council or Dallas Independent School District (DISD) elections.[20]

The Catholic diocese historically has not played a prominent role in city politics or in developing civic leaders among the Hispanic communities of the city. A shortage of priests has limited the time they have available for engagement in political action, although some parishes have become involved in political action groups such as Dallas Area Interfaith. Successful Hispanic evangelical churches are often sponsored by and remain heavily dependent upon Anglo churches for their survival. One Dallas Hispanic leader opined, "You can't really say what you want to say because the funding stops . . . No one wants to offend the Pope of the Baptists, Dr. [W. A.] Criswell."

There are two notable exceptions to the separation of church and politics in today's Dallas. The first, and oldest, is St. Luke Community United Methodist Church, led by Pastor Zan Holmes. St. Luke's hosts a weekly leadership luncheon for black elected officials and other leaders, where issues are discussed, strategy is incubated, and guests are invited to explain policies and submit themselves to close questioning by participants. The leadership luncheon has exerted a strong influence on its regular attendees and has become one of the most important civic meetings in the minority community and the city as a whole. It frequently serves as a venue for resolving differences among black politicians and, often with Holmes's influential brokering, the construction of alliances among sometime adversaries, such as the agreement of County Commissioner John Wiley Price to support the Trinity River project of Mayor Ron Kirk. Holmes is widely respected throughout the city, and is often involved in mediating disputes and brokering compromises among officials, races, and religious communities. A former member of the State House of Representatives, a powerful preacher, and former member of the Board of Regents for the University of Texas System, he maintained his authenticity in both the radical and moderate camps in the black community while his influence among Anglos steadily grew.

Dallas Area Interfaith (DAI), an interdenominational and interracial organization modeled on the Southwest Voters Project of San Antonio, and affiliated with the Alliance of Industrial Organizations,[21] built a grass roots, faith-based organization in the inner city during the 1990s. Some sixty churches and schools belonged to DAI in 1998. The organizational members included a number of north Dallas mainline Protestant denominations, such as Presbyterians, Methodists, and Lutherans, as well as southern Dallas congregations and some Catholic parishes serving Hispanic congregations.

Using organizational strategies derived from labor unions and community action organizations, it mobilized support behind a focused program derived from one-on-one and community discussions and then secured public pledges of support from officials for them. Its most important work was in neighborhood organization, which required the recruitment and training of leaders in group self-help and political action strategies. Program success was critical in building trust and self-confidence among these grass roots operatives so they could see that participation mattered. Therefore, DAI set specific goals that could be achieved in reasonable periods of time. Its insistence on public commitment and accountability produced some uneasiness among city officials and business leaders because of its willingness to use confrontational tactics, both to secure the commitments and to call attention to failures to produce as promised. Interfaith's approach violated the civic culture's value of conflict avoidance. It was, however, one of the few organizations in Dallas that could fill a Council chamber or school board meeting room with a well-informed and racially mixed crowd. In a city without strong local party organizations or labor unions with interests in development of grass roots leaders, DAI was almost alone in organizing ordinary citizens around a broad-based local agenda and training them for leadership responsibilities. Its unwillingness to recruit and endorse candidates, however, limited its effectiveness.

The Progressive Voters League, which operated voter education programs, registration and get out the vote drives among blacks from the 1930s into the early 1990s fell into disuse after internal squabbles. The Dallas County Branch of the NAACP, after years of internecine battles and conflict with the national headquarters over litigation strategy and chapter management, lost much of its influence and broad base among the city's African-Americans. It became a platform for a faction of black activists frequently aligned with Commissioner John Wiley Price.

La Raza, a Mexican-American political party that developed a substantial following in south Texas, never attracted a large following in Dallas. The League of United Latin American Citizens (LULAC) is active in Dallas, but has not become a major institution for development of civic capital among Hispanics. The Mexican-American Legal Defense Fund (MALDEF) has played an important role in school, housing, and voting rights litigation, but it is not a mass organization. There are a growing number of Hispanic community organizations, such as Casa Guanajuato, which serves immigrants and other residents with ties to that central Mexican State.

Both the historic ethnic civic institutions and those of more recent vintage, serving other communities such as the Korean, Chinese, Vietnamese, and Cambodian communities, have lacked resources, permanent staff, and sustained leadership. They have provided, in recent years, vehicles for aggressive advocates of causes or vocal support for individuals and issues of interest to them. Most cannot survive on dues from members and in recent years many have lost support from Anglo donors as other avenues opened for the advancement of minorities in business and mainstream institutions. Combative styles of leadership caused some former sympathizers to withhold support. Except for organizations like DAI, which can draw on external support, only the ethnic chambers of commerce, which in tone and operation mimic the once all-Anglo Greater Dallas Chamber of Commerce, provide broad civic experience for their members.

The Black and Hispanic Chambers of Commerce provide networks and services for their members. The Black Chamber is the oldest and largest of its kind in the United States. Under the leadership of its organizer and first executive secretary, A. Maceo Smith, it was a central force in black Dallas during the years of legal segregation. Smith made the Chamber a key player in the advancement of civil rights for blacks. He helped organize the Progressive Voters League, threatened economic boycotts to gain concessions from white business leaders, and hosted meetings of civil rights attorneys and organizers.

Until the mid-1970s, the Black Chamber's focus tended to be on major social issues affecting the black community. Today, however, it is largely a service organization and advocate for its members—most of them black-owned small businesses. Its focus has been on economic development in southern Dallas and business opportunities for black businesses. In particular, the chamber has taken advantage of the changes in federal law that demand minority business participation to expand contracting and supplier opportunities with major Dallas corporations. A chamber leader explained how they operated to take advantage of the Dallas way of doing business:

> The good old boy system is alive and well. It is particularly so in construction. Allied General Contractors is largely a white organization. They had a number of tutored minority businesses that saw no need to be members of the Black Chamber. Most minority businesses don't have this opportunity. They are not a part of the group on a social or a business qualification basis. They can't take advantage of the network. So sometimes we go down with John [Wiley Price] and walk around with signs. Other times we call government agencies. . . . You can't divorce business from politics. It is an evolutionary process for Nations Bank to see that there are [investment] opportunities out here [in South Dallas]. Dallas has been lucky in the absence of turbulence. But I would much rather sit at a table and work out the problem than take a more strident approach.[22]

In the new environment in which it now works, the Black Chamber often must walk a fine line between advocacy of the interests of the black business community and its increasing need for contributions from major corporations to help support its small permanent staff and public service activities. Of the 617 business members in 1994, almost half—290—were not minority-owned. One of its officers' most important tasks is cultivation of memberships and donations from the area's largest non-minority firms.

Its problems were exemplified by one of its most successful community programs, designed to encourage black teenagers to excel in school. The Philip Morris Tobacco Company annually provided funds for one hundred high-priced pairs of sneakers, which the Black Chamber awarded to outstanding black students in the DISD. Miller Brewing Company was also a major contributor to its programs. Smoking and alcohol consumption are chronic problems in the black community, and the chamber was criticized for accepting support from these companies. But it was in a poor position to refuse the help without another sponsor, which it could not find among its members.

The Greater Dallas Hispanic Chamber of Commerce is a much younger organization than its black counterpart, but shares many of the older organization's problems and frustrations. Because so many of the city's Hispanic-owned businesses are also marginal operations, it, too, depended upon the support of major corporations for funding. Until the mid-1980s, it had no professional staff, relying instead on its presidents, other officers and volunteers to manage its affairs. Unlike the Greater Dallas or North Dallas Chambers, where corporate executives on the board of directors or serving as committee chairs have large staffs to keep their businesses running while they devote time to Chamber and civic work, many Hispanic business owners have no one to whom to delegate tasks. The absence of other strong Hispanic organizations in the city places additional burdens on the president of the Hispanic Chamber to serve as the "representative" of the Hispanic community in Anglo business and civic circles. As one former president put it: "It's like you became the god of the Hispanic community the day after your election."[23]

The Greater Dallas Chamber of Commerce now includes the chairpersons of the ethnic chambers on its board of directors. While some that have served in this role disparage it as "window dressing,"[24] it has provided an important forum for advancing the interests of minorities and their firms. It has broadened the social connections among minority and non-minority business leaders. Since the residue of the "good old boy" system remains an important aspect of doing business in Dallas, connections are important. The opportunity for minorities to serve on the Greater Dallas Chamber's committees contributes to the civic education of both Anglo and minority members. For the minority members, however, it can impose special burdens. Because there are still so few of them operating within the peak business organizations, they are in demand to satisfy the need for ethnic diversity on a large number of boards and task forces. This adds to an already difficult problem of balancing civic commitments with maintaining business and family obligations. Also, as their businesses and practices grow, they have even less time to devote to civic affairs in a city that traditionally looked to business executives for leadership. Several interviewees reported a serious burnout problem, making development of a political class and institutions to sustain it crucial.

The leadership problem of minority communities was exacerbated by the absence of a critical mass of business and professional people. There has been a remarkable increase in the number of minority professionals in Dallas in recent years, but compared to Anglos, the number with sufficient incomes and leisure to devote to public affairs is disproportionately small. While committees of member-volunteers provide experience in problem solving and group processes, the legacy of discrimination in Dallas continues to constrain the advancement of many talented minorities into the mainstream of business and civic leadership.

The CEOs of most of the city's major corporations have become strong advocates of equal opportunity and workforce diversity. Most have joined the Dallas Together Forum to pledge more jobs and contracts for minorities. Minority business leaders remain skeptical, however, of both the pace and extent of progress. As they tend to see it, the CEOs are committed, but they pass the job of implementing their corporate commitments to underlings who continue to do business as usual. This may overstate the degree of inertia, for there has been an increase in the numbers of minorities moving up the career ladders in Dallas corporations, and minority businesses are increasingly able to compete for business. Few believe, however, that the playing field is level.

The Vanishing Electorate

About three-fourths of the million residents of Dallas were of voting age in 1998. Approximately 450,000 were registered to vote.[25] Anglos, with slightly less than half of the population, were still a slight majority of voting age population and 53 percent of registered voters. Thirty-eight percent of those registered were black, and about nine percent were Hispanics. No more than 27 percent of all those registered voted in any municipal, school board, or bond referendum election since 1980. On average, less than one voter in five participated in mayoral elections during that twenty-year period. In contrast, more than twice as many voters—an average of 45 percent—voted in partisan elections for County Judge [presiding officer] of the Dallas County Commissioners' Court, notwithstanding the relative obscurity of that office. Special elections to fill a vacancy on the City Council or school board sometimes attracted only a few hundred voters. Some precincts have reported no votes at all in special elections.

Even in an era of low voter participation, Dallas presents an extreme case of voter neglect. Several factors may explain the high levels of nonvoting. Nonpartisanship and off-year elections clearly account for some of the low turnout. A contested mayor's race can increase turnout, as the 1987 contest between Annette Strauss and Fred Meyer, and the three-way race in 1995, suggest. The first election under the 14–1 system in 1991 produced greater voter interest, as every council seat was contested even though the mayor's race was not regarded as close. Other years, in which most Council incumbents were reasonably secure or unopposed and there was no mayoral election saw participation rates shrink to single digits. The 1998 special election to fill a school board vacancy brought out only 3.5 percent of the voters, even though four candidates competed for the office. In the 1999 mayoral election, Ron Kirk had no significant opposition in his bid for re-election. Even though there were a few contested Council elections, only 6.7 percent of the city's voters cast ballots.

Dallas voters find referenda no more compelling than mayoral and Council elections. Participation in eight referenda held between 1981 and 1993, shown in Table 10.1, averaged 19.5 percent, but varied widely. The highest turnout was 27 percent in the November 1991 referendum on collective bargaining for police officers and a non-binding referendum on whether members of the DART board should be elected. The lowest rate, 12 percent, occurred in the 1989 referendum on bonds to finance the Central Expressway reconstruction and flood control measures. Although three-fourths of those voting approved both bond issues, they amounted to only 9 percent of the registered voters of Dallas.

Municipal and school elections are often of particular interest to property owners, as tax rates are affected by decisions of elected officials. In 1981, widespread hikes in the assessed values of residences produced a large increase in turnout over previous elections, as protests spread across the city and a number of council members with political bases in homeowners groups were elected. Homeownership explains some of the disparity in Anglo and non-Anglo voting. Anglos own almost three-quarters of all owner-occupied dwellings in Dallas. African-Americans and Hispanics, respectively, own only 16 and 9 percent of such homes.[26] Income is also highly correlated with participation, and the 1994 survey of household conditions in Dallas found that overall, homeowners' household income was twice that of renters.[27]

When voters sense that their votes do not matter, they tend to stay home. There have been no surveys that measure Dallas voters' sense of efficacy, but the anecdotal evidence suggests that it is low. Several Council members interviewed for this book expressed their frustration at their inability to get the city government to respond to citizen concerns and asserted that many voters had concluded that voting had little effect on the course of city government. Participation in school pol-

Table 10.1 Voter Turnout and Behavior, Selected Referenda, 1981–1993, by Race

Date & Subject	*Participation Rate*			*Votes "For" (Pct.)*		
	City	*Sample Precincts: 75% White*	*Sample Precincts: 75% Black*	*City*	*Sample Precincts: 75% White*	*Sample Precincts: 75% Black*
Power Distribution						
1/81—Term Limits	23	32	13	67	81	14
4/83—Council Pay	n.a.	25	4	37	37	62
8/83—Create DART	n.a.	33	11	55	72	19
5/89—Police Rev. Bd	18	21	11	26	12	89
12/90—14-1 Council	21	23	20	49.8	33	98
Council Pay				43	30	88
11/91—Police Bargain	27	44	25	40	37	30
Elect DARTBd.				67	61	75
5/91—14-1 Council	25	31	14	59	55	86
Council Pay				36	38	53
Fiscal Issues						
1/81—Prop. tax Limit	23	32	13	32	37	9
6/88—DART Debt	17	27	7	45	43	77
8/92—Fair Park Tax	13	14	9	40	37	60
Public Works Bonds						
8/82—Symphony Hall	n.a.	29	4	57	70	55
Fair Park Improvement				64	68	71
11/85—Buy Arts Dist.	n.a.	21	7	59	69	60
Trinity Parks				53	60	59
11/89—Central Expwy.	12	12	16	75	83	75
Flood Control				77	77	93
Mean Participation	**19.5**	**26**	**13**			
Median Participation	**19.5**	**25**	**11**			

Source: Victor Biggerstaff, Referenda and Civic Functions in Dallas, 1981–1993: The Effects of Race (unpublished paper, 1994). Turnout and voting behavior were derived from Dallas County Elections Department and City of Dallas City Secretary's Office. Precincts in north and south Dallas were selected from 1990 Census tracts in which 75 percent of the population or more were, respectively, non-Hispanic white or non-Hispanic black. The twelve elections and nineteen propositions were selected on the basis of media attention. The 1989 referendum on the 10-4-1 Council districting plan discussed in detail below, was not included. The 1991 DART Board referendum was a non-binding advisory referendum.

itics was affected when many Anglos withdrew their children from the public schools. They continued to pay school taxes on their property, but so long as tax rates did not dramatically change, they had little reason to take an interest in school board or bond elections. The fact that the school system was under federal court supervision for such a long period may also have added to voters' sense of inefficacy.

The frequency of elections in Dallas induces voter fatigue.[28] It is not uncommon to have as many as ten elections in a year, including referenda and special elections to fill vacancies on the Council or School Board. Separation of municipal from state and federal elections and the get-out-the-vote efforts of political parties and statewide candidates[29] reduce participation. It makes regular voting a chore. When these structural impediments are added to the perception, especially among minorities, of the futility of voting in a system that underrepresented them, nonvoting seems like rational behavior to economize time and energy. But at its worst, it is an expression of civic neglect, born of disillusionment, distrust, cynicism and indifference—a withdrawal from the urban public.[30]

Black participation in elections and referenda is generally much lower than that of Anglos. Because of their higher degree of dispersal throughout the city, it is more difficult to estimate Hispanic participation, but it appears to be lower even than that of blacks. A study of matched precincts in Anglo northern and black southern Dallas for eight referenda between 1981 and 1993 found that the average turnout in the southern precincts was about half that of the northern precincts. Precincts were selected in which the population was at least 75 percent Anglo or black, respectively. Black participation, as shown in Table 10.1, reached or surpassed 20 percent only twice during this period. In the December 1990 referendum on the 14–1 redistricting plan for the City Council and on increasing council compensation, a fifth of the registered voters in the southern precincts voted, almost equaling the 23 percent who turned out in the northern precincts. The police collective bargaining referendum of November 1991 drew a quarter of all voters in the southern precincts.[31]

Bond referenda were rarely defeated in Dallas. In part this was due to the generally conservative approach to bond issues and the careful structuring of campaigns in support of them, led by notable citizens and featuring well-financed public relations efforts that targeted those most likely to vote favorably. In most of these referenda the difference in the level of white and black voter participation did not affect the outcome. Black participation was lowest in bond elections, which until the 1998 arena and Trinity River project referenda, were pitched primarily to Anglo voters.

Substantial majorities of both the white and black precincts voted for each of the public works referenda. Black and Anglo voting patterns diverged in the three referenda involving fiscal issues shown in Table 10.1. Black voters tended to oppose a cap on property taxes more strongly than Anglos in the 1981 referendum. Blacks favored granting the Dallas Area Rapid Transit Authority (DART) the power to issue bonds for long-term debt, while Anglo voters in northern Dallas opposed it.

By 1988, blacks saw DART as a source of jobs and improved transportation, while Anglos rebelled at the agency's mismanagement and high costs. Black voters favored imposing a 0.5 percent sales tax to finance refurbishment of Fair Park and some improvements to the black neighborhoods surrounding the park in South Dallas. A majority of Anglo voters opposed the tax. Few Anglos voted, but the even lower black turnout allowed the Anglo opposition to prevail.

Racial polarization was most pronounced in referenda dealing with the distribution of political power. Blacks saw the 1981 referendum limiting members of the Council (then composed of eight district and three at-large positions) to three terms as a means of limiting their ability to develop effective political leaders in city government. Anglo voters have generally opposed increasing the compensation of Council members above the $50-per-meeting level. Blacks have supported pay increases for the Council to make it possible for people with modest incomes to serve. The only exception to this voting pattern occurred in the 1989 Charter referendum. Blacks voted against the compensation proposition as well as all other charter amendments as part of a strategy of defeating the 10–4-1 redistricting scheme. Ironically, this was the only time north Dallas Anglos have supported increased council pay.

The 1990 referendum on the 14–1 Council redistricting scheme was the defiant last stand of Anglo voters against increased minority representation. Black turnout nearly matched that of Anglos, with the proposition losing by only 372 votes. An increase of 1 percent in the black vote could have changed the outcome. Anglos finally joined blacks in confirming the 14–1 system in May 1993; two years after the federal court had imposed it.[32]

In 1991 both Anglos and blacks voted against the right of the police to bargain collectively and for an advisory referendum on whether to elect members of the DART board, but for different reasons. Anglos opposed union collective bargaining as weakening the authority of the city manager to control the city administration and set budgetary priorities. Blacks feared that granting the police the right to collective bargaining would increase the power of a force that they regarded as hostile to them. Support for election of DART board members by Anglos reflected frustration at the mismanagement of the transit agency by an appointed board. Black support reflected a desire for greater political influence on the board and better transit service for their neighborhoods.

A Foundation for a New Politics?

The election of Ron Kirk as mayor in 1995 without a run-off and the 1998 arena and Trinity referenda suggest the possible emergence of a new calculus in Dallas politics that could bridge the politics of color. Minority voter turnout and strong support determined the outcome in each of those elections. The 1995 mayoral election is the only time in Dallas history when black turnout exceeded that of Anglos (25 to 21 percent, respectively).[33] Kirk's share of the black vote was estimated at 97 percent but he also received a substantial Anglo vote. Neither the 1995 mayoral nor the two 1998 referenda campaigns were racially polarized, although Kirk appealed directly to his base constituency to increase its turnout in all three campaigns. But he did so without overtly appealing to racial stereotypes.

As was suggested in Chapter 9, these elections raise the possibility of a stable and mutually beneficial electoral alliance between minority voters and the downtown business interests of the largely Anglo executives and professionals. Minority votes were critical to achievement of their interests in all three elections. Kirk needed business support to legitimate his initial candidacy. By championing projects dear to business and successfully rallying minority support for them in the face of serious opposition among Anglo voters, he enlarged his business support while solidifying his electoral base. As he approached re-election the business community needed him more than he needed it. What remained uncertain was whether the alliance Kirk engineered could be institutionalized to endure after his second and final term. That would seem to depend upon the development of new intermediary institutions to generate a succession of authentic leaders with effective bargaining skills and a cadre of citizens whose disciplined participation is a product of informed deliberation, instead of a politics of identity and manipulation.

Creation of a social production system capable of creating a multi-racial public must overcome the basic value of Dallas civic culture that regards citizens as consumers rather than governors. This attribute runs even deeper than the institutional and racial factors that have depressed participation and stifled development of robust local politics. As was pointed out in Chapter 2, the language of Dallas politics is that of individual commercial transactions, not shared responsibility for government. City government is regarded as apart from politics, a corporate monopoly that supplies a fixed array of services that should not be subject to electoral whim. It is about means, not ends. This attitude was captured by City Manager John Ware's assertion that: "Dallas City government is not the answer to everything. It is not the answer to housing. It is not the answer to schools. I have never had a person come in saying, 'I need a house.' The city government should be involved in service delivery. . . ."[34]

In such a system, citizens are not expected to play much of a role in the design of services. City administrators tend to be possessive of programs and expect that if citizens are allowed a significant role in their design or administration they will cause them to be inefficient, more expensive, and induce delays. This attitude extends to federally funded programs that require a citizen participation component, such as the Neighborhood Renaissance (NRP) and the Enterprise Community programs. Comparing the swiftness with which in-town housing grants were dispensed with the slow pace of the NRP, which involved citizen committees in the selection of projects, Ware argued that the in-town housing program worked well because it was managed top-down, directly from city hall. The NRP, on the other hand, required extensive citizen involvement at the grass roots level.[35]

One of the explicit federal goals of the Enterprise Community program is empowerment of neighborhood citizens through involvement in the design and management of the programs it sponsors. The Dallas program was designed entirely by staff, although a consultant was retained to hold a series of community meetings to discuss its possible objectives and priorities and meet the federal requirements for citizen involvement. Once approved by the U.S. Department of Housing and Urban Development, the program was administered directly from an assistant city manager's office. A citizen advisory panel met infrequently to be updated on the projects initiated by the staff.

Although the services provided by the program were well designed and effective, they were essentially client services. Clients could accept or decline some of them, such as job training and tax credits for employment of newly trained workers. Others, such as community policing involved some continuing participation by residents of the Enterprise Community.

An effort spearheaded by local university, health care, and other community organizations to create a community information system foundered when city agencies would not release some critical data and the City Manager's office would not accede to control of the project by citizens and nonprofit organizations. The project would have made available on-line information from city and other agencies about conditions in neighborhoods, such as crimes, code violations and enforcement actions, mortality and morbidity data, and city expenditures for services and facilities. This information would have been accessible by geographic areas defined by the users, who could download and analyze it themselves, or use a number of on-line analytical programs. There was little capacity in city hall for this sort of analysis, which integrates information from a variety of sources and estimates effects of different variables on neighborhood conditions, thus informing debate on how to tailor programs to deal with them. Creation of such a capacity in the neighborhoods threatened the managerial regency's monopoly of technical information and the legitimacy of expert rule.

The paternalism of the city bureaucracy and the rear guard of the business establishment have fostered a civic environment in which each person is encouraged to think and act as an individual consumer of a monopoly produced good. Neither the formal electoral and representative systems nor informal institutions of collective action provide a viable means of shaping the public agenda or influencing public policy. A civic culture that abhors group protest and direct confrontation also eschews thorough deliberation of alternative measures and tends to view almost all forms of collective action except those undertaken by the established formal and informal organs of governance as not legitimate. This relegates civic action to consumer choice. Individual consumer choice, however, is almost always ineffective. Without the intermediation of institutions, aggregation of individual choices remains vulnerable to manipulation through appeals to fear and desire, envy, and vicarious association with celebrities and powerful endorsers.

Citywide elections and referenda rely heavily on mass advertising and other public relations techniques. They appeal to the public as consumers, often with a subtext of free ridership. The new arena was "sold" as a benefit without cost to Dallas taxpayers, since the bonds that financed the city's participation were to be retired by a sales tax on rental cars and hotel rooms paid, allegedly, by nonresidents. Prominent business and sports figures were lined up to endorse the "product" and write op ed columns extolling its virtues. Opponents were dismissed with attacks on their character or motives. Their objections were ignored in the interest of keeping "on message" by repeating the content empty slogan: "Say Yes! To Dallas." Opponents of the arena, on the other hand, while having cogent arguments to make about the financing, location, and even the need for the facility, yielded to the simplification: "Vote No. It's a Bad Deal!" Their most telling assertion was that the city had become the willing victim of two of its richest and sharpest operators. Neither side engaged in reasoned discourse about the merits of an arena for the city, although an effort was made by some opponents to do so.

Assertion and attack rather than argument and engagement in discourse are hardly unique to Dallas. As Kathleen Hall Jamieson has documented in distressing detail, they have become the common coin of campaign advertising and speech.[36] In a city like Dallas, however, where levels of distrust and cynicism were already high, the use of consumer marketing of policy further undermined the development of horizontal networks and institutions of civic engagement, which must necessarily be founded on mutual trust. Consumers are hardly the equivalent of citizens. Citizens share responsibility for policy. Dallas voters are rarely asked to share. They are urged to buy. And too often, they discover they have purchased a defective product. It is not an experience that builds trust and civic capital. It sustains Dallas as a city without a public.

11

Race, Representation, and Legitimacy

> The history of minority participation in the political process of Dallas is not one of *choice;* it is a record of what blacks and Hispanics have been *permitted* to do by the white majority.
>
> U.S. District Judge Jerry Buchmeyer

The System in Crisis

When Council member Al Lipscomb threw his chair and stalked out of the Council chamber on May 11, 1991, it was a symbol of more than the frustration and outrage of blacks at one more delay in Dallas's tortured journey toward compliance with the federal Voting Rights Act. Throwing chairs was a good metaphor for the way in which the city dealt with the problem of redesigning Council districts so that blacks and Hispanics, who made up half of the population by 1990, had a chance to elect Council members they preferred. The struggle to create a fairer system of representation provides a remarkable opportunity to understand how Dallas civic culture influenced the city's approach to a key institution for developing civic capital.

From 1975, when eight single member districts and three at-large council positions were created, until 1991, black voters were "packed" into two districts. Blacks had comprised about 30 percent of the total population since 1980 but no black had ever been elected to any of the three at-large seats.

Hispanics, who comprised one-eighth of the population in 1980, never had a "safe" district, although Hispanics had been elected from time to time in one of the single-member districts. Business-supported Hispanics had also been elected to an at-large seat. The use of numbered positions for the at-large council seats prevented bullet voting by minorities to elect independent candidates whom they favored. The cost of citywide campaigns inhibited minority candidates from even seeking election at-large.

The 8–3 system of representation had been designed to render moot a lawsuit brought by Lipscomb against the at-large system following the 1970 census. As the 1990 Census approached, minority leaders realized that for the first time, the combined black and Hispanic population could exceed the Anglo population. But unless the system was changed substantially, the Council was unlikely to reflect the demographic shift. The U.S. Supreme Court had recently interpreted the 1982 amendments to the Voting Rights Act to require that electoral systems provide minorities with an opportunity to elect representatives of their choice if it were proved that electoral schemes and patterns of voting were racially polarized and resulted in discrimination.[1] Dallas black activists began to threaten legal action.

These threats, along with the dramatic racial confrontations involving the police, brought the city to crisis. There was widespread agreement among opinion leaders that some further accommodation of minority demands for fairness was necessary. Mayor Annette Strauss consulted with business and minority leaders and, in 1988, convened "Dallas Together," a tri-ethnic task force of over eighty members, and charged it with making recommendations to improve racial harmony. In its final report, Dallas Together targeted education, employment opportunities, and minority representation on the City Council as central interracial issues the city must address. As the report was being written, two black civic gadflies, Roy Williams and Marvin Crenshaw, filed suit in federal district court, alleging that the 8–3 system violated minority rights under the Voting Rights Act. Hispanic plaintiffs soon intervened in the suit. It was clear that if the city did not reform its system of Council representation it faced the unwelcome prospect of having it done by a federal court.

The Charter Advisory Committee[2]

After receiving the task force report in late February 1989, the City Council appointed a Charter Advisory Committee to recommend revisions to the council election system that could be approved by the voters, rendering the lawsuit moot. The mayor chose Ray Hutchison to chair the committee. Hutchison, a senior partner of one of the city's large law firms, and a leading figure in business and public affairs, had chaired the representation subcommittee of Dallas Together, which strongly recommended scrapping the 8–3 system for a system that would be more representative of the city's diverse population. A native of Dallas's working class Pleasant Grove community, he seemed an ideal choice. He had been one of the first Dallas Republicans elected to the Texas Legislature and later chaired the state party. He was known as politically astute, forthright, and inventive in crafting solutions to difficult problems. As a leading Republican, he would be a credible messenger to Dallas's fading business establishment and the conservative voters of North Dallas of the bad news that they would have to share power with minority voters.

The committee started work in early 1989 with two serious handicaps: its membership and its deadline. Each Council member appointed one member. Mayor Strauss appointed five members: a credible rainbow of Anglo, black, Hispanic, and Asian community leaders, including Hutchison. Generally, Council members picked people of stature from their districts. But three appointed themselves: Lipscomb, the other black council member, Diane Ragsdale, and Jerry Rucker, an at-large Anglo member from North Dallas, who frequently tangled with Ragsdale and Lipscomb. Both black politicians were allied with the lead plaintiffs in the lawsuit. Several of the Anglo members of the committee interpreted their self appointments as tactics designed to preserve the issues in the lawsuit where many blacks thought there was a chance of greater political gain than through a committee that was still Anglo dominated. Thus, from the moment of its appointment, the committee was divided by mutual suspicion of bad faith, especially between blacks and Anglos.

In its charge to the committee, the Council asked for a report by late April, which provided less than two months to solve a difficult and divisive issue. The ostensible reason for the short deadline was that city elections were to be held in May, and the Council wanted the report in time to vote on it rather than leave the redistricting scheme to their successors. Moreover, under Texas law, there were only a few dates during the year when a charter referendum could be held, and the Council wanted to get the matter on the ballot as soon as possible, the better to quash the lawsuit. As the committee convened, U.S. District Court Judge Jerry Buchmeyer granted the city's request for postponement of the trial until the representation issue could be put to referendum.

The deadline meant that Hutchison would have to keep the committee on a fast track, compressing the fact-finding and hearing stages of the process, and cramming the decision-making stage into two or three sessions. This tight schedule, imposed by the chair, contributed to the atmosphere of mistrust within the committee. Generally, blacks assumed that Hutchison and his allies had a secret agenda they planned to ram through the committee that would still short change minorities. Hutchison and others assumed that the only role of Ragsdale, Lipscomb and other black members (and some of the Hispanics) was to cause the committee to fail in order to keep the lawsuit alive.

During the first month of its deliberations, the committee argued about procedure and elected black and Hispanic vice chairs: Pettis Norman, a businessman and former star of the Dallas Cowboys, and Joe May, a community activist and self-made demographer. It heard presentations about different forms of representative systems. The heart of its deliberations, however, was on the practical issues of how many seats would there be on the Council, how would they be elected, and most important of all, how many would be safe for each ethnic and racial group.

Early on, Ragsdale and Lipscomb took the position that nothing but a system composed entirely of single member districts would be acceptable. Most other blacks on the committee and some of the Hispanics endorsed this view, but the exceptions were significant. Pettis Norman insisted on keeping his options open, and some Hispanics feared that with a more widely dispersed Hispanic population, a system that relied solely on single member districts would limit their representation and political influence. There was considerable sentiment among Anglo members for retaining some at-large seats or for some other means of providing for a scheme of representation that would help preserve neighborhood and citywide interests.

The city staff and Joe May, independently, presented the committee with an array of districting plans containing between ten and fourteen districts. Since the 1990 census had not been taken, the only data available at the census tract or block level was from the 1980 census. These data could not reflect the substantial changes everyone acknowledged had occurred in the population of all three major population groups. Thus, the committee agreed on some overall population assumptions (which turned out to be significantly low for Hispanics), but it could only guess at how the population might be geographically distributed. This meant that the committee could not draw district lines that could be tested in court or by the Justice Department before the 1990 census became available in early 1991. All it could do was decide on the number of seats and the manner of election. Because of the geographic concentration of blacks and Anglos, some pretty fair guesses could be made of the number of members each might elect if the redistricting followed federal requirements. Estimating the number of Hispanic seats was more problematic, depending on assumptions about the size, dispersion, political solidarity, the proportion of the population that was eligible to vote and would actually participate in elections.

As the deadline for a decision approached, Hutchison developed what he regarded as a compromise, crafted to give minorities more seats and still be palatable to North Dallas voters and the Anglo business community. He proposed a two-tiered plan. The first tier consisted of ten single-member districts. The second tier divided the city into "quadrants," each of which would elect one council member. Council members would continue to be elected for two-year terms. The mayor would be elected at large for a four-year term. Hutchison argued that under this 10–4-1 approach, three of the first tier districts would contain black majorities and one would have a Hispanic majority. In the second tier, the majority of voters in one of the four quadrants would be black, two would be Anglo, and the remaining one would be a multi-racial "minority-majority" district.

Ragsdale and Lipscomb viewed Hutchison's proposed compromise as an attempt to maintain Anglo hegemony. From their perspective, the quadrant districts were no better than the hated at-large seats. Their size—about 250,000 people each—would prevent any but wealthy candidates or those financed by business interests to be elected from them. By their reckoning, eight of the fourteen council seats and the mayoralty would end up in Anglo hands, for a Council of nine Anglos and six minorities for a decade, even though the committee had agreed that by 1990 Anglos would constitute less than half of the city's population. They and most other minority members of the committee held out for a system composed of twelve single-member districts, with the mayor elected at large.

The minorities on the committee were not united, however. Norman saw merit in the 10–4-1 proposal. He believed it could produce opportunities for minority candidates to develop multi-racial political constituencies. He was not convinced, in the absence of credible data, that blacks and Hispanics would fare less well under Hutchison's proposal than they would with a straightforward single member district system. May opposed Hutchison's plan, but the other Hispanic committee member felt that the dispersal of Hispanics in the city gave them a better chance of capturing an additional seat with the quadrant overlay than if all districts were the same size.

In an effort to solidify the minority position, black members held a caucus the night before the committee was due to vote on a plan to present to the City Council. Norman, in particular, was subjected to intense pressure to support the 12–1 alternative. He refused to yield, however. The next day, when the committee convened, Hutchison announced that he had learned of the caucus. He suggested that those who convened it were trying to undercut the work of the committee in order to preserve the lawsuit. He then accepted a pre-arranged motion to recess the committee, subject to the call of the chair. The motion quickly passed, and amid mutual recriminations, the committee members retired to their press conferences.

Three weeks later, the original April deadline for a report having passed, Hutchison reconvened the committee to approve its final report to the Council. It promptly voted down the 12–1 proposal and adopted Hutchison's 10–4-1 plan. All the opposition came from minority members, although Norman and one Hispanic member voted with the majority. In addition to the basic plan, the committee recommended two charter amendments designed to placate Lipscomb and Ragsdale. The first increased compensation for council members. While the recommended change would keep Council pay well below the median for the twenty largest cities in the country, it would more than double the current annual compensation rate, enabling more minorities that were not retained by their businesses to serve on the Council. The second amendment extended the limit on council service from three to four two-year terms. This amendment was important to Ragsdale and Lipscomb, as both were approaching election to their third full terms, and under the current charter they would be ineligible to seek a fourth term. A third amendment lengthening the mayor's term from two to four years, with a two-term limit, was adopted with almost no comment.

Hutchison and those supporting his plan assumed the committee's recommendations would appear on the referendum ballot as a single package of charter reforms, which voters would either accept or reject with a single vote. This strategy was undone when the city attorney ruled that each amendment must appear on the referendum ballot as a separate question. Unbundling of the amendments made it possible for Anglo voters to vote for 10–4-1 and against the increase in Council compensation and for minority voters to do the opposite. The city attorney's ruling destroyed any chance, however slight, of building tri-racial support for the charter amendments as a package.

Redistricting Referenda

Round One: 10–4-1

By the time the committee's recommendations reached the Council, the May elections had replaced four members, including Jerry Rucker and the only Hispanic member, Al Gonzalez. Only one of the new members and one re-elected member joined Ragsdale and Lipscomb in opposition to sending the 10–4-1 plan to referendum. The new member, Jim Burger, had run for mayor in 1987 and was generally expected to try again in 1991. He was an outspoken advocate of a 12–1 redistricting plan. The fourth vote came from Lori Palmer, who represented a "progressive" and racially mixed midtown district. The Council majority placed the 10–4-1 plan before the voters in an August special election.

Hutchison and Mayor Strauss cobbled together a coalition of notable business and civic leaders to provide support for approval of the plan. The campaign's main targets were North Dallas voters. They assumed that the opposition of the elected black leaders and the division of opinion among Hispanics would mean that there would be strong opposition in black and Hispanic precincts to the 10–4-1 proposition and that its approval would depend on a strong Anglo vote. Their judgement proved correct. 10–4-1 was approved in a racially polarized vote. North Dallas voted in favor and southern Dallas voted against it in overwhelming numbers. The only surprise was the defeat of the Council pay increase. Conservative north Dallas voters narrowly favored it, but not by enough to offset its rejection in black and other working class precincts.[3] The amendments dealing with term limits and extending the term of the mayor to four years were approved.

Williams and Crenshaw now moved for a hearing of their case in federal district court. The Council submitted the adopted charter amendments to the U.S. Department of Justice for clearance under the Voting Rights Act. The Department responded that it could not act on the 10–4-1 plan until it saw districts based on the 1990 census. Legally, this left the city in the position of having to defend the old 8–3 system in court, since it was the existing system of representation.

The city's defense of the existing system was just short of a confession of judgment. The mayor and other members of the Council who were called to testify, along with Hutchison, said they felt the 8–3 system discriminated against minorities and should be replaced. Plaintiffs presented virtually uncontested evidence of polarized voting in Council races where there were minority candidates, packing of minority voters into as few districts as possible, foot dragging at changing the representation system, and the difficulty minority candidates had in financing at-large campaigns.

In light of the evidence before the court, Judge Jerry Buchmeyer's finding that the 8–3 system violated the Voting Rights Act was hardly surprising. Although the 10–4-1 plan was not technically before him, Buchmeyer expressed his doubt that it could pass muster under the Supreme Court's standards for enforcing the Voting Rights Act.

Having found the existing system illegal, the court turned to the issue of a remedy. The plaintiffs requested a system of fourteen single-member districts with the mayor elected at large. While this was two more districts than they had originally wanted, there was logic to it: the pending charter amendments created fourteen seats, albeit four of them were "quadrant" seats, so the city was officially committed to a Council of that size.

Round Two: 14–1

The City Council was divided over whether to accept the likely order of the court to create fourteen single-member districts, or to appeal and try to secure approval for the 10–4-1 plan. Glenn Box, a newly elected member from an East Dallas district, argued that since the voters had approved 10–4-1 the Council was honor bound to defend the will of the majority of city voters. Mayor Strauss had strongly supported 10–4-1 as the best system of representation for the city and one that she believed would heal its racial wounds. Now, however, she proposed a compromise: the Council would put the 14–1 plan to referendum. If it prevailed, the city would not have to appeal, since a majority of voters would have committed the city to it. Although Box and others opposed the move, Strauss prevailed, and the Council set a December 1990 date for the referendum, which in addition to the 14–1 proposal, contained another separate question on increasing council pay.

Once again Strauss helped orchestrate a committee of community notables to back the referendum. Former Council Member Al Gonzalez, a Hispanic businessman, chaired the committee. The same public relations firm that had designed the successful 10–4-1 campaign was now retained to sell 14–1 to the same voters. Perfunctory endorsements were obtained from the Dallas Citizens Council, the Greater Dallas Chamber of Commerce, and the other usual suspects. The Mayor endorsed 14–1 with the same fervor she had shown for 10–4-1 some 16 months earlier, and went on vacation.

Williams and Crenshaw, together with other black leaders, organized a separate grass-roots effort in the black community to support the plan, contending that the establishment campaign was not designed to appeal to black voters, but geared only to winning support in North Dallas. Hispanic community leaders also mounted a pro-14–1 campaign.

While there had been no organized Anglo opposition to the 10–4-1 referendum in 1989, the new campaign was not so lucky. Glenn Box allied himself with Tom Pauken, a conservative businessman, newspaper columnist, and Reagan administration operative, and Pat Cotton, a local Republican political consultant, to form a group to oppose 14–1. With Pauken taking the leadership of the "Just Say No to 14–1" campaign, the group stressed a popular sovereignty theme, arguing that a liberal federal judge (Buchmeyer was a Carter appointee) had no right to overturn a decision of the people expressed at referendum. Pauken condemned the idea that the city, if the suit were settled, would pay the legal costs of the plaintiffs, estimated at $750,000. Under federal law, plaintiffs' attorneys, if successful, were entitled to have their fees paid by the defendants. This subtlety did not burden Pauken. A skilled polemicist, he characterized the 14–1 proposal as a racial quota system, dwelling on the understanding that had been reached between the city and the plaintiffs that if the people approved the referendum, at least four seats would be created that would be safe for black candidates. Given the population distribution patterns in Dallas, it would have been be difficult to create fewer than four districts with substantial black majorities under either the 14–1 or 10–4-1 plans.

As the campaign progressed, it was evident that Pauken's group was making an effective appeal to many Anglo voters. It was also reasonably clear that although the peak business organizations endorsed 14–1, their endorsement was less enthusiastic than it had been for the earlier 10–4-1 referendum. The mayor, who was being criticized for being absent from the city during much of the campaign, then made a mistake that played into Pauken's judge-bashing strategy. Strauss called Judge Buchmeyer to verify that he had told attorneys in the case that if the city did not approve the referendum he would impose a 14–1 plan. The judge, after checking with the plaintiffs' attorneys, affirmed that he would indeed do that. It was unclear whether he checked with the city's counsel—but then the mayor was the "head" of city government. He admonished the mayor not to discuss her conversation with him.

In a television debate with Pauken, the mayor asserted that one of the reasons for voting for 14–1 was that the judge "has said" that if the city did not, he would impose it. Pauken asked her how she knew what the judge would do; had she spoken with the judge? The mayor lied, saying she had not, but that the judge had told that to the attorneys (which was true). She later admitted, however, that she had called the judge and he had told her what he would do if the referendum failed. Pauken seized on this admission to blast Buchmeyer again as an arrogant federal judge, interfering in the right of the voters of Dallas to determine for themselves what kind of representation system they would have. He demanded that Buchmeyer remove himself from the case. He and Box petitioned the Court of Appeals for the Fifth Circuit to remove Buchmeyer for prejudice. The Court of Appeals subsequently found no prejudicial action by Buchmeyer, noting only that his talking to the mayor was "unwise," but the issue served Pauken and his allies well during the remainder of the campaign.

Another event reinforced the "Just Say No" campaign's racial strategy. During the campaign, County Commissioner John Wiley Price was involved in two incidents. An off-duty and out of uniform police officer, jogging past Price's home, shouted a racial insult. As a result of many challenges of police behavior, Price had earned a reputation for being hot-tempered and confrontational. The animosity between him and many police officers was mutual. At the insult, Price leaped into his car, chased down the officer, and holding an air gun (witnesses differ on whether he held it to the officer's head), collared him. This incident made the front pages and threatened for a time to generate a broader conflict. Price rallied his supporters, the police chief investigated the behavior of the officer, and the Dallas County District Attorney considered whether to revoke Price's probation resulting from a previous escapade in which he defaced liquor billboards in southern Dallas.

Although this latest Price adventure was resolved through intervention by his pastor, Zan Holmes, Price made an indelible impression on many Anglo voters as the kind of black elected official they might expect in multiple if more Council seats were provided for minorities. Ragsdale and Lipscomb were often mentioned with disfavor by Anglo voters because, like Price, they were confrontational and garrulous, and affronted Dallas's image of itself as a city that got things done quietly and efficiently.

A week before the election, Price was involved in a second altercation, this time before television cameras. While picketing a local TV station for its alleged failure to hire more minorities for its on-camera jobs, Price stepped in front of a van driven by a suburban woman who was coming to the same building to pick up a child. She recognized Price, and knowing of his reputation, was apparently frightened. After an increasingly angry exchange, he refused to move out of her path, and she inched the van forward. He grasped the windshield wipers and bent them back. A police officer at the scene intervened and stopped the confrontation. Price was charged, on the woman's complaint, with a misdemeanor property offense. Pauken's committee did not need to say anything specific about the incident to capitalize on it. It fit well into the coda of "racial quotas" the campaign was already emphasizing.

The 14–1 plan was rejected by less than 400 votes. Although black precincts had a higher turnout than in previous special elections—almost doubling past votes in some cases—and voted heavily in favor of 14–1, Anglo precincts in north Dallas delivered a fatal blow to its chances. Voters refused legitimacy to the attempt by a majority of the Council to bring an end to the long redistricting conflict. The margin of defeat was small, but it was a clear defeat. The city was back at square one. Now it would be even harder than before the referendum to settle the lawsuit. Plaintiffs, who were adamant that 14–1 be implemented, had a federal court decision behind them. The role of the attorneys' fees in the referendum campaign also made it politically difficult for the city to agree to a settlement that would cost it heavily.

The Court Jerry-Manders Dallas

Frustrated in their attempts to settle the suit, the plaintiffs returned to court, and after a short hearing on remedies, Judge Jerry Buchmeyer ordered the Council to redistrict the city into fourteen single-member council districts. To carry out this task, he commandeered the city's own redistricting commission, which had been appointed by the Council to draw up a 10–4-1 plan. In addition, he appointed two "experts" to assist the commission: Robert Greer, the city's staff demographer, and Richard Engstrom, a political scientist from the University of New Orleans and an authority on Voting Rights redistricting issues. The order to redistrict was issued in February 1991. The earliest date possible for municipal elections was

May 4. Buchmeyer, in consultation with the city's attorneys, gave the commission two weeks to complete its work in order to allow enough time before the election for candidates to file and campaign.

Like the 1989 charter revision committee, the Council had picked the redistricting commission. Each member chose one commissioner; the mayor selected five and named one of them, Robert Oberwetter, as chair. Vice President for Public Affairs of Hunt Oil Company, Oberwetter had managed the mayoral campaign of Strauss's 1987 opponent. Her other appointees included Tom Laszo, the Chairman of the Hispanic Chamber of Commerce, and Sheryl Wattley, a young black attorney with no close political connections to Dallas's black politicians. Laszo and Wattley were selected as commission vice-chairs at its organization meeting prior to the court order to create fourteen districts. The commission was the third tri-ethnic committee formed in two years to solve the redistricting puzzle.

Once Buchmeyer decided that the city would have fourteen single-member districts, he asked Oberwetter to poll the commission to see if its members would be willing to work for the court instead of the city. All agreed to do so. Meeting in chambers with Oberwetter and representatives of the parties, and after receiving assurances from Greer that he could produce the maps in that time, Buchmeyer set a deadline of two weeks for a final report from the commission. The judge gave the commission no further instructions or guidance. He never talked to Engstrom.

Judge Buchmeyer was clear, once he had found the violation of the Voting Rights Act, that it should be remedied at the first available opportunity. May 4 happened to be the normal date for municipal elections and he saw no reason, once the city assured him that it was physically possible to draw districts in that time, for any delay in holding Council elections under the new plan. He was determined to use the city's processes and election calendar rather than appoint a master or set new election dates.

Greer and Engstrom saw their roles as staff advisers and implementers for the commission. At its first meeting, Engstrom laid out his understanding of the basic guidelines or rules of thumb the U.S. Department of Justice and federal courts had used in assessing specific redistricting plans. He advised the commission that appellate courts rarely had approved districts that varied in population more than a two percent deviation from the average for court-ordered plans, in contrast with permitting as much as five percent variation from the mean in plans drawn by legislative bodies. He also reported that the U.S. Department of Justice used a rule of thumb of 65 percent as the level of minority population a district needed to ensure that candidates favored by minority voters could be elected. The commission accepted both the 2 percent deviation and the 65 percent minority population level as working rules it would use in drawing districts.[4]

Even without explicit directions from the court, the commission understood its task to be the creation of a system of districts that would correct the racially discriminatory pattern found by the court. To them this meant creating a system that as nearly as possible provided a number of safe black and Hispanic districts proportional to the black and Hispanic population of the city. Thus of fourteen seats, blacks, with 30 percent of the population were "entitled" to 4.2, Hispanics with 21 percent of the population, to 2.9, and Anglos to the remaining seven. All members of the commission appeared to have thought that the proportionate distribution of seats among the racial and ethnic groups was their primary duty. Once that was assured, several felt that they should do what they could to protect incumbent council members.

The "first count" 1990 Census data became available the week Buchmeyer issued his order. The Bruton Center for Development Studies of the University of Texas at Dallas, using its Geographic Information System, supplied Greer and the Commission with maps showing the number and percentage of Anglos, blacks and Hispanics in each census block. Information at this scale was crucial, because to obtain the "right" percentages of population for each district, the commission had to split census tracts into smaller components. The maps made it possible for Greer and members of the commission to move lines around blocks to include or exclude voters of one race or another.

Looking at the maps, it was clear to the commission that its most difficult task was to create "safe" Hispanic districts for a population that was not as highly concentrated as blacks and Anglos. The Hispanic commissioners called a summit caucus of community leaders, which, after reviewing the situation, agreed that the two Hispanics on the commission should demand two safe Hispanic districts and fight to preserve them at all costs. Accepting this demand at its next meeting, the commission instructed Greer and Engstrom to produce the two strongest Hispanic districts possible. The black members then declared that if the Hispanics wanted only two districts, there should be five black districts. This would produce a council equally divided between Anglos and the two legally protected minority groups and roughly reflecting the 1990 population of the city. Again the full commission concurred.

Working with the maps and computer programs, Greer and Engstrom produced two districts that contained safe Hispanic majorities. But each required tortuous boundary drawing, tracking around blocks, splitting recognized neighborhoods and established voting precincts, and creating thin "bridges" of land between separated pockets of Hispanic settlement. Greer confessed that he thought the form of these districts and their division of local communities was so outrageous that the commission would never accept them. It did so virtually without discussion.[5]

This decision drove the remainder of the process. The commission now asked Greer and Engstrom to develop five safe black districts. Four black districts could be easily created in southern and west Dallas, but drawing a fifth safe black district proved difficult. Many middle class families moved from the black ghetto in southern Dallas during the 1980s into formerly Anglo or mixed race neighborhoods on the eastern, southwestern, and northern fringes of the city. Except for southwest Dallas, these areas were fairly remote from the historic center of the black population. Moreover, two important communities south of I-30—Oak Cliff and Pleasant Grove—had large numbers of Anglos, but their neighborhoods were surrounded or integrated by blacks and Hispanics. Two Anglo council members who planned to run for reelection represented these communities. Both had effective spokespersons in their appointees on the redistricting commission.

Concern over the 12–1 redistricting plan, which probably would have divided Oak Cliff into two districts and made unlikely the election of an Anglo in either of them, had provided part of the impetus toward the 1990–1991 Oak Cliff secession movement discussed in earlier chapters. Oak Cliff was proudly multi-ethnic, although its integration is more in the aggregate than block by block. The Anglo core of Oak Cliff was Kessler Park-Stevens Park, a handsome middle class community. South and west of this enclave, Hispanics occupied many older homes, and to the north, east, and south, Oak Cliff has been home for many upwardly mobile black families. Its historic business district, centered on Jefferson Street, contains the city's largest concentration of Hispanic-owned businesses. North of Oak Cliff, West Dallas contained the city's largest and most notorious public housing project, the subject of another long trial and expensive settlement in Judge Buchmeyer's court. The virtually all-black "project" was adjacent to neighborhoods with the highest concentration of low-income Hispanics in the city.

Many Oak Cliff residents were proud of the fact that their community had become diverse while remaining stable. Middle class residents from each ethnic group were committed to maintaining a diverse community. Community leaders feared that a system of representation based on race would divide their community politically and reduce its influence in city affairs. Some undoubtedly feared that the loss of an Anglo representative would discourage some Anglos from staying and other households or firms from locating in Oak Cliff.

Across town in Pleasant Grove, a working class community in southeast Dallas, a substantial degree of racial change had occurred. Many blocks that were almost completely Anglo in 1980 had high percentages of new black or Hispanic families by 1990. There was no mass exodus of Anglos, but as families aged and left for other accommodations or died, upwardly mobile minority families replaced them. The result was a checkerboard pattern of settlement that made it virtually impossible to keep Pleasant Grove intact if its black population was needed to provide the "safe" margin for one or more adjoining districts. If current population trends continued, a district anchored in Pleasant Grove could probably elect an Anglo (assuming voter polarization along racial lines) immediately following the 1990 redistricting. After a short time, however, the district would become competitive for black or Hispanic candidates.

With Oak Cliff and Pleasant Grove complicating the problem of drawing five black districts, the work of the commission was divided between northern and southern Dallas. Greer worked on districts for the northern half of the city with the Anglo members. They had only two principal concerns—protection of incumbents by avoiding districts that forced them to run against each other, and keeping as many as possible of the city's "progressive" voters out of Glenn Box's conservative district. Greer satisfied the second concern by creating a 13-mile long district that stretched from Love Field in northwest Dallas to the city limits on the east side of town. Only a block or two wide in places, this district looked safe for Lori Palmer, the progressive incumbent. It also circumnavigated Box's home, leaving him an opening to the more conservative northeastern neighborhoods.

Engstrom was still struggling to find a fifth safe black district south of I-30. He was competing with the Oak Cliff commission member who was working to devise a plan that would protect the Anglo incumbent, Charles Tandy. Because of the difficulty in creating the fifth black district, the commission decided to ask Buchmeyer if he would approve a plan in which some district populations deviated from the average by four rather than two percent. The judge agreed to the commission's representation that without it, five safe black districts could not be created. He extended the deadline for reporting to him by several days to allow the commission to complete its work.

Engstrom began a new search for the fifth district. During an all night work session with Sheryl Wattley, he discovered that a fifth district could be created by a pincers movement around Pleasant Grove, connecting a line of blocks on the eastern boundary of the city with black neighborhoods to the south and southwest. This produced a plan that a majority of the commission accepted.

The final plan was adopted with dissents from one black and two Anglo commissioners. One of the Anglos submitted a minority report with an alternative plan, which protected the Oak Cliff incumbent. The black dissenter was upset by the decision of Wattley and other blacks on the commission, after a long and acrimonious caucus, to the district containing Al Lipscomb's residence because it included a large number of middle class neighborhoods. The district was overwhelmingly black, but its higher income residents were less likely to support Lipscomb's style of politics. Its work completed, the commission presented its recommendations to the court. After a perfunctory hearing, Judge Buchmeyer ordered it into effect.

While the commission was going about its work, members of the City Council were debating whether to accede to the court's order and end the dispute or to appeal it. Burger and the two black Council members urged an immediate settlement to end the city's agony, however unpopular that might be with voters who had just rejected the court-ordered plan. Mayor Strauss now took the position that the city should respect the decision of the voters and appeal the district court's rejection of the 10–4-1 plan. This position was championed by Box, who continued to belabor Buchmeyer's "intervention" into city affairs and to insist that since 10–4-1 had been approved twice by the voters the City Council was honor bound to defend it to the bitter end.

Thus, over strenuous objections from Lipscomb, Ragsdale, Palmer, and Burger, the Council voted to draw a 10–4-1 plan and submit it to the Justice Department for clearance. Simultaneously, they petitioned the Court of Appeals for the Fifth Circuit to overrule Judge Buchmeyer's order. In deciding to appeal, the Council also removed the case from the city attorney. Box and Jerry Bartos, a north Dallas Council Member who had opposed the 14–1 referendum, felt that the city attorney had not aggressively defended the city in the initial case. Although Box had made much of the cost of plaintiffs' attorneys' fees in the recent referendum, he supported a motion to commit the city to pay more than $250,000 to retain a special counsel to handle the appeal.

As the legal battle continued, candidates for Council scrambled to find out in which districts they lived so they could file for the May 4th election, which presumably would be held under the court-ordered 14–1 plan. In a surprise to local political observers, Congressman Steve Bartlett announced he would resign his seat in the U.S. House of Representatives to run for mayor after Annette Strauss announced she would not seek a third term. Then, just a few days before the March filing deadline for Council candidates, the U.S. Court of Appeals for the 5th Circuit stayed Judge Buchmeyer's order to give the Justice Department time to review a specific 10–4-1 plan. The election was postponed.

The Council directed Greer, who was still catching up on his sleep from the round-the-clock work for the redistricting commission, to prepare a 10–4-1 plan to submit to the Justice Department. He prepared several alternatives, and the Council selected one that provided three black and one Hispanic districts in the ten first tier districts. Anglos would dominate two and blacks one of the four second tier quadrant districts. The fourth quadrant was racially mixed, with blacks and Hispanics together outnumbering Anglos. The Council did not use the redistricting commission it had originally appointed for the express purpose of drawing up a 10–4-1 plan. It was now regarded as an instrument of the court.

The Dallas chapter of the Southern Christian Leadership Conference announced a boycott of the city as a result of the Council's action. Lipscomb, Ragsdale, and Burger again urged their colleagues to settle the suit. They predicted that the Justice Department would reject the 10–4-1 plan because it diluted Hispanic voting strength and did not do as well for blacks as the 14–1 plan approved by Buchmeyer. Minorities were enraged by special counsel Mike McKool's recommendation that the city retain Bradford Reynolds, who had headed the Civil Rights Division in the U.S. Justice Department during the Reagan administration, to represent it before the Justice Department. Reynolds' reputation as a foe of affirmative action and other civil rights policies made him an anathema to minority leaders. After a raucous hearing, the Council decided not to retain him.

Since Justice Department review of redistricting schemes is not a formal adjudicatory process, various delegations went to Washington to lobby the Civil Rights Division in its review of the Council's handiwork. Taking the full sixty days allowed by law, the Justice Department notified the Council in early May that it had rejected their 10–4-1 plan.

Once again in a familiar mess, the Council met in executive session with its attorneys to figure out what to do next. Box and others wanted to appeal the decision of the Department or to draw a new 10–4-1 plan. Some members wanted to see if it would be possible to reach a settlement with the plaintiffs, an idea that now seemed attractive to a tentative majority. Discussions with the plaintiffs ensued, and the weary Greer was ordered to draw up more 14–1 alternatives, this time with a view to saving a seat in Oak Cliff for Charles Tandy, and if possible, the Pleasant Grove seat of incumbent John Evans. Since the plaintiffs insisted on five black districts, Greer could save one incumbent, but not both. The "compromise" plan he developed, which seemed acceptable to the plaintiffs, preserved Tandy's seat (and, therefore, his vote for it), but sacrificed Evans, dividing Pleasant Grove among three new districts, two of them with a majority of black residents.

The suit seemed at the brink of settlement. Lawyers' fees had ballooned since December. Not only would the plaintiffs' attorneys be entitled to more, but the city now had incurred almost a million dollars in legal costs of its own through the fruitless work of McKool. But everything unraveled in the executive session that preceded the May 11th council meeting at which Lipscomb threw his chair. Mayor Strauss and Council Member Harriet Meiers joined the two North Dallas members, plus Box and Evans, to cast six votes for a different plan Greer had been ordered to draw, which provided only four black districts, apparently preserving seats for both Tandy and Evans.

This action torpedoed any chance of settling the case, but gave McKool something to take back to the Justice Department. Again, he sought Council support for a Washington representative to help make the city's case before the Office of Civil Rights. This time he suggested Jervis Leonard, a Nixon Administration assistant attorney general, who had no negative association with civil rights issues. It turned out, however, that Leonard had been involved in a questionable business deal in Texas and was, consequently, unacceptable to the Council. But word soon filtered back to McKool that the Justice Department was not enthralled with the latest submission, and he informed the Council that it probably would not be approved because it was clear that a fifth black and seventh minority district could be created. This time, over Box's objections, the Council threw in the towel. Greer was sent back to his computer, laying out options. The plan finally adopted by the Council and approved by the Court is shown in Figure 11.1. It preserved an Oak Cliff district that could elect an Anglo, but was far less favorable to Anglo chances in Pleasant Grove.

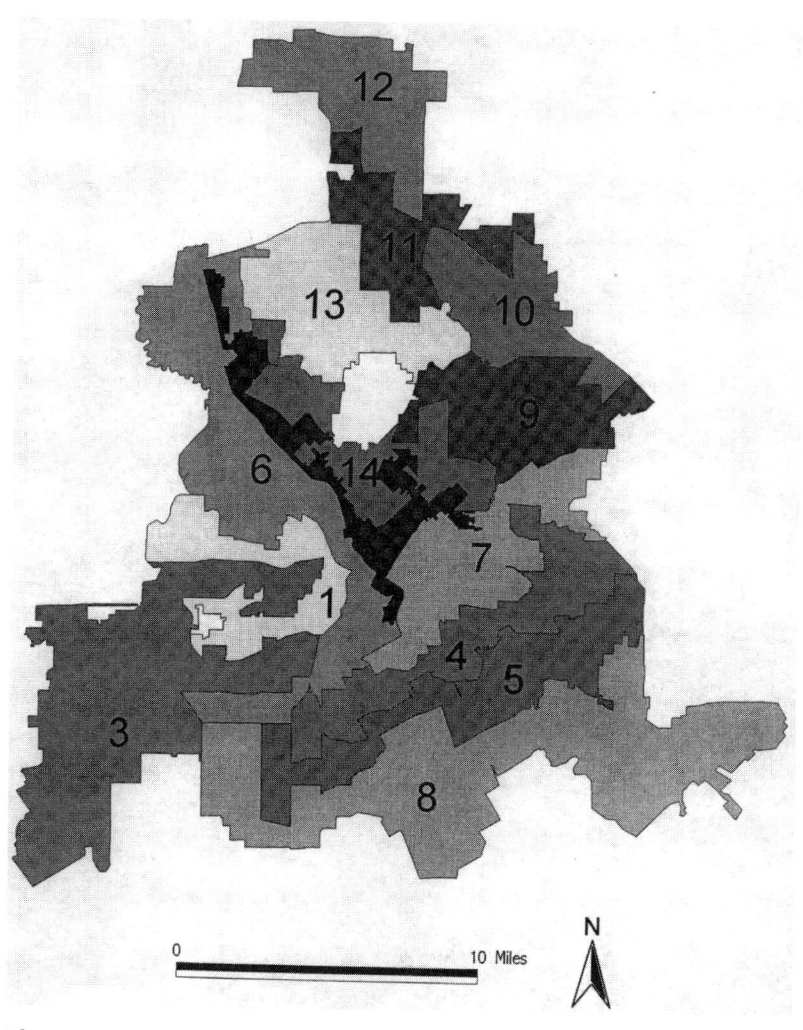

Figure 11.1. Dallas city council districts

The World Does Not End

Fifty-seven candidates filed for the fourteen new Council seats. Every seat was contested. Two incumbents were defeated. In the 5th District, John Evans, the Anglo who had represented Pleasant Grove, lost in the first round to Don Hicks, a black tax and civil rights attorney. Ragsdale lost in a bitter 6th District run-off to Charlotte Mayes, the black candidate supported by most of the Breakfast Club's members, none of whom lived in the district. In the 4th District, which had been drawn to provide a fifth safe black seat, Marvin Crenshaw, the co-plaintiff in the redistricting lawsuit, lost in a run-off to Larry Duncan, the Anglo president of the Homeowners League. Domingo Garcia, who had intervened in the lawsuit on behalf of Hispanic voters, won the 1st District seat, and Chris Luna, also with Breakfast Club support, won the run-off against another Hispanic in the 2nd District, which had been created as the second safe Hispanic district. Lipscomb was elected to a fourth term. Thus, the new Council contained four blacks, two Hispanics, and nine Anglos, including Steve Bartlett, who easily won the race for mayor.

Redistricting and Civic Capital Formation

Assessing the significance of the Dallas experience with redistricting for the formation of civic capital requires distinguishing the process from the result. It is hard to argue that the painful and expensive process by which the city reached its result increased the civic skills of many that participated in it. On the other hand, the new Council, however problematic the design of its districts, provided greater opportunities for the civic engagement of people previously excluded from effective roles in city governance.

Redistricting involves the redistribution of power in the community and lies at the heart of the fundamental question of politics: Who gets what, when, and how? The existence of legal constraints on how districts may be drawn makes drawing them no less political. Therefore, the means selected for carving up the political map of the city are crucial to the outcome. In the Dallas case, the choice of litigation to force consideration of minority interests set in motion alternative processes that were more congenial to the civic culture. These included the creation of Dallas Together task force, the Charter Review Committee, the Redistricting Commission, involvement of the City Council, and use of referenda to legitimate decisions. Thus, the redistricting effort proceeded on two tracks: one political, under control of incumbent and traditional interests with voices but little influence for minorities; the other legal, driven by the *Williams* plaintiffs in federal court. The political track was designed in part to avoid a court-ordered result unsatisfactory to traditional interests; and the legal track was taken to prevent a redistricting scheme that continued to deny minorities their rightful share of political power under the Voting Rights Act.

Both tracks provide textbook examples of the adage that the answers one gets depend upon the questions asked. In both venues, the issue was primarily one of racial equity. The political track framed the question as one of accommodating the justified legal demands of minorities in ways that could be accepted by the Anglo majority. The legal track defined the issue simply as one of full vindication of minority rights. Neither track framed the question as one of how to fashion a fair representative system that could work and advance the development of civic capital in a modern, racially and economically diverse city. In fact, neither process was well designed to deal with such a question.

The charter revision committee's membership and deadline interacted to contribute to its ultimate failure. In part, the deadline was a response to the pending litigation; in part, it was an innocent misjudgment about the difficulty of finding a consensus solution. The lawsuit undoubtedly stimulated serious interest on the part of the Council and the city's economic leaders in resolving the problem expeditiously. But the deadline generated an atmosphere of haste in which there was no time for doubting or for opposing members of the committee to explore fully the consequences of the 10–4-1 proposal or any other alternatives. The squelching of genuine deliberation by the committee compressed any time for public education about that approach. Most committee members felt compelled to reach a quick decision. Minority members who entered the process warily became even more distrustful as they perceived the chair to be brushing aside their proposals and railroading through a prearranged plan designed to preserve Anglo power. Hutchison and his allies looked on the behavior of Ragsdale and Lipscomb as insincere and designed only to preserve the court case.

The atmosphere of time pressure and distrust within which the committee worked made real negotiation impossible. The blocs took positions early in the process, and there was little exploration of how their respective interests might be accommodated. The presumption of the minority members that a court would probably insist on a straight single-member district plan buttressed their intransigence to consideration of other options. Although some of them appeared open to a trade-off that would have increased the number of minority seats and guaranteed increased compensation for Council members in return for some form of mixed or two-tiered system, there was insufficient trust among key members to pursue such approaches. The tendency of each side to fix on a particular size for the Council was exacerbated by the absence of data that could show the consequences of choosing any particular number of seats or pattern of districts.

In a sense, the Charter Revision Committee represented a traditional Dallas approach to symbolic accommodation of minority complaints without surrendering actual power. Rather than negotiate a redistricting plan with minority members,

Hutchison shut down the committee following the minority caucus and recalled it only when he had the votes for the 10–4-1 plan. Even though he sweetened the medicine by including a recommendation for increased compensation for Council members, both the proposed change in the representative system and the procedure by which it was reached disappointed or offended key minorities, not least of whom were the *Williams* plaintiffs.

Approval of the two-tiered plan by a narrow majority of voters in a racially polarized referendum guaranteed that minorities would regard the 10–4-1 plan as a non-legitimate response to their complaint of political exclusion. However fair it seemed to those about to share a little of their power, it seemed grossly unfair to those demanding full recognition of their right to equal political opportunity. Because the 10–4-1 plan was adopted without any data to support its assertions of racial equality, its approval in the 1989 referendum ensured that the lawsuit would proceed. The major accomplishment of the referendum was to delegitimate the old 8–3 system, making it all but impossible for the federal court to find against the plaintiffs. The referendum provided faux legitimacy for those resisting change and gave cover for the subsequent racially polarized campaign against the 14–1 plan.

Once the matter was in court, there was no room to trade off the array of neighborhood, economic, incumbency, and other interests with legitimate claims to fairness in the representative system. The Voting Rights Act spoke only to the issue of racial fairness. The Totality of Circumstances Test, which the Supreme Court laid out for assessing voting rights complaints, dealt with nonracial claims for representation only to the extent that they did not impinge on racial equality. Thus, the scope of the issues before the court was narrow. The question Judge Buchmeyer had to decide was whether the city's history of districting, voting, and policy actions had the effect of diluting the opportunity of minority voters to elect candidates of their choice to the council. If the answer to this question was "yes," the court had to find a violation of the Voting Rights Act.

Having easily done so, the next job of the court was to impose a remedy that cured the violation. Although the Voting Rights Act admonishes that it does not require that the number of seats be proportional to the minority population, such a remedy would, on the face of it, end the discrimination. Also, once racial discrimination was found, it was hard for the court to accept a plan that provided for fewer black and Hispanic districts than it was technically feasible to produce.

Without ever saying so, the law placed pressure on the commission to make race its primary consideration in drawing districts. The irony of this result was that such districts could institutionalize racially polarized voting by segregating voters by race into Council districts. Although the Supreme Court, in *Shaw v. Reno,*[6] subsequently recognized this defect, it did not resolve the dilemma that there seemed to be no other practical cure for the problem of dilution of minority voting strength so long as single-member districts were used.[7]

Judge Buchmeyer, though much criticized by those who opposed the 14–1 system, acted with considerable restraint. His order was limited to the correction of the discrimination he had found, and to which the city had admitted. Finding the remedy proposed by the city inadequate to cure the evil, he accepted the remedy proposed by the plaintiffs. While he increased the number of Council positions from eleven to fourteen, the latter number had already been agreed upon by the Council and approved by the voters in the 10–4-1 configuration. Rather than undertake the drawing of districts himself, he employed the commission the Council had selected to perform that task. Using race as the primary criterion, the commission produced fourteen districts, most of which were racially homogeneous. The majority-minority districts, in particular, were creative polygons that traversed the city, cutting across neighborhoods and precincts, severing some communities into as many as three separate districts. Nevertheless, Buchmeyer accepted the commission's recommendations without change as the basis for his final order. It was not appropriate for the court to consider problems of representative government that were not before it.

The Council, having accepted the 10–4-1 scheme engineered by its Charter Review Committee and having secured its approval at referendum, was unable to reverse course to obtain the approval of a 14-district plan. The rejectionist bloc on the Council was joined by the wavering centrists in the fumbling attempt to use the referenda as a rationale for refusing to settle the lawsuit, appealing Buchmeyer's order, and seeking Justice Department approval for a 10–4-1 design. The Council faced reality only after the appeal was denied and the Justice Department rejected the plan submitted to it. The Council's modifications to the court-approved 14–1 were designed to protect two incumbents, and were only half successful.

The adage that no one should watch laws or sausage being made could have been coined for the Dallas Council attempting to redistrict itself. If the process did little to increase the capacity of those who partook of it to solve complex public issues or to build trust among officials or between them and their publics, that may be beside the point if the resulting system of representation worked to build civic capital.

The 14–1 system enabled some people to serve on the Council who could not have succeeded under either the old 8–3 system, and probably not under the 10–4-1 scheme. At least four members of the first Council elected under the new scheme would have had great difficulty winning without single-member districts, which made personal campaigning possible. Three of the districts that had been designed to be "safe" for minority candidates elected candidates not favored by most of the minority voters in those districts. In two districts, the contributions of the Breakfast Club and a higher turnout of Anglo voters were significant. Charlotte Mayes survived a recall election engineered by supporters of Diane Ragsdale and was later re-elected three times in District 7. Chris Luna also was re-elected twice before retiring from the Council in 1997. District 4 elected Larry Duncan, an Anglo who in subsequent elections received a majority of African-American votes, and was re-elected three times. These candidates and others—notably Don Hicks, who won the 5th District, which had been designed to give incumbent John Evans an opportunity for re-election—managed to build and maintain multi-racial constituencies.

In some respects, the sheer artificiality of the districts required incumbents to "work" them assiduously through town hall meetings, issue forums, and other forms of personal contact. Council members became reasonably skilled in securing resources for their districts, producing a more acceptable distribution than in the past. Most became effective advocates for the needs of their constituents. Duncan and Barbara Mallory, who was elected in District 6 in 1993, cooperated to create a 400-member citizens task force on the Trinity Corridor, which developed proposals that were eventually co-opted by Mayor Kirk as the basis for the 1998 bond referendum. Several other southern Dallas Council members cooperated to demand and receive greater attention by city government to the problems of southern Dallas, although the Council as a whole remained highly attentive to the interests of the business community and the revitalization of the downtown area.

None of this activity appears to have increased voting, although it encouraged other forms of political participation, such as attendance at community meetings. Most incumbents have been secure in their positions. Only two of those originally elected in the new districts were defeated in bids for re-election. After the first wide-open Council election, competition and turnout declined as incumbents built reputations and resources to discourage potential challengers. Elections in years when there was no race for mayor tended to produce lower voter turnout, giving an advantage to incumbents who had greater name recognition and access to campaign funding. Term limits may also have inhibited potential challengers who could wait for an incumbent to be forced into retirement before seeking the position.

The councils elected since 1991 have been more racially diverse, and there have been more disagreements among minority representatives than in previous years. To the extent that racial and ethnic discord and under-representation of minorities was the most salient issue in the city at the beginning of the decade, the creation of single-member districts can be said to have ameliorated that problem. While it is usually near the top of the political and policy agendas in Dallas, race competes with a wide variety of other issues for voter and official interest. Neighborhood stability takes up a considerable amount of Council and staff time, and animates many voters. Economic development, transportation problems, infrastructure maintenance, policing, environmental quality, and animal control are often matters of intense dispute. Some of these issues are infused with racial overtones, but some are relatively free of them. None of them can be "fixed" without engagement in a substantive and sustained discourse.

The new representative system appears to have been an important factor in reducing intergroup conflict in Dallas, but it did not materially change the general drift of the city's governance. It can be credited with support for the development of programs such as community policing, expanded opportunities for minority contractors, and efforts to increase investment in southern Dallas and the central business district, but it has not shown more competence in dealing with other issues. Lacking any independent support staff, the Council has deferred to the city manager on most operational, financial, and infrastructure issues. It ceded the initiative for long-range planning to a private organization, the Dallas Plan. Occupied primarily as caseworkers for their districts, Council members have been primarily reactive rather than anticipatory in their policy roles. Until Laura Miller was elected in 2002 to fill the remainder of Ron Kirk's term as mayor after he resigned to run for the U.S. Senate, no district council member had been able to build a citywide constituency.[8]

During the Bartlett mayoralty from 1991 to 1995, the Council remained fractious, substantially abetted by Bartlett's shortcomings as a leader. Following the election of Ron Kirk, the adoption of new rules of procedure and tighter control of the agenda by the mayor improved Council decorum and shortened meetings. Kirk was also acknowledged by his Council colleagues to be an extraordinarily gifted consensus builder and presiding officer. Unlike Bartlett, who often surprised his colleagues with proposals, engendering mistrust even among potential allies, Kirk worked carefully to prepare members for his initiatives and had a reputation for keeping his word. Even those who were not "team players" and found themselves with less important committee assignments, or bereft of chairs they had hoped to occupy, begrudgingly conceded the mayor's effectiveness and leadership skills.

At the end of the 1990s, there was general acceptance of single-member districts for the Council. Most members of the Council tended to see little need for further change. They were satisfied with their roles and resisted any effort to increase the powers of the mayor. As one former member put it: "The city manager has to satisfy at least six of us to keep his job. A strong mayor would only have to satisfy himself."[9] Both mayors Bartlett and Kirk, however, were frustrated by the weakness of their office and their inability to meet the expectations of the public that they run the city.[10] In 1997, Kirk suggested strengthening the office of mayor, but abandoned any effort to amend the Charter after many members of the Council, including African-American and Hispanic members, voiced strenuous opposition. They liked the mayor's position the way it was: weak.

Perhaps most telling, the Council gave no thought to the next cycle of redistricting, due in 2001 following the census. Charter-imposed term limits placed the next redistricting beyond the concerns of over half of the Council members serving in 1999, as they were ineligible for re-election in 2001. No one interviewed for this book had given thought to how the city might address the next round of redistricting in light of the *Shaw* doctrine. This lack of foresight in adapting to new circumstances and consequent resort to ad hockery is a pattern common to Dallas; one that springs naturally from a civic culture that continues to rely on certain ways of resolving complex problems.

V

Conclusions and Reflections

12

How Dallas "Solves" Problems

> Urban regimes . . . become locked into a way of seeing the world and applying solutions to the problems they isolate. . . . These solution-sets . . . are as important as the participants in defining that regime.
>
> BRYAN D. JONES

Solution Sets

People engage in collective political activity through interest groups and other intermediary institutions to resolve particular public problems. Civic capital is produced when officials and citizens receive positive feedback from their participation in the form of policy successes, personal satisfaction, and development of civic skills that can be applied to other issues. Civic capital formation in a complex and diverse city depends substantially upon a public environment that fosters a sense of political efficacy across classes, races, and interests. Because no one group can be expected to prevail on all issues or all of the time, one of the key elements in the development of civic capital is experience in the formation and maintenance of alliances and coalitions to resolve problems.

Conversely, if participation is restricted or produces negative feedback that engaging in public affairs is fruitless and personally not efficacious, the development of civic capital will be stunted. Substantial segments of the population learn to shun political life rather than embrace it. The pool from which leadership can be drawn will be shallow, and the legitimacy of policies and the government itself may be compromised.

Whether the experience of those who seek to participate in the public life of the city is productive of civic capital or not, certain systemic tools tend to be employed. When these tools are used in patterned ways, they may be characterized as "solution sets," which reflect the understandings of the governing elite about the causes of problems and how they should be addressed.[1] These solution sets become culturally imbedded as the appropriate ways of conducting public business. When new problems emerge, there is a tendency to apply techniques that appear to have worked in the past. There are, in all cultures, methods that are regarded as appropriate, and more likely to be employed than others that a disinterested observer might think were more rational.[2]

The use of solution sets presupposes a "normal" state of affairs, the equilibrium of which is occasionally punctuated by some event or activity that brings an issue onto the public and institutional agendas, thus demanding a response from the political system.[3] In this sense, most solution sets are reactive rather than anticipatory. They are what a city does in dealing with problems that are regarded as out of the ordinary. They may be used even after they repeatedly fail to resolve issues and be counterproductive of civic capital formation. Six distinct solution sets can be derived from the description of decisions in earlier chapters. Each affects the way civic capital is developed in Dallas.

Managed Care—The Good Housekeeping Standard

Policy equilibrium in Dallas is governance on automatic pilot under the managerial regency. Managers are responsible for routine services and incremental initiatives of modest scope and controversy. Consistent with a civic culture that assigns political amateurs to short-term poorly compensated service on the governing boards of the city and school district, little policy creativity is expected of them. Although they have no independent staff support, their job is to oversee the managers of extensive bureaucracies, provide a sounding board for citizens, make modest adjustments in the policy recommendations of managers, and legitimate their actions with the imprimatur of representative government. Dallas has enjoyed the services of a number of able city managers such as George Shrader and Richard Knight, who combined strong professional and technical competencies with finely tuned political sensitivities.

Under the banner of "implementation" of policy, the manager as the chief executive officer of the city exercises wide discretion in administering the day-to-day affairs of city agencies and in bringing proposals to the Council. While the elected officials clearly matter, and occasionally make a substantial difference in the direction and tone of policies, the normal state of Dallas governance is one of managed care—inexpensive, prudent, incremental, and occasionally innovative.

The most effective managers have been problem solvers like Richard Knight, whose reputation as the city's "Mr. Fixit," was tested in the Civilian Police Review Board and police shootings crises discussed in Chapter 6. In dealing with these crises, Knight operated on two levels. On the first, he played a traditional role. He secured the prompt resignation of a chief who had lost the confidence of both the Council and the police force. Fully and publicly exercising his authority under the Charter, he undertook a nation-wide search for a new chief, to the consternation of the Dallas Police Association (DPA), and in the face of concern of some council members who clearly favored selection of a chief from inside the department. His refusal to discuss increasing the size of the police force with representatives of the Dallas Police Association was calculated to emphasize the point that he alone was responsible for recommending the number of positions and the budget for the force. He also effectively denied the DPA *de facto* recognition as a bargaining agent for police officers. Together, these actions re-established Knight's authority over a department that seemed to some to be on the verge of spinning out of control.

In all his actions, Knight took care to work within his clearly established authority and Dallas custom. There was some complaining but his right to act as he did was never challenged. While the issues of departmental management were highly politicized, they were undisputedly the manager's to resolve. Had he not acted, he risked being fired.

In the Review Board matter Knight operated at a second, essentially political level. His key role in brokering the agreement that ended the dispute foreshadowed John Ware's characterization of the manager's role: "I don't manage. I am a facilitator and referee."[4] But Knight was more than a mere good office through which the parties could work. He devised the compromise that had eluded the mayor and Ross Perot, whose support for it made possible withdrawal of the Police Association's threat to force a referendum on the powers of the Review Board. Knight's stature in the African-American community and the importance to it of supporting the city's most prominent black official were critical to acquiescence in an outcome that some minority politicians feared would weaken oversight of the police. Finally, his agreement to recommend a significant increase in the size of the police force, but a smaller one than demanded by the Police Association, asserted his managerial prerogatives and provided a base for reform of the department with a significant infusion of new personnel.

The evolution of policing in Dallas under successive city managers and police chiefs illustrates how artfully those professional managers used the powers bestowed on them by both the City Charter and the deferential political culture of Dallas to ameliorate the chronic problem of police-community relations. What Knight began in response to a near breakdown in departmental legitimacy and morale and a high level of public conflict among politicians and interest groups was ultimately carried out by Chief Ben Click with a minimum of political interference. The hierarchical discipline of the manager system, combined with the paramilitary command structure of the police department, made possible relatively rapid adaptation to change in the character and distribution of political influence in the city. In such traditional service areas, where the authority of the manager is essentially uncontested, the managed care solution set is most likely to be employed and appears to work well.

The Dallas system of governance, however, forces the manager into enhanced leadership positions on a wide range of policies. The advent of single-member districts and the demise of any policy-centered endorsement group have produced a Council composed of members focused sharply on the needs of their districts. While the mayor can use the visibility of the office to sponsor or support discrete policy initiatives, like the Dallas Plan or a bond issue, recent mayors have had neither a reliable political coalition in the Council nor the personal staff resources to initiate or carry out proposals. They can advance projects that have an external constituency, like the sports arena, when they have the cooperation of the manager. But the manager remains the official with the power to negotiate a deal for the city, although he may stay in the background while the mayor leads the public campaign for approval by the Council and the voters. As Ware's role in finding financing for in-town housing reveals, "facilitator" is far too passive a description for the manager's role in Dallas.

While the Council must acquiesce in the recommendations and decisions of the manager or his subordinates, it is primarily reactive to the manager's initiative. Only the manager has the legal authority and access to staff and other resources necessary to initiate projects that involve substantial organizational effort and technical competence. So long as the managers contain the crises and avoid new disruptions that threaten the image or stability of the city, they are unlikely to encounter sustained or serious opposition.

The role of the General Superintendent of Dallas Public Schools is more complicated. Theoretically, the superintendent has even broader authority than the city manager does, due to a legal framework that sharply limits the school board's power to oversee administration. This is abetted by the lower visibility and tenuous political legitimacy of the school board, and a board presidency that is weaker institutionally than even the mayor, since serving in that office depends upon the support of a majority of the board. With the exception of Sandy Kress, few school board chairs have seen themselves as much more than presiding officers. Under normal circumstances the confluence of these factors gives the superintendent extensive authority to run the school system, virtually without effective political oversight.[5]

Dallas Public Schools, however, have not operated under normal circumstances for more than forty years. The superintendent's authority has been circumscribed by federal court supervision of the school system and persistent racial conflict among trustees. The primary focus of the court on desegregation has often subordinated or stifled other administrative actions that superintendents might have taken to improve overall school performance. As Chapter 5 pointed out, court supervision has also given minority members of the School Board substantial leverage on superintendents' discretion in personnel, construction, and organizational decisions.[6]

Although schools, like police, are "coping" organizations,[7] they lack the paramilitary discipline and cultural solidarity of the police. This produces a system that is centralized only on paper. In the real world of educational politics, change cannot be engineered easily from the top. Teachers have greater individual autonomy and are less visible to the public when at work than are the police. They are better organized and more experienced in using their political muscle and entrenched bureaucratic procedures to prevent or delay actions they regard as contrary to their interests. In this environment, it is harder for superintendents to be "left alone" to "manage" the system by the board, the court, or their employee-constituents. Consequently, school affairs, unlike much of city affairs, have been in a state of disequilibrium for almost half of the twentieth century.

Power Plays and Market Makers

Managers may act as policy entrepreneurs, but ultimately they lack the legitimacy, legal power, or autonomy necessary to achieve certain objectives on their own. Some issues fall outside recognized managerial authority. And there are situations when the organizational routines of the managerial regency are inadequate. Special cases, such as the near death of Dallas Area Rapid Transit (DART), involve both managerial and policy failure. Other problems, like school performance, are chronic and evade containment through management strategies.

Where there is a substantial consensus of key officials and leaders of peak business organizations on the policy objective, the preferred solution set can be characterized as a power play by market makers. Key figures use their civic and business reputations and slack resources to sell policy or candidates to a largely unmobilized public. The power play has been a prominent feature of Dallas politics, at least since the concerted business-led Charter campaign of the 1930s. Other legendary examples include the creation of the CCA, the Centennial Exposition of 1937, the symbolic integration of schools in 1961, and the installation of Erik Jonsson as mayor. The power play is almost always the solution set of choice for the support of bond issues and charter amendments, which are subject to voter referenda.

City Council approval of a bond referendum is normally preceded by several months of publicity and preparation during which the manager, mayor, and Council members identify major infrastructure needs of the city and orchestrate news stories about the sorry state of facilities and particular needs.

When a major item has come onto the agenda, such as the Arts District, dredging of White Rock Lake, or the 1998 Trinity River Corridor project, it has almost invariably been accompanied by substantial preparation of the opinion leaders for its scale and importance to the city. This includes pronouncements by the mayor, endorsements by the peak business organizations, and feature articles and editorials in the *Dallas Morning News*.

The power play then follows a standard ritual. The bond issue itself is proposed by the City Manager. There usually is a short time between the manager's submission and the deadline for Council action and a short time between that action and the referendum date. This makes it difficult for those who oppose the measure to mobilize. Traditionally, the mayor plays a key leadership role lining up endorsements by business, political and civic notables, and in raising an intimidatingly large campaign fund for the drive. In the words of former mayor Bob Folsom: "On bond issues, the mayor needs to have a good sense of the city. . . . You should know that there is a lot of leadership who will support it. You try to organize; get Council members to work their districts."[8] Jack Evans, also a former mayor, echoed Folsom in speaking of the politics of putting together a bond issue: "The mayor has to have a feel for community, know its needs. Each council member has his own thing. The mayor has to get them together."[9]

The "Vote Yes!" campaign is launched when the mayor announces formation of a blue ribbon committee, chaired by the mayor or a prominent business leader. In recent years, black and Hispanic co-chairs have become standard elements of such campaigns. The Citizens Council and the respective Chambers of Commerce issue their endorsements. All former mayors attest to the importance of an affirmative vote. A public relations firm is employed to produce a marketing campaign, which sells the referendum through appeals to Dallas's greatness as a city and stresses the most popular benefits of the bond issue. The *Dallas Morning News* provides news coverage and editorial support. The bond drive chair, the mayor and other supporters become available for talk shows, TV interviews, and town hall meetings organized by Council members and other endorsers.

When serious but underfunded opposition forms, as in the arena and Trinity River cases, it typically is dismissed by the mayor and other campaign spokespersons as composed of marginal cranks and enemies of progress, growth, and the Dallas aspiration to become a "world class" city.[10] On rare occasions, as in the DART referendum, when the opposition may be relatively well financed and skillfully led, the power play may not work, as it depends for success as much on apathy as on any demonstrated ability to actually influence voters. The defeat of the DART and 14–1 referenda and the close calls in the arena and Trinity Corridor bond issues, where the opposition was poorly financed—and in the case of the Trinity, not even organized—suggest that city voters have grown increasingly weary of doing as "the best people" advise. Business solidarity has decayed and North Dallas voters are no longer as reliable or dominant as they once were.

Minority voters have become a new market that remains an enigma to many power players. In the arena and Trinity referenda it ultimately was southern Dallas voters, especially blacks, who followed the leadership of the Mayor, black council members, and a late endorsement by Commissioner John Wiley Price, to provide the margins of victory. For the first time in the city's history, minority voters demonstrated that they could be the deciding factor for projects favored by the economic elite. Votes from black precincts nearly carried the 14–1 referendum. It would appear, in light of this experience, that future power plays in Dallas must be more inclusive and take more careful account of the changing political calculus of the city. Making the market for policies and projects will require multi-racial strategies. What remains unclear, in light of past practice, is whether inclusion will involve real sharing of power and, therefore, assist in the development of civic capital among minorities, or will require only a better targeted sales pitch to a different bloc of voters.

Tri-Ethnic Committees

The growing importance of minorities in legitimizing decisions has been recognized symbolically in the increasing use of tri-ethnic committees as a Dallas solution set. The earliest example of this approach was Judge William Taylor's appointment in 1971 of five members of each major ethnic group to advise the court on implementation of its school desegregation order. Given official status by the court, the tri-ethnic committee exercised substantial influence in shaping the court's subsequent orders, placing it in frequent conflict with the school board.[11]

The tri-ethnic Dallas Alliance operated for two decades following its organization by some of the more progressive and younger business leaders of Dallas to find an acceptable resolution of the school desegregation crisis. Under the sponsorship of the Greater Dallas Chamber of Commerce, the Alliance was a large consultative body, with equal membership drawn from the three major ethnic groups. For the first time, independent black and Hispanic leaders met on an equal basis with business executives. The Alliance eventually broadened its scope to embrace a broad agenda of civic issues. In 1986 it provided the forum for resolution of a dispute over the disposition of a lead smelter that had become a source of community concern and racial conflict in west Dallas. Its study of the implications of community conditions for intergroup relations[12] helped influence Mayor Annette Strauss to appoint the multi-ethnic Dallas Together task force to address the chronic racial tensions of the city. The report of Dallas Together led directly to appointment of the racially balanced Charter Review Committee. It, in turn, spawned a third tri-ethnic committee: the redistricting commission eventually co-opted by Judge Buchmeyer.

Tri-ethnicity became an almost universal politically correct response to city issues. The character and membership of tri-ethnic committees have evolved from the days when the business elite designated the minority members, to a system in which the respective groups are canvassed to identify independent and authentic leaders from each community to increase the legitimacy of committee decisions or recommendations. Some minority leaders feel that many of these committees still tend to select non-confrontational minority members. County Commissioner John Wiley Price, for example, argued that they are still composed of "safe" minorities: "Anglos will choose people like them. You won't see me on a board. Anything I'm elected to, black people elected me."[13] Justice of the Peace Cleo Steele, one of the pioneer black elected officials of Dallas, agreed: "The Dallas Citizen Council wants blacks from the corporate world—not the Al Lipscombs and the Diane Ragsdales. Those whom the black community sees as leaders are not the same people the whites recognize. Blacks who go through the Citizens Council are not called by the black community to serve. There is a question whether the black community would accept them."[14]

Enduring alliances that reach across a broad range of issues have yet to develop among ethnic groups. The ad hoc tri-ethnic committees have, however, provided a critical forum for exchange of views and the development of interracial understandings on specific problems. As the Hispanic population has grown in size and influence in city affairs, tensions have developed between its leaders and blacks, although they continue to cooperate in many matters, such as minority employment and business opportunities. New self-organizing groups, such as Dallas Area Interfaith (DAI), have begun to emerge and to develop a grass roots agenda focused on human capital and neighborhood improvement issues.

Cooperation among ethnic groups, always fragile, has been frayed by posturing over the allocation of power and resources in conflicts over issues such as appointment of a new school superintendent. Tri-ethnic committees hold out the possibility of introducing a new dynamic into Dallas political life. Thus far, no bottom-up multi-ethnic group, including DAI, has evolved into a significant political force and the general aversion to direct political action in the form of electioneering and candidate endorsements may continue to constrain development of more than ad hoc mobilizations around specific issues or projects. The Dallas Alliance, which might have provided a base for a broad effort, viewed its mandate as limited to facilitation of intergroup understanding and limited problem solving. It could not justify continuing to exist when it concluded that enough other organizations were addressing intergroup problems and the Chamber of Commerce withdrew staff support.

Tri-ethnicity in Dallas was too often a means of maintaining the status quo of social control through modest accommodation, rather than a means of building civic competence and capital, although that has often occurred as an unplanned by-product. The single-member district system provides an additional barrier to development of a broad-based tri-ethnic group with a comprehensive political agenda. With few exceptions among the current districts, Council incumbents and candidates have limited incentives to join continuing citywide alliances that cross racial boundaries.

Waiting for Erik

In the wake of the confrontation between blacks and Hispanics and general disarray within the School Board and the school administration, following the resignation and conviction of General Superintendent Yvonne Gonzalez, the *Dallas Morning News* editorialized:

> . . . FOR THE SHORT TERM: Some trustees would like to bring on board a seasoned business executive who could address the most pressing management problems facing the Dallas schools.

> That's a prudent idea. A veteran administrator, experienced in turning around troubled businesses, could take on the widespread business and personnel crises outlined in the corruption probe.
>
> Such an interim chief could overhaul the current process and restore fiscal responsibility to the district. Former mayor Jack Evans was instrumental in bringing credibility to Dallas Area Rapid Transit when he served briefly as the agency's chief executive officer.[15]

Business leaders, however, had little stomach for assuming even advisory, let alone executive, responsibility for the school system. Several business executives reported disillusionment with the school board and its divisive racial politics. Others were concerned for the effects on their businesses if they took prominent positions on issues before the board.[16] Almost a year later, in November 1998, *Dallas Morning News* education reporters interviewed a number of local and national executives, civic leaders, and educators about how to "fix" the Dallas Public Schools. They reported a consensus that radical steps were needed, but none on exactly which steps to take. No one was willing to accept the honor of instituting them. Each person interviewed nominated some other generic person to "take charge." Tom Luce, the persistent reformer, said he was not available, but suggested a nontraditional outsider, such as a retired general. Mayor Kirk declined to assume a role similar to that of the mayor of Chicago, who had been given responsibility for the schools by the Illinois Legislature. "We've got all that we can say grace over right now," said the mayor,[17] who had elsewhere conceded that education was the city's most important problem.[18]

"Waiting for Erik," the call for a business leader to "take charge" in a time of crisis, is a common Dallas solution set. It recalls the drafting of Erik Jonsson to rescue a desperate city from its "dark hour of the soul" following the assassination of President Kennedy. The civic folklore of Dallas is replete with stories of business executives who stepped forward in time of need to serve the city and its institutions.[19] But few ventured into politics, especially in the last two decades, and most focused their efforts on discrete projects—usually physical improvements—that could be accomplished in a reasonable time. No business executive has served as mayor since 1987. The last two mayors—Bartlett and Kirk—have been politicians.

As happened in response the *Dallas Morning News'* call for an "Erik" to clean up the malignant school district, no one volunteered to set aright the manifold problems besetting the city. Even when someone can be recruited for tasks that are increasingly thankless and often intimidating in their political and technical complexity, their *noblese oblige* may be greeted with skepticism, if not outright hostility. Don Williams, the Chairman of Trammel Crow Companies, is, perhaps the most recent "Erik," in his effort to stimulate economic development in South Dallas. Dedicating 40 percent of his time to initiatives he developed after extended conversations with citizens of the area, Williams created a foundation to work with communities in South Dallas-Fair Park to stimulate investment in housing, employment and business opportunities, and services. He helped organize and fund an industrial park development corporation and hired consultants to identify business opportunities for investors in the area. While welcomed by some, Williams' efforts were suspected by others of being self-serving or misdirected and insufficiently attentive to the needs of current residents.[20]

Following the Yvonne Gonzalez debacle, Ross Perot met individually with school board members and offered to bring in a New York consulting organization to survey teachers, parents, and others to identify needed changes in the system. Although the board initially accepted his offer, the help was postponed because of objections from several quarters who perceived the offer as patronizing, and one over which Perot and not the stakeholders in the system—parents, teachers, etc.—would have control.[21]

"Waiting for Erik" reflects not only the rich heritage of business involvement in the affairs of the city, but a culture of dependency nourished by an oligarchic system that brooked little discussion and even less dissent. The business leadership was perceived as the patron that would provide for Dallas. In return, it was conceded control. But the old oligarchs were succeeded by a new generation of multi-national executives who were more residents (and some not even that) than builders of the city. Changes to the city and in their businesses dampened CEO passion for either control or good works. A tradition of social control in which power was not shared faded into a system that had little power to share. The trouble with waiting for Erik was that even if an "Erik" showed up, he came immediately under suspicion if not attack, failed to comprehend why no one seemed grateful for his attentions, and retreated to sullen immobility.[22]

Limited Liability Private-Public Partnerships

One solution set that still seems to work well in Dallas is the Limited Liability Private-Public Partnership. This approach usually involves an initiative by a private or nonprofit organization, the success of which depends upon a direct or tax subsidy and a high level of inter-sector cooperation. In some cases the private sector organization may actually fund and perform limited or enhanced public services under contract to the city.

The best example of this solution set is the tax increment district for the central business district (CBD) and use of the Central Dallas Association as a mechanism for allocating these resources to improve amenities and services in the downtown area. Part private government, part CBD business lobby, and part promotional organization, the CDA provided an effective means of focusing the attention of key stakeholders on the most valuable real estate in the city, and a means of deliberation on the changing economic functions of the CBD.[23]

The CDA represents the most sophisticated form of the private-public partnership. While not unique to Dallas, it fit the Dallas cultural tradition of private sector leadership in development issues. It made possible the mobilization of slack private resources in combination with an "invisible" public subsidy generated by the revenue increments from increased property values in the tax increment district, and used the combined resources to enhance the business environment. It served a public objective through a largely private device, finessing what might otherwise be a sharp conflict with other claimants for city resources.

More problematic are the private-public partnerships the city entered into with individual entrepreneurs as incentives for construction or renovation projects on the assumption that municipal tax abatements or direct subsidies to development would generate jobs or growth in revenues from increased property values, related development, and sales. Some of these so-called "partnerships"—the arena is a prominent example—were little more than inducements to a developer to select a Dallas site rather than one in a neighboring jurisdiction.

A final variant of the limited liability partnership can be found in the Dallas Plan. Rather than build and rely on its own professional staff and the Plan Commission to prepare development and infrastructure plans for the city, the Dallas Plan ceded the initiative in development policy to a self-perpetuating private group. While this gave its recommendations legitimacy in the business community, it posed serious problems of legitimacy for other publics. Even though the Dallas Plan staff made a good faith effort to engage neighborhood and community groups in the planning process, it shared ideas rather than power. Like other civic tools and solution sets of Dallas, Limited Liability Private-Public Partnerships tend to remain instruments of social control rather than means of broad civic engagement and social production.

Leaving It to Barefoot and Jerry[24]

Where the issues are complex and controversial, and the stakes are high, the ordinary solution sets of Dallas governance often failed. None of them was very effective in resolving issues where the rights or interests of disadvantaged racial or ethnic groups were at issue. Tri-ethnic committees can claim some successes but they tended to be ad hoc, unofficial, and advisory. They facilitated mutual trust across racial and ethnic lines, and fostered long term friendships among those who participated in them.

The School Board and Council now have members identified with each of the three principal ethnic communities. This would appear to make the need for tri-ethnic committees less urgent, but elected representatives have exacerbated intergroup conflict as often as they have overcome it to work harmoniously on issues of common interest. The School Board, especially, where issues of power, resource allocation, and educational policy remain overtly racial in content, has rarely risen above division based on identity. In contrast, the Council under the leadership of Mayor Kirk appears to have begun to surmount some of the historic divisions.

The era of strong men who could be called from the helms of business or genteel retirement to "solve" problems appears at an end. Specific projects within the purview of city hall can be left to the professional managers, but their legitimacy is limited to matters that can be defined as within their expertise, and those in which hierarchies still work. Private-public limited partnerships have never tackled the most tangled issues confronting the city, and as they depend so heavily on a fusion of private business and public interests, they seem uniquely unfitted to do so. Their attention span seems limited in both scope and time.

The vacuum has so often been filled by litigation in federal court that it must be counted as a major solution set used by those whose interests were ignored or denied by the city's policy institutions. Resort to litigation is strong evidence of the incapacity of the city's civic institutions to resolve them through democratic processes. But as their use in school desegregation, public housing, and council redistricting illustrates, courts remain uncertain instruments for the resolution of complex issues.[25]

The independence of the federal judiciary made it an essential instrument, in the face of intransigent local officials, for establishing and enforcing rights of disadvantaged individuals and classes and protecting them from further discrimination. But in spite of its undoubted value as a solvent of obstructive governance, its use in Dallas as a solution set is fraught with problems. Paradoxically, judicial procedure and the adversary process can inhibit and prolong the resolution of policy controversies, even as they are necessary to crystallize issues and serve as catalysts for action.

First of all, the aim of a public interest lawsuit is to affix liability to officials for a violation of rights. When they are sued, officials with the power to address the complaints of the class are converted into defendants who must defend the legality their actions or inaction. Policy issues that should have been settled through political compromise and voting are transformed into legal issues. While the officials erect their legal defenses, they can use the processes of litigation to excuse further inaction, claiming they are precluded from acting by the pending lawsuit, all the while engaging in dilatory motions and appeals, as was done in the desegregation and housing cases. Or, as in the school and redistricting cases, they may serially offer inadequate measures and force each one to be litigated, drawing out the process and hoping to exhaust and impoverish the plaintiffs or wear down the judge.

The court's job is to adjudicate the controversy, assign liability for any legal wrong and impose a remedy, which might be fashioned by the parties in the form of a consent decree. Even if the original order is overruled or modified, the trial judge may still have considerable latitude in fashioning a final order. The plaintiffs (including any plaintiff-intervenors), who have selected themselves as the agents of change, through interaction with their counsel, play a critical role in the fashioning of the court's decrees. Since the court is focused on rectifying the injury to plaintiffs it has before it, the remedies it approves are designed to serve that end.

But courts are also constrained in how they may respond. As the non-elected branch of government, federal courts are wary of overreaching in cases that impinge on normal political processes and powers of elected or appointed officials. Consequently, their approaches tend to be restrained and incremental. In the Dallas cases the judges first issued declaratory judgments, retaining jurisdiction to give the local officials an opportunity to meet the requirements of the Constitution or federal law. The next step, after finding noncompliance or intransigence, might be an injunction, followed, after months or years of more noncompliance, with an affirmative order. In the school desegregation case, officials appealed several orders before buckling down to implement the court's decree in good faith. In the housing case, appeals of various intervening defendants, including the U.S. Department of Housing and Urban Development, and refusals to concur in a consent decree delayed a final order and compliance. Both cases dragged on for years—and in the case of schools, for decades.

Even with the aid of masters and monitors, the courts remain dependent upon the defendant bureaucracies to correct the problem. In the school case, the end result of over forty years of court intervention was a de facto re-segregated system, which the court was powerless, under Supreme Court doctrine, to prevent, and which it cannot correct. In the *Walker* housing case, implementation depended on the City and the Dallas Housing Authority. In both cases the courts succeeded in forcing re-allocations of resources and dismantling systems of officially sanctioned racial segregation. At last, after years of litigation, the public agencies began good faith implementation of the final decrees, but it is hard to argue that the problems were actually resolved. Both cases produced second order consequences and events beyond the control of the courts that required administrative and political responses that could move faster, more flexibly and with greater nuance than even the most dedicated judges.

In the redistricting cases, the issues were simpler and the solutions less complex, requiring little bureaucratic action. Even there, however, the city resisted the court's order until there were no other options. The case presents other concerns for the use of the courts as substitutes for regular political processes, even when it is necessary to use them. The court's ability to fashion remedies was restricted by the kind of questions it could address. The case highlights the problem of the self-selection of plaintiffs, who may or may not be able to represent the interests of a class in more than a symbolic way. In *Williams,* some defendant officials regarded the plaintiffs as nuisances, gadflies with no substantial constituencies or capacity to speak for the "class" in whose interest they sued. Nonetheless, the decision in their favor gave them immediate status as equal negotiators with the city on a new system of representation. The lawsuit framed the issue narrowly and produced second order consequences the city would confront as it dealt with the results of the 2000 Census and subsequent Supreme Court decisions governing the role of race in redistricting decisions.[26]

In summary, the courts have been a necessary, if slow-working catalyst for change in Dallas. The lawsuits and their defense absorbed time and resources dealing with political issues that were contorted into legal ones. In each area of policy that fell to the courts to resolve, the political leadership of the city abdicated to its attorneys. The importance of the issues taken to court and the frequency with which they were decided there rather than in the forums of the political system were powerful indicators of civic dysfunction.

Learned Incapacities

Dallas has a reputation for being well managed. It is not well governed. Neither city government nor the school system has exhibited the capacity to perform effectively the most basic civic functions. These include representing the increasingly diverse interests of the city, mobilizing public opinion to resolve conflicts and deal with the urgent and difficult problems, engaging in reasoned deliberation, developing leaders, and legitimating policy choices.

During the ascendancy of the "Garchs," the formal government institutions provided a shell of legitimacy for a system of social control. With the dissipation of the entrepreneurial regime, the incapacity of official governmental institutions was made manifest. Most of the solution sets used to deal with complex public policy problems were extra-governmental. They represented ways in which various stakeholders in Dallas overcame or circumnavigated the frailties of official processes. But the extra-governmental solution sets increasingly did not work, or did not work very well. In continuing to use them the city learned behaviors that impaired rather than advanced the formation of civic capital and the capacity for self-governance.

The Legacy of Dependence

The system of social control exercised by the corporate leaders of Dallas for almost two generations created a politics of patronage and dependency. It relied on low rates of participation, political passivity in the general population, tutoring and anointing agreeable leaders, and the suppression of competing bases of power. The system was reinforced by frequent nonpartisan elections and referenda and limits on tenure in inherently weak offices; this combination made building independent political bases virtually impossible. A maverick mayor could occasionally be elected, but was essentially bereft of any capacity to lead or govern without the support of reliable allies on the Council and access to the slack resources of the business elite. The successes of the twentieth century's two great mayors, R. L. Thornton and Erik Jonsson, were rooted in their status in the business world rather than their reputations as political leaders.

One legacy of the era of oligarchy is the continuing dependence of community organizations on the patronage of corporate leaders. Socially prominent institutions such as hospitals, arts and cultural organizations, and the United Way rely on corporate support in any city. In Dallas the patronage runs deeper, enveloping the ethnic chambers of commerce and a wide array of community improvement and civic groups that look to corporations rather than their members or community-oriented foundations for their financial lifelines and leadership. A consequence of this condition is a dearth of independent thinking in the civic arena. Challenges to conventional wisdom are rare. So deeply imbedded is the civic culture of looking to business for leadership and succor, that although the cohesion and power of the commercial regime has dramatically declined, it is hard for many in Dallas to imagine acting without approval from the ephemeral "business community."

The fading half-life of the oligarchy continues to stifle a robust urban politics. In part this is a function of the immaturity of Dallas philanthropy. Dallas is home to several well-endowed foundations but few have professional staff. Almost all foundation boards remain in control of the first or second generation of the donor families. They tend to operate as appendages of the corporations or individuals that created them, and they have yet to provide a substantial independent presence in fostering policy innovation and development of civic leadership. Thus, Dallas philanthropy remains quite personal and politically safe. Grants are idiosyncratic far more often than they are programmatic. References are usually more important than the merit of projects.

With rare exceptions, regular political party organizations have paid only intermittent and marginal attention to city and school politics. Since the demise of the Citizens Charter Association (CCA), there have been no local "parties" to recruit or endorse candidates openly for local offices. Party activists have occasionally recruited themselves for council positions,[27] and party affiliation, or suspected affiliation, can be important in voting behavior and campaign strategy. A base in a political party can help a candidate recruit workers, raise money, and mobilize voters. The 1987 mayoral race between Annette Strauss and Fred Meyer was, to some, a partisan battle, as both had well-known party affiliations. In 1991, Steve Bartlett's prominence as a Republican congressman was surely helpful in garnering financial and other support. But it was probably less significant than "the word" that he was the candidate of Ray Hunt and the residue of the business establishment, or that he could attract substantial black support in spite of the strong Democratic credentials of one of his principal opponents.

In 1995, two of the three major candidates for mayor were clearly identified as Democrats, but Darrell Jordan, a well-regarded attorney with strong ties to business, was unable to parlay his Republican identity into significant support against Democrat Ron Kirk. It could be argued that nonpartisanship makes it possible for candidates like Kirk to win, even in a city with a weak Democratic Party and strong, though not entirely reliable Republican proclivities.

For many years, the highly exclusive system for the preparation of promising white business executives for leadership positions in the governance of Dallas gave senior leaders of the Dallas Citizens Council and the CCA an opportunity to observe a person's capacity and commitment to the "Dallas way." As the Council changed under the onslaught of court-imposed districts, the old system of business-guided ascension yielded to a system of self-nomination of free lancers for Council seats. Remnants of the commercial regime such as the Breakfast Club pay no attention to grooming prospects for public service. Instead they use campaign contributions to exercise quiet influence in a few elections and strategically important appointments. The lack of any public political organizations to support candidates and advocate programs makes such leverage disproportionately effective.

In the minority communities, there is a paucity of strong organizations and networks to prepare their members for the exercise of political influence. Some are little more than vehicles for the personal advancement of their "leaders." Others depend upon the patronage of Anglos but do offer their active members some opportunities to develop group skills. Some minority business owners are independent of the Anglo elite due to the nature of their clientele, but with rare exceptions they lack comparable resources or business stature.[28]

Segregation denied blacks and Hispanics access to the mainstream professions, from which political leadership normally arises. The absence of a highly regarded black college in Dallas[29] stunted the development of a critical mass of professionals in law, medicine, architecture, and engineering, which provided a solid core of black middle class leadership in other southern cities. Since the 1970s, however, there has been a substantial increase in black and Hispanic professionals and administrators. Some are natives returning home; others have come to the Dallas area to join professional firms and corporate staffs actively engaged in diversifying their work forces to serve national and global markets. Government agencies have also actively recruited minorities for professional positions. This new minority middle class provides a pool of talented individuals who have begun to enter civic life laterally, rather than struggle up the civic ladder in the more traditional minority organizations. Mayor Ron Kirk is the most prominent example.

Many black and Hispanic professionals remain heavily dependent upon the favor of the firms or other institutions that employ or do business with them, however.[30] There is not always a close connection between many of the new professionals and native Dallas blacks and Hispanics.[31] Many locate in north Dallas or in the suburbs and have only a weak identification with the traditional minority communities and their problems. There is also a growing trend of middle class black families, in particular, moving from the historic ghettos of Dallas into integrated or higher income but largely black communities throughout the Metroplex, taking advantage of the relaxation of discrimination in the housing market that has accelerated in the past decade. This "hollowing out" of the inner city tends to exacerbate the problems of civic leadership and social stability in those communities.[32]

Dallas black and Hispanic civil rights organizations did not attain the influence in their respective communities that they did in some other U.S. cities. Churches, traditional bases of minority political development, have only recently begun to produce more independent and militant pastors and lay leaders. The Southern Christian Leadership Conference supported a field worker in Dallas and played a supporting role in several skirmishes with the city, but never became a major catalyst of a civil rights movement, as natural allies in the black Interdenominational Ministerial Alliance were co-opted by the Anglo business leadership. The Catholic Church in Dallas was largely Anglo until recently, and historically, was not a strong advocate of Mexican-American interests in city affairs. Mainline Protestant churches serving Hispanic congregations are often missions of Dallas Anglo churches. The interdenominational Greater Dallas Community of Churches has been a consistent but generally moderate voice on social issues, but has not taken an overt role in electoral politics or in the development of civic leadership among its congregations.[33]

In some areas of the city, homeowners or community associations have provided a base from which candidacies and civic leaders can develop, although such organizations have tended to be less developed in working class and minority neighborhoods. In other areas, geographically concentrated interest groups, such as gays and lesbians, or ad hoc organizations created to oppose a development project[34] or to respond to an issue such as lax code enforcement may offer a springboard for a candidacy or a substantial and steady source of financial and political support. Few of these organizations, however, function even at a Council district level, let alone on a citywide basis. While all of these groups provide limited leadership experience for active members, none are consciously in the business of developing and supporting candidates for local office.

The Dallas system produced antipoliticians with no debts to their constituents, but who were dependent upon their firms, families, or quiet benefactors for the support necessary to seek and hold city office. The baleful effect of this system for minority leadership was revealed in the bribery trial of Council Member Al Lipscomb, whose defense involved testimony by prominent black leaders that Dallas civil rights activists routinely accepted secret payments from white benefactors.[35] Several Anglo business executives also testified that they had made such payments to Lipscomb.[36] Even if one assumes no *quid pro quo,* acceptance of such gratuities compromised minority leaders, undermined their authenticity, and implied Anglo control over their actions. A less charitable interpretation of this "wink-wink system" is that the implicit threat to withdraw support or to publicize it is an element of a continuing system of social control.

The central irony of Dallas politics is that a culture of dependency has persisted so long in a city where there remains almost no one upon whom to depend.

The Politics of Identity

If there is no one upon whom to depend, there *are* groups and places with which to identify. In general, Dallas is not a city of strong neighborhoods, like those in Chicago or Pittsburgh,[37] but it is a city of strong racial and ethnic identities, reinforced by a sense of historical discrimination and neglect. The "hidden transcripts"[38] of the black and Hispanic communities in

Dallas contain a litany of resentments and suspicions that are often obscured in what passes for civic discourse. Complaints run the gamut from racial insensitivity and slurs by police and bureaucrats to neglect of poor minority neighborhoods while courtesies and services are lavished on well-to-do Anglo North Dallas.

The politics of racial identity are reinforced by class but it is by no means confined to poor blacks or Hispanics. Many middle class and professional minorities feel threatened by the power of the business elite to influence their incomes or stymie their careers if they fail to conform to what is expected of them in role and manners.[39] There remains deep suspicion that "they"—powerful Anglos—are intent on crushing "uppity" minorities. Thus, when the U.S. Attorney in 1998 initiated criminal investigations of black Council members and one former member, there was suspicion that the potential prosecutions were aimed at destroying successful black politicians. Even after the initial cases brought were against an Anglo school board member, who was acquitted, and an Anglo Council member, who entered a plea of guilty before the case could go to the jury, the suspicion continued that the investigations were racially motivated. Al Lipscomb, while under indictment for bribery and extortion, won re-election in 1999 over token opposition with 80 percent of the vote.

In recent years, black and Hispanic groups, respectively, have increasingly pursued divergent interests, as demonstrated in the battles over school policy, appointment of a new superintendent, and their alignment in the dispute between Superintendent Gonzalez and Matthew Harden. Such schisms in the two major minority groups befuddle well-meaning Anglos, who often appear amazed that "minorities" can have divisions of interest. When a letter surfaced from the chairs of the Dallas Citizens Council and the Greater Dallas Chamber of Commerce, urging Gonzales to retain Harden, the system's black chief financial officer and the proximate cause of Gonzalez' downfall, Hispanic leaders threatened to boycott the grocery stores of the Chamber's Chair, Liz Minyard. Meanwhile, black activists disrupted board meetings demanding selection of a black superintendent to succeed Gonzalez.

A key element in the wariness between blacks and Hispanics is a strong sense among more active blacks that they had borne the brunt of the struggle for civil rights and dignity in a deeply hostile city, a struggle in which Hispanics, as late arrivals in Dallas, were free riders. Better able to assimilate into the dominant Anglo "business" culture of the city, and to disperse among its neighborhoods, Hispanics are now displacing blacks and allying with Anglos to frustrate black achievement just as it seemed within reach. While blacks recognize that they have more power than before, they still see the Anglo business community as "anointing" the leaders of their choosing, rather than accepting those selected by the blacks themselves. Mexican-Americans, on the other hand, carry the residue of historic resentment at being driven from power in Texas by the Anglos in the War of Texas Independence, and relegated for generations to second class status in the state, isolated by language and poverty from the economic and social mainstreams.

The Anemia of Civic Discourse

Dallas solution sets rely very little on civic discourse and deliberation as a prelude to decision or action. Residents are not engaged in a civic dialogue in which they take shared responsibility for the policy choices made by the city. Rather, the modern variant of single option politics prevails. Citizens are approached as consumers of services or projects and urged to "buy" the only package being offered, usually presented as a bargain complete with jobs, growth, no tax increase, and blessed by the best people and a tri-ethnic conclave.

Arbitrary deadlines for decisions are often set when they are not necessary. Proposals are made, often in sketchy form, with little time for discussion before decision. Council or

School Board members are briefed, rarely given an alternative, and pressed to approve, showing that Dallas remains a "can do" city. Council and Board members have no institutional or professional staff with the skills and knowledge necessary to conduct independent analyses of policy proposals. They must either accept staff information and analyses as valid, resort to poorly informed cross-examination, or find an alternative source for analysis. Such behavior marks one as not a team player, or worse, as meddling in administration rather than confining oneself to the development of "policy." A substantial number of former Council members regarded staff information as often self-serving and unreliable, but appeared unable, under the strictures of the city charter against interfering in "administration," to imagine ways in which they might obtain countervailing information and the leverage it provides.[40]

The obsessive concern for the "business climate" and the city's competitive position for economic growth have nurtured a deep aversion to political conflict. But the aim is less to resolve conflict than to suppress it. Mayor Ron Kirk's stock campaign speech included a pledge to "stop the blame game." His first act as mayor was to push for the adoption of rules of Council decorum designed to expedite business and eliminate disruptions and demonstrations from members or visitors. He worked successfully to establish strong bonds with the city manager, to build consensus on the Council for major initiatives, and to hold the trust of both business leaders and his core of black support. The objective was to convey an image of a diverse but harmonious city, dedicated to growth and progress.

Single options, little discussion or dissent, and a hard sell to voters, with occasional blessing from a tri-ethnic committee or incantations of private-public partnership, smother debate of both ends and means. Policy analysis in Dallas tends to follow decisions, thus providing a *post hoc* confirmation of the wisdom of the policy rather than an aid to decision making.[41]

The institutionalization of conformity and almost morbid fear of open discussion of racial interests squelches informed debate and the sort of robust political conflict that attracts a widening circle of participants to the argument. Instead of engaging in civic discourse, those who are excluded from the consensus must either resort to "acting out" their frustration in outbursts or demonstrative behavior. This, of course, reinforces the determination of the keepers of the city's image to tighten the gag. Unable to gain a hearing, much less redress of grievances, those who do not resign their citizenship and turn to sullen neglect may convert their frustration into a lawsuit. While this at least forces debate, it occurs in a venue once removed from civic discourse and one that substitutes the clarity of winners and losers from the ambiguity and compromises of political discussion. There is ample evidence that in Dallas the legitimacy of judicial determination is no substitute for the legitimacy of democratic processes.

Conclusion

The way Dallas performs its civic functions falls well short of the ideal of local governance as a school for democracy. Dallas governance suffers from a cultural and institutional hangover that poses a substantial barrier to its capacity to adapt to the transformation of its environment. The formal institutions of government were designed to frustrate participation and the broad mobilization of interests. This institutional barrier reinforces and is reinforced by a political culture that fostered a politics of exclusion and dependency, further inhibiting the kinds of civic engagement that build experience in power sharing, public deliberation, and conflict resolution. The legacy of segregation and its attendant behaviors of first ignoring then under representing and patronizing minorities produced a legitimacy crisis for both the institutions and policies of the city. The result is a disjunction among latent and emerging sources of political power, slack economic resources, and legitimacy. Dallas is a classic case of civic dysfunction.

The fixation on social control worked only so long as the corporate elite could maintain solidarity and the city's minorities did not attain a critical mass of political influence and leadership. Once geographic diffusion and economic restructuring fractured business solidarity, the ability and the will to control dissipated. The national rights revolution prohibited continued exclusion of the growing minority populations from posts of formal power, but those posts are so circumscribed in power and resources that the experience they offer the emerging political class is often as frustrating as it is enlightening. The private sector still holds the bulk of the city's slack resources, but now lacks the leadership or cohesion to deploy them effectively. It retains, however, an inchoate ability to legitimatize public actions as good for the business climate. Its problem is the disappearance of a coherent vision or a strategy of how to attain it. And it perpetuates a civic system that is incompetent to conduct serious policy analysis or to plan. Thus, it proceeds ad hoc, almost at random; still relevant but no longer in command.

The emerging middle, professional, and political classes among minorities have not yet attained the financial independence necessary for substantial involvement in public affairs, and public offices in Dallas do not provide sufficient compensation to sustain even a modest lifestyle. Consequently, officials must depend upon the generosity of employers, partners, family, or others to engage in public service. This fact of political life can compromise the reputation of an elected official for integrity, and may well attract the attention of the Public Integrity Section of U.S. Attorney's office.

Because there are so few interracial intermediary institutions in Dallas, and those that exist are so weak, new, or apolitical, a new base for political cooperation and power sharing has not yet emerged. Each office holder tends to be a freelancer, who must build and maintain his or her own constituency. Race-based districting reinforces an emphasis on the politics of identity. While the scramble for ethnic equity in representation and bureaucracies is an important step in opening access to power and in providing the opportunity for civic learning by all groups, its vulnerability to racial demagoguery complicates development of political trust. Moreover, the past heavy reliance on the courts to vindicate minority rights against a resistant city, while a necessary tactic in forcing entry into the system, is at best a cumbersome strategy for governing.

In its transition from the old regime to a new one, the Dallas managerial regency epitomizes the plight of the information age city. The historic umbilical connection to the economic power brokers of the city has been severed. Those with access to economic resources capable of shaping the fortunes of the city have little stake and less presence in it. Those with a high stake in its future are gaining political power but lack substantial economic resources. Some distrust the managers because of their historic ties to the economic elite. Others prefer to maintain the regency—the strength of which increasingly depends upon the ability to satisfy weak politicians—than to risk creation of strong independent institutions of political leadership that may not have to accommodate them. At the same time the legitimacy of the managers, which depended upon hierarchy and technical monopolies, is vitiated in all but a few arenas by the flood of information now accessible to publics through computer and telecommunications technologies.

In this environment, most of the solution sets Dallas has employed in the performance of its civic functions have proved inadequate to the task of helping citizens and officials of the city learn to share rather than hoard resources and power. Most have, in fact, encouraged widespread neglect of civic responsibilities and contributed to a culture of consumerism, in which salesmanship supersedes deliberation.

The Dallas experience suggests that advancing the civic function of cities requires greater attention from both theorists and practitioners of urban governance. Those who see value in local self-government must re-examine the premises upon which governance systems are built. There is reason for discontent with theory that purports to explain and classify regimes, but cannot suggest how change might be induced in a particular cultural and institutional context to enhance a city's capacity to perform its most essential role in a democratic society.

13

Reflections

What we need . . . is a political unit of more truly human proportions in which a citizen can acquire confidence and mastery of the art of politics, that is, of the arts required for shaping a good life in common with fellow citizens.

ROBERT A. DAHL

The Dallas Paradox

The political economy of Dallas poses a paradox. Its private sector is charged with entrepreneurial energy. Through peaks and troughs of business and technology cycles Dallas firms have been leading innovators, creating new products and services, swiftly adapting to new markets. Its public sector is seized with institutional entropy. It resisted adaptation to the changing population and economy, holding fast to its machine-age model of governance as the Dallas economy hurtled into the information age.

The economic and political systems of Dallas, once fused, have slowly decoupled. The remnant of the entrepreneurial regime that once dominated city affairs remains influential but no longer governs. A new generation of CEOs exhibits faint interest in governing the city. They are more focused on their own corporate careers and the global marketplace than on Dallas. Their corporate parks dot the suburbs. Proximity to the airport is more important than to the central business district.

The scope of their shared interests is much wider than the city, or even the region. Decisions made in Dallas area headquarters affect the fortunes of cities around the world. Reciprocally, on many matters, the welfare of the city depends heavily upon corporate decisions made elsewhere. Even if Dallas could stretch its boundaries to encompass all the buildings that carry the logos of the region's multinational firms, it still could not enclose the virtual economy upon which it increasingly depends.[1] Many key actors and stakeholders do not live in Dallas. Both resident and virtual corporate citizens owe overlapping allegiances to parent and subsidiary enterprises, suppliers and customers, other governments, non-local organizations, professional and occupational peers, family and friends, religious and social groups. Their civic actions flow from a mixture of self-interested preferences and obligations their roles establish.[2]

Meanwhile, the minority population of Dallas reached critical mass and a new political class emerged, anchored to the city's political geography and group identities. But lacking the independent resources or political discipline essential to cement stable alliances and confronted with institutional barriers to effective political mobilization, its purchase on governance is tenuous. In the long twilight of the old regime, a regency of managers governs within bounds set by federal judges.

The paradox of a catalytic private sector and a paralytic public sector is rooted in a civic culture that looks upon government as a necessary inconvenience, the sole purpose of which is to promote and protect the interests of business. The notion that the public interest is privately held is deeply imbedded in the civic consciousness, including much of the city's minority communities. It has been at the core of the system of social control exercised by the entrepreneurial regime during its ascendance and during its decline by the regency. Ironically, running the city as a closely held corporation in the interest of business resulted in a system that worked against that interest as it failed to resolve problems of education, race relations, and governance. And as the city's governance system failed to address effectively its most critical problems, it lost legitimacy. Anglos as well as minorities withdrew from participation in the civic arena. Treated as consumers, they acted as such and many who did not or could not move withdrew from city affairs. For those with more stamina or access to lawyers willing to take cases on contingency, litigation became an alternative form of politics. The largest of local functions, education, remained under judicial supervision as the twentieth century drew to a close, as did public housing. Providing equal representation for minorities on the City Council also required court intervention.

To be sure, there was no general collapse of government. Going concerns kept going. It remained possible to achieve specific development projects through the use of the city's well-established solution sets. Bond issues could be won through power plays, symbolic tri-ethnic committees, and appeals to consumer interests and the city's world class image. A dwindling business elite could still influence elections, appointments, and policy with well-placed campaign contributions and income supplements. Private-public limited liability partnerships provide creative ad hoc approaches to complex development and revitalization problems. And the professional managers of some agencies, such as the police department, were still able to use their bureaucratic autonomy and tight hierarchies to reengineer their agencies and the services they provide.

These achievements—some of them both substantial and important, others of dubious value—were products of a system that historically relied on social control. The great failure of Dallas governance has been its resistance to evolution toward a system based on social production; one that engages people in a stable governing alliance that offers mutual benefits and fosters development of civic capital.

Building the Public Sector's Capacity to Govern

Dallas epitomizes Stone's observation that: "If society lacks high coherence and formal authority is weak, then a capacity to govern cannot be taken as a given."[3] The question then, is: what might be done in Dallas to increase social coherence, formal authority, or both? First of all, so long as the diminished business interests can achieve their limited goals through the tactical use of their slack resources, they have little incentive to support major changes in the system. They will accommodate other interests with symbolic goods or side payments to achieve specific objectives, but give up established practices of social control for a social production coalition only if they must. Creating the conditions under which such an arrangement becomes imperative would seem to be the first task for those interested in improving the city's capacity to solve problems.

Shifting from its current, dysfunctional governance system to a social production regime with power to solve problems will require attention to the public, private, and independent sectors. The public sector needs first of all the capacity for comprehensive and independent action together with the broad political base and cohesion necessary to give its actions legitimacy in the major ethnic, economic, and geographic constituencies of the city. The private sector needs new means of reaching policy positions that are more transparent and inclusive, as well as approaches to deployment of its slack financial resources that are less narrowly self-interested. This suggests an enhanced, even critical role for the independent sector. Given the complexity of the city's problems, effective governance calls for a regime composed of strong, rather than weak, partners.

The most daunting task in forming a social production regime in Dallas is to create a city government with the capacity to govern. An emerging political class now holds most of the formal elective offices in Dallas, but lacks the cohesion, independence, and resources required for effective governance. The pervasive anti-politics of the civic culture and the inherent weakness of elected officials render even the most ambitious and energetic politicians institutionalized "morning glories."[4] Their politically and administratively emasculated offices deny them capacity to do much more than respond passively to the initiatives of mangers or private policy entrepreneurs. Their power is essentially nugatory, exercised primarily through delay or inaction. The redistricted City Council and School Board symbolize the importance of tri-ethnic endorsement for the legitimacy of public actions, but neither separately nor in conjunction can they be said to govern.

Overcoming Identity Politics and Amateurism

A principal barrier to establishing a government capable of participating in an effective regime coalition is the politics of ethnic identity. Some ethnic competition and conflict is probably unavoidable, even healthy in a city with Dallas's racial history. The formal institutions of government could be rearranged, however, to provide more opportunities for interracial coalitions than for political separatism. Single-member districts drawn primarily on racial criteria can exacerbate tendencies in both minority and Anglo districts to emphasize ethnic antagonisms and grievances. While airing these concerns and electing council members who could articulate them may be regarded as a necessary therapeutic catharsis for Dallas, maintenance of such districts into the next decade is problematic for both political and constitutional reasons.

Politically, single-member districts tend to be designed to protect incumbents and ensure the election of a council with approximately the same racial and ethnic distribution among its members as the population of the city. But statistical representativeness is not equivalent to political representation.

Legally, current U.S. Supreme Court doctrine forbids the use of race as the primary factor in the design of representative districts. Thus, a new system of representation based primarily on non-racial factors could provide an opportunity to build multi-ethnic political alliances. This could be done in several ways that ensure politically significant and cohesive interests can have voices in the policy process in reasonable proportion to their strength, whether those interests are grounded in ethnic identities, geographic communities, corporate interests, economic class, religious affiliation, or something else.

Compact single-member districts could be drawn with mixed constituencies. Changing ethnic settlement patterns make this difficult but more likely as a practical matter than in 1991. Such districts could be legally suspect, however, if they reduce the opportunity for black and Hispanic voters to elect representatives of their choice. In any event, reversion to more traditional redistricting criteria, such as compactness and protection of incumbents (itself a criterion of dubious merit) is likely to produce more districts in which community concerns outweigh those heavily freighted with race.

An alternative approach would be to use multi-member districts and some form of proportional representation, such as cumulative voting. In cumulative voting, each voter has a number of votes equal to the number of offices to be filled. Those votes may be distributed among candidates in any way the voter chooses; e.g., one for a candidate for each position, or all of them for one candidate. Cumulative voting allows any substantial minority bloc—whether based on race, class, or ideology—with sufficient cohesion and discipline to elect a representative it favors by casting all votes for that candidate. The virtue of cumulative voting is that it does not artificially induce racial voting. It permits it where race is the salient issue for a significant group of voters. At the same time, racially diverse districts could be expected to encourage many candidates to adopt electoral strategies designed to build coalitions among ethnic groups and encourage candidates with different ethnic identities and constituencies to form slates that share campaign costs and improve their respective electoral prospects. Thus, cumulative voting systems offer successful city politicians experience in multi-ethnic coalition building.

The principal problem with the multi-member districts necessary for a cumulative voting system is that, unless the size of the Council is substantially increased, they would be larger than the single-member districts currently in use, making campaigns more costly for candidates not affiliated with a slate. This could present an opportunity for well-financed interest groups like the Breakfast Club to exercise disproportionate influence on an election through strategic contributions to specific campaigns. Of course that possibility exists in the present system and has been practiced. Such cherry picking of candidates by narrow interest groups can be offset through development of broad-based district or citywide endorsement groups and pooling of campaign costs by the endorsed candidates. Campaigning as a slate, either at the district level, or in affiliation with a candidate for mayor, also lays a basis for cooperation on a common policy agenda by the members who are elected.

No electoral arrangement can, of itself, assure cooperation across racial, ethnic, or other policy lines for either campaigns or setting the policy agenda. Electoral arrangements can, however, structure opportunities and barriers to cooperation, facilitating or impeding the management of conflict. The present system tends to exacerbate conflict and limit cooperation to symbolic inclusion or ad hoc manipulation designed to procure compliance. Without change in the formal governmental structure it will be hard to produce a stable set of officials with enough power and experience to engage effectively in informal collaboration with the private sector and enough diversity to legitimate the fruits of that collaboration in addressing the city's most pressing problems.

While redesigning the representative system could be an important element in making a social production regime possible, standing alone it is unlikely to be sufficient. City officials not only need integrated electoral bases that are independent though not exclusive of traditional business interests, they need the institutional capacity to govern. This entails recognition that the conduct of city business is not a job for amateurs. The legitimacy of the government is undermined more by the dependence of Dallas elected officials on external support to enable them to serve than by dependence on large donors for campaign contributions. Paying the mayor and council members salaries commensurate with their responsibilities for the conduct of city business could enable a wider pool of people to seek office as well as reduce the potential for and appearance of conflicts of interest. Whether officials are subsidized by their firms or through secret emoluments such as those that led to the conviction of Council Member Al Lipscomb, they undermine the real and apparent independence of officials and, therefore, their capacity as members of a governing coalition.

Capacity to govern requires the capacity to deliberate, which in turn, requires the access to the information and other resources necessary to shape and consider alternative policy options. So long as the city manager is the sole source of staff support for the Council, its members are denied the independent capacity for fiscal and policy analysis they need for effective oversight of the administration and evaluation of its policy initiatives. The accommodation Council members reached with the managers allows them to micromanage in small matters pertaining to their respective districts, but generally to do as they are advised on larger issues where the manager is presumed to have better information and greater expertise. Some members occasionally bridle, but the Council usually accepts the single option the manager presents, lacking any capacity to generate alternatives or undertake a careful analysis. Ironically, the diffusion of information that has weakened the legitimacy of the managerial regents with the public has not materially weakened their roles in the guidance of elected officials. Without staff of their own, council members must depend on the manager or others outside of government, remain susceptible to manipulation, and are unable to command mutual respect as part of a governing regime. They lack the resources and powers essential for performing their most important task, deliberation on the content of the public interest for the city.

Creating an Institutional "Erik"

The managers govern Dallas largely by default. There simply is no one else to do it. But the foundations of the regency in both city government and the school system have eroded. Once the cohesion and deep engagement of the business establishment faded, the managers' role as its surrogate has also gradually diminished. It has been replaced by a new role as policy entrepreneur and advocate, forcing managers into controversies that risk their reputations for neutral competence and professionalism. The risk is heightened by the loss of the monopoly on information on which the regency and its expert professionals relied for their legitimacy and influence.[5] Shorn of both their economically powerful patrons and the presumption of superior expertise, constrained by court orders and whipsawed by the politics of identity, managers have increasingly found themselves distrusted by some as the tool of the "establishment" and by others as overly cautious careerists. To maintain their positions, they tread an uncertain path between responding to the service requests of council members and framing visions of the city's future for which there may be no constituency. But because of the conventions that define their role, city managers are in a poor position to be catalysts for a multi-ethnic regime.

The Council-Manager Plan made apparent sense for Dallas so long as it could be assumed that the mayor would be a part-time official with a private business to run, and could depend upon a like-minded, cohesive, and equally part-time Council. Such assumptions are no longer valid. Mayors and most Council members are now drawn from the growing and diverse political class. The demands of constituents and the complexity of urban problems, in both their political and technical dimensions, turn even reluctant officials into full-time public servants. The public visibility of the office makes the mayor the lightning rod if not the dynamo of city affairs. In the words of Mayor Ron Kirk: "People think the mayor is responsible for what happens in the city, whether I am or not."[6]

In recent years, mayors have become directly involved in a wide range of significant negotiations, especially on major development projects, that technically fall within the domain of the city manager. The mayor alone has the political stature to lead negotiations with global corporations, local officials, the governor and state legislature, or federal officials. Ultimately, it is the mayor, as the only citywide official, who can place non-routine or non-emergency matters on the public and institutional agendas of the city and keep them there. The city manager cannot speak consistently with clear authority for the city on any matter where Council support is uncertain or its position ambiguous. Under the current Charter, the mayor is equally encumbered, and carries the additional millstone of not being the city's chief executive.

There is merit in the argument that even with its ceremonial mayoralty, Dallas has produced several exceptional leaders, whose personal forcefulness overcame the inherent weakness of the office. Their power, however, was grounded in their economic roles. There is no guarantee that a strong office will always attract effective leaders. But it would seem more likely to do so than the current system because it would afford an opportunity to make a difference in the city and to build a political reputation.

The critical difference in the present office and an invigorated one with real power and public expectations for accomplishment is that it institutionalizes "Erik." As a *political* executive, a strong mayor would be expected to exert leadership in both the inside and outside games of urban politics.[7] Inside Dallas, the mayor's central role would be the catalyst to form and maintain a governing regime, bringing its resources and powers to bear on the city's most pressing problems. There is, for example, widespread agreement that the most urgent inside problem of Dallas governance involves redesign and invigoration of public education as it emerges from court supervision. Few expect the moribund system to be resuscitated by revolving superintendents and an institutionally dysfunctional school board. Neither has the political capacity to frame the education issue in compelling terms that connect it to the welfare of the city, mobilize opinion and resources, reengineer the delivery system to drastically improve performance, and focus political and professional accountability for producing results. An empowered mayor does, as mayors in several other cities are beginning to demonstrate. This would require a transfer of responsibility for public education to the city government, greatly increasing the stakes of mayors and council members, and by extension their constituencies and supporters, in public education. It could lead to a more effective integration of education with other social services and development policies, and with the leadership of a resourceful mayor with Council and private sector allies, provide a broader basis for a social production regime. Achieving substantial progress on this most frustrating of city problems could have a profound effect on reestablishing citizen trust in the city's governance system and foster the formation of civic capital among those engaged in the reforms.

Outside Dallas there is the continuing challenge of regional and intergovernmental collaboration to ensure that the city shares fairly in the benefits and costs of the regional economy's growing role as a command and control center of the international urban system. Mayors have always played a role in regional and intergovernmental affairs, but their influence has been circumscribed by the limitations of the office and their access to private resources. With the disappearance of the magnate mayors, reputation for the ability to marshal public opinion and the resources of city agencies is critical if the city is to seize intergovernmental opportunities and acquire timely infusions of private capital. Building such a reputation takes more than a well-worked jawbone. It requires executive authority.

A traditional objection in Dallas to the establishment of an institutionally strong mayor is that an effective political leader may be a poor manager. But there is no reason for the city to deprive itself of either talent. Many cities and urban counties require their elected executives to appoint, with the consent of the Council, a chief administrative officer or deputy mayor. This official, often an experienced city manager, serves at the pleasure of the mayor and is responsible for the day-to-day administration of programs and departments.[8] Such an arrangement provides the city with the benefits of both strong political leadership and professional management.

Managing Conflict

A strong mayor ensures some institutional conflict with the Council, and Dallas civic culture eschews conflict as a danger to the city's economic welfare. But as March and Olsen point out, "democratic institutions are built on a presumption of conflict."[9] These include conflicts between ideals of unity and diversity, among political and economic interests, between political preferences and expert knowledge, and among organs of governance and their officials. Conflict serves important democratic purposes. It attracts interest and participants as they are drawn to take sides in the contest.[10] Adversaries hone their persuasive skills and are induced to give reasons for their positions that their colleagues and the public can judge against standards of public interest and experience. Reason giving and analysis are foundations of civic learning and the development of public trust as preferences are challenged and modified, and consensus forms based on consent rather than compliance.

The real secret of a government of separated and divided powers is not the purity of the distinctions between the branches and levels of government. Rather, it lies in the necessity it creates for officials to cooperate, compromise, and resolve their differences in order to accomplish a substantial portion of their aims. This not only tempers excesses to which unchecked power can occasionally tempt officials, it provides a spur to consultation, consensus-building and the development of informal ways of sharing power and responsibility. Whether the city reverts to partisan elections for mayor and Council or retains the nominally nonpartisan system, the need for the mayor to build reliable alliances with Council members should provide incentives to conduct joint campaigns. The cooperation required to construct electoral slates may carry over into the organization of the Council and its policy agenda, helping produce a system of collective accountability, including a built-in opposition, which takes its business to be holding the administration and council majority to public account for its actions.

Within a diverse Council and voting public, competition for the support of median voters and for the added legitimacy that a larger majority or consensus bestows on policy and its sponsors places bounds on conflict and pushes politicians toward the center and unity. Moreover, a system in which no one interest is always the designated loser and none can be sure of always winning, places a premium on civility, as one can ill afford to alienate today's adversary, who may be tomorrow's decisive ally.

The governance system sketched here institutionalizes conflict, but it also provides means of managing it. The use of cumulative voting increases the likelihood of contested elections for the Council and the probability that it will contain representatives of diverse interests. Contested elections tend to offer policy choices and attract increased participation in campaigns and elections. Higher turnout could also have the effect of increasing the legitimacy of the government, and result in further increasing participation as voters' sense of efficacy increases.

Other measures might also increase voter turnout above the abysmal levels common in Dallas. Reducing the frequency of elections and holding municipal elections concurrently with state elections would undoubtedly increase turnout. Making council terms the same as the mayor's, and limiting referenda to general elections could further reduce voter fatigue and neglect. Longer council terms could have additional benefits. They provide greater opportunities for Council members to concentrate on the merits of policies as opposed to calculations of their electoral impact. It could encourage joint campaigns by mayoral and council candidates based on commitment to common policy goals. Such endeavors could lead to the development of multi-ethnic grass roots political organizations to provide the infrastructure, financial, public relations, and other components necessary for successful campaigns and for establishing an authentic popular and independent base for elected officials. Such intermediary organizations provide means of giving citizens practical experience in politics. They also would introduce a more public means of identifying future political leaders and recruiting candidates than the current system of self-nomination. This would give greater stability to the system and provide a means of preparing competitors and successors to current elected officials.

Reinventing the Role of the Private Sector

Remaking the formal political organs of city government to make it an effective force in Dallas governance is only part of the task of building a social production regime. Reorienting the city's private institutions of governance from their fixation on social control to one of sharing responsibility for social production will be difficult in the context of Dallas civic culture.

The Dallas Citizens Council offers the most promising opportunity for that reorientation and the greatest obstacle to it. Since the late 1980s its membership has been broadened. Its leadership includes a new generation of executives, whose corporate responsibilities limit the time they can devote to Dallas affairs, but whose global experience makes them among the region's most sensitive people to issues of social equity and urban quality. It has developed an agenda that embraces a wide range of educational and social concerns.

The Citizens Council remains the most influential voice of business interests in today's Dallas. On the other hand, it remains averse to open and public discussion of its activities, preferring to work behind the scenes and to exercise influence through confidential communications with officials or through surrogate organizations. This mode of operation impairs the development of trust in both the Citizens Council and the officials who are discovered to have collaborated with it, regardless of the merits of an action. Also, the growing dependence of the Citizens Council on its own regent—its full-time president—to identify issues and handle lobbying chores, diminishes the extent to which involvement in its work builds civic capital among its own members. Many, in fact, appear clueless about how to approach major city issues and most are timid at the prospect of being publicly identified with controversial issues, especially those with racial implications. Few have either the time or patience for long, occasionally acrimonious meetings with racial, environmental, and other civic activists to reach consensus on complicated problems. They send their vice presidents for community relations to these sessions. The latter lack authority to commit the boss, who also may lack the autonomy to say "yes or no" without checking with the home office in another city.

In their 1989 report on the condition and future of Dallas, Neal Pierce and Curtis Johnson suggested a radical transformation of the Dallas Citizens Council into a regional citizens' organization.[11] Modeled on the Twin Cities (Minnesota) Citizens League, they envisioned an organization funded primarily by corporations and foundations, but open to any individual willing to pay nominal dues. Members of the organization would elect its board. It would sponsor policy studies and initiatives developed by committees open to any willing participant and staffed by policy experts employed by the organization. As it works in the Minneapolis-St. Paul region, the new civic league's positions would be shaped by its committees and its agenda would embrace the most critical social, economic and governance issues of the region, including those of the central city.

Its influence would not stem solely from its representation of the top business firms, as is the case of the Citizens Council. Rather, it would also flow from the merit of its analyses, its capacity to build consensus from the array of economic and social, geographic, and virtual interests making up its membership, and its ability to mobilize both corporate and community support for its proposals.[12] Such a transformation of the Dallas Citizens Council would represent an abandonment of its private club character and move it well beyond its token expansion to the heads of professional firms, plus a few women and minority executives. It would become a semi-public institution. Corporate executives would lose their exclusive power over its agenda. By sharing power, however, they would gain a broader and different kind of influence, tempered by a more realistic immersion in and deeper understanding the problems of the city. And they could begin to build something of enormous value to them and their firms over the long run: mutual trust across lines of class and race.

The most important component of private sector involvement in a governing coalition is the ability to mobilize slack resources to achieve specific goals. When it comes to large-scale development projects, their success increasingly depends upon public powers and investments. Clearly, that has been the case in recent Dallas history. At the same time, major public initiatives, such as the Dallas Museum of Arts, the Arboretum, Symphony Hall, improvements to the zoo, and downtown parks and amenities have relied heavily on infusions of private capital. The Central Dallas Association, Southern Dallas Development Corporation, the Dallas Initiative, and the Southwestern Medical Center all have drawn on a rich mixture of public and private resources. In each instance, private funding has been idiosyncratic and there is no systematic means of allocating major slack resources of corporations and philanthropies to achieve strategic objectives.

Dallas has a number of small community-oriented foundations, a number of which operate through the Dallas Foundation. Corporate and major private individual and foundation funding, though often generous, is not coordinated, except for gifts administered through the United Way and the Greater Dallas Community Council. As more of the extraordinary wealth in Dallas moves into foundation endowments there may be an opportunity to mobilize these resources to influence profoundly the quality of the city for a vast number of its residents. A community foundation following a strategic agenda does not preclude individual foundations pursuing their own interests, but it does provide a means by which a substantial portion of the endowment resources of the city can be channeled to projects and purposes that have been subjected to thoughtful analysis and deliberation. A number of cities have created community foundations that coordinate corporate and foundation giving in accordance with a strategic agenda, so that the slack resources made available can have the greatest leverage on public funding and community efforts.[13]

Bringing the independent sector into the governing regime could have a salutary effect. It would introduce a protagonist with significant resources and the perspective of a trustee for the public interest rather than the economic self-interest (however enlightened) or political goals of the corporate sector. The independent sector is uniquely positioned to inject concerns for development of social and civic capital into deliberations about the city's welfare and to reinforce its moral arguments with resources that facilitate development of a rich network of intermediary social and civic institutions. There are overtly political tasks that the independent sector cannot perform without risk to its tax-exempt status but it can do some things that neither business nor government is equipped to do.

It will require changes from current practice to make the Dallas nonprofit sector a stable element in a governing regime, but there are mechanisms in place that could promote that transformation. The Nonprofit Resource Center established by the Meadows Foundation in the Swiss Avenue historic district, or the Dallas Foundation could serve as catalysts for an expanded role for the city's current and future foundations. The aim is not to impose a system in which all foundations conform, but only one in which there is a higher level of coordination based on thoughtful deliberation about strategic city priorities and the appropriate role of the granting and operating foundations in performing that role. In time, such an approach could be expected to demonstrate its capacity to assist materially in solving critical problems of the city. This, in turn, should encourage new donors to appreciate the value of entrusting a substantial portion of their endowments to coordinated endeavors rather than confine all of them to future uses that primarily serve their current interests. A part of the role of a coordinated independent sector is the education of potential benefactors in the virtues of so leveraging their trust assets.

Formation of Civic Capital

The reform of citywide governmental, business, and independent sector institutions sketched above would arguably provide a basis for a new governing regime with an enhanced capacity to solve problems and engage in social production for those participating in regime deliberations and decisions. It may be possible for the regime to solve problems, however, without engaging in the formation of civic capital among the broader population, thus failing to perform one of the core functions of city governance. Capacity to solve problems is critical to building trust, but it is not, of itself, sufficient to rejuvenate participation in political life, diffuse civic skills widely among the public, and displace the passive consumerism of Dallas with engaged citizenship.

Changing the Approach to Governance

For that to happen, deliberation on things that matter and authority to make or at least participate in decisions will need to be diffused to the community level. This could be done in a number of ways, either in the alternative, or in some combination. Whatever the ultimate resolution, it will mean a fundamental change in the way in which Dallas is governed, abandoning the hierarchical and structured accountability approaches of machine age corporate management for the looser networks and consultative processes of the information age.

First, the argument for strengthening the mayor and council and for giving the city government more comprehensive authority, including responsibility for public education, does not imply that the central organs of city government should attempt to run the city from City Hall. A looser touch and a more collegial organization are better suited to the information age. It can also empower a wider range of people to work on solving the problems of the city and share more broadly the responsibility for governance.

The central organs of the city government might be primarily concerned with strategic planning; setting goals and performance standards; providing the tools and processes that enable effective, responsive, and ethical administration; ensuring that resources are available and allocated to meet those standards and goals; and coordinating intergovernmental and inter-sector activities. It may be useful to distinguish between the roles of *providing for* services or development activities and actually *producing* all of them.[14] The latter function may be performed by a wide variety of entities—subordinate units of the city government, operating foundations and nonprofit organizations such as community development corporations, and private vendors—in addition to government agencies.

If the City should move toward a system in which its central agencies focus on planning and providing for services, as distinct from being the monopoly producer of them, it will need to take care to retain the staff and information it needs to be a "smart buyer."[15] Basically, this entails knowing what it is trying to achieve, having the capacity to set performance standards and to hold the producers it selects—whether public, nonprofit, or private organizations—accountable for the quality of their performance.

Creating Institutions of Community Governance

Deconcentrating the production of public goods has a number of advantages in a city as large, diverse, and complex as Dallas. It permits adaptation to a variety of circumstances arising from the spatial and virtual politics of the city. It recognizes that there are both economies and diseconomies of scale that cannot be addressed by a single administrative structure or a completely unitary system. It allows for more experimentation with new approaches to services and development and can use market discipline, broaden choices, and control costs.

Dallas has a number of self-conscious communities with fairly well defined and traditional boundaries. These include Oak Cliff, East Dallas, South Dallas-Fair Park, Pleasant Grove, Lake Highlands and Oak Lawn, among others. The current system of single-member district representation generally makes relatively little use of these communities, the integrity of which is important to the development of civic consciousness and public trust. These traditional communities could serve as nuclei for establishing a community tier of governance with responsibility for the provision and production of services at a more intimate scale. Community governance would also make it possible to respond more sensitively to local variations in needs and preferences for levels or types of public goods and services. One community may place a high priority on improvement of reading skills in its schools while another seeks enhanced community policing and a third is primarily concerned with code enforcement, street and sidewalk maintenance, or animal control.

Theoretically, a central government can make these spatial adjustments, but Dallas history does not inspire confidence that it will. The community governments envisioned here would not be like the neighborhood advisory councils that have been established in some cities, such as Atlanta, which tend to fall into disuse and become objects of cynicism as people realize they are not influential on things that matter. Nor are they a variation of "neighborhood city halls" where representatives of city departments hang out with the neighbors and try to adjust their activities to be more responsive to local needs.

If the boards of community governments have responsibilities and powers that make competing for positions on them worthwhile, they can contract with city agencies or other producers of services, or in some cases, produce the services themselves. The City might also contract with the community governments for the production of area-sensitive programs. City agencies might use the communities as their basic administrative districts, but the objective is to give the community governments enough power to be forces to be reckoned with, incorporating them into the governing regime. It cannot be persuasively argued that community governments would be too small to be effective. Most would be larger in area and population than most of the suburban governments throughout the Dallas area. No one seems to doubt the capacity for governance of small cities like Addison or DeSoto or to discount the advantages they derive from certain diseconomies of scale and close relationships between citizens and officials.

For such a system to work, it will be necessary for the city to provide core funding based on a formula that ensures that each community government has sufficient resources to administer its basic functions. Additional funds above the basic support level could be provided through proposals made as a regular part of the budget process, delegation of authority to impose a surtax on municipal rates, or through fees that enable the communities to enrich services and undertake unique and innovative approaches to localized problems.

The arrangement between the City and the Central Dallas Association suggests one way in which a community tier of governance could be financed and a model of how such organizations might function to set policy objectives and undertake programs with some combination of self-help and financial assistance. Another model is the nonprofit foundations of planned communities, which represent both homeowners and renters, and use compulsory fees assessed against property owners to maintain common property and operate a variety of facilities and programs.[16] Consistency in form is less important than capacity to address local concerns effectively and represent those concerns and needs forcefully in citywide forums.

Whether the community governments are subdivisions of the general government of the City or nonprofit organizations, each could be held accountable for the performance of its agreed upon tasks through the budgetary process, performance standards in contracts, regular audits, and requirements for professional management of the activities it undertakes. The City could also retain the authority to override or suspend certain kinds of decisions and negotiate their modification when they negatively affect neighboring or city-wide interests. Election of community government board members, the use of competition for service contracts, and requirements for transparency in deliberations and decision-making could ensure accountability to residents of each community and to the city at large for the funds it dispenses. Perhaps the most important benefit of the establishment of a tier of community governance is the opportunity it would provide for wider participation in the processes of governance for a substantial body of citizens. This diffusion of opportunity for direct experience in governing can broaden the pool of potential political and civic leaders for city and state affairs and provide channels for formation of civic capital throughout the city.

The Virtues of Sharing Power

The approach to governing sketched here has a number of advantages for a large city like Dallas. First of all, it allows the City government to take advantage of the special strengths of a wide array of producers. Second, it makes effective use of competition to lower costs and improve the quality of services by denying any one producer—including the city's central agencies—a permanent monopoly. Third, it provides a mechanism for consciously fostering community-based urban laboratories for the resolution of problems through the development of indigenous organizations. These may include localized programs of improvement, such as charter schools, community development corporations, community and employer-based job training programs, public safety and antidrug initiatives, nonprofit housing corporations, and services to groups that are often underserved or overlooked by central government agencies. Fourth, experience in grass roots governance strengthens the civic capital of the city by engaging a broader cross section of citizens in public processes and empowering them with both experience in governance and access to resources. Fifth, sharing power with independent sector organizations often leverages public monies with other financial and in-kind contributions.

Given its imbedded culture of social control, the hard trick for Dallas will be to create a new ethic of shared power, mutual trust, and reciprocal responsibility. The voluntary group that enters into an arrangement with the city is no longer a totally free agent, but it is more than a mere instrument of the government. It has a responsibility to perform as agreed. The government, in turn, has a responsibility to provide clear guidance and oversight of the manner in which public resources are used, and to resist the temptation to co-opt the organization for its own political aims. Most importantly, the City will have to work on treating grass-roots groups with respect, even when they are inconveniences and, occasionally, nuisances.

Finally, sharing power avoids the natural resistance to critical oversight inherent when the same organization is responsible for the provision, production, and evaluation of public goods. The unitary, hierarchical, and monopolistic design of the Council-Manager/Board-Superintendent systems contains an inherent conflict of interest. The elected bodies cannot oversee their administrative creatures without confronting their own failures of judgment. And since they are dependent entirely upon their appointed executives for personal staff, policy analysis, and program evaluation, they tend to find it difficult to hold their managers accountable, or even to criticize them constructively. When one member or a small faction uses independent sources of information, conflicts in personal style, debatable allegations of ethical transgressions, or ideological perspectives as the basis for criticism, they are often ostracized for not being team players. The consequence is acquiescence in single options, often with little serious consideration of alternatives or implications; a focus on means rather than ends; the neglect of central strategic capacities such as planning; and obsession with maintaining control of matters that might be performed better through systems of delegation and accountability.

The Special Case of Education

These considerations are nowhere more critical than in the governance of urban public education. Because the future of the city in an information age rides on its human capital, it makes sense to place ultimate responsibility for education on the most visible officials of the city rather than permit them to shirk it. But making them responsible does not require them to conduct public education as a monopoly enterprise or administer it as if it were a mass production industrial plant. Rather, there are strong reasons to believe that policy tools should be selected for the production of educational services that offer a wide range of choices to parents and students as means of assuring both accountability and high quality performance.

Texas law is generous in its openness to the establishment of charter schools, which permit existing school faculty or others to form nonprofit organizations to operate public schools under performance contracts. These schools receive the per-pupil fund allotment that would otherwise go to the student's traditional school, and they must meet the basic requirements of public schools—nondiscriminatory enrollment, secular education, and mastery of core subject matter. But they are relieved of most administrative regulations in return for contractual obligations to perform effectively in educating their students.[17]

Whether the delivery mechanism is charter schools, more conventional approaches to school choice, or the use of contract vendors to deliver special programs such as reading instruction for disadvantaged students, the important point is that the objective is to preserve the core values and enhance the effectiveness of *public education*. It is not to protect the traditional structure and organization of the *public school system*. In thus preserving the faith without necessarily protecting the church, the city will need room to innovate, to experiment with different organizational and substantive approaches.

Forging New Tools of Civic Engagement

The governance system sketched above recognizes the diversity of Dallas, and the demands it produces for specialization and variety in the organs through which the public's business is conducted. At the same time, specialization and diversity require wide access to information and argument about issues so that citizens can make informed choices and officials can be held accountable to them. Reliable information is even more crucial to the effective operation of democratic governance than it is to the functioning of free markets. The flow and surges of information influence the salience of issues and permit both officials and citizens to make reasoned and responsible choices.[18]

For an urban democracy to work, raw information alone is not sufficient. There must be public deliberative forums where facts and ideas are connected to reasons, which are offered as justifications for proposals and tested in debate. Civic discourse in a democracy is essentially an exercise in public ethics.[19] It may be passionate, occasionally hyperbolic, and thus, requires rules by which adversaries must show respect for the dignity of those who doubt their wisdom if not their evidence. Proponents of policies should offer reasons for what they would have government do in the form of factual evidence and moral arguments that make claims that they are palpably in the public interest. This requirement for justification denies legitimacy to policies that are self-interested, products of corrupt influence, or reflections of no more than the exercise of raw power.

The forms of respect are hollow without the substance of respect. At a minimum that requires equal and ready access to information and the specialized knowledge for gathering, organizing, and interpreting it. For Dallas, equalization of policy information and access to knowledge would represent a substantial change in its way of conducting public business. Clearly, it would mean modifying the Power Play/Market Maker solution set and the affinity of its practitioners for single policy options and the dismissive marginalization of antagonists. At best, it would involve transparency in the development of policies. This would include disclosure of both assumptions and the evidence in support of proposals, critical analysis prior to decisions rather than window dressing reports to justify decisions after they have been made, wider consultation, and more thorough debate on the merits before action.

This is not a prescription for paralysis by analysis as the antidote to the "ready, fire, aim" approach that too often characterizes the city's policy making. It simply recognizes that almost every effort to withhold information tends to generate mistrust, and in many cases it engenders litigation that delays decisions or their effect far longer than would result from open deliberations. The formidable financial cost of mistrust is reflected in the hundreds of millions of dollars paid by Dallas in court judgments against the city. The cynicism and civic neglect of citizens is far more damaging in the long run to the legitimacy and effectiveness of the government.

The separation of legislative and executive powers induces a more open information environment. It removes any incentive for the Council to be protective of information in the administration's possession. Equipping the Council with its own information technologies and analytical capacity can only further its inquisitiveness. A tier of community governance will produce a demand for comparative information about community services and performance levels. The use of nongovernmental organizations to carry out many programs will also require more transparency to dispel concerns of inside dealing and favoritism.

More than ever, the electronic age demands the careful cultivation of public forums for civic discourse in which advocates expect to engage one another's arguments rather than hurl sound bites. One can sense possibilities in CSPAN and internet discussion groups. Public television and access channels are a greatly underused resource for public debate, and cities have done little more with them than broadcast official meetings. Both conventional and advancing technologies in telecommunications—much of it invented and produced in the Dallas region—offer exceptional opportunities for creating new tools of civic information and engagement that can be used by ordinary citizens.

Public television and radio and public access cable TV channels have been under-used as media for news, analysis, and special in-depth documentaries dealing with city issues. Interactive telecommunication can make possible the simultaneous engagement of many different groups throughout the city in the same discussion at the same time. This can improve understanding of issues and different perspectives on them, and enhance mutual trust and responsibility, particularly if the encounters are designed to foster skills in listening, problem resolution, negotiation, and leadership. Such experiences are vital to urban governance and provide the human relationships that can make it possible to transcend the anonymity and ennui of the virtual city. The promise of the new technologies is that they can be used to convert couch potato consumers into networking citizens.

Creation of a community information system that can be accessed through the internet offers another means by which spatially-coded information could be made available through schools, libraries, and community centers to neighborhood organizations and citizens. Prototypes of such information systems exist in other places, such as Kansas City and Philadelphia. For geographic levels from neighborhood to region, they can provide data on population, households, employment, crime, health, and employment, as well as information on budget allocations, capital expenditures and private investments, services, and code enforcement. Such systems can offer basic programs for analyzing the information, comparing probable outcomes of alternative policy scenarios, and making further inquiries and registering comments.[20]

Richer mass media coverage of city affairs and a working community information system could be important contributions of the city's philanthropic institutions to development of civic capital. These kinds of information resources empower citizens and organizations to participate in city affairs on a more equal basis with the experts of the bureaucracy and well-financed interest groups. While they undoubtedly complicate the lives of officials in the short run, they can improve their work lives in the long run. They force decisions to be well-grounded in evidence and meticulously defended in public, improving their effectiveness as well as public understanding, confidence and trust. They create an environment of accountability, both in the processes of decision making and in the quality of the decisions themselves.

If information technologies are to become tools of the civic enterprise, access to them must be widespread and not dependent entirely upon wealth. Unlike print media, the civic channels and bulletin boards should be viewed as part of the city's commons. Access to the Internet must eventually become as ubiquitous as access to the telephone, and its navigation and civic uses will have to become a part of the public school curriculum. Those without access or ability to use telecommunications technology will be effectively denied full citizenship.

Toward Governing in the Public Interest

For the foreseeable future the core problems of Dallas will have to be addressed by the city if they are to be addressed at all. To address effectively issues of service and development, Dallas must concurrently increase its capacity to perform its civic function and adapt its political system to the new economy and the social realities of urban life in a new century. That will require breaking the old cycle of institutions reinforcing civic culture, reinforcing institutions. Nonpartisanship, term limits, penurious stipends for elective office, and managerialism—all fruits of a civic culture fostered to maintain social control in the service of a narrow conception of commercial interest—impoverished the city's capacity for effective problem solving and sustained political leadership once the old entrepreneurial regime withered. Culturally imbedded anti-governmentism, dread of conflict, and affinity for single-option policy-making deadened the interest of even the attentive publics, anesthetized political creativity, and suppressed the arts of compromise. The politics of identity and widespread civic neglect took their place.

The powerful and pervasive economic and demographic forces that transformed Dallas created a new kind of city with far-reaching implications for its governance. Economic restructuring produced a leadership vacuum that could not be filled by either an emerging political class, managerial regents, or the federal courts. The result is a system in which no one is in charge, no one is responsible, and no one can be held accountable for the performance of the government. It embodies the two great paradoxes of governance in the information age. The first arises from the necessity of sharing power: How do we get everyone in on the act and still get some action? The second results from the twilight of hierarchy: Who is responsible when no one is in charge?[21]

In designing a new system of urban governance for Dallas, given its civic culture and the dominant role of business in its past governance, there is special resonance in Wallace Sayre's observation that "public and private management are fundamentally alike in all unimportant respects."[22] Government is not a business. Citizens are not merely customers, shopping for best buys of tax and service packages. Nor can urban government be justified as little more than the operator of the local growth machine.

Thus far, the course of Dallas governance has not followed the civic republican or urban democracy paths advocated by Tocqueville, Mill, Dewey,[23] Elkin, and Putnam. Rooted in the Greek polis, their view held that the core function of local self-government is formation of civic capital through public-regarding civic engagement, which engenders a reciprocity of trust, loyalty, and shared responsibility[24] among citizens and officials. Dallas instead followed the Roman Imperial tradition of local government, which tends to view local government primarily as an administrative instrument of the state—an efficient means of providing services locally.[25] Social control and efficiency have been valued more than equity and justice. Individual and group self interest have been prime motivators of public behavior. The result has been a pinched understanding of the city's commercial public interest. Reform is the more difficult because none of the city's established institutions is much interested in it and its basic solution sets are designed to quash the kind of open deliberation and consensus building that is a necessary precursor to change.

Institutionalizing competent performance of civic functions will take more than a few months of socialization through a tri-ethnic committee followed by ratification of a single option or the fortunate election of a few competent and honest officials. New formal governmental institutions are a necessary but hardly a sufficient basis for democratic development.[26] Structural changes are necessary because structures constrain the mobilization of publics and the capacities to decide and act. They can make a difference in the quality of performance of civic functions. They are not sufficient because it is possible to pervert any institutional arrangement through poor or misguided leadership. Although some structures can reduce the risks of inadequate and corrupt officials and enhance the value of exceptional and virtuous leaders, the formal sector of governance is at best enabling, at worst confining.

The informal sector gives the forms life through its network of mediating institutions. Dallas is not bereft of interest groups. It has a fairly rich array of clubs, churches, leagues, and associations, within which bonds of trust have been established. What it lacks are non-governmental institutions built on enduring coalitions that include significant participation from different ethnic groups and economic levels. Such institutions, whether political parties or civic leagues, can help extend mutual trust, and fuse financial and political resources in pursuit of common objectives. Competition between such institutions, within the bounds of civic patriotism, can also foster political talent and leadership, crystallize issues for resolution, and manage conflict.

Democratic governance presumes that people will try to imbed their own interests in both formal and informal arrangements. But it also presumes that institutions can be designed to ameliorate the excesses of self-interest by balancing interests against each other so that none has full or permanent control. Thus, to govern, power and, ultimately, responsibility must be shared. This requires those who would govern to appeal to the "public interest," essentially an ethical justification that others are obliged to honor and meet with similar argument. A product of this kind of arrangement is the propagation of certain civic virtues. Among these are toleration of differences of conscience and expression; equality of individual dignity; freedom of association; consent based on informed deliberation; the rule of law and its just administration; fairness in the management of common resources and public goods; and accountability to the public. Therefore, democratic governments are designed consciously to impair their subversion to narrow interests by employment of a variety of institutional barriers to the control of policy by a narrow faction and by procedures that promote toleration, transparency, deliberation, and compromise in pursuit of the public interest. In many respects this is the antithesis of the governance institutions of Dallas.

Institutions and cultures are creatures of history and experience: they are more products of evolution than revolution. But evolutionary paths can be altered by either harsh environmental realities that force adaptation, or by conscious decisions. Dallas has willfully changed its civic course in the past, invented its history, and created a distinctive civic culture. Dallas was then, however, a simpler city and susceptible to simpler approaches than are now required for one of the nation's great urban centers.

Dallas must find a way to adapt more effectively to the transformations of its population, economic institutions, and technology than it has done so far. Dallas is less in control of its own destiny than ever before. Reinventing its governance and adapting democratic institutions and processes to cope better with complexity is not surrender to chaos. It represents instead coming to grips with reality, shedding the old civic myths and the affinity for social control for a new vision of the city as a diverse seedbed of democracy, civic virtue, and entrepreneurial energy. What is not practical, in the truest construction of that term, is to continue a system that neither works nor advances the practice of urban democracy.

NOTES

Chapter 1

1. For more detail, see Ladd and Yinger, *America's Ailing Cities*; and Hanson, *Rethinking Urban Policy*.

2. Clark and Dear, *State Apparatus*.

3. Stone, *Regime Politics*, p. 10

4. Elkin, "State and Market in City Politics"; G. Stoker, "Regime Theory and Urban Politics"; Stone, *Regime Politics*.

5. Hicks, "Beneath the Surface," p. 25.

6. Berry, *Long Wave Rhythms*.

7. Elkin, *City and Regime*.

8. Stone, *Regime Politics*.

9. In *Left Coast City*, Richard Edward DeLeon describes the inability of the coalition members in San Francisco's progressive regime to achieve internal coherence or reach mutually acceptable accommodations in the face of societal change and economic restructuring that led to its collapse.

10. In Chapter 14 of *Politics of Urban Development* (272–74), Stone developed a typology of regimes based on the requirement that they must be able to mobilize resources commensurate with their main policy agendas. He identified four major types: caretaker coalitions that are devoted to provision of services and seek to preserve the status quo; corporate regimes that act to promote the development interests of downtown businesses; progressive coalitions that seek to control growth and its adverse externalities; and lower class coalitions that seek expansion of opportunities and protection of neighborhoods. Also see G. Stoker, p. 61.

11. Stone, *Regime Politics*, p. 9.

12. March and Olsen, *Rediscovering Institutions*, p. 18.

13. Ibid., p. 22–23.

14. Ibid., p. 23.

15. Stone, *Regime Politics*, p. 227.

16. Tocqueville, *Democracy in America*, p. 310.

17. Elkin, *City and Regime*, p. 10. In *Democracy in America*, Tocqueville wrote: "Municipal institutions constitute the strength of nations. . . . They bring

[liberty] . . . within the people's reach, they teach them how to use and enjoy it" p.63. In *Representative Government* (p. 468), John Stuart Mill similarly argued that such institutions are essential to the "public education of citizens."

18. Elkin, *City and Regime,* p. 11.

19. Ibid., p. 15.

20. Stone, *Regime Politics,* p. 241.

21. Putnam, *Making Democracy Work,* p. 157.

22. Elkin, *City and Regime,* p. 15.

23. Ibid., p. 11.

24. In *Bureaucracy: What Government Organizations Do and Why They Do It,* James Q. Wilson distinguishes production, procedural, craft, and coping organizations, based on the extent to which it is possible for superiors to view them at work and measure the effect of their activity on outcomes.

25. Salamon, ed., *Beyond Privatization,* p. 29.

26. "Solution sets" is a concept that recurs in the writings of Bryan D. Jones, including "Social Power and Urban Regimes" (1993); *The Sustaining Hand* (1993, with Lynn W. Bachelor); and *Reconceiving Decision Making in Democratic Politics* (1994).

27. Elkin, *City and Regime.*

Chapter 2

1. Hill, *Dallas: The Making of a Modern City,* p. xvii.

2. Erik Jonsson, "Dallas: City with a Heart," p. 8.

3. Ibid., p. 12.

4. Weber, *The City;* Mumford, *The City in History.*

5. The real first generation of Dallas oil barons was more interesting and less influential than the fictional Ewing family. See Jane Wolf, *The Murchisons: The Rise and Fall of a Texas Dynasty.* See also a profile of H. L. Hunt in A.C. Greene, *Dallas USA,* pp. 120–142.

6. Kelly, "Ron Kirk." *Dallas Morning News,* April 21, 1996, p.10J.

7. Ibid.

8. "Leadership." *Dallas Times-Herald,* May 16, 1971, p. 1 of the special section. See also oral histories taken from such notables as R. L. Thornton, John Stemmons, and Woodall Rogers, located in the Dallas Section of the Jonsson Library in Dallas, and Warren Leslie's *Dallas: Public and Private,* especially chapter 3, "The 'Yes or No' Men," pp. 60–85.

9. "School Board," *Dallas Morning News,* January 18, 1996, p. 18A.

10. Two articles from the same magazine, spaced 40 years apart, well represent this viewpoint: see McCombs and Whyte, "The Dydamic Men of Dallas,"

in *Fortune,* February 1949, and Kenneth Labich, "The Best Cities for Business," in *Fortune,* October 23, 1989.

11. For example, see Dallas, City of, *The Dallas Advantage,* a brochure published to promote business in Southern Dallas.

12. Kelly, "Ron Kirk." *Dallas Morning News,* April 21, 1996. P. A1.

13. The archetypal case, enshrined in the civic myth, is the high-pressure approach used by R. L. Thornton to raise the funds required to secure the Texas Centennial exhibition for Dallas. See Chapter 4 of this volume.

14. Schutze, *The Accommodation: The Politics of Race.*

15. Only seven of thirty council members who served from 1950 to 1995, who responded to a question on factors they considered in first seeking election to the council listed "starting a political career" as important or very important.

16. Earl Cabell resigned as mayor to run successfully for Congress in 1964. Steve Bartlett served in Congress after being a member of the Council. In 1990, he resigned his seat in Congress to run for mayor.

17. The level of skill of mayors has varied considerably. Robert Folsom and Jack Evans, for example, who served as mayors in the late 1970s and early 1980s, were generally successful in maintaining a majority in support of measures they advanced. Mayor Annette Strauss (1987–1991) presided over a far more fractious council at a time of racial confrontations over various policies, including police conduct toward minorities and council redistricting. Mayor Steve Bartlett (1991–1995), the first mayor elected under the 14–1 system tended to operate without sufficient deference and consultation with his colleagues, resulting in considerable in fighting among members and contentious council sessions. His successor, Ron Kirk, demonstrated considerable skill in working with members of the Council to maintain decorum and consensus and in maintaining support of civic and business groups. He was re-elected in 1999 without serious opposition.

18. The staff for the mayor's office, like that of other members of the Council, are members of the civil service who have been assigned by the Office of the Manager to serve as staff assistants to the mayor. The mayor neither chooses them nor has the authority to remove them, although it would be unusual for a City Manager to refuse such a request.

19. Interview with former mayors Jack Evans, Annette Strauss, and Robert Folsom, 1993.

20. Elkin, *City and Regime.*

21. James Aston, one of the city's early managers, became president and later CEO of the First National Bank of Dallas. George Shrader created his own firm. Richard Knight became a Vice President of Caltex, and Jan Hart entered the brokerage firm of Bear Stearns as a municipal bond expert, and later became president of the Greater Dallas Chamber of Commerce. John Ware became the chief executive of a new investment firm financed by Tom Hicks, CEO of Hicks

Muse Tate and of the Dallas Stars NFL Hockey franchise. Assistant Manager Dan Petty became an executive of Hunt Petroleum's local development subsidiary, the Woodbine Corp., and later served as the President of the North Texas Commission. Richard Douglas, another former assistant city manager, served subsequently as president of the Greater Dallas Chamber of Commerce.

22. From interviews and conversations with current and former city council members.

23. For the current Dallas council-manager system to work it is important for the city manager to rest easy on the formal powers of the office rather than insist rigidly on the prerogatives of the manager, such as the rule that staff can receive direction only from a majority of the Council, communicated through the Manager. Jan Hart, who was manager during the first years of the Steve Bartlett mayoralty, relied heavily upon her powers under the Charter and had a prickly relationship with the mayor and the council, which resulted in her resignation. Her successor, John Ware, was far more flexible in his relationship with both Mayor Bartlett and Mayor Ron Kirk, essentially sharing the power of policy initiation and accepting anonymity when credit for accomplishment was being assigned. At the same time, he exercised tight control over the bureaucracy of the city.

24. Hill, *Dallas: The Making of a Modern City,* pp. 109–127.

25. Ibid.

26. Scott, *Domination and the Arts of Resistance.*

27. Interview, Anonymous source. September 21, 1993.

Chapter 3

1. Holmes and Saxon, *The WPA Dallas Guide,* p. 38, ff.

2. Holmes and Saxon, *The WPA Dallas Guide,* p. 150–153; also, Saunders, "Boats Along the Trinity," in *Sketches of a Growing Town,* pp. 51–65.

3. Holmes and Saxon, *The WPA Dallas Guide,* p. 137; B. Peterson and D. Davis, "Winning the Railroads," in *Sketches of a Growing Town,* pp. 39–40.

4. B. Peterson and Davis, "Winning the Railroads," pp. 44–45; Holmes and Saxon, *The WPA Dallas Guide,* p. 137.

5. Holmes and Saxon, *The WPA Dallas Guide,* p. 139.

6. Holmes and Saxon, *The WPA Dallas Guide,* pp. 124–129; Hill, *Dallas: The Making of a Modern City,* p. 4.

7. Alexander Cockrell and his widow, Sarah, are described by Darwin Payne (*Sketches of a Growing Town,* pp. 23–35) as the first capitalists of Dallas.

8. Holmes and Saxon, *The WPA Dallas Guide,* pp. 286–290.

9. Dallas was the principal supplier of cavalry saddles to the U.S. and

British armies during World War I (Holmes and Saxon, *The WPA Dallas Guide,* pp. 127–134).

10. Holmes and Saxon, *The WPA Dallas Guide,* pp. 167–172.

11. Holmes and Saxon, *The WPA Dallas Guide,* pp. 161–166.

12. Payne, *Big D: Triumphs and Troubles,* pp. 49–52.

13. Payne, *Big D: Triumphs and Troubles;* Greene, *Dallas USA,* p.144; 122–123; Wolf, *The Murchisons.*

14. Greene, *Dallas USA,* p. 75.

15. Payne, *Big D: Triumphs and Troubles,* pp.115–122.

16. Greene, *Dallas USA,* pp. 217–224.

17. Payne, *Big D: Triumphs and Troubles,* p. 218.

18. Payne, *Big D: Triumphs and Troubles,* p. 30; Kessler, *A City Plan for Dallas.*

19. Prince, *A History of Dallas: From a Different Perspective,* p. 119; Williams and Shay, *Time Change,* pp. 70–71.

20. Greene, *Dallas USA,* pp. 168–169; Payne, *Big D: Triumphs and Troubles,* 256 ff.

21. See Waddell, Berry, and Hoch, "Residential Property Values in a Multinodal Urban Area," in *Journal of Real Estate Economics,* (7)2:117–141 (1993), and Waddell, *1990 Appraisal Ratio Study.* A 1992 study of the Dallas County residential property values (Bruton Center, *State of the Region 1992,* pp. 52–53)found that, holding constant the size and age of housing, there was a depreciation of value of almost 20 percent for homes in neighborhoods that were over 70 percent black or Hispanic, compared with those that were less than five percent black or Hispanic.

22. The "Stemmons Corridor" is named, as is Interstate 35-E, for its principal land owner and promoter, John Stemmons, a stalwart of the Citizens Council.

23. Altwegg, "Economy aims at 4 in a row," *Dallas Morning News,* January 19, 1964, p. 9–1.

24. Waddell and Shukla, "Employment Dynamics," in *Geographical Analysis,* (25)1:35–52 (1993).

25. Waddell, *1990 Appraisal Ratio Study.*

26. Waddell and Shukla, "Employment Dynamics"; Melosi, "Dallas-Fort Worth: Marketing the Metroplex," in *Sunbelt Cities,* pp. 162–195.

27. Brown, "1979: The year of the real estate boom," *Dallas Morning News,* January 6, 1980, p. H-1.

28. U.S. Bureau of the Census, *Selected Labor Force Statistics* (1962, 1970, 1990).

29. Ibid.

30. Noyelle and Stanback, Jr., *Economic Transformation of American Cities;* Hanson, ed., *Rethinking Urban Policy,* pp. 11–58.

31. Bruton Center, *State of the Region 1992*, pp. 11–13.

32. Bruton Center, *State of the Region 1992*, p. 36.

33. Bruton Center, *State of the Region 1992*.

34. General Motors subsequently sold EDS back to its local management.

35. Hicks, "Beneath the Surface and Beyond the Borders," in *State of the Region 1992*, p. 25.

36. Ibid., p. 26.

37. Jacobs, *Cities and the Wealth of Nations*, pp. 35–42; 171–172.

Chapter 4

1. Elkin, *City and Regime*; Stone, *Regime Politics*.

2. See Hill, *Dallas: The Making of a Modern City*, pp.23–90, for an excellent account of the political climate of turn-of-the-century Dallas. See also Payne, *Big D: Triumphs and Troubles*, pp. 29–114, for a discussion of this period from a slightly different perspective. The following section relies upon these narratives.

3. Prince, *A History of Dallas*, pp. 56–121; Payne, *Big D: Triumphs and Troubles*, pp. 70–73; Hill, *Dallas: The Making of a Modern City*, pp. 44–51; Williams and Shay, *Time Change*, pp. 46–53.

4. Hill, *Dallas: The Making of a Modern City*, pp.101–107; Payne, *Big D: Triumphs and Troubles*, pp. 67–82.

5. Holmes and Saxon, *The WPA Dallas Guide*, pp. 91–92; Payne, *Big D: Triumphs and Troubles*, Chapter 4, "Embracing the Ku Klux Klan," pp. 67–96.

6. Hill, *The Making of a Modern City*.

7. Ibid.; Hill, *Dallas: The Making of a Modern City*, pp. 102–104.

8. Hill, *Dallas: The Making of a Modern City*, pp. 105–110.

9. For a full discussion of the role of the *Dallas Morning News* in the Charter movement, see Barta, *The Dallas News and Council-Manager Government*.

10. Woodrow Wilson, "The Study of Administration," in *Political Science Quarterly* (2)2:197–222 (1887); Goodnow, *Politics and Administration*; Childs, "Principles Underlying the City-Manager Plan," in *Basic Literature of American Public Administration*, p. 97; National Municipal League, *Model City Charter*.

11. Payne, *Big D: Triumphs and Troubles*, pp. 126–132.

12. Ibid.

13. Ibid., pp. 133–134.

14. Cheney, *Dallas Spirit*, p. 60.

15. Payne, *Big D: Triumphs and Troubles*, pp. 153–175.

16. Interview, Stanley Marcus, 1996.

17. Leslie, *Dallas: Public and Private*, p. 63.

18. Payne, *Big D: Triumphs and Troubles*, pp. 172–173; Hill, *Dallas: The Making of a Modern City*, pp. 122–125.

19. Interview, Stanley Marcus, 1996.

20. Thometz, *The Decision-Makers*, pp. 27–37; Hill, *Dallas: The Making of a Modern City*, Chapter 5.

21. Elkin, "State and Market in City Politics," in *The Politics of Urban Development.*

22. Hill, *Dallas: The Making of a Modern City.*

23. Payne, *Big D: Triumphs and Troubles,* p. 279.

24. Payne, *Big D: Triumphs and Troubles,* p. 309.

25. Payne, *Big D: Triumphs and Troubles*, pp. 305–317; Leslie, *Dallas: Public and Private*, pp. 152ff.

26. Quoted in Payne, *Big D: Triumphs and Troubles,* p. 322.

27. Payne, *Big D: Triumphs and Troubles,* p. 323.

28. These included Jerry Junkins, the CEO of Texas Instruments, who pushed initiatives to improve education in the Dallas Public Schools, but not his successor, who focused almost exclusively on repositioning the company for global competition in a new generation of digital processors. Ray Hunt, whose downtown holdings were substantial, enjoyed the respect of his business associates and a social legitimacy denied his father, the flamboyant reactionary, H. L. Hunt. Ray Hunt led the revival of the Citizens Council in the late 1980s, stepped in as chairman of the SMU board of trustees to clean up after a football scandal in 1987, and was involved in almost as many behind the scenes political and economic transactions as he was rumored to be. McDonald "Don" Williams, the Chairman of the Board of Trammell Crow Companies, devoted enormous personal energies to race relations and improvement of housing and neighborhood conditions in the inner city.

29. Schutze, *The Accommodation: The Politics of Race.*

30. Holmes and Saxon, *The WPA Dallas Guide*, p. 291.

31. The memoir of Dr. Robert Prince, *A History of Dallas,* describes life in Black Dallas from the 1930s to the 1980s. Substantial documentation of the extent and effects of segregation can be found in the opinions of the Federal District Court in a trio of cases, dealing, respectively, with desegregation of schools, segregated public housing, and violations of the Voting Rights Act in city council representation: *Tasby v. Estes,* 412 F. Supp. 1192 (N.D. Texas, 1976); *Walker v. Dallas Housing Authority,* 734 F. Supp. 1289 (N.D. Texas, 1989); *Williams v. Dallas,* 734 F. Supp. 1317 (N.D. Texas 1990). Other accounts include Payne, *Big D: Triumphs and Troubles,* especially Chapters 9 and 12; Williams and Shay, *Time Change*; and Schutze, *The Accommodation: The Politics of Race.*

32. Waddell, "The Paradox of Poverty Concentration." The phenomenon is not unique to Dallas. See Jargowsky, *Poverty and Place.*

33. Green, *Washington: Capital City*; Stone, *Regime Politics,* pp. 18–21.

34. Prince, *A History of Dallas*, pp. 74.

35. *Ibid.*, pp. 117, 137–138.

36. North Texas Commission, *Workforce Skills and Competencies.*

37. For the war against unions, see Hill, *Dallas: The Making of a Modern City*, pp. 130–161.

38. *Ibid.*, p. 99.

39. Payne, *Big D: Triumphs and Troubles,* p. 182.

40. Schutze, *The Accommodation: The Politics of Race*, p. 94.

41. *Ibid.*, pp. 94–96.

42. *Ibid.*, pp. 69–74; Payne, *Big D: Triumphs and Troubles,* pp. 255–263.

43. Holmes and Saxon, *The WPA Dallas Guide*, "Little Mexico: Outpost for Manãna," pp. 306–308.

44. Ibid., p. 306.

45. Interview, Pedro Medrano, 1994.

46. Interview, Adelfa Cajello, 1993; Frank Hernandez, 1993

47. This conflict is discussed in Chapter 5 of this volume.

48. Schutze, "St. Al: Will he die in prison for the sins of the plantation?" in *Dallas Observer,* April 18, 1998, pp. 35ff.; Miller, "Clueless," in *Dallas Observer,* May 30, 1996. Related articles can be found at www.dallasobserver.com.

49. One prospective Hispanic candidate reported that following a meeting with business leaders at which he was implored not to run, he returned to his office to learn that his bank loans had been called. Interview, Frank Hernandez, 1993.

50. Ellis, *Judicial Assumptions of Remedial Law*, pp. 146, 157–158. One such group of business contributors operated as The Dallas Breakfast Group, discussed in Chapter 11 of this work.

51. Stone, *Regime Politics*, pp. 11–12.

52. Ibid., 226–229.

53. The 1989 amendments made the mayor the only council member elected at-large and for a four year term. They also gave the mayor power to appoint city commission chairs. Under council rules, mayors appoint council committees, name the chairs, and prepare, with the assistance of the city manager, the agenda for council meetings.

54. Mayor Steve Bartlett's strongest supporter was Ray Hunt, whose properties included the Reunion complex and other valuable downtown properties.

55. Interview, Ron Kirk, August 11, 1998.

56. Interview, Alex Bickley, 1994.

57. Interview, Donna Halstead, 1998.

Chapter 5

1. Bruton Center, *Community Needs Assessment*; Bruton Center, *Housing Conditions,* 1993. The latter study also found a high correlation between unwill-

ingness to invest in housing repairs and crime rates. The importance of schools in decisions to remain or relocate in metropolitan areas is confirmed by other research. See Percy, Hawkins, and Maier, "Revisiting Tiebout," in *Publius,* (24)4:1–17 (Fall 1995).

2. Payne, *Big D: Triumphs and Troubles,* pp. 251–263.

3. Linden, *Desegregating Schools in Dallas,* pp. 19–20.

4. *Bell v. Rippy,* 133 F.Supp. 811 (ND Tex. 1955).

5. *Brown v. Rippy,* 233 F.2d 796 (5th Cir. 1956).

6. *Bell v. Rippy,* 146 F.Supp. 485, 487 (ND Texas 1956).

7. Ibid.

8. Ibid.

9. *Borders v. Rippy,* 247 F.2d 268 (5th Cir. 1957). The school system claimed the following: it needed more time to formulate plans for integration that would be in the best interests of the district, its children, and the community; immediate integration would result in mixed classes in all but one high school and many elementary schools; most schools were full of white children who would have to be displaced to let Negro children come in; differences in scholastic aptitude of whites and blacks would impose undue burdens on the schools to provide enough teachers; and plaintiffs had not exhausted their state administrative remedies.

10. Ibid. at 271.

11. *Rippy v. Borders,* 250 F.2d 690, 691 (5th Cir. 1957). Judge Atwell's order is not reported in the Federal Supplement, but is quoted in the circuit court opinion reversing him.

12. Ibid. at 692–693.

13. Linden, *Desegregating Schools in Dallas,* pp. 26–32.

14. *Boson v. Rippy,* 275 F.2d 850, 853 (5th Cir. 1960).

15. Ibid. at 417.

16. *Borders v. Rippy,* 184 F.Supp. 402 (ND Tex. 1960).

17. Ibid. at 403.

18. Ibid. at 407.

19. Ibid. at 413.

20. Ibid. at 419.

21. Ibid. As an example of a good thought, Judge Davidson cited Joe Louis' decision not to work for an organization encouraging black tourists to visit Cuba, after it was brought to his attention that Cuba had propagandistic designs on the project.

22. *Boson v. Rippy,* 285 F.2d 43, 45–46 (5th Cir. 1960).

23. Ibid. at 47–48.

24. *Borders v. Rippy,* 195 F.Supp. 732, 733 (ND Tex. 1961).

25. Ibid. at 734–735.

26. Linden, *Desegregating Schools in Dallas,* p. 32.

27. Ibid.

28. *Cooper v. Aaron,* 358 U.S. 1 (1958).

29. Linden, *Desegregating Schools in Dallas,* pp. 27–28.

30. Linden, *Desegregating Schools in Dallas,* pp. 40–46. Also see Brophy, "Active Acceptance—Active Containment," in *Southern Businessmen and Desegregation,* pp. 139–140.

31. Linden, *Desegregating Schools in Dallas,* pp. 40–48.

32. *Britton v. Folsom,* 348 F.2d 158 (5th Cir. 1965)

33. *Britton v. Folsom,* 350 F.2d 1022, 1023 (5th Cir. 1965)

34. 78 Stat. 241

35. 42 U.S.C. § 2000d

36. Rosenberg, *The Hollow Hope,* pp. 85–93.

37. *U.S. v. Jefferson County Board of Education,* 372 F.2d 836 (5th Cir. 1966), *affirmed en banc,* 380 F.2d 836 (5th Cir. 1966).

38. In *Griffin v. County School Board,* The U.S. Supreme Court told a school district that had delayed, then resorted to abolishing its public schools as a means of avoiding integration that: "The time for mere 'deliberate speed' has run out." 377 U.S. 218, 234. Citing *Griffin,* the Court, in *Green v. County School Board of Kent County, Virginia,* 391 U.S. 430 (1968) emphasized that: "The burden on a school board is to come forward with a plan that promises realistically to work, and promises realistically to work *now . . . until it is clear that state-imposed segregation has been completely eliminated.*" 391 U.S. at 439. (Italics in the original). Still, obstruction and dilatory tactics, similar to those practiced in Dallas, continued. The Court, in *Alexander v. Holmes County Board of Education,* 396 U.S. 19 (1969) restated the obligation to remedy the existence of dual systems and said, "a standard of 'all deliberate speed' for desegregation is no longer constitutionally permissible. . . . [T]he obligation of every school district is to terminate dual school systems at once and to operate now and hereafter only unitary schools." 396 U.S. at 20. Finally, in *Swann v. Charlotte-Mecklenburg Board of Education,* 402 U.S. 1 (1971), the Court unanimously stated that: "the remedy must be implemented *forthwith.*" 402 U.S. 1 (1971). (Italics in the original)

39. 402 U.S. 1, 15. These remedies included busing, redrawing attendance zones, racial mix quotas for schools, integration of faculties, enhancement of programs, etc.

40. Linden, *Desegregating Schools in Dallas,* pp. 57–59.

41. Ibid., p. 61.

42. Although the stair step plan was put into effect, it merely involved the elimination of racial criteria for admission to each grade level. DISD had not been ordered to take affirmative action to remove the vestiges of its dual education system. In the meantime, desegregation jurisprudence was changing as the federal courts grew increasing impatient with the dilatory tactics and outright resistance

of local school boards to discharging their constitutional duties under *Brown*. In 1965 the Circuit Court twice ordered the DISD to desegregate its twelfth grade no later than September of that year. *Britton v. Folsom*, 348 F.2d 158 (5th Cir. 1965); *Britton v. Folsom* (350 F.2d 1022 (5th Cir. 1965). Again, DISD took no steps beyond those strictly required of it by the court's order.

43. *Tasby v. Estes*, 342 F. Supp. 945 at 948 (USDC, ND Tex., 1971).

44. Ibid. at 954.

45. Ibid. At 952.

46. *Tasby v. Estes*, 517 F.2d 92 at 104.

47. Ibid. At 109.

48. Ibid. At 110.

49. 517 F.2d 92 at 106, 107 citing *U.S. v. Texas Education Agency, Austin Independent School District*, 467 F.2d 848 (5th Cir. 1972).

50. The appeals court excluded, on the authority of the Supreme Court's decision in *Milliken v. Bradley*, 418 U.S. 717 (1974), any remedy that involved other school districts in the Dallas metropolitan area unless they also were found to operate dual systems or to have contributed to the operation of the dual system in DISD. Highland Park ISD was specifically excluded from any remedy, as the trial court found, and the appeals court concurred, that this small district—and the wealthiest in Texas—had eliminated all vestiges of a dual system by 1958, when it permitted the fewer than a dozen black children living in the district to attend its schools rather than send them to DISD's black schools for their education. *Tasby v. Estes*, 412 F.Supp. 1192 (ND Tex. 1976); remanded, 572 F.2d 1010 (5th Cir. 1978); cert. dism. sub nom *Estes v. Metropolitan Branches of Dallas NAACP*, 444 U.S. 437 (1980).

51. A good discussion of the role of the Alliance can be found in Linden, *Desegregating Schools in Dallas*, pp. 110–120.

52. The complete text of Judge Taylor's order can be found at 412 F.Supp. 1192, 1210–1221. The key elements are also summarized in the opinion of Judge Barefoot Sanders in *Tasby v. Wright*, 520 F.Supp. 683, 688 (ND Tex. 1981).

53. The court emphasized that all of the plans submitted by litigants, except one submitted by plaintiffs, left East Oak Cliff as a predominantly black subdistrict. That plan, which would have established an exact racial balance in each school in the district, would have entailed busing 49,000 students. Substantial physical improvements had been made to the schools in this area by DISD and they were the sites of innovative educational programs. Taylor believed these programs could be sufficiently enriched to equalize educational opportunity for the black students and, thus, provide a practical means, without busing, of meeting constitutional requirements even though some schools in the desegregated district might remain "one race" schools. 412 F.Supp. 1192, 1204. There was a basis for his view in the Supreme Court's dicta in *Swann v. Board of Education*, 401 U.S. 1, at 26ff. (1970).

54. The district was ordered to create at least two "exemplary" development and demonstration classes for children in the East Oak Cliff area. These evolved into Learning Centers, with low student-teacher ratios and highly enriched programs for the primary grades.

55. *Estes v. Metropolitan Branches of Dallas NAACP,* 444 U.S. 437 (1980).

56. Linden, *Desegregating Schools in Dallas,* pp. 140–141.

57. The system was designed so that low-performing schools could "succeed" by setting reasonable goals for improvement above the past year's performance.

58. Interview, Linus Wright, July 7, 1998.

59. Ibid.

60. Ibid.

61. *Tasby v. Wright.* 520 F.Supp.2d 683 (1981); aff'd in part and rev'd in part, 713 F.2d 90 (5th Cir. 1983).

62. Linden, *Desegregating Schools in Dallas,* pp. 157–167.

63. *Tasby v. Wright,* 520 F.Supp. 683

64. *Tasby v. Wright,* 713 F.2d 90 (1983)

65. Wright's achievement is even more remarkable when it is viewed in the context of both the racial controversies that were swirling about the board over educational techniques and the necessity of hiring and training a large number of teachers—many of whom were scarcely qualified. Wright reported that of 15,000 teachers he hired to fill positions in the system, only 3700 could initially pass the national teachers examination. Interview, Linus Wright, 1998.

66. Linden, *Desegregating Schools in Dallas,* pp. 177–187.

67. Dallas Independent School District, Executive Summaries.

68. 418 U.S. 717 (1974).

69. *Tasby v. Edwards,* 807 F. Supp. 421(1992). The effects of the learning centers on development of cognitive skills remain uncertain. Some reported substantial progress, but with approaches that could not be widely replicated throughout the system—such as extremely small classes and computer-assisted learning, reinforced with intensive tutoring programs.

70. Kathlyn Gilliam was defeated in 1996 after twenty-six years on the Board. Yvonne Ewell died in 1998.

71. The Supermagnet campus was to be located in southern Dallas and consolidate almost all of the separate magnet schools at one location. The idea behind the proposal was that it would not only assist the desegregation agenda by locating the most attractive educational programs in a minority neighborhood; it would benefit from the economies of scale by allowing the different magnet programs to share certain common programs, staff, and facilities.

72. The system, proposed by epidemiologist Robert Haley, of The University of Texas Southwestern Medical Center, and modified by William Webster,

the Assistant Superintendent for Research, used statistical techniques to factor out the usual excuses for poor performance, such as prior preparation of students, poverty, and non-English speaking. For the court, standardized test scores provided a significant measure of progress toward the school district achieving unitary status. The need to compile the test data by race, even with the omitted students, continued to show a significant gap between the achievement of the Anglo and African-American or Hispanic students. Regardless of its imperfections, the accountability project sharpened the focus of educators, parents, and external constituencies on the importance of developing reading skills during the early years as the most cost-effective way of improving student performance and ultimately reducing drop out rates.

73. Interview, Sandy Kress, June 10, 1998.

74. Ibid.

75. Interviews with Sandy Kress June 10, 1998 and Rebecca Bergstresser, May 26, 1998.

76. Elementary and Secondary Education Act of 1964.

77. Interview, Sandy Kress, June 10, 1998.

78. The general perception of the ineffectiveness of the program led Congress to amend the statute in 1994, permitting a more diffuse use of the funds.

79. The plan was a response to research findings that the most successful schools involved parents, allowed the principal and teachers budgetary and programmatic flexibility to respond to parental concerns and student needs, and held them directly responsible for the results in student achievement. See Bliss, Firestone, and Richards, *Rethinking Effective Schools*; Chubb and Moe, *Politics, Markets, and America's Schools*.

80. The system did not, of course, work as neatly as this suggests. Principals often did not know the amount of their Title I allocations until well after the start of the school year, and there were many conflicting "suggestions" about how they should use their flexibility.

81. See Farkas, *Human Capital or Cultural Capital?*.

82. Using data from DISD records of individual students and teachers, Farkas and his colleagues isolated the factors that contributed to the development of cognitive and noncognitve skills in students of different socioeconomic backgrounds. See Farkas, Grobe, Sheehan, and Shuan, "Cultural Resources and School Success," in *American Sociological Review* (55):127–142.

83. Key elements in the effectiveness of the program were the intensive training and close supervision of tutors; the independence of the program's management from the school's personnel rules, which made it possible to replace unreliable or poorly performing tutors quickly; and the work of the in-school coordinator who provided quality control among the tutors, worked with teachers and principal to minimize disruption of classes and other activities, and han-

dled the tedious tasks of record keeping and report writing. For a description of the management system used by the program and its implementation in DISD schools, see Kinheman, *Implementation of Reading One-One*.

84. Farkas, Fischer, Vicknair, and Dosher, *Can All Children Learn to Read at Grade-Level?*. Also see the editorial praising the program in *Dallas Morning News*, February 21, 1997, p. A-26.

85. Much of this story is told in Farkas, *Human Capital or Cultural Capital*. Other aspects I directly observed as the dean of the School of Social Sciences, of which Farkas was a faculty member.

86. Farkas, *Human Capital or Cultural Capital?*

87. *Tasby v. Woolery*, 869 F. Supp. 454 (1994).

88. Texas law at that time permitted the State Board of Education to establish twenty charter schools. These would be public schools but autonomous of the local district and exempted from many of the regulations that restricted innovation in curriculum, teacher requirements, etc. Instead they would be held to performance goals, and for each student they enrolled they would receive the state per capita assistance that otherwise would flow to the school district.

89. When she had been appointed superintendent, Gonzalez had renovated her office, explaining that she needed to increase its security. When questioned about the cost, she claimed, with Hardin's endorsement, that the complete renovation had cost only $16,000. The figure was important because she had just disciplined and demoted a black administrator for spending $9000 to build a new restroom in her office. Hardin now claimed that the remodeling had cost at least $90,000.

90. Wertheimer, "Expert advises trustees about roles, power," *Dallas Morning News*, March 24, 1999.

91. March and Olsen, *Rediscovering Institutions*.

92. The independence of federal judges stems from their appointment to serve during "good behavior"—in effect, for life or until they voluntarily retire. Only Congress can remove a federal judge, and only by impeachment. Federal courts, however, have no automatic means of enforcing their decisions. They can issue contempt citations and injunctions, but if those subject to them do not voluntarily comply, the courts depend upon the executive branch to enforce their orders. The Congress can limit or expand their statutory jurisdiction, and affect them in other ways through the appropriations process and the confirmation of judges.

93. From 1987, when the city entered a severe economic recession, until 1993, the tax base of the district actually declined. The school tax rate doubled during the same period. The DISD could sustain losses in enrollment without suffering a proportionate loss of income because property owners continued to pay the school tax. The district would lose some *per capita* intergovernmental

assistance if enrollment declined, but aid based on the income of families served by the schools would increase if there were more poor students. In fact, the worse the district performed, the more funding it might expect from some sources, such as the federal government.

94. Edward Cloutman, for example, was the Neighborhood Legal Services attorney who filed the *Tasby* case, and was still handling it in 1994, long after the Tasby children had graduated from high school and had children of their own in the Dallas schools.

95. For a more extensive elaboration of the history and the problems of the federal courts generally, see Cooper, *Hard Judicial Choices*; Rosenberg, *The Hollow Hope;* Wood, *Remedial Law.* One feature of the judicial system's process of appeals is that the circuit courts and the Supreme Court begin to see patterns emerge from similar cases appealed from a cross section of district courts. Especially in the Fifth Circuit, which included most of the states of the deep south in addition to Texas, noncompliance with desegregation orders, ranging from attempts to end the public school system in order to avoid integration to the token compliance in Dallas.

96. In 1986, the court set magnet guidelines at 40 percent black, 40 percent Anglo and other, and 20 percent Hispanic. By 1993 the ratios had to be reset at 32 percent each for blacks, Anglos and Hispanics, and four percent for other racial groups. In that year, 8,195 students attended all magnet schools. The racial mix was 18 percent Anglo, 55 percent African-American, 24 percent Hispanic, and less than four percent "other." *Tasby v. Woolery,* 869 F.Supp. 454, 464.

97. Quoted in Wood, *Remedial Law,* pp. 86–87.

98. J. Q. Wilson, *Bureaucracy,* pp. 168–171.

99. The research on this subject is extensive, with numerous studies attempting to measure the effects on student performance of a wide array of cognitive and non-cognitive factors. See Farkas, *Human Capital or Cultural Capital?*.

100. For a complete explanation of these typologies, see J. Q. Wilson, *Bureaucracy.*

101. March and Olsen, *Democratic Governance.*

102. Nathan and Doolittle, *The Consequences of Cuts.*

103. In the 1994–1995 test cycle, over three of every four Hispanic children in grades one through three were not tested. Some 80 percent of these children were to be tested the following year with a Spanish language test and their scores would be added to those of the English speaking children in the respective schools. Unfortunately, most of those who scored well on the Spanish language test remained dysfunctional in English.

104. Superintendent Yvonne Gonzalez, in her first address to Dallas business leaders, pointed out that statistics that purport to measure success can conceal serious problems. She pointed out that reported annual drop out rates appear to

be as low as two percent, but that when student histories are traced over their final four years, they come closer to 20 percent. (*Dallas Morning News* [February 26, 1997] p. B-1.) Although most of their schools showed "improvement" over the prior year, Farkas and colleagues estimated that for the 1994–1995 school year, 78 percent of third graders, 70 percent of second graders, and 64 percent of first graders could not read at grade level. (Farkas, et al, *Can All Children Learn to Read?* p. 7.)

105. See Behn, "Linking Measurement and Motivation," in *Advances in Educational Administration,* pp. 15–58.

106. Ray Marshall has pointed out that urban schools based on an industrial manufacturing model are inapposite to the needs of an information age society. See Marshall and Tucker, *Thinking for a Living.*

107. Stone, *Regime Politics,* pp. 226–233.

108. Examples include the late Jerry Junkins of Texas Instruments who devoted considerable amounts of his personal time, staff, and company financial resources to both general improvements in education and specific school projects, such as the Frazier Elementary School Learning Center in South Dallas, and support of the Reading One-One tutoring program. Other executives have worked diligently with individual schools, some motivated by a general concern for the quality of education and the Dallas labor force, others drawn to improve the schools for their own children. A number of firms participate in the Communities in Schools program, although it is no longer funded by the school system through the Greater Dallas Chamber of Commerce.

109. These include activists like Woodbine Development's John Scoville and attorney Tom Luce, who have lobbied for a wide range of educational improvements and reforms for more than twenty years. Luce put forward an agenda for educational reform in *Now or Never: What We Must do To Save Our Schools,* coauthored with Chris Taylor.

110. After leaving the Board, Kress wrote an op-ed article for the *Dallas Morning News,* in which he pointed to the progress the district had made, and challenged the business community to become involved. Two weeks passed, and there was no response. The silence was such that the nonagenarian Stanley Marcus, in his column in the paper, commented on the nonresponse to Kress' plea. No one responded to Marcus, either.

111. Dallas Citizens Council, *Strategic Agenda Progress Report,* 1994.

112. Farkas, *Human Capital or Cultural Capital?.*

113. Liz Minyard, CEO of a grocery chain, faced threats of boycotts of Minyard Stores when a letter she had written in support of Matthew Hardin surfaced during the controversy over his lawsuit against Superintendent Yvonne Gonzales.

Chapter 6

1. Prince, *A History of Dallas,* pp. 123–124.

2. Ibid. Prince reports the level of distrust was so high that blacks were reluctant to give evidence to the police.

3. Ibid.

4. Payne, *Big D: Triumphs and Troubles.*

5. U.S. Commission on Civil Rights, *Administration of Justice in the Southwest;* Texas Advisory Committee, *Civil Rights in Texas.*

6. Achor, *Mexican Americans in a Dallas Barrio,* p. 103.

7. Ibid., pp. 106–107.

8. For more detailed accounts of the two Rodriguez affairs, see Achor, *Mexican Americans in a Dallas Barrio,* pp. 106–108; 148–153.

9. Based on interviews with Rene Martinez; Adelfa Cojello; Frank Hernandez; Pedro Medrano; Domingo Garcia.

10. Williams and Shay, *Time Change.*

11. Ibid.

12. Howlett, "Man testifies he kicked, hit officer in fight." *Dallas Morning News,* December 9, 1986, p. 232.

13. Dallas City Ordinance No. 19818 (1988)

14. While this fear had a problematic foundation, it was nonetheless one that was clearly genuine on the part of DPA officers and members, based on interviews with Sr. Cpl. Monica Smith, the DPA president.

15. Manry and Hanson, Dallas Police Review Board, p. 5.

16. Interview, Diane Ragsdale, 1993.

17. Manry and Hanson, Dallas Police Review Board, p. 9.

18. Donald Byrd, who served from 1973 to 1979, had left the DPD in 1971 to become chief in Albuquerque, New Mexico, but returned to Dallas as second in command in 1973. Glen King (1979–1982) began his career in Dallas, then served from 1969 on the staff of the International Association of Chiefs of Police in Washington, D.C. until his appointment as chief.

19. Manry and Hanson, Dallas Police Review Board, p. 7.

20. Vines was later acquitted of the charge.

21. Hart also sent a strong signal to the Department that she would not tolerate obfuscatory explanations of police shootings. After a young officer, responding to a 911 call, shot a black businessman, mistaking him for a prowler, Hart admonished the then acting chief that she wanted a direct and frank explanation of the incident, not an excuse that the officer "feared for his life." Interview, John Ware, July 24, 1998.

22. Camina, "Rathburn quits: 3rd Dallas chief to leave," *Dallas Morning*

News, January 29, 1993. pp. 1A, 20A. Price was quoted as saying: "I think that Bill Rathburn has the potential to be a really good chief and a really good man. . . . I guess I'm a little upset that we keep going through our damn chiefs like pantyhose or something. . . . It's a snake pit that surrounds him. . . . It's the same snake pit that surrounded Mack Vines." Quoted in Nagorka, "Rathburn quits: Surprise, anger, frustration." *Dallas Morning News* (January 29, 1993) p. 22A.

23. Unless otherwise noted, the sections that follow are based on an interview with Chief Ben Click, July 8, 1998.

24. Dallas, City of, *Performance Report* (1991)and *Performance Review* (1992).

25. Interview, Ben Click, July 8, 1998.

26. Peters and Waterman, *In Search of Excellence*. Peters and Waterman argue for a "loose-tight" approach in which management is clear about ends but loose as to the means used. Click's approach varies in that he emphasizes that in policing, means are often as important as ends. A botched handling of evidence in an investigation, for example, can easily defeat the end of removing a dangerous criminal from society.

27. Interview, Ben Click, July 8, 1998.

28. Interview, Capt. Jerry McDonald; Sergeant Neelie Lewis; Deputy Chief Terrell Bolton, January 13, 1998.

29. Interview, Charles O'Neal, Vice President of the Black Chamber of Commerce, March 4, 1998, conducted by L. Shane Hall.

30. Interview with Bolton, McDonald, and Lewis; see note 28, above.

31. J. Q. Wilson, *Bureaucracy*.

32. Interview, Ben Click, July 8, 1998.

33. Ibid.

Chapter 7

1. The power to regulate land uses for their compatibility with adjacent uses was established in *The Village of Euclid v. Ambler Realty Co.*, 272 U.S. 365 (1926), in which the Supreme Court based its approval of the use of the police power to regulate land uses on analogy with the common law of nuisance, which, said the Court, "may be merely a right thing in the wrong place,—like a pig in a parlor instead of a barnyard." 272 U.S. at 388.

2. Boortz, *Boom and Bust in Dallas*. For a more entertaining discussion, see Barna, *The See-Through Years*.

3. Ausubel and Herman, *Cities and Their Vital Systems*.

4. All "public" infrastructure may not be produced by the government. Developers often produce local streets, sewerage and water systems, parks and trails, and even build schools as part of planned communities. Even when they

internalize these costs in the prices of the improved space they sell, however, they remain dependent upon public infrastructure for access to their communities, and for much of the other public capital improvement necessary to provide a level of service that makes the development marketable. While adequate public facilities are a necessary condition for private development at a substantial scale, public infrastructure alone is not a sufficient condition to induce private investments. There must also be a market. (Bamburger, *The Capital Connection.*)

5. Dallas, City of, *Financial Report,* 1997. As was the case with the street system, neither the value of schools nor the value of any state or county-financed facilities were included in this estimate of city-owned property.

6. Dallas, City of, *Performance Report,* 1997.

7. Ibid.

8. Pagano and Bowman, *Cityscapes and Capital,* p. 44.

9. Stone and Sanders, *The Politics of Urban Development.*

10. Peterson, *City Limits.*

11. Logan and Molotch, *Urban Fortunes,* p. 32.

12. Ferman, *Challenging the Growth Machine*; Swanstrom, *The Crisis of Growth Politics*; DeLeon, *Left Coast City.*

13. Payne, *Big D: Triumphs and Troubles,* p.3.

14. For a recapitulation of Stanley Marcus' successful campaign to allow the Dallas Museum of Arts to show contemporary art that right wing political and religious groups asserted was "communist," see Schutze, *The Accommodation: The Politics of Race,* pp. 99–103. The Philistinism of some of Dallas's first generation of leaders is the stuff of legend, such as R. L. Thornton's purported reply to the request to support the symphony: he would contribute if he did not have to go (Wallace, "What Kind of Place is Dallas?" in *Life Magazine* 31 [January 1964], p. 68). The city, however, has retained a deep strain of native moralism, abolishing its Board of Film Censors only in 1993.

15. Lee, "Sculpture garden to boost economy." *Dallas Morning News,* April 9, 1997, p. 1A.

16. Payne, *Big D: Triumphs and Troubles,* p. 284.

17. Barna, *The See-Through Years.* Dallas's notable architecture includes a number of outstanding buildings designed by the nation's leading architects, including Fountain Place, the Dallas City Hall and the Morton Meyerson Symphony Hall.

18. About the only criticism one ever hears in Dallas of Erik Jonsson is that he let Clint Murchison build Texas Stadium in Irving, instead of finding some way to keep the Dallas Cowboys, "America's Team," in the city by replacing the Cotton Bowl with a more modern stadium.

19. In defending a plan for a dual, four-lane "parkway" straddling the Trinity floodway, supporters of the project defended its "overriding principle . . . :

To create along the Trinity a world-class design that would distinguish Dallas from its global competitors." (Chris Kelley, "Big problem big solution," *Dallas Morning News* [July 9, 1997], pp. 1A, 9A.)

20. Kain, "Deception in Dallas" *Journal of the American Planning Association* (Spring 1990):184–196.

21. Stanley Marcus is reported to have said that subsidizing a downtown sports arena made no more sense than subsidizing Nieman-Marcus to retain a downtown location for its flagship store. Interview, Jerry Bartos, July 16, 1998.

22. The expenditure of the bond proceeds was contingent upon federal funding for extension and raising of the levee system by the Corps of Engineers, approval of highways by the Texas Tollway Authority, and land swaps with the city by the State Parks Department. The Corps of Engineers had not completed its study of the levee system; the feasibility of constructing and managing a toll road to "parkway" standards inside the levees had not been determined; the State Parks Department had not agreed to a necessary land swap with the city; the number and characteristics of the lake or lakes were still at a conceptual stage; and access to recreation areas located on opposite sides of the river remained unsettled.

23. Brown, "Office leasing accelerates," *Dallas Morning News,* July 2, 1998, p. 1D.

24. In May 1997 the Dallas County Central Appraisal District reported a 10 percent growth in the tax base. The figure was later revised to slightly more than 8 percent.

25. Oak Cliff Chamber of Commerce, *Deannexation Study*.

26. Brown, "Heading Uptown" *Dallas Morning News,* March 13, 2000. Dallas Plan, Long Range Capital Improvements Strategy. City Council Workshop presentation, June 15, 1993. Available centrally located and uptown sites were undergoing development in 2000, however, with the resurgence of the economy.

27. In the years immediately following World War II, Dallas acquired water rights in the Trinity watershed and built a series of reservoirs designed to meet regional water supply needs well into the twenty-first century. Its interstate highway system created new nodes for development on the periphery of the city, and the new international airport, developed jointly with Fort Worth, was designed to meet anticipated passenger travel demands for a generation.

28. Boortz, Boom and Bust in Dallas.

29. Jenkins, *Office Location in a Post-Industrial Urban Environment*, p. 68. In the 1970s, 28 million square feet of new office space were built outside the central business district (CBD) in Dallas county, and in the 1980s, an additional 75 million square feet were constructed. In 1970 a majority of the office space in Dallas County was still in the CBD. By 1980, the CBD contained only a third of the county's office space, and by 1990, its proportion of the increased total dropped to 26 percent.

30. Ibid.

31. Bruton Center, *The State of the Region 1992*, pp. 44–45. The CBD, Stemmons Corridor, and the North Central Corridor, combined lost employment during both the boom and bust. In absolute numbers, employment declined between 1983 and 1987 from 288,587 to 244,393. The CBD alone gained 4,512 jobs between 1983 and 1985, but then lost 22,411 in the next two years. Its percentage of total metropolitan employment fell from 8.87 percent in 1983 to 7.54 percent four years later.

32. Republic and First National Bank had previously merged, but due to excessive real estate loans, the new institution was insolvent and was sold to NCNB, of Charlotte, North Carolina, and later renamed Nations Bank, Texas, as part of a new multi-state banking system. Texas Commerce Bank retained its name, but its ownership changed from a Texas corporation based in Houston, to the Chemical Bank of New York. M-Bank, the former Mercantile Bank established by R. L. Thornton, also was declared unsound by federal regulators and was purchased by a Columbus, Ohio, holding company and renamed Bank One. A large number of Savings and Loan institutions were liquidated by the federal Resolution Trust Corporation, as part of the resolution of the savings and loan debacle.

33. Two of the largest planned communities in the Dallas suburbs were sold by their original owners. Las Colinas, between the city and the airport, was sold by the Carpenter family, which had become financially overextended. In Collin County, north of Dallas, 6,230-acre Stonebridge Ranch was placed under the management of the FDIC and sold from Chapter 11 bankruptcy to the Mobil Land Development Company.

34. Plano, for example, attracted J. C. Penney's corporate headquarters (from New York City) as well as Frito-Lay (from its former location in Dallas) to the Legacy Park development owned by EDS, which had moved its headquarters there from North Dallas. EXXON and GTE located their headquarters in Las Colinas, in Irving.

35. Arter & Hadden, *Dallas First*, p. *i*.

36. Interview, Rick Douglas, July 28, 1998.

37. Elizar, *American Federalism*.

38. In legal terms, real property is more than a piece of the earth. It consists of a "bundle of rights" and obligations, which are enforceable at law. (*Kaiser-Aetna v. United States,* 444 U.S. 164, 176 [1979].) The bundle includes the right to possess, exclude, alienate, and use beneficially. The obligations include duties to use in ways that do not waste the resource or create nuisances to neighboring holders of property. In the United States, private property has two great constitutional protections, guaranteed by the Fifth and Fourteenth Amendments to the Federal Constitution. A person may not be deprived of property without due process of law, and government cannot "take" property for a public use without paying its owner "just compensation."

39. The only such planning director in the city's history, Weiming Lu, served only a short time in the 1970s before resigning in frustration to take a position in St. Paul, Minnesota.

40. The position of Planning Director was filled by the Director of the Department of Economic development, an architect, who made a condition of her appointment that she would continue to manage the city's in-town housing program.

41. Interview, James Reid, March 28, 1997.

42. Illustrations of this process include the ordinances for protection of historic districts and regulations governing the use of $25,000,000 in Section 108 in-town housing funds, which provided for tax abatements in return for provision of 15 percent of the units for rent to low and moderate income households.

43. Interview, Susan Mead, July 17, 1998.

44. Examples of developer-owners in this group: Ray Nasher, Trammell Crow, Lincoln Properties, John Stemmons, John and Jere Thompson (Southland Corp.) , Robert Folsom, Ben Carpenter, David Fox.

45. Boortz, *Boom and Bust in Dallas.*

46. Ibid.

47. Ibid. In chapters 5 and 6, Boortz describes the effect of national policies, including deregulation of savings institutions and banks, on the Dallas real estate market. Also, the Economic Recovery Tax Act of 1982 introduced new depreciation schedules that made real estate investment through syndicates more attractive and helped finance a speculative bubble that burst when the Tax Reform Act of 1986 limited the use of tax shelters that had been an "unintended consequence" of the 1982 Act.

48. The Dallas reputation of Nation's Bank was that "everything has to go through Charlotte." Interview, Larry Fonts, April 14, 1997.

49. Interview, Max Wells, July 27, 1998.

50. Wolf, *The Murchisons.*

51. Originally called North Park Bank, Ray Nasher's bank later was merged into Cornerstone Bank, and then Compass Bank.

52. Ellis, *Judicial Assumptions of Remedial Law*, pp. 119–123. Twenty of the thirty current and former council members responding to a question about the importance of factors in their successful campaigns rated finances as important or very important. In four council elections from 1987 to 1993, winning candidates consistently spent more on their campaigns than other candidates.

53. Ibid., pp. 134–148.

54. Payne, *Big D: Triumphs and Troubles*, p. 293. The phrase "Keep the dirt flying" was the slogan of R. L. "Uncle Bob" Thornton, whose eight years as mayor saw the initiation of more public works than any previous period in the city's history.

55. Fielding pled guilty to charges of fraud, extortion, and abuse of office involving a rezoning application by EDS. He also was convicted of fraudulently creating minority enterprises and then demanding that clients of his factoring firm, which had business to do with the city government, use them as suppliers of goods or services. There was, of course, a great deal of private corruption associated with the Savings and Loan scandals of the late 1980s, but none of it involved bribery of public officials.

56. Pederson, "The wink-wink system," *Dallas Morning News*, January 30, 2000. Lipscomb's prosecution hinged on unreported payments by a taxi cab company to the councilman.

57. Interview, Cherryl Peterman, July 21, 1998.

58. These agencies include the City's departments of streets, sanitation, water utilities, and parks and recreation; County roads; The Texas Department of Transportation and the Texas Turnpike Authority; Dallas Area Rapid Transit District; and the U.S. Corps of Engineers. All possess their own planning and design units, and all are oriented toward the accommodation and servicing of growth.

59. In 1997, the issue of Love Field traffic expansion was again opened with several challenges to the Wright Amendment, which was crafted by Representative James Wright to protect Dallas/Fort Worth International Airport from competition. Senator James Shelby (R. Ala.) offered amendments that would have opened Love Field to flights to Alabama. A new airline took advantage of a long-forgotten provision of the Wright Amendment that allowed long-haul flights with aircraft seating fewer than fifty passengers. Continental and American Airlines announced that they would enter Love Field; and the City of Fort Worth sued Dallas for enforcement of the original agreement between the two cities that restricted Love Field traffic.

60. Interview, Lori Palmer, 1993.

61. Ibid.

62. Interview, Donna Halstead, July 17, 1998. Lake Highlands residents viewed this kind of development as incompatible with their single family community and as not responsive to a market but to the tax incentives then available for apartment construction.

63. Ibid.

64. Ibid.

65. Interviews, Steve Bartlett, July 25, 1998; Donna Halstead, July 17, 1998; Max Wells, July 27, 1998; Susan Mead, July 17, 1998; Cherryl Peterman, July 21, 1998.

66. Interview, Donna Halstead, July 17, 1998. There are some cases, given the configuration of council districts, that clearly affect more than a single district. And, according to some who have served on the Council, distinctions are

made between routine rezoning cases and those that have city-wide, or at least multi-district significance. An example would be the rezoning of the so-called Nasher tract at the corner of Northwest Highway and the North Central Expressway, near North Park Plaza. After many years and many attempts to rezone it, the Council agreed to rezone it for a planned mixed use development of moderate density, meeting both the concerns of neighboring residents and the interest of the city in development of sufficient scale to make a significant addition to the tax base.

Chapter 8

1. Interviews, Larry Fonts, April 11, 1997; Dan Petty, April 22, 1997; Max Wells, July 27, 1998.

2. This process of connecting issues to champions was described by a number of association executives in interviews.

3. In 2000, the executives of the peak business organizations—the Dallas Citizens Council, the Greater Dallas Chamber of Commerce, the Central Dallas Association, and the North Texas Commission—all had long experience in the private, nonprofit, and/or public sectors working with top executives and boards of notables, either in Dallas or other cities. They enjoyed easy access to both executive suites and city hall.

4. For example, McDonald Williams, Chairman of Trammell Crow Companies devoted 40 percent of his time, and considerable financial resources to the physical and social development of South Dallas-Fair Park, including funding a community foundation to work with residents. David Biegler, the Chairman of Lone Star Gas Company, has served in a variety of civic posts.

5. For example, the goal of neighborhood improvement was not permitted to stand in the way of expansion of Fair Park, even though it required condemnation of adjacent homes occupied by African-Americans.

6. Dallas Citizens Council, *Strategic Agenda*, 1989.

7. "Governmental affairs" was an euphemism for exercising more influence in policy decisions of city government, including issues of racial equity and regional planning.

8. Dallas Citizens Council, *Strategic Agenda Progress Report*, 1994, p.12.

9. The Dallas Plan, "A Draft for Community Discussion," *Dallas Morning News*, October 24, 1993, Section Q.

10. Interview with Richard Anderson, Greg Campbell, and Robert Hoffman, March 24, 1994.

11. Ibid.

12. Ibid.

13. Dallas City Plan, Inc., *The Dallas Plan*, p. 5–1. The Plan defined the core

assets as the library system, Fair Park, the Arts District, White Rock Lake, the Zoo, McComus Landfill, the transportation and water systems, and D/FW, Love Field, and Redbird Airports. Admitting that this was a somewhat disparate list, the Plan explained, "These are the assets that make Dallas unique. . . . The core assets represent very significant investments made in the past by city leaders. . . . Each of these core assets has the potential to be a catalyst for additional economic and community growth."

14. Ibid., pp. 5–4 to 5–6.

15. Ibid., p. 5–11.

16. Ibid., p. 7–16; also interview, Robert Hoffman, March 24, 1994.

17. In 1998, they proposed that the city devise a program of incentives to encourage development of the biomedical industry in Dallas in the vicinity of UT-Southwestern Medical Center.

18. Interview, Robert Hoffman, March 24, 1994.

19. Founders included Henry Gilchrist, John Gardner (Mercantile Bank), John Scoville (Woodbine Corp.), Bill Morman, Dan Petty (Woodbine), George Shrader, John Adams (Texas Commerce Bank), David Biegler (Lone Star Gas).

20. Interview, Larry Fonts, President of The Central Dallas Association, April 11, 1997.

21. Central Dallas Association, *Annual Report,* 1994.

22. The source of this quotation requested anonymity.

23. In 1997 the assessment was $.08 per $100 of assessed value.

24. The bicycles and personal equipment for the officers cost $1500 each. Fonts sold the idea to his members by pointing out that each bike unit they donated brought an extra police officer to patrol the CBD. After about 5000 miles the bicycles end their useful lives as police vehicles. They are then returned to CDA, which has them repaired and repainted for the police department to give to Dallas Public Schools students who have perfect attendance records.

25. Fonts reported that the arrest rate for bicycle-mounted officers was twenty times that of officers responding in patrol cars.

26. Central Dallas Association, *Annual Report,* 1997.

27. The intervention of the CDA appears to have been crucial, as it provided testimony and argument in behalf of the business operators in the area, rather than have the case be seen merely as one of oppressive governmental action against disadvantaged citizens. Fonts interview; see note 20, above.

28. Interview, anonymous source, 1997.

29. Interview, Cherryl Peterman, July 21, 1998.

30. Central Dallas Association, *Progress Report,* 1996.

31. Interview, Fonts, July 24, 1998. The CDA had no plans, as of 1998, to bring residential representatives on to its board.

32. Interview, Rick Douglas, July 28, 1998.

33. This is a mild characterization of their views.

34. Bachelor's degree programs in business and accounting, education, and criminal justice, and an MBA degree were approved by the Coordinating Board.

35. For example, the Oak Cliff Chamber of Commerce asserted in 1990 that since 1962, 80 percent of all bond-supported infrastructure construction had occurred in northern Dallas. (Oak Cliff Chamber of Commerce, *Deannexation Study*.) The City countered that, when central business district, city-wide expenditures, and other expenditures not related to specific geographic areas are excluded, the southern sector received about 40 percent of city expenditures between 1967 and 1989. (Letter from Ted Benevidas [City of Dallas Budget Director] to Lucy Billingsley, January 23, 1991.)

36. The Southern Dallas Development Corporation took over the charter of the Housing and Economic Development Corporation of Dallas, which had been incorporated as a tax-exempt organization in 1984, but had been dormant until reconstituted as SDDC.

37. The description of the SDDC is based on an interview with Jim Reid, President/CEO of Southern Dallas Development Corporation, March 28, 1997.

38. Stewart, "Organizational Assessment Report for Southern Dallas Development Corporation."

39. Southern Dallas Development Corporation, *Annual Report*,1996.

40. Reid, Notes for speech to Salesmanship Club, March 13, 1997.

41. Southern Dallas Development Corporation, *Developments,* June 1998.

42. City of Dallas Business Development Corporation, *The Dallas Initiative Report,* May/June 1997.

43. Interview, Bob Moss, July 24, 1998.

44. Southern Dallas Development Corporation, *Developments,* June 1998.

45. An Oak Cliff Gateway TIF (tax increment financing) had been established.

46. The Dallas Enterprise Communities program allocated approximately $1 million to each program.

47. "Bond funds by city council district," *Dallas Morning News,* May 1, 1998. p. 26A. (The article includes a map showing allocations by Council District).

48. The improvement of Main Street has been an example of serious attention to the public amenity of the central business district. Construction of Pegasus Plaza, including a central urban park, street plantings and furniture, and flags, have helped transform a forbidding urban streetscape into a pleasant promenade. Thanksgiving Square, a fountain-filled private plaza in the central business district, is another well-used pedestrian refuge. There are other oases of repose and beauty in downtown Dallas, but they are often tucked away as part of a private courtyard or complex. A notable exception will be the two-acre Nasher Sculpture Garden, adjacent to the Dallas Museum of Arts.

49. There are, of course, managers who are exceptions to these characterizations. The only Dallas managers who might be called planner friendly were Charles Anderson and Richard Knight. Both served during the 1980s and employed talented professionals as their planning directors. Even they did not provide much in the way of analytical support to the department. After Knight resigned, the Planning Department atrophied during the administrations of his successors, Jan Hart and John Ware. It was during Hart's administration that the Dallas Plan was undertaken, with her concurrence. Under Ware, the Planning Director position went unfilled for several months.

50. Responses to Council Questionnaire.

51. Interview, Cherryl Peterman, July 21, 1998.

52. Dallas was one of the cities that participated in the Urban Institute's Urban Infrastructure Network , and was regarded as a city with an aggressive program of effective infrastructure maintenance and management. See Godwin and G. Peterson, *Guide to Assessing Capital Stock Condition,* and Hatry and Steinthal, *Guide to Selecting Maintenance Strategies for Capital Facilities.*

53. Such a requirement is common among U.S. cities.

54. See note 50.

55. Max Wells, who served on the council from 1988 to 1997, listed as his proudest achievement keeping the city's bond rating high during the recession years. (Interview, July 27, 1998.)

56. The journal, *Financial World,* twice in the 1990s named Dallas as the "best managed city in America" largely on the strength of its financial practices and bond rating. The truly sobering thought is that they may have been right.

57. Ladd and Yinger, *America's Ailing Cities,* p. 203.

58. In fiscal year 1998, the tax base of Dallas grew at a rate of 8.2% compared with rates of over 10 percent for the suburbs.

59. Interview, Richard Anderson, September 1994.

60. Interview, Steve Bartlett, July 25, 1998.

61. In 1989, the Council augmented the role of the city manager in development policy when it established the Department of Economic Development, and charged it to work with the Chamber of Commerce and other business organizations, such as the Central Dallas Association and community development corporations, such as SDDC. The Department put together information and incentive packages to attract relocation prospects to Dallas and to retain businesses and jobs in the city. It was given responsibility for recommending various subsidy programs, such as tax abatements and freeport zones to induce location of new projects in the city and to retain existing firms. As an agent of the city manager's office, the role of the Department of Economic Development is primarily coordination of the activities of other bureaucracies of the city, and the maintenance of liaison with external organizations and firms. Its authority derives

from the extent to which it enjoys, or is seen to enjoy, the confidence of the Manager.

62. Interview, John Ware, July 24, 1998.

63. Interview, Cliff Keheley, August 18, 1995.

64. Interview with former mayors Annette Strauss, Jack Evans, and Robert Folsom, April 7, 1994.

65. Ibid.

66. Interview, Steve Bartlett, July 25, 1998.

67. Interview, Max Wells, July 27, 1998.

68. Dillon, "Arena location is short-sited choice," *Dallas Morning News,* November 18, 1997, p. 1C.

69. The name was sold to American Airlines for $125 million.

70. The city rolled the outstanding debt of Reunion into a refinancing of additions to the Dallas Convention Center.

71. Igrassia, "Land talks may be heading toward condemnation fight." *Dallas Morning News,* December 4, 1997, p. 32A.

72. Igrassia, "Council sets vote on taxes to put arena near TU plant." *Dallas Morning News,* November 15, 1997, p. 17A.

73. Gillman, "Pro-arena side reports $2.5 million in gifts," *Dallas Morning News,* July 15, 1998, p. 21A. The pro-arena campaign spent approximately $38 for each vote they won.

74. Ibid. Over half the opposition contributions came from three car rental companies that would be subject to the new taxes.

75. Dallas Bond Campaign, "We Love Dallas," p. 10.

76. Quoted in Kelley and Ingrassia, "Trinity plan could hinge on voter trust," *Dallas Morning News,* April 12, 1998, p. 20A.

77. Quoted in Ingrassia, "Mayor calls on blacks to back Trinity project," *Dallas Morning News,* April 2, 1998, p. 1A.

78. Ibid., p. 13A.

79. Ingrassia, "Trinity victory called sign of southern Dallas clout," *Dallas Morning News,* May 4, 1998, p. 8A.

80. Ingrassia, "Trinity proposal critics disrupt council meeting," *Dallas Morning News,* April 23, 1998, p. 1A. The mayor had earlier called the League of Women Voters' opposition to the Trinity plan "abominable." (Ingrassia, "League takes stand against Trinity plan." *Dallas Morning News,* April 14, 1998, p. 13A.)

Chapter 9

1. Elkin, "State and Market in City Politics," in *The Politics of Urban Development,* p. 27.

2. Interview, Rick Douglas, July 28, 1998.

3. Wolman, Hanson, Hill, Howland, and Ledeber, "National Economic Development Policy," *Journal of Urban Affairs* (14)2:220 (1992).

4. See Chapter 11.

5. Stone and Sanders, *The Politics of Urban Development*, p. 297.

6. The phrase is Robert P. Stoker's. See: "Baltimore: The Self-Evaluating City," chapter 13 in Stone and Sanders, *The Politics of Urban Development*.

7. Ibid., pp. 250–251.

Chapter 10

1. This is consistent with observations by Bryan D. Jones and Lynn W. Bachelor that: "Most city governments are characterized by multiple policy arenas, and each arena can have considerable independence . . . . Moreover, the city's governing coalition often has little interest in many urban policy arenas, even though those affected by policies formulated in that arena are very concerned." (*The Sustaining Hand: Community Leadership and Corporate Power*, p.17.)

2. Schattschneider, *The Semi-Sovereign People: A Realist's View of Democracy in America*.

3. Tocqueville, *Democracy in America*, p. 310.

4. Putnam, *Making Democracy Work*.

5. Ibid.

6. Interview, Ron Kirk, August 11, 1998.

7. Dallas has little modern experience with a competitive party system. During the era of Democratic hegemony in Texas, most local notables were registered as Democrats and voted for conservative members in the party primary, the election that mattered. When the state, and especially North Texas, began to vote Republican in national and state elections, many of the old guard Democrats were able to switch parties without changing their points of view.

8. Interviews with Council Members Mary Poss, Don Hicks, Larry Duncan. The ability to challenge information provided by the city manager's staff depends upon personal research, analytical, and computing skills of individual Council Members. The city does not furnish council members or the Council as a whole with computers or policy analysis staff.

9. Dewey, *The Public and Its Problems*.

10. See Burns, *Leadership*.

11. Interview, Max Wells, August 3, 1998.

12. Interview, Jerry Bartos, July 16, 1998.

13. Daniel, "Bootstrap Politics."

14. Interview, Guadalupe Garcia, November 16, 1993.

15. Gelsanliter, *Fresh Ink*. Robert Decherd, the CEO of the Belo Corporation,

owner of the *Dallas Morning News,* was an organizer of the Breakfast Club, and the author of its innocuous name.

16. See chapter 5 for discussion of the school board majority led by Sandy Kress.

17. Letter from Ray L. Hunt, John R. Johnson, George A. Shafer, and William T. Solomon. Copy of the letter is in author's files. Three of the signers are former chairmen of the Dallas Citizens Council.

18. Ibid.

19. Interviews with Lee Simpson, Delia Reyes, Domingo Garcia, Diane Ragsdale, Lori Palmer, Donna Halstead.

20. Over time, a number of quite conservative Anglos have been elected to the City Council from North and East Dallas with support from religious fundamentalists, but there has been no overt effort to "gain control" of either the Council or school board in Dallas.

21. Interview, Rev. Gerald Britt, August 25, 1995.

22. Interview with Black Chamber of Commerce officers, April 7, 1994.

23. Interview, Guadalupe Garcia, November 16, 1993.

24. Ibid.

25. The City Secretary's office did not have an exact number. The figure of 450,000 registered voters is based on their estimate that about half of the registered voters of Dallas County live in the city.

26. Bruton Center, *Housing Conditions in the City of Dallas: Comprehensive Technical Report*, p.44, Table 13.

27. Ibid., pp. 44–45. Average household income for owners was $67,646; for renters it was $33,190. Almost two-thirds of owners were above moderate income levels, while a third of renters were classified as very low income.

28. Gillman, "Off to the polls—again." *Dallas Morning News,* March 12, 1998, pp. 1A, 14A.

29. Consolidated, general elections would surely produce long ballots in Texas, where voters elect a dazzling array of obscure officials with even more obscure duties, and a battery of judges no one ever heard of, except for the plaintiff and defense bars. In addition, the primary and general election ballots regularly present voters with a mind-numbing menu of referenda on policy marginalia, often expressed in incomprehensible language. Shortening the ballot by the elimination of some offices altogether, or by making them appointive rather than elective would be a separate and worthy cause.

30. Lyons, Lowery, and DeHoog, *The Politics of Disatisfaction.*

31. Biggerstaff, "Referenda and Civic Functions in Dallas 1981–1993."

32. The May 1993 referendum on the 14–1 council plan was largely symbolic, bringing the Charter in line with the court-ordered redesign of the Council. Nonetheless, Anglo voters turned out in significantly larger numbers than

in 1991, and this time, endorsed the inevitable. Black turnout was lower than in the highly charged 1991 referendum, but those who voted heavily favored the change.

33. McGonigle, "Voters cross racial lines to elect Kirk," *Dallas Morning News,* April 23, 1995, pp. 1, 11A.

34. Interview, John Ware, July 24, 1998.

35. Ibid.

36. Jamieson, *Dirty Politics.*

Chapter 11

1. *Thornburg v. Gingles,* 478 U.S. 30 (1986)

2. Unless otherwise noted, the information in this section is based on direct observation by the author and participation in discussion with principals as an adviser to the committee.

3. For an explanation of voting strategy on the charter amendments, see Chapter 10.

4. Interview, Richard Engstrom and Robert Greer, March 8, 1991.

5. Ibid.

6. *Shaw v. Reno,* 113 S.Ct. 2816 (1993).

7. The use of "traditional" criteria, such as compactness, may appear to be race-neutral, but can be used deliberately to dilute minority voting strength. Gerrymanders can be neat as well as bizarre.

8. Domingo Garcia ran for mayor in 1995 and was later elected to the State House of Representatives. Lori Palmer, on retirement from the Council, ran unsuccessfully for County Judge, and Donna Halstead lost a race for the State Senate before becoming President of the Dallas Citizens Council. Glenn Box was an unsuccessful candidate for Congress.

9. Interview, Sandra Crenshaw, May 28, 1998.

10. Interviews: Mayor Ron Kirk, August 11, 1998; Steve Bartlett, July 25, 1998.

Chapter 12

1. Jones and Bachelor, *The Sustaining Hand.*

2. March and Olsen, *Rediscovering Institutions.*

3. Baumgartner and Jones, *Agendas and Instability in American Politics.*

4. Interview, John Ware, July 24, 1998.

5. In 1998, outside audits and investigations by the U.S. District Attorney discovered contracts signed by the Board Secretary on behalf of the President

of the School Board, apparently without the knowledge or authorization of the President or the Board.

6. In 1998, the Texas Education Agency admonished the Dallas School Board to restrain itself from micromanaging matters that were consigned by law or regulation to the superintendent and to devote itself more fully to making "policy." This advice proved difficult for the board to follow.

7. J. Q. Wilson, *Bureaucracy*.

8. Interview with former mayors Annette Strauss, Jack Evans, and Robert Folsom, April 7, 1994.

9. Ibid.

10. Lee, "Arena foe reflects on intense grass roots fight," *Dallas Morning News,* January 19, 1998, p. 10A. For example, in the 1998 referendum on bonds for a new arena, a former council member who supported the arena characterized the leader of the anti-arena campaign as "divisive and strident and shrill."

11. Interview, Rene Martinez, August 15, 1993.

12. School of Social Sciences University of Texas at Dallas, *The State of the Community*.

13. Interview, John Wiley Price, August 4, 1995.

14. Interview, Cleo Steele, November 24, 1993, conducted by Theresa Daniel.

15. "Dallas Schools." *Dallas Morning News,* October 10, 1997, p. 30A.

16. Stahl, "DISD looks to business," *Dallas Morning News,* January 25, 1998, pp. 37A, 41A.

17. Drew and Suhler, "DISD problems call for drastic action," *Dallas Morning News,* November 15, 1998, p. 26A.

18. Interview, Ron Kirk, August 11, 1998.

19. Their names are on freeways and buildings—R. L. Thornton, who organized the 1936 Texas Centennial and created the Dallas Citizens Council, then served as mayor in the 1950s; John Stemmons, whose donations of land made possible the I-35 highway and, incidentally the Stemmons Corridor office and industrial area; his son, who led the effort to create the Dallas County Community College District; Ray Hunt, builder of Reunion, reorganizer of the Citizens Council after its decline in the 1980s and who helped reorganize the Southern Methodist University's Board of Trustees and administration after its football program received the "sudden death" penalty from the NCAA for paying its players; Jack Lowe, who organized the Dallas Alliance; Jack Evans, who ended his retirement to rebuild the DART management following the disastrous 1989 referendum; Ross Perot, who led the fund raising for the Morton Meyerson Symphony Hall and helped resolve the police crisis; and Jerry Junkins, the CEO of Texas Instruments, who, at the time of his death was deeply involved in trying to strengthen reading education in Dallas schools. These and many others, to whom

the city can point, contributed their time and reputations to improvement of the city.

20. Interview, Jon Edmonds, April 2, 1998. Observation, Dallas Area Interfaith, April 5, 1998.

21. Tatum, "Even a survey raises suspicions in schools." *Dallas Morning News,* April 8, 1998, p. 17A. The questionnaire was later distributed.

22. An example of this behavior is the response of business leaders to an invitation, after the Gonzalez crisis, from the new school board president, Hollis Brashear, to resurrect the "partnership" with business that had flourished during the Jonsson years. Amidst the inability of the board to define the role of a business advisory committee and doubts by business leaders about the efficacy of their involvement, the initiative foundered. "It's difficult to be a cheerleader right now. The district's got to earn back the trust," said John Scovell, a Woodbine Development Corp. executive with a long history of DISD involvement. "I don't think any of the cheerleaders can improve the team on the playing field. . . . You're going to see some people make some decisions about involvement that revolve around the downside rather than the upside [of participation]. I don't think we should draw and quarter them for trying to check how deep the water is before they get involved" (Stahl, "DISD looks to business," *Dallas Morning News,* January 25, 1998. pp. 37A, 41A.)

23. Central Dallas Association, *Progress Report,* 1997. Interview with Larry Fonts, April 11, 1997.

24. U.S. District Court Judges Barefoot Sanders and Jerry Buchmeyer.

25. Wood, *Remedial Law*; Rosenberg, *The Hollow Hope.*

26. In *Shaw v. Reno* and its progeny, the Supreme Court held schemes that use race as a primary factor in the design of districts violate the Equal Protection Clause of the Fourteenth Amendment of the U.S. Constitution, substantially vitiating *Gingles v. Thornburgh,* without overruling it.

27. Interviews with former Council members Lee Simpson, Domingo Garcia, Lori Palmer, 1993.

28. Guadalupe Garcia, for example, owns funeral homes serving the Mexican-American community. "I don't bury a lot of Anglos," he said, which made it difficult for anyone in the economic elite to threaten his business. Similarly, Comer Cottrell, CEO of Pro-Line, a manufacturer of cosmetics for the black market, could assert his independence as the first African-American member of the Board of Directors of the Dallas Citizens Council. (Interviews, Guadalupe Garcia, November 16, 1993; Comer Cottrell, 1993.)

29. Bishop College, a church-related black institution, relocated to Dallas in the 1960s, but was weak academically and chronically underfinanced. It failed in the 1980s. Its campus was acquired by Comer Cottrell, the city's most prominent black business executive, and Paul Quinn College moved to Dallas from

Waco in 1990. In spite of considerable support from Dallas corporations and philanthropists, it has struggled to maintain its accreditation and provide a solid program of higher education.

30. Mayor Kirk is no exception, as his law partners essentially support his public service, since his pay, as mayor is only $50.00 a meeting. Bartlett had an independent business, which provided income to him during his years as mayor.

31. Interview, James Washington, March 1, 1994.

32. Paul Waddell, "The Paradox of Poverty Concentration." For a broader view of this phenomenon, see W. J. Wilson, *The Truly Disadvantaged*; and Jargowsky, *Poverty and Place.*

33. A four-year effort sponsored by the Community of Churches—The Council of Leaders—tried to provide a series of policy education programs for lay leaders in member congregations. The objective of the programs was to bring to bear the ethical concepts of religious faiths on serious public issues confronting the city. Program series were developed on child hunger, intergenerational equity, racism, welfare reform, and the death penalty. Attendance at meetings was low, rarely exceeding thirty people, and the program was suspended in late 1997.

34. Interview, Lori Palmer, 1993.

35. Flournoy, "Secret gifts are unusual, scholars say." *Dallas Morning News,* February 1, 2000.

36. Ibid.; see also Pederson, "The wink-wink system," *Dallas Morning News,* March 1, 2000.

37. Ferman, *Challenging the Growth Machine.*

38. Scott, *Domination and the Arts of Resistance.*

39. Interview, Mary Sias, November 17, 1993.

40. Survey of City Council members, 1995.

41. A notorious example is the "feasibility" study of the proposed DART system conducted after the 1989 referendum had been called. (Kain, "Deception in Dallas," *Journal of the American Planning Association,* Spring 1990, pp. 184–196.) Another is the DeLoitte-Touche report on the economic impact of the new arena. Such studies typically use the assumptions the city has given the contractor.

Chapter 13

1. Barnes and Ledebur, *The New Regional Economics.*

2. March and Olsen, *Democratic Governance.*

3. Stone, *Regime Politics,* p. 231.

4. The phrase was used by Tammany Sachem George Washington Plunkitt to characterize reformers that "looked lovely in the mornin' and withered up in

a short time" as they encountered the difficulties of governing (Riordan, *Plunkitt of Tammany Hall,* p. 17).

5. See Hanson, *The Next Generation in the Management of Public Works;* Reschenthaler and Thompson, "The Information Revolution and the New Public Management," *Journal of Public Administration Research and Theory,* (6)2:125–143.

6. Interview, Ron Kirk, August 11, 1998.

7. For a discussion of these "games," see Rusk, *Inside Game Outside Game.* Rusk is pessimistic, however, about the willingness of mayors to participate in the outside game of building regional coalitions to address critical urban issues. While by no means sanguine, I am more optimistic, provided the office is designed with incentives to engage in "urban foreign policy."

8. Some charters, such as that for Baltimore County, Maryland, give the chief administrative officer a term of office that expires six months after the commencement of an executive's term. This provision was designed to give the administration continuity from one executive to the next, and an opportunity for a newly elected executive to work with the incumbent CAO and reappoint him or her if a good relationship is established. Even in cities with strong mayors and no CAO it is not uncommon for a newly elected mayor to retain most of the department heads from the outgoing administration. Fears of patronage hacks populating top positions in city governments are largely misplaced. Incompetent administrators are dangerous to the political health of elected mayors. In the words of former Mayor Richard J. Daley of Chicago, "Good government is good politics."

9. March and Olsen, *Democratic Governance,* p. 193.

10. Schattschneider, *The Semi-Sovereign People.*

11. Pierce and Johnson, *Citistates.*

12. The experience of the Twin Cities Citizens League is impressive testimony to the added value of sharing power to move and shake local and state affairs. It has for over thirty years been the chief policy entrepreneur of the region, providing the leadership for such reforms as the Twin Cities Metropolitan Council, tax base sharing among municipalities, and school choice, to mention but a few of its signal accomplishments.

13. The Greater Cleveland Foundation and the Kansas City Association of Trusts and Foundations are two of the oldest and most successful such efforts. In the 1980s, corporations and foundations in Philadelphia created Philadelphia First as a means of increasing the effectiveness of philanthropy in addressing critical urban problems.

14. Kolderie, "Two Different Concepts of Privatization," *Public Administration Review* 46:285–291.

15. Kettl, *Sharing Power.*

16. A discussion of private governments of planned communities can be found in Hanson, *New Towns: Laboratories for Democracy.*

17. Hassel, "The Case for Charter Schools," in *Learning from School Choice.*

18. Jones, *Reconceiving Decision-Making in Democratic Politics.*

19. L. Stoker, "Interests and Ethics in Politics," *American Political Science Review,* (86)2:369–380; Guttman and Thompson, *Democracy and Disagreement.*

20. Such a community information system, designed in the mid-1990s by a coalition of organizations led by the Bruton Center for Development Studies of the University of Texas at Dallas and specialists at Parkland Hospital, foundered due to the concerns of city administrators for control of the system. It could be activated by the willingness of the city to produce and share the program and service data needed at appropriate geographic levels. There are important issues concerning the confidentiality of some administrative data, which can be addressed in modern Geographic Information Systems.

21. Cleveland, *The Knowledge Executive*; and Cleveland, "The Twilight of Hierarchy," *Public Administration Review* (45):185–195 (January-February 1985).

22. Quoted in Allison, Jr., "Public and Private Management," in *Current Issues in Public Administration,* p.6.

23. Dewey, *The Public and Its Problems.* Dewey, like the others cited, essentially embraces the Greek tradition of the *polis,* which was reflected in the medieval city states and, in many respects, in the constitutional development of Britain and the United States. His approach is more democratic than republican, however.

24. March and Olsen, *Democratic Governance.*

25. For a discussion of these traditions, see Waldo, "A Theory of Public Administration Means in Our Time a Theory of Politics Also," in *Public Administration: The State of the Discipline.*

26. Putnam, *Making Democracy Work: Civic Traditions in Modern Italy,* points out that there is great variety among governments with identical governmental structures.

BIBLIOGRAPHY

Achor, Shirley. 1979. *Mexican Americans in a Dallas Barrio*. Tucson, AZ: University of Arizona Press.

Allison, Graham T., Jr. 1994. "Public and Private Management: Are They Fundamentally Alike in All Unimportant Respects?" in Frederick S. Lane, ed., *Current Issues in Public Administration,* 5th edition. New York: St. Martin's Press.

Altwegg, Al. January 19, 1964. "Economy aims at 4 in a row: Dallas reshaped in golden sixties," *Dallas Morning News,* 9–1.

Arter & Hadden. 1990. *Dallas First: A Comprehensive Economic Study on the City of Dallas and Its Suburbs*. Dallas, TX: Arter & Hadden.

Ausubel, Jesse H. and Robert Herman, eds. 1988. *Cities and Their Vital Systems: Infrastructure Past, Present and Future*. Washington, DC: National Academy Press.

Bamburger, Rita. 1984. *The Capital Connection: Interpreting the Economic Consequences of Urban Infrastructure Decline*. Washington, DC: George Washington University, Master's Thesis.

Barna, Joel Warren. 1992. *The See-Through Years: Creation and Destruction in Texas Architecture and Real Estate 1981–1991*. Houston, TX: Rice University Press.

Barnes, William R. and Larry C. Ledebur. 1997. *The New Regional Economics: The U.S. Common Market and the Global Economy*. Thousand Oaks, CA: Sage Publications, Inc.

Barta, Carolyn Jenks. 1970. *The Dallas News and Council-Manager Government*. Austin, TX: University of Texas at Austin, Master's Thesis.

Baumgartner, Frank R. and Bryan D. Jones. 1993. *Agendas and Instability in American Politics*. Chicago: University of Chicago Press.

Behn, Robert D. 1997. "Linking Measurement and Motivation: A Challenge for Education," in Paul W. Thurston and James G. Ward, eds., *Advances in Educational Administration: Improving Educational Performance: Local and Systemic Reforms*. Greenwich, CT: JAI Press.

Berry, Brian J. L. 1991. *Long Wave Rhythms in Economic Development and Political Behavior*. Baltimore, MD: The Johns Hopkins University Press.

Biggerstaff, Vic. 1995. "Referenda and Civic Functions in Dallas 1981–1993: The effects of race." Unpublished paper.

Bledsoe, Timothy. 1993. *Careers in City Politics: the Case for Urban Democracy.* Pittsburgh, PA: University of Pittsburgh Press.

Bliss, James R., William A. Firestone, and Craig E. Richards, eds. 1990. *Rethinking Effective Schools: Research and Practice.* New York: Allyn & Bacon.

Boortz, Charles C.L. 1993. *Boom and Bust in Dallas: 1983 to 1993—A Case Study.* Richardson, TX: University of Texas at Dallas. Doctoral Dissertation in Political Economy.

Brandl, John. 1998. "Governance and Educational Quality," in Paul E. Peterson and Bryan C. Hassel, eds., *Learning from School Choice.* Washington, DC: Brookings Institution Press.

Brophy, William. 1982. "Active Acceptance—Active Containment," in Elizabeth Jacoway and David Colburn, *Southern Businessmen and Desegregation.* Baton Rouge, LA: Louisiana State University Press.

Brown, Steve. January 6, 1980. "1979: the year of the real estate boom," *Dallas Morning News,* 9–1.

———. July 2, 1998. "Office leasing accelerates: Dallas-area demand doubled in first half, surveys show," *Dallas Morning News,* 1D.

———. March 13, 2000. "Heading Uptown: Office builders flocking to central Dallas," *Dallas Morning News.*

Bruton Center for Development Studies. 1992. *State of the Region 1992.* Richardson, TX: University of Texas at Dallas.

———. 1993. *Housing Conditions in the City of Dallas.* Dallas, TX: City of Dallas Department of Housing and Neighborhood Services.

———. 1994. *Housing Conditions in the City of Dallas: Comprehensive Technical Report.* Dallas, TX: City of Dallas Housing and Neighborhood Services Department.

———. 1995. *Community Needs Assessment: Dallas County.* Dallas, TX: United Way of Metropolitan Dallas, 1995.

Burns, James McGregor. 1978. *Leadership.* New York: Harper and Row.

Camina, Catalina. January 29, 1993. "Rathburn quits to take Olympics Job: He's 3rd Dallas chief to leave since '88." *Dallas Morning News,* 1A, 20A.

Central Dallas Association. 1994. *Annual Report.* Dallas, TX: Central Dallas Association.

———. 1996. *Progress Report.* Dallas, TX: Central Dallas Association.

———. 1997. *A Progress Report.* Dallas, TX: Central Dallas Association.

Cheney, Allison A. 1991. *Dallas Spirit: A Political History of the City of Dallas.* Dallas, TX: McMullan Publishing Co.

Childs, Richard S. 1981. "The Principles Underlying the City-Manager Plan." In Frederick C. Mosher, ed., *Basic Literature of American Public Administration, 1787–1950.* New York: Holmes and Meier.

Chubb, John and Terry Moe. 1990. *Politics, Markets, and America's Schools.* Washington, DC: Brookings Institution Press.

City of Dallas Business Development Corporation. May/June 1997. *The Dallas Initiative Report.*

Clark, Gordon L. and Michael Dear. 1984. *State Apparatus: Structures of Language and Legitimacy.* Boston: Allen & Unwin, Inc.

Cleveland, Harlan. 1985. "The Twilight of Hierarchy: Speculations on the Global Information Society." *Public Administration Review* 45:185–195.

———. 1985. *The Knowledge Executive: Leadership in the Information Society.* New York: Dutton.

Cooper, Phillip J. 1988. *Hard Judicial Choices: Federal District Court Judges and State and Local Officials.* New York and Oxford: Oxford University Press.

Dahl, Robert A. 1967. "The City in the Future of Democracy," *American Political Science Review,* 61 (December):953–970.

Dallas Bond Campaign. 1998. "We Love Dallas." Dallas, TX.

Dallas Citizens Council. 1989. *Strategic Agenda: Long Term Strategic Priorities for the Dallas Citizens Council.* Dallas, TX: Dallas Citizens Council.

———. 1994. *Strategic Agenda Progress Report: An Update on the Long-Term Strategic Priorities for the Dallas Citizens Council.* Dallas, TX: Dallas Citizens Council.

———. February 1994. *Strategic Agenda Progress Report: An Update on the Long-Term Strategic Priorities for the Dallas Citizens Council.* Dallas, TX: Dallas Citizens Council.

Dallas, City of. 1991. *Performance Report.* Dallas, TX: City of Dallas Office of Budget and Research.

———. 1992. *Performance Review.* Dallas, TX: City of Dallas Office of Budget and Research.

———. 1997. *Performance Report, 1997.* Dallas, TX: City of Dallas.

———. 1989. *The Dallas Advantage.* Dallas, TX: City of Dallas Economic Development Department.

———. 1997. Financial Report. Dallas, TX: Department of Taxation and Revenue.

Dallas Independent School District. 1989. "Executive Summaries of Research and Evaluation Reports." Dallas, TX: DISD Department of Research Evaluation and Information Systems.

Dallas Morning News. January 18, 1996. "School Board: Kress decision raises new challenges," 18A.

———. October 10, 1997. "Dallas Schools: Trustees should look for a strong interim leader," 30A

Dallas City Plan, Inc. 1994. *Dallas Plan.* Dallas, TX

Dallas Plan. October 24, 1993. "A Draft for Community Discussion." *Dallas Morning News,* Section Q.

Dallas Times-Herald. May 16, 1971. "Leadership," special section, 1.

Daniel, Theresa. 1994. "Bootstrap Politics: Hypotheses on the Development of Black and Latino Leadership in Dallas." Unpublished paper delivered at the Southwestern Political Science Association Meeting, San Antonio, TX.

DeLeon, Richard. 1992. *Left Coast City: Progressive Politics in San Francisco, 1975–1991*. Lawrence, KS: University of Kansas Press.

Dewey, John. 1927. *The Public and Its Problems*. Denver, CO: Henry Holt and Company.

Dillon, David. November 18, 1997. "Arena location is short-sited choice," *Dallas Morning News,* 1C.

Drew, Duchesne Paul and Jayne Noble Suhler, November 15, 1998. "DISD problems call for drastic action, some say: State takeover, district split mentioned." *Dallas Morning News,* 26A.

Elizar, Daniel J. 1984. *American Federalism: A View from the States,* 3rd edition. New York: Harper & Row.

Elkin, Stephen L. 1987. *City and Regime in the American Republic*. Chicago: University of Chicago Press.

———. 1987. "State and Market in City Politics: Or, The 'Real Dallas." In Clarence N. Stone and Heywood T. Sanders, eds., *The Politics of Urban Development*. Lawrence, KS: University Press of Kansas.

Ellis, Margaret E. 1995. *Judicial Assumptions of Remedial Law: An Empirical Analysis of the Single-Member District Remedy for Voting Rights Act Violations*. Richardson, TX: University of Texas at Dallas Dissertation in Political Economy.

Farkas, George. 1996. *Human Capital or Cultural Capital: Ethnicity and Poverty in an Urban School District*. New York: Alpine De Gruyter.

Farkas, George, Jim Fischer, Keven Vicknair, and Ralph Dosher. 1995. *Can All Children Learn to Read at Grade-Level by the End of Third Grade?* Richardson, TX: Center for Education and Social Policy, The University of Texas at Dallas.

Farkas, George, Robert Grobe, Daniel Sheehan, and Yuan Shuan. 1990. "Cultural Resources and School Success: Gender, Ethnicity, and Poverty Groups within an Urban School District." *American Sociological Review* 55:127–142.

Ferman, Barbara. 1996. *Challenging the Growth Machine: Neighborhood Politics in Chicago and Pittsburgh*. Lawrence, KS: University of Kansas Press.

Flournoy, Craig. January 28, 2000. "Secret gifts are unusual scholars say: Lipscomb allies testified that payments to civil-rights activists were common." *Dallas Morning News,* 23A.

Gelsanliter, David. 1995. *Fresh Ink: Behind the Scenes at a Major Metropolitan Newspaper*. Denton, Texas: University of North Texas Press

Gillman, Todd J. March 12, 1998. "Off to the polls—again. Democrats, Republicans agree on one thing: primary's low turnout result of voter fatigue. *Dallas Morning News,* pp. 1A, 14A.

———. July 15, 1998. "Pro-arena side reports $2.5 million in gifts: Supporters' funds outdistanced foes' by 28-to-1." *Dallas Morning News,* 21A

Godwin, Stephen R. and George Peterson. 1984. *Guide to Assessing Capital Stock Condition—Guides to Managing Urban Capital Series, Vol. 2.* Washington, DC: The Urban Institute.

Goodnow, Frank J. 1900. *Politics and Administration.* New York: Macmillan.

Constance Green, 1963. *Washington: Capital City.* Princeton, NJ: Princeton University Press.

Greene, A.C. 1984. *Dallas USA.* Austin, TX: Texas Monthly Press.

Gurwitt, Rob. September 1997. "Nobody in Charge," *Governing,* p. 24.

Guttman, Amy and Dennis Thompson, 1995. *Democracy and Disagreement.* Cambridge, MA: Harvard University Press.

Hanson, Royce. 1970. *New Towns: Laboratories for Democracy.* New York: Twentieth Century Fund.

———. 1987. *The Next Generation in the Management of Public Works: Getting Some of It Together.* Washington, DC: National Academy of Public Administration.

———, ed. 1983. *Rethinking Urban Policy: Urban Development in an Advanced Economy.* Washington, DC: National Academy Press.

Hassel, Bryan C. 1998. "The Case for Charter Schools." In Paul E. Peterson and Bryan C. Hassel, eds., *Learning from School Choice.* Washington, DC: Brookings Institution Press.

Hatry, Harry P. and Bruce G. Steinthal. 1984. *Guide to Selecting Maintenance Strategies for Capital Facilities—Guides to Managing Urban Capital* Vol. 4. Washington, DC: The Urban Institute.

Hicks, Donald A. 1992. "Beneath the Surface and Beyond the Borders: New Dimensions of Dallas Area Economic Development." In Bruton Center for Development Studies, *State of the Region 1992.* Richardson, TX: University of Texas at Dallas.

Hill, Patricia Evridge. 1996. *Dallas: The Making of a Modern City.* Austin, TX: University of Texas Press.

Holmes, Maxine and Gerald D. Saxon, eds. 1992. *The WPA Dallas Guide and History.* Dallas, TX: University of North Texas Press.

Howlett, Tom. December 9, 1986, "Man testifies he kicked, hit officer in fight," *Dallas Morning News,* 23A.

Ingrassia, Robert. November 15, 1997. "Council sets vote on taxes to put arena near TU plant. Site draws praise; new costs criticized," *Dallas Morning News,* 17A.

———. April 2, 1998. "Mayor calls on blacks to back Trinity project: Business leaders endorse bond plan; some African-Americans fault Kirk." *Dallas Morning News,* 1A.

———. April 14, 1998. "League takes stand against Trinity plan." *Dallas Morning News,* 13A.

———. April 23, 1998. "Trinity proposal critics disrupt council meeting: Tensions run high in debate on river plan." *Dallas Morning News,* 1A.

———. May 4, 1998. "Trinity victory called sign of southern Dallas clout: Analyst says business-minority alliance emerging." *Dallas Morning News,* 8A.

Jacobs, Jane. 1984. *Cities and the Wealth of Nations: Principles of Economic Life.* New York: Random House.

Jamieson, Kathleen Hall. 1992. *Dirty Politics: Deception, Distraction, and Democracy.* New York: Oxford University Press.

Jargowsky, Paul A. 1996. *Poverty and Place: Ghettos, Barrios, and the American City.* New York: Russell Sage Foundation.

Jenkins, Lyssa A. 1996. *Office Location in a Post-Industrial Urban Environment.* Richardson, TX: University of Texas at Dallas, Doctoral Dissertation in Political Economy.

Jones, Bryan D. 1993. "Social Power and Urban Regimes." *Urban News* 7(3):1–2.

———. 1994. *Reconceiving Decision Making in Democratic Politics.* Chicago: University of Chicago Press.

Jones, Bryan D. and Lynn W. Bachelor. 1993. *The Sustaining Hand: Community Leadership and Corporate Power.* Lawrence, KS: University Press of Kansas.

Jonsson, Erik. 1981. "Dallas: City with a Heart." In Donald F. Mitchell, ed. *Profile of Dallas: Love Affair with a City.* Dallas, TX: Turtle Creek Gallery.

Kain, John F. 1990. "Deception in Dallas: Strategic Misrepresentation in Rail Transit Promotion and Evaluation." *Journal of the American Planning Association.* Spring 1990: 184–196.

Kelley, Chris. April 21, 1996. "Ron Kirk," *Dallas Morning News,* 10J.

———. July 9, 1997. "Big problem big solution: $1 billion downtown traffic plan faces first hurdle." *Dallas Morning News,* 1A.

Kelley, Chris and Robert Ingrassia. April 12, 1998. "Trinity plan could hinge on voter trust: Proposal called gem, fantasy." *Dallas Morning News,* 20A.

Kessler, George E. 1911. *A City Plan for Dallas.* Dallas, TX: City of Dallas Board of Park Commissioners.

Kettl, Donald. 1993. *Sharing Power: Public Government and Private Markets.* Washington, DC: Brookings Institution Press.

Kinheman, Nancy. 1995. *Implementation of Reading One-One in Dallas Public Schools.* Richardson, TX: The University of Texas at Dallas. Ph.D. Dissertation in Political Economy.

Kolderie, Ted. 1984. "Two Different Concepts of Privatization." *Public Administration Review* 46:285–291.

Labich, Kenneth. October 23, 1989. "The Best Cities for Business." *Fortune*. Unpaginated reprint.

Ladd, Helen F. and John Yinger. 1991. *America's Ailing Cities: Fiscal Health and the Design of Urban Policy,* updated edition. Baltimore, MD: The Johns Hopkins University Press.

Lee, Christopher. April 9, 1997. "Sculpture garden to boost economy, city leaders say," *Dallas Morning News,* 1A.

———. January 19, 1998. "Arena foe reflects on intense grass roots fight." *Dallas Morning News,* 10A.

Leslie, Warren. 1964. *Dallas: Public and Private*. New York: Grossman Publishers.

Linden, Glenn M. 1995. *Desegregating Schools in Dallas: Four Decades in the Federal Courts*. Dallas, TX: Three Forks Press.

Logan, John R. and Harvey L. Molotch. 1987. *Urban Fortunes: the Political Economy of Place*. Berkeley, CA: University of California Press.

Luce, Tom, and Chris Tucker. 1995. *Now or Never: What We Must do To Save Our Schools*. Dallas, TX: Taylor Publishing.

Lyons, W.E., David Lowery, and Ruth Hoogland DeHoog. 1992. *The Politics of Disatisfaction: Citizens, Services, and Urban Institutions*. Armonk, N.Y.: M.E. Sharpe, Inc.

Manry, Lynn and Royce Hanson. 1989. "Dallas Police Review Board." Richardson, TX: School of Social Sciences, University of Texas at Dallas. Unpublished case study.

March, James G. and Johan P. Olsen. 1989. *Rediscovering Institutions: The Organizational Basis of Politics*. New York: The Free Press.

———. 1995. *Democratic Governance*. New York: The Free Press.

Marshall, Ray and Marc Tucker. 1993. *Thinking for a Living: Education and the Wealth of Nations*. New York: Basic Books.

McCombs, Holland and Holly Whyte. February, 1949. "The Dydamic Men of Dallas," *Fortune,* 98–103, 162–66.

Melosi, Martin V. 1983. "Dallas-Fort Worth: Marketing the Metroplex." In Richard M. Bernard and Bradley R. Rice, eds., *Sunbelt Cities: Politics and Growth Since World War II*. Austin, TX: University of Texas Press.

Mill, John Stuart. 1951. *Utilitarianism, Liberty, and Representative Government*. New York: E.P. Dutton & Co.

Miller, Laura. May 30, 1996. "Clueless." *Dallas Observer*.

Mumford, Lewis. 1938. *The Culture of Cities*. New York: Harcourt Brace.

———. 1961. *The City in History*. New York: Harcourt, Brace & World.

Nagorka, Jennifer. January 29, 1993. "Rathburn quits to take Olympics job: Colleagues, officials voice surprise, anger, frustration." *Dallas Morning News* 22A.

Nathan, Richard P. and Frederick C. Doolittle and Associates. 1983. *The Consequences of Cuts: The Effects of the Reagan Domestic Program on State and Local Governments*. Princeton, NJ: Princeton University Press.

National Municipal League. 1927. *Model City Charter*. New York: National Municipal League.

North Texas Commission. 1989. *Workforce Skills and Competencies*. Arlington, TX: North Texas Commission.

Noyelle, Thierry J. and Thomas M. Stanback, Jr. 1984. *The Economic Transformation of American Cities*. Totowa, NJ: Rowman & Allanheld, Publishers.

Oak Cliff Chamber of Commerce. 1990. *Oak Cliff Deannexation Study, Summary Report*. Dallas, TX: Oak Cliff Chamber of Commerce.

Pagano, Michael A. and Ann O'M. Bowman. 1995. *Cityscapes and Capital: The Politics of Urban Development*. Baltimore, MD: The Johns Hopkins University Press.

Payne, Darwin. 1994. *Big D: Triumphs and Troubles of an American Supercity in the 20th Century*. Dallas, TX: Three Forks Press.

———, ed. 1991. *Sketches of a Growing Town: Episodes and People of Dallas from Early Days to Recent Times*. Dallas, TX: Southern Methodist University.

Pederson, Rena. January 30, 2000. "The wink-wink system." *Dallas Morning News,* 21.

Percy, Stephen L. Brett W. Hawkins, and Peter E. Maier. Fall 1995. "Revisiting Tiebout: Moving Rationales and Interjurisdictional Location." *Publius* 24(4):1–17.

Peters, Thomas J. and Robert H. Waterman. 1982. *In Search of Excellence: Lessons from America's Best-Run Companies*. New York: Harper & Row.

Peterson, Byrdette and Della J. Davis, 1991. "Winning the Railroads, 1872 and 1873," Chapter in Darwin Payne, ed., *Sketches of a Growing Town: Episodes and People of Dallas from Early Days to Recent Times*. Dallas, TX: Southern Methodist University.

Peterson, Paul. 1981. *City Limits*. Chicago: University of Chicago Press.

Pierce, Neal and Curtis Johnson. 1993. *Citistates: How Urban America Can Prosper in a Competitive World*. Washington, DC: Seven Locks Press.

Prince, Robert. 1993. *A History of Dallas: From a Different Perspective*. Dallas, TX: Nortex Press.

Putnam, Robert D. 1993. *Making Democracy Work: Civic Traditions in Modern Italy*. Princeton, NJ: Princeton University Press.

Reid, James. March 13, 1997. Notes for speech to Salesmanship Club, Dallas, TX.

Reschenthaler, G.B. and Fred Thompson. April, 1996. "The Information Revolution and the New Public Management." *Journal of Public Administration Research and Theory,* 6(2):125–143.

Riordan, W. L. 1905. *Plunkitt of Tammany Hall*. New York: McClure, Philips.

Rosenberg, Gerald N. 1993. *The Hollow Hope: Can Courts Bring About Social Change?* Chicago: University of Chicago Press.

Rusk, David. 1999. *Inside Game Outside Game: Winning Strategies for Saving Urban America*. Washington, DC: Brookings Institution Press.

Salamon, Lester M., ed., 1989. *Beyond Privatization: The Tools of Government Action*. Washington, DC: The Urban Institute Press.

Saunders, Judith. 1991. "Boats Along the Trinity." In Darwin Payne, ed., *Sketches of a Growing Town: Episodes and People of Dallas from Early Days to Recent Times*. Dallas, TX: Southern Methodist University.

Schattschneider, E .E. 1960. *The Semi-Sovereign People: A Realist's View of Democracy in America*. New York: Holt, Rinehart and Winston.

School of Social Sciences University of Texas at Dallas. 1988. *The State of the Community: Implications for Intergroup Relations,* Vols. I & II. Dallas, TX: The Dallas Alliance.

Schutze, Jim. 1986. T*he Accommodation: The Politics of Race in an American City*. Secaucus, NJ: Citadel Press.

Schutze, Jim. April 18, 1998. "St. Al: Will he die in prison for the sins of the plantation?" *Dallas Observer,* 35, ff.

Scott, James C. 1990. *Domination and the Arts of Resistance: Hidden Transcripts*. New Haven, CT: Yale University Press.

Southern Dallas Development Corporation. 1996. *Annual Report*. Dallas, TX: Southern Dallas Development Corp.

———. June 1998. *Developments*. Dallas, TX: Southern Dallas Development Corp.

Stahl, Lori. January 25, 1998. "DISD looks to business: Executives' help sought in repairing credibility." *Dallas Morning News,* 37A, 41A.

Stewart, Patricia Gordon. 1996. "Organizational Assessment Report for Southern Dallas Development Corporation." Dallas, TX: The Center for Nonprofit Management.

Stoker, Gerry. 1995. "Regime Theory and Urban Politics." In David Judge, Gerry Stoker, and Harold Wolman, *Theories of Urban Politics*. Thousand Oaks, Calif.: Sage Publications, Inc.

Stoker, Laura. 1992. "Interests and Ethics in Politics." *American Political Science Review* 86(2):369–380.

Stoker, Robert P. 1987. "Baltimore: The Self-Evaluating City." In Clarence N. Stone and Heywood T. Sanders, eds., *The Politics of Urban Development*. Lawrence, KS: University Press of Kansas.

Stone, Clarence N. 1989. *Regime Politics: Governing Atlanta 1946–1988*. Lawrence, KS: University Press of Kansas.

———. 1987. "Summing Up: Urban Regimes, Development Policy, and Political Arrangements." In Clarence N. Stone and Heywood T. Sanders, eds., *The Politics of Urban Development*. Lawrence, KS: University Press of Kansas.

Stone, Clarence N. and Heywood T. Sanders, eds. 1987. *The Politics of Urban Development*. Lawrence, KS: University of Kansas Press.

Swanstrom, Todd. 1985. *The Crisis of Growth Politics: Cleveland, Kucinich, and the Challenge of Urban Populism*. Philadelphia, PA: Temple University Press.

Tatum, Henry. April 8, 1998. "Even a survey raises suspicions in schools," *Dallas Morning News,* H1.

Texas Advisory Committee to the U.S. Commission on Civil Rights. 1970. *Civil Rights in Texas*. Washington, DC: U.S. Government Printing Office.

Thometz, Carol Estes. 1963. *The Decision-Makers: The Power Structure of Dallas*. Dallas, TX: Southern Methodist University Press.

Tocqueville, Alexis de. 1955 (1835, 1840). *Democracy in America,* Vol. I. New York: Vintage Books.

U.S. Bureau of the Census. 1962, 1970, 1990. *Selected Labor Force Statistics*.

U.S. Commission on Civil Rights. 1970. *Mexican Americans and the Administration of Justice in the Southwest*. Washington, DC: U.S. Government Printing Office.

Waddell, Paul. 1990. *1990 Appraisal Ratio Study*. Dallas, TX: Dallas County Central Appraisal District.

———. 1996. "The Paradox of Poverty Concentration: Neighborhood Change in Dallas-Fort Worth from 1970 to 1990." Working Paper 96–11. Richardson, TX: School of Social Sciences, University of Texas at Dallas.

Waddell, Paul and Vibhooti Shukla. 1993. "Employment Dynamics, Spatial Restructuring and the Business Cycle." *Geographical Analysis* 25(1):35–52.

Waddell, Paul, Brian J. L. Berry, and Irving Hoch. 1993. "Residential Property Values in a Multinodal Urban Area: New Evidence on the Implicit Price of Location." *Journal of Real Estate Economics* 7(2):117–141.

Waldo, Dwight. 1990. "A Theory of Public Administration Means in Our Time a Theory of Politics Also." In Naomi B. Lynn and Aaron Wildavsky, eds., *Public Administration: The State of the Discipline*. Chatham, NJ: Chatham House Publishers, Inc.

Wallace, Robert. 1964. "What Kind of Place is Dallas?" *Life Magazine* 31 (January): 68.

Weber, Max. 1962. *The City*. New York: Collier Books.

Wertheimer, Linda K. March 24, 1999. "Expert advises trustees about roles, power," *Dallas Morning News,* 27A.

Wertheimer, Linda K. and Rick Klein. July 9, 2000. "Experts say DISD should move slowly: Harmony with new chief called key." *Dallas Morning News,* 1A

Williams, Roy H. and Kevin J. Shay, 1991. *Time Change: An Alternative View of the History of Dallas*. Dallas, TX: To Be Publishing Co

Wilson, James Q. 1989. *Bureaucracy: What Government Organizations Do and Why They Do It*. New York: Basic Books.

Wilson, O. W. 1950. *Police Administration*. New York: McGraw-Hill.

Wilson, William Julius. 1989. *The Truly Disadvantaged*. Chicago: University of Chicago Press,

Wilson, Woodrow. 1887. "The Study of Administration." *Political Science Quarterly* 2(2):197–222.

Wolf, Jane. 1989. *The Murchisons: The Rise and Fall of a Texas Dynasty*. New York: St. Martin's Press.

Wolman, Harold, Royce Hanson, Edward Hill, Marie Howland, and Larry Ledeber. 1992. "National Economic Development Policy." *Journal of Urban Affairs* 14(2):220.

Wood, Robert, ed. 1990. *Remedial Law: When Courts Become Administrators*. Amherst, MA: University of Massachusetts Press.

Cases, Statutes, and Ordinances

Alexander v. Holmes County Board of Education, 396 U.S. 19 (1969).

Bell v. Rippy, 133 F.Supp. 811 (ND TX 1955).

Bell v. Rippy, 146 F.Supp. 485 (ND Texas 1956).

Borders v. Rippy, 184 F.Supp. 402 (ND TX 1960).

Borders v. Rippy, 188 F.Supp. 231 (ND TX 1960).

Borders v. Rippy, 195 F.Supp. 732 (ND TX 1961).

Borders v. Rippy, 247 F.2d 268 (5th Cir. 1957).

Boson v. Rippy, 275 F.2d 850, 853 (5th Cir. 1960).

Boson v. Rippy, 285 F.2d 43 (5th Cir. 1960).

Britton v. Folsom, 348 F.2d 158 (5th Cir. 1965).

Britton v. Folsom (350 F.2d 1022 (5th Cir. 1965).

Britton v. Folsom, 348 F.2d 158 (5th Cir. 1965)

Britton v. Folsom, 348 F.2d 158 (5th Cir. 1965).

Britton v. Folsom, 350 F.2d 1022, 1023 (5th Cir. 1965)

Brown v. Rippy, 233 F.2d 796 (5th Cir. 1956).

Cooper v. Aaron, 358 U.S. 1 (1958).

Dallas City Ordinance No. 19818 (1988)

Elementary and Secondary Education Act of 1965.

Estes v. Metropolitan Branches of Dallas NAACP, 444 U.S. 437 (1980)

Griffin v. County School Board Prince Edward County, 377 U.S. 218 (1964).

Green v. County School Board of Kent County, Virginia, 391 U.S. 430 (1968).

Kaiser-Aetna v. United States, 444 U.S. 164, 176 (1979).

Milliken v. Bradley, 418 U.S. 717 (1974).

Plessy v. Ferguson, 163 U.S. 537 (1896).

Rippy v. Borders, 250 F.2d 690, 691 (5th Cir. 1957).
Shaw v. Reno, 113 S.Ct. 2816 (1993).
Swann v. Charlotte-Mecklenburg Board of Education, 402 U.S. 1 (1971).
Tasby v. Edwards, 807 F. Supp. 421 (N.D. TX 1992)
Tasby v. Estes, 342 F. Supp. 945 (USDC, N.D. TX, 1971).
Tasby v. Estes, 412 F.Supp. 1192 (N.D. TX 1976).
Tasby v. Estes, 517 F.2d 92 (5th Cir. 1975).
Tasby v. Estes, 572 F.2d 1010 (5th Cir. 1978)
Tasby v. Woolery, 869 F. Supp.454 (N.D. TX 1994).
Tasby v. Wright, 520 F.Supp. 683 (N.D. TX 1981).
Tasby v. Wright, 542 F. Supp. 134 (N.D. TX 1982).
Tasby v. Wright,. 713 F.2d 90 (1983).
Tasby v. Wright, 585 F.Supp. 453 (N.D. TX 1984).
Tasby v. Wright, 630 F.Supp. 597 (N.D. TX 1986).
Tasby v. Woolery, 869 F.Supp. 454 (1994).
Thornburg v. Gingles, 478 U.S. 30 (1986)
U.S. v. Jefferson County Board of Education, 372 F.2d 836 (5th Cir. 1966), *affirmed en banc,* 380 F.2d 836 (5th Cir. 1966).
U.S. v. Texas Education Agency and Austin Independent School District, 467 F.2d 848 (5th Cir. 1972).
Village of Euclid v. Ambler Realty Co., 272 U.S. 365 (1926).
Walker v. U.S. Department of Housing and Urban Development, 734 F.Supp. 1289 (N.D. Texas, 1989).
Williams v. Dallas, 734 F. Supp.1317, (N.D. Texas 1990).
18 U.S. 717 (1974).
42 U.S.C. § 2000d
Civil Rights Act of 1964, 78 *Stat.* 241

Interviews

All interviews were conducted in Dallas, unless otherwise noted.

Anderson, Richard. March 24, 1994.
Barta, Carolyn. 1995.
Bartlett, Steve. July 25, 1998.
Bartos, Jerry. July 16, 1998.
Bedford, Luis E. March 22, 1994.
Bergstresser, Rebecca. May 26, 1998. Richardson, TX.
Bickley, Alex. February 22, 1994.
Blair, Fred. November 16, 1993.
Bolton, Terrell. January 13, 1998.
Britt, Gerald. August 25, 1995.

Cajello, Adelfa. July 28, 1993
Campbell, Greg. March 24, 1994.
Cheek, Kyle. April 25, 1997. Richardson, TX.
Click,Ben. July 8, 1998.
Cloutman, Edward. July 23, 1993. Richardson, TX.
Cotton, Pat. February 1, 1991.
Cottrell, Comer. 1993.
Crenshaw, Sandra. May 28, 1998.
Douglas, Rick. July 18, 1998.
Duncan, Larry. May 28, 1998.
Dunning, Tom. March 1, 1994.
Edmonds, Jon. April 2, 1998.
Engstrom, Robert. February 8, 1991. Richardson, TX.
Estrada, Robert. April 6, 1994.
Evans, Jack. April 7, 1994. Richardson, TX.
Folsom, Robert. April 7, 1994. Richardson, TX.
Fonts, Larry. April 11, 1997. Richardson, TX.
Garcia, Domingo. 1993.
Garcia, Guadalupe. November 16, 1993.
Greer, Robert. February 8, 1991. Richardson, TX.
Halstead, Donna. June 17, 1998.
Hernandez, Frank. September 15, 1993. Richardson, TX.
Hicks, Don. August 4, 1998.
Hoffman, Robert. March 24, 1994.
Holcombe, Craig. 1989. (Interview conducted by Lynn Manry)
Holmes, Zan. September 2, 1993.
Houston, Tom. April 7, 1994.
Hubner, Mark. 1995.
Johnson, Curtis. 1991.
Johnson, Sam. April 7, 1994.
Keheley, Cliff. August 18, 1995.
Kirk, Ron. August 11, 1998.
Knight, Richard. August 1998.
Kress, Sandy. June 10, 1998. Austin, TX (via telephone).
Laszo, Frank. February 1991. Richardson, TX.
Lewis, Neelie. January 13, 1998.
Marcus, Stanley. October 25, 1995.
Martinez, Rene. August 5, 1993.
McDonald, Jerry. January 13, 1998.
Mead,Susan. July 17, 1998.
Medrano, Pancho. October 6, 1993.

Miller, Laura. August 15, 1998.
Mitchell, Beverly Brooks. March 8, 1994.
Molberg, Kenneth. October 12, 1993.
Moss, Bob. July 24, 1998.
O'Neal, Charles. March 4, 1998. (Interview conducted by L. Shane Hall.)
Oberwetter, Robert. February 1991. Richardson, TX.
Palmer, Lori. June 1993.
Peirce, Neal. 1991.
Peterman, Cherryl. July 21, 1998.
Petty, Dan.
Poss, Mary. May 21, 1998.
Price, John Wiley. August 4, 1995.
Quigley, Tom. 1995.
Ragsdale, Diane. September 14, 1993.
Reid, James. March 28, 1997.
Reyes, Delia. November 30, 1993.
Schutze, Jim. November 2, 1993.
Shaw, Rufus. June 30, 1995.
Shivers, Brian. November 9, 1993. Richardson, TX.
Sias, Mary. November 17, 1993.
Simpson, Lee. July 23, 1993. Richardson, TX.
Stahl, Lori. August 17, 1995. Richardson TX.
Steele, Cleo (Conducted by Theresa Daniel). November 24, 1993.
Stevens, Christine. October 13, 1995. Richardson, TX.
Strauss, Annette. April 7, 1994.
Tatum, Henry. 1995.
Walz, Karen. July 8, 1998.
Ware, John. July 24, 1998.
Washington, James. October 27, 1993; March 1, 1994.
Wattley, Cheryl. February 1991; December 14, 1993.
Weiser, Dan. December 1, 1993.
Wells, Max. July 27, 1998.
West, Royce. December 2, 1993.
Wright, Linus. July 7, 1998.

INDEX